PEOPLE, MARKETS, GO
ECONOMIES AND SOCIETIES 1
Volume 12

CW00549849

The Age of Machinery

PEOPLE, MARKETS, GOODS:
ECONOMIES AND SOCIETIES IN HISTORY

ISSN: 2051-7467

Series editors
Barry Doyle – University of Huddersfield
Steve Hindle – The Huntington Library
Jane Humphries – University of Oxford
Willem M. Jongman – University of Groningen
Catherine Schenk – University of Oxford

The interactions of economy and society, people and goods, transactions and actions are at the root of most human behaviours. Economic and social historians are participants in the same conversation about how markets have developed historically and how they have been constituted by economic actors and agencies in various social, institutional and geographical contexts. New debates now underpin much research in economic and social, cultural, demographic, urban and political history. Their themes have enduring resonance – financial stability and instability, the costs of health and welfare, the implications of poverty and riches, flows of trade and the centrality of communications. This paperback series aims to attract historians interested in economics and economists with an interest in history by publishing high quality, cutting edge academic research in the broad field of economic and social history from the late medieval/ early modern period to the present day. It encourages the interaction of qualitative and quantitative methods through both excellent monographs and collections offering path-breaking overviews of key research concerns. Taking as its benchmark international relevance and excellence it is open to scholars and subjects of any geographical areas from the case study to the multi-nation comparison.

PREVIOUSLY PUBLISHED TITLES IN THE SERIES ARE
LISTED AT THE BACK OF THIS VOLUME

The Age of Machinery

Engineering the Industrial Revolution, 1770–1850

Gillian Cookson

THE BOYDELL PRESS

The right of Gillian Cookson to be identified as
the author of this work has been asserted in accordance with
sections 77 and 78 of the Copyright, Designs and Patents Act 1988

First published 2018
The Boydell Press, Woodbridge

ISBN 978-1-78327-276-1

The Boydell Press is an imprint of Boydell & Brewer Ltd
PO Box 9, Woodbridge, Suffolk IP12 3DF, UK
and of Boydell & Brewer Inc.
668 Mt Hope Avenue, Rochester, NY 14620–2731, USA
website: www.boydellandbrewer.com

A catalogue record for this book is available
from the British Library

The publisher has no responsibility for the continued existence or accuracy of URLs for
external or third-party internet websites referred to in this book, and does not guarantee
that any content on such websites is, or will remain, accurate or appropriate

This publication is printed on acid-free paper

Typeset by BBR Design, Sheffield

Printed and bound in Great Britain by
TJ International Ltd, Padstow, Cornwall

Contents

Illustrations

Map

Plates

Figure

Tables

Acknowledgements

The power of networking, the idea that collaborating and sharing knowledge repays the sharer many times over, is an inspiring thought. Through their generosity, many friends and acquaintances, old and new, enthusiastic and encouraging, ever ready with information and suggestions, have proved the truth of it. Thanks to them, the book is all the richer, far more rounded and coherent than it could otherwise have been, and I hope gives some return.

The start of my fascination with textile engineers, the point when I realized how little was known, came in 1985–87 when I worked as researcher alongside Colum Giles and the late Ian Goodall on the Royal Commission on Historical Monuments (England) project on Yorkshire textile mills. Colum and Ian, before his untimely death in 2006, continued to support and encourage over the years. Very recently, Barbara Hahn of Texas Tech University transmitted to me some of her energy and perspective while working on 'Rethinking Textiles' as incoming international fellow in the University of Leeds, 2014–16. In between, there are so many people to thank, some of them multiply, not least for their friendship and patience with me.

For their specific expertise – in engineering or other industrial, social, economic, local and regional history – I acknowledge with great thanks the help of Chris Aspin, Derek Bayliss, Richard Byrom, Stanley Chapman, Alan Crosby, Ron Fitzgerald, the late David Hey, George Ingle, Kenneth Jackson, David Jeremy, Muriel Lord, Ted Milligan, Göran Rydén, John Suter and Tony Woolrich. My DPhil benefited greatly from contact with a clutch of distinguished textile historians: Douglas Farnie, John Iredale and Philip Townhill, all of whom have since died; and my supervisor David Jenkins. The influence of Maurice Beresford, who died in 2005, lives on through what he taught me as an undergraduate about the industrial history of Leeds.

Determined to better understand the context and technical demands of machine-making, I started on this book in 2013. There followed many museum visits and conversations with curators, mostly in 2014. It is a great concern that few of the key early machines survive, and even so their futures are uncertain following recent museum closures. One beacon of hope is the reopening Calderdale Industrial Museum, where Derek Bird and Jeff Wilkinson gave me significant help. Thanks too to Philip Butler (Lancashire

County Council Museums Service) and Ian Gibson, formerly of LCCMS, expert advisor to the Stepping Up record of textile machines in Lancashire museums collections; to Liz McIvor (Bradford Industrial Museum); Daniel Martin, formerly of Leeds Industrial Museum; Pieter Neirinckx (MIAT, Ghent); Andrian Paquette (Slater Mill, Pawtucket, Rhode Island); and Margaret Tylee, Barry Tylee and Ted Young, volunteers at the excellent Wortley Top Forge.

Countless librarians and archivists have helped me over the years. I am particularly indebted to those of West Yorkshire Archives Service; and to Ian Dewhirst, formerly of Keighley Library; Gail Mitchell (Business and IP Centre, British Library); Mike Chrimes, now director of engineering policy and innovation at the Institution of Civil Engineers; David Hunter of the West Yorkshire Historic Environment Record; Kirsty McHugh, then of the Yorkshire Archaeological and Historical Society; and Harriet Sandvall, previously of the United Grand Lodge of England.

Since my DPhil research, serious and proficient work by family historians has contributed enormously to what is known about their machine-making ancestors. I have to thank, for kindness in sharing work that is largely unpublished, and for patiently dealing with my questions, Paul Murray Thompson (Matthew Murray); Stephen Wordsworth (Joshua Wordsworth); Clive Thompson (William Carr); Bob Gamble (the Tempest family of millwrights); David Andrew and Paul Schoon (the Hattersleys); and Christopher S. H. Smith, whose mother was a Hattersley and father descended from William Smith.

To the Economic and Social Research Council, who supported my doctoral research in the University of York, 1990–94, I am eternally grateful. The University of Leeds School of History, where I was once an undergraduate, greatly facilitated the latter stages of this project by awarding an honorary research fellowship.

Megan Milan, Rohais Haughton and Nick Bingham (Boydell & Brewer), and Amanda Thompson (BBR Design), steered the production process with great efficiency, patience and good humour.

For encouragement and friendship over the years, thank you to Brian Barber and colleagues at the Yorkshire Archaeological and Historical Society; to Malcolm Chase, Pat Hudson, Chris MacLeod, Alison Morrison-Low, Andy Nicholson, Alessandro Nuvolari and Mary Rose. Special words of thanks to John Cantrell, Ernie Freeman, Cormac Ó Gráda and Peter Sowden; and to Francis Cookson for producing the map and photographs.

It is a great regret that Katrina Honeyman, who inspired and encouraged all around her, died too soon to see this. I am not sure that it could have happened without her. She is much loved and missed

But this is for my boys, Joe and Frank, babies when it began, and now men; and for Neil, whose constant companion this has been, these thirty years.

Abbreviations

BL	British Library
Borthwick	Borthwick Institute, University of York
Brotherton SC	Brotherton Library Special Collections, University of Leeds
Dir.	Directory
DNB	*Oxford Dictionary of National Biography* (Oxford University Press, 2004, with online updates)
HE	Historic England
NEIMME	North of England Institute of Mining and Mechanical Engineers, Newcastle upon Tyne
NYCRO	North Yorkshire County Record Office, Northallerton
OED	Oxford English Dictionary
PP Artisans and Machinery	PP (HC) 1824 (51) V, Select Committee on Artisans and Machinery
PP Exportation of Machinery	PP (HC) 1841 (201) VII, Select Committee on the Operation of Laws affecting the Exportation of Machinery
RCHME	Royal Commission on the Historical Monuments of England
TNA	The National Archives
UGLE	United Grand Lodge of England, Freemasons' Hall
UMIST	University of Manchester Institute of Science and Technology
VCH	Victoria County History
WYAS	West Yorkshire Archive Service
YAHS	Yorkshire Archaeological and Historical Society collections in Brotherton Library Special Collections

Note on Conventions

Places mentioned in the text and index are noted by their pre-1974 county.

Pre-decimal currency is denoted in pounds, shillings and pence (£ s. d), in which £1 (one pound sterling) = 20s. (twenty shillings), and 1s. (one shilling) = 12d (twelve pence).

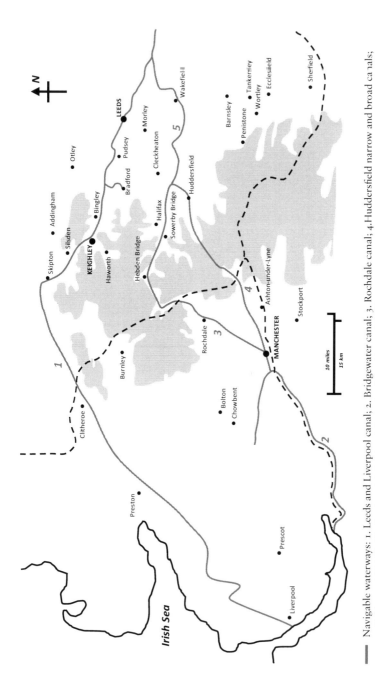

Navigable waterways: 1. Leeds and Liverpool canal; 2. Bridgewater canal; 3. Rochdale canal; 4. Huddersfield narrow and broad canals; 5. Calder and Hebble Navigation, joining Leeds branch of the Aire and Calder Navigation.

Pre-1974 boundaries of the counties of Lancashire (to the west) and West Riding of Yorkshire (to the east).

Land above 800 ft (250 m).

Northern England, showing places mentioned in the text and contemporary waterways

Introduction

Big engineering attracts most attention, but the promise of resolving larger questions about industrialization lies in the smaller-scale. Pre-factory engineering, particularly in subcontracting, innovation-chasing, cash-limited, resource-constrained textile engineering, holds all the interest. Without it, how could industrialization have happened at all? Machines were fundamental to industrial change in the eighteenth century. What we call the industrial revolution is not to be understood without appreciating how they came to be imagined and built.

Yet historians have not confronted early textile engineering. As a research topic, it has not found its place. Various approaches have been tried: this is a 'submerged sector' with virtually no useable sources, so as an industry it is unknowable beyond the familiar great men and famous firms; or it is a matter of technology, a question in metal and wood, nuts, screws and bolts, a progression towards mechanical efficiency, in which those same great men represent human input; or it is a sideshow of the textile industry, whose energy fed it and led it; or it was essentially quite static, operating in almost the same way at the end of the transformative century as it had at the beginning. As lines of enquiry, none of these is sufficient.

It is the outcomes of textile engineering which draw us in; that is, its products and their global impact. But these outcomes are not a route into understanding the hows and the whys of early textile engineering. Failures, culs-de-sac and false dawns are as much part of the process of discovery, indications of just what it took to succeed. Still there is no well-worked history of the engineering industry in the northern English textile districts – no study fully focused on the machine and component manufacturers who fed the booming needs of textiles before 1840. Nothing adequately pictures, in any depth, colour and glory, the progression, the chronological development, the speed of adoption, of textile technology in places at the eye of the storm of industrialization. Nor is much known about the social context within which technology was generated. Yet the surrounding culture – social, local, industrial, technical – was everything; its readiness to face uncertainty and complexity the key to innovating.[1]

---

1 Nowotny, *Cunning of Uncertainty*, xi, 2–3, 8.

The vacuum around this culture has instead generated many assumptions, and these tend to rest unchallenged. So, machine-making was part of the textile industry; clock-makers built machines; great inventors solved all the technical issues; jealousy, spying and secrecy characterized early engineering. None of this is true, as historians worked out some long time ago; just how flawed it is, remains to be told. On all the points, the sources actually tell a great deal, if allowed to do so.

The course of industrialization was one of startling disconnects within a lengthy, ill-defined period of gradual change. Textile engineering was a powerhouse of transformation, inspiring relentless innovation and symbolizing revolution. Paradoxically, the new engineering itself was slow to consolidate. It trailed behind its customer industry, textiles, in any resemblance to a modern industry. Its manufacturing processes appear absurdly traditional in contrast with its cutting-edge (as they must then have seemed) products.

The new industry took perhaps a half-century to fully fledge, from the first spread of spinning jennies, flying shuttles and water frames, into a largely factory-based, steam-powered, modern shape. The first part of this story is about finding ways to make and do novel things, activity built on human and local connection. The end point is more of a disconnect: transforming methods and systems of fabrication, concentrating and specializing, achieving something much more structured and (in modern senses) businesslike. Three or four phases of creativity are recognizable: first, the 'best possible', marshalling any available resources before 1800; then, specialization growing from the 1790s; integrating operations in powered factories, from around 1820; followed from the mid-century by a new chapter, engineering as very big business. Creativity was increasingly institutionalized. While the needs for human resourcefulness were undiminished, they certainly shifted with each new phase.

The central question I set out to answer is this: how, with engineering products and manufacturing processes both stretching any contemporary possibility, had it been possible to build a new high-tech industry practically from scratch? Textile engineering's role in industrialization was so exceptional that it can never be just a case study. Its history is uniquely enlightening, about the nature of innovation, about how the essential components of a technical business were assembled, and about the dynamics and ethos of the pioneering communities in which it developed.

'Why here?', we might also ask. Northern England was well-endowed with water-power, and suitable iron and coal to support engineering's transition to maturity. Specific skills, in iron and mechanics, were heavily supplemented from neighbouring regions and from places further afield, in particular south Yorkshire, Tyneside and Glasgow.[2] None of this explains exactly why textile

2   Hudson, *Industrial Revolution*, 113–15.

engineering germinated here, except that the watercourses, and a growing local expertise in processing various fibres, generated particularly strong textile clusters in Lancashire and Yorkshire. These well-resourced textile industries held exceptional significance, particularly in the early impetus they delivered, arising from their urgent need to escape the tensions of the putting-out system and replace it with something more manageable and reliable. Once this process, this focus upon innovation, was in motion, then proximity of machine-makers and machine-users was paramount in making technology work and develop effectively.

Understanding historically

Chronology is critical to understanding this industry. Actors and their actions should be seen in context, within the trades, know-how and social structures of their own time and place, in a landscape explored without hindsight. Why does this need to be stated at all? Because the history of engineering has had a particular issue with an inclination to work backwards, accepting too readily a Whiggish perspective that progress inevitably prevails. Stories are told through the prism of a mature mid-nineteenth-century industry, a triumphal end point which comes to be seen as entirely foreseeable.

This approach is not helpful in understanding early engineering. There is really only one way to establish its history – take nothing for granted; set the narrative in a solid context of 'what was', not 'what was coming later'; and deal with the shortage of easy information through a meticulous focus upon localities. Historians, said Kuhn, by studying the process of research rather than working backwards from finished scientific achievement, have the power to transform our understanding of science.[3] In describing 'a sketch of the quite different concept of science that can emerge from the historical record of the research activity itself',[4] Kuhn identified something equally true for the history of technological ventures.[5]

Kuhn later wrote about the importance of 'the community structure of science'. While his scientific communities are differently constructed from those of textile engineers, the point transfers. Essentially he advocates case studies.

> Scientific knowledge, like language, is intrinsically the common property of a group or else nothing at all. To understand it we shall need to know the special characteristics of the groups that create and use it.[6]

3 Kuhn, *Structure of Scientific Revolutions*, 1.
4 Kuhn, *Structure of Scientific Revolutions*, 1.
5 And of other things: see below, Ankarloo's critique of the new institutional economics.
6 Kuhn, *Structure of Scientific Revolutions*, 176, 210, additions to 2nd edn.

Here is a reminder of terminology's potential to confuse. A new trade producing a new technology set will fumble towards settling its own language. The vocabulary used, or not used, by machine-makers to refer to themselves, each other, and their products, has to be considered as a facet of historical evidence, a source revealing subtleties of the engineers' world. What, for instance, did contemporaries recognize in the terms millwright, clock-maker, tinker – and what does that say of how they worked and interrelated?

The corollary is that certain terms in modern usage, especially relating to business and innovation, come with implied values attached. This received wisdom may be inappropriate to past contexts, and muddle our under-standing of the historical situation. In absorbing modern orthodoxies, words might imply relationships and circumstances quite foreign to the past. During the period of industrialization, a particular problem attaches to the word 'entrepreneur', which was not in currency in Britain at the time. It is incongruous, an anachronism, and tends to pre-judge (or at least inhibit the debate on) what textile engineers were about.[7] 'Community' is also to be used advisedly – although here is an opportunity to define what 'community' might have meant to early machine-makers, and the enabling power of mutuality.[8]

Given the context and dynamics of this early industry, there is little doubt that engineering 'communities' – perhaps defined by locality, or united in skill and knowledge – were inspired by the possibilities around them. Resources were very limited, yet somehow held potential to generate the high-tech industry of greatest importance to industrialization. And whatever the inspi-ration or imagined futures at the start, the engineers involved can have had no realistic concept of outcome, no notion of the cataclysm to follow. So what was their motivation?

There are echoes of Kuhn in Ankarloo's criticism of the new institutional economics, where 'history is understood in light of the present, rather than the present understood in the light of history'.[9] Here, by habitually overlooking history, the grip of orthodox thinking has been further reinforced. But history, especially within the context of community, is a tool to challenge conven-tional moral assumptions within classical economics. History enables us to understand how capitalist economies have developed. In revealing this past, universal possibilities are rediscovered, because how people actually behave, and behaved, in life is not consistent with how economics textbooks say they should.[10] Whether demand or supply, organization or technology, were the driving forces, is a sterile and uninteresting sideshow compared with exploring the human and social dynamism in action. But can we ever pin this down, to

7   While 'textile engineer' is an anachronism, it is unambiguous.
8   See below, pp. 183–7.
9   Ankarloo, 'New Institutional Economics', especially 28–9.
10   Thaler, *Misbehaving*.

be confident in knowing the motivations, the purposes, of eighteenth- and nineteenth-century innovators and industrialists? The question 'why' may not indeed be answerable. Yet intelligent speculations are possible. Asking 'what' does at least produce better evidence on which to base conjecture.[11]

So we seek human explanations in the industry's early advance, and to illuminate the working of communities – local, industrial, social, spiritual – in which engineers lived and worked. The social context was multifaceted, and the nature of innovation itself immensely varied. Industrialization, after all, amounts to rather more than a dataset. Above all, it concerned relationships, within and around engineering, in a setting of families, neighbours and co-workers. Connections really mattered, not only for self-advancement, but as a hedge against disaster in an unforgiving environment. To possess a trade and build a family business might offer some protection in a world with so little security. The experiences of early engineers are testament to the fact that even a trade and business could not guarantee prosperity. Why, then, would these men take on additional risk in branching away from familiar work into the new engineering? The answer is that the risk was generally proportionate to their existing activity. The commissions that came along, at least in the earlier phases of machine-making, tended to supplement other income. This was sensible business practice and in most cases presented no threat to personal well-being and wider contentment. Uncertainty was (in both senses) vital, as inspiration and necessity for this scale of innovation.[12] There were constant, rousing, fresh challenges. Here were also good prospects, the reassurance of familiar frameworks and groups, and a sense of an intelligent community solving immediate problems. But how consciously this occurred, how mutual the support, to what degree the process was orchestrated – these are the questions.

Complexity and completeness

The early history of textile engineering is particularly complicated, for it was heavily enmeshed with other sectors. Of these, more is known of the customers – textile manufacturers – than of the obscured metal trades supplying components and services. This latter group is largely impenetrable, certainly not sufficiently knowable to be able to count, track or analyze details of production and sales. Even for contemporaries in the mid-nineteenth century, when the shape and organization of engineering grew much clearer, the trade proved close to unquantifiable.

11   Nowotny, *Cunning of Uncertainty*, 47–8.
12   Uncertainty is not the same as risk: Nowotny, *Cunning of Uncertainty*, viii, 63, and *passim*.

Textile engineers dealt in capital goods, for which demand can lag behind general economic cycles. But because machines were specific to one process and one branch of textiles, and mainly the technology evolved at some pace before settling to a consistent and acceptable performance, other forces might prevail. In certain cases, textile manufacturers, afraid to miss an opportunity, bought even in a downturn. Once the technology was better resolved, demand became more predictable. The industry's fortunes through many decades are therefore interwoven with technical improvement within textiles. For textile engineers, these were *products*. There is a very considerable literature, starting in the nineteenth century, about technological change in the different branches of textiles, across the many operations needed to transform fibre into finished cloth. Those early antiquarians provide local contexts, information about ventures – and venturers – in new types of textile working, and offer clues about how the needs for machinery were first met.[13]

Then a second technological transformation was in progress within machine-making: machine tools and new working systems revolutionizing the *process* on its own shop floors. This advanced engineering branch was curiously slow in adopting its own technology, taking to factories and production lines some considerable time after textiles had done so. Engineers, it seems, were cautious, waiting until demand for machines was sufficiently secure to make the investment safe.

Of course technology – textile, machine-tool and production – was a major element in machine-making's advance. It is, though, just one factor in the dynamic, only partially explaining what drove industrial change. For nuts, bolts, descriptions and drawings of machinery, the reader is by and large referred, via footnotes, elsewhere. But for the wider view, contextual chapters define, and give substantial weight to, the textile industry's own needs, and to the communities within which machine-makers worked. In this setting, the industrial was personal, the personal industrial. To understand the forces of change, then, means embracing a group of industries (not least iron, and older hand crafts), and the social relationships within the proto-engineering trades. Taking the social standpoint of machine-making provides a larger perspective for economic and industrial questions.

The problem of sources

With its fragmentary and deficient source material, early textile engineering is far from unusual among industries of its time and place. Difficult sources, though, are an occupational hazard for historians, and no excuse to undersell

---

13   See app. 1 and 2.

an important subject. After all, this was the essential transformative industry, a leader in establishing lasting economic development of global significance.

The lack of notice given to this new engineering first struck me during earlier research, supporting a survey of Yorkshire textile buildings in the mid-1980s.[14] Finding clear definitions or analysis of early engineering proved nigh on impossible. Nineteenth-century chroniclers had written about advances in textiles and machinery, though generally with the hindsight of a century or more. There was nothing comprehensive to be found about the founding phases of textile engineering, no substantial work defining the larger process of adjustment, no understanding of how one new industry was delivered and another recast. So it was a desire to understand more about early machine-making which stirred the first phase of my own research, starting in 1990.[15]

It was never in doubt that more information was there to be found, and that creative thinking and imaginative searching could extend the view behind the scenes. Tiny, shifting, adapting businesses, under the radar and perhaps only fractionally engaged with machine-making, if they came to historians' notice at all, could not offer records sufficient for a conventional, institutional kind of history. It is fairly clear why there has been so little previous investigation, and why the familiar tales of invention – of Crompton, Hargreaves and Arkwright, Cartwright, Roberts and the rest – proved so appealing, not least to authors. But it took more than a concept to produce a working machine. A wider world of engineering thrived beyond the easy fame of a few innovators, and this broad fringe was the dynamic heart of mechanical progress.

In fact the evolution of mechanical engineering overall has been little studied.[16] Collectively, the small firms characterizing Sheffield's early steel industry made up a sector of immense importance, but because every fragment about them is hard-won, they too have suffered neglect.[17] Without study of small workshops and their interrelationships, though, there is no way into understanding eighteenth- or early nineteenth-century business. This model, groups of small units constituting large and significant industries, was common, and not restricted to engineering and metal trades.[18]

Though much data is piecemeal, its scope and scale is actually substantial. Indeed, since digitized family records and newspapers appeared online, these fragments together threaten to overwhelm. Additional sources have been

14   RCHME survey of textile mills, 1985–87, published in Giles and Goodall, *Yorkshire Textile Mills*.
15   Cookson, 'West Yorkshire textile engineering industry'.
16   MacLeod and Nuvolari, 'Glorious Times', 216–17.
17   Tweedale, *Steel City*, 11.
18   Berg, *Age of Manufactures*, *passim*.

newly discovered or identified. While inevitably there are gaps in evidence, and matters impossible to reconcile, enough has materialized to present an essentially new work here, based only loosely in the 1994 doctoral thesis. Since 2012 it has been re-researched, reworked and rethought.

The approach has not fundamentally changed, for really there is no route into early engineering other than the community focus. There are a few engineering business records, but even the better sets lack completeness. This applies to the relatively large Kirkstall Forge, as much as to the small but influential Richard Hattersley. What these archives immediately show is the prevalence of subcontracting and casual work, and the level of engagement with a wider industrial community. So their information can be tracked outwards into other networks, connected and seen within a time frame, and from this emerges some clarity. That said, a substantial measure of hypothesizing will follow. But having found some context and chronology, the hypothesis becomes more coherent and credible.

Contexts

The contexts – localities, trades, families and technologies – are much overlapping. Where they meet is the heart of the dynamic, in the places where textile production was mechanized.

In the way that witnessing an early machine in action helps us to understand the process, so defining the setting of early engineering – the needs *of* new machinery as well as those *for* new machinery, and how they were met with resources locally available – is the route to explaining the industry's foundations. For the process was apparently organic – largely instinctive, immediate and artless, devoid of grand strategy. Here is an attempt to characterize the contexts, comprehensively and coherently, and to reflect on how they could generate remarkable outcomes.

Were the results really so exceptional? Arguably, the eighteenth-century transformation in textile production was organizational as much as technological. Producing cloth involved a complex set of operations, some done by machine, much by hand – the whole requiring considerable orchestration. It would take some further decades before complicated areas of textile production became absorbed within the machines themselves. The machines are totemic, as are the textile factories, but their consequence in the early days was more than just mechanical. The crux was how a machine was accommodated within existing systems, how it fed into workshops and community production within (above all) textile districts of northern England, that is, parts of Yorkshire, Lancashire and the north Midlands. Though symbolic of change, the eighteenth-century generation of machines were basic, and appreciating how they were made – the skills and materials involved in producing them – is basic to analysing the historical process.

What of analysing the industrial community? Community sources are not a poor substitute for absent business records. In fact this evidence is not at all a substitute, for community is where machine-making happened. The exercise is not source-led, but rather accepts the actuality. Both engineering and textiles were then immersed in local society, and human considerations – personal, familial, social relationships – mattered. Sometimes they outweighed technical and commercial factors. Friendships and kinships at times explain business and career decisions that would otherwise be puzzling.

The potential to reveal such networks has been transformed by the online explosion, and by searchable electronic databases. These possibilities have brought to light substantial new material, and inspired serious and accomplished family historians to write about machine-makers of whom little was previously known. In Yorkshire, important early engineers like Matthew Murray, Richard Hattersley, William Smith, John Jubb and Joshua Wordsworth were long recognized, but pinpointing origins, tracing careers, defining the nature of achievement, had seemed difficult to the point of impossibility. Of many others involved, some quite significant and with careers extending past 1850, very little has previously been discoverable.

It transpires, though, that the cohort of early textile engineers, even when very marginal firms are included, was small.[19] And as this was a start-up industry, a high proportion became casualties, falling by the wayside before 1820 – for a variety of interesting reasons – their misfortunes revealing what it took to succeed, or at least what it took to not fail. Removing these losses from the equation reduces the machine-making corpus further still. Generally, then, description works better than statistics, and discursiveness reveals unexpected connections, between engineers and localities, and with older craft industry.

So a starting point is biography, the research building upon a small exercise in prosopography. Family dynamics and extra-family relationships were important, though not necessarily in ways beneficial to business. Company histories sponsored by successful firms tend towards myth, rose-tinting and more Whiggishness. Often they omit embarrassing setbacks – bankruptcy, strife, incompetence, failures of planning. Focusing here on lives and relationships makes it possible for significant misreadings – and misleadings – to be rectified.

Keighley and Leeds were by 1850 the West Riding's principal textile-engineering centres. Before that, as early as c. 1780, clusters of machine- and component-making emerged in those places. In Keighley, a smaller town more

---

19   See app. 1 and 2.

discrete and fathomable as an industrial community, almost the whole of the early industry can be captured; and then the chains of succession into fewer, larger, firms active in c. 1850. Leeds is a counterpoint, bigger and industrially complex, with earlier engineering factories and a focus on woollens and flax (while Keighley dealt in cotton and worsteds). Still, the Leeds industry was grounded in its community, and many small and transient engineering firms are distinguishable. Leeds, as an urban centre, also traded with a greater range of foundries and forges. Ironmaking and ironworking matter in defining the early networks: self-evidently significant to engineering, and part of the inter-connection of trades and families leading back from west to south Yorkshire, these underpin the foundations of engineering in both Leeds and Keighley.

The detail of this research, including family relationships which are convoluted and not always fully substantiated, is set out in appendices. While evidence is sometimes circumstantial, together it is nonetheless weighty and suggestive. Thus we are immersed in engineering's 'submerged' sector,[20] of people and businesses which left little clear trace, a bloc encompassing downright failure, modest achievement, lack of ambition, and withdrawal through choice, bad luck, or for other reasons. Information comes from parish records and registers, rate books, family bibles, probate papers, militia rolls, newspaper announcements, antiquarian accounts, museum artefacts, and just occasionally from business records, which bring to life trading networks, subcontracting arrangements, products and processes.

And so empirically, driven by fragmented but compelling evidence, a context is constructed from which we deduce why people might have acted in certain ways, under certain circumstances. To understand these dynamics is to understand the potential of societies – communities – to address great questions in modern as well as historical eras. The case of the northern machine-makers shows how groups with direction and a supportive environment, though skills and resources are restricted, may yet rise above themselves, beyond any expectations, into a realm of undreamt-of achievement.

20   The phrase belongs to Floud, *British Machine Tool Industry*, 6.

I

The Coming of Machinery

In 1907, the first national census of British manufacturing confirmed textile-machine making as the largest single engineering branch. The nation's textile engineers presented 'an overwhelmingly dominant force in world trade', exporting 45 per cent of what they made. On the eve of the Great War, the industry employed 40,000, almost all of these men or apprentices. The United States was alone in the world in not relying upon Britain for most of its machines. Even so, just one Yorkshire town, Keighley, monopolized the American market in worsted machinery.[1]

Machine-making holds a special place within the narrative of industrialization. The eighteenth century's breakthrough textile machines have become familiar because they are held to symbolize that great industrial and social upheaval. But the industry that produced these and later marvels, laying the foundations of mechanical engineering as we know it, lingers in the shadows. A century before its dominance was officially established in 1907, textile engineering was still a work in progress, in the process of configuring itself into a standalone trade. The industry's rudiments were worked out over the course of half a century, from perhaps 1770, in the textile districts of northern England. Here, individuals of limited education, with few financial resources and in general possessing no more than rough and ready skills, embarked upon an extraordinary creative endeavour that (it is no exaggeration to say) shaped today's world.

How could such achievement emerge from apparently unpromising beginnings? Here was an artisan trade picking up the sharp edge of technology, catching a wave of innovation, working out techniques and creating tools, cultivating a skilled labour force, and raising a generation capable of developing a complex new institutional framework. Textile engineering was more than just another new manufacturing industry: it was also the source of innovation, its role to develop and supply new kinds of technology to apparently eager users in the textile industry. An intriguing dynamic was at work. Demand could be generated through innovation – an efficient machine launched upon

1   PP (1912–13) CIX c. 6320, Final Report on the First Census of Production of the United Kingdom, 1907; Saul (ed.), *Technological Change*, 142–4.

the textile industry was likely to find a market. Minds were open to change, and as the process of mechanizing textiles accelerated from the mid- to late-eighteenth century, the possibilities must have excited. A further impetus was the booming demand for textile products, with merchants and manufacturers seeking more and better machinery in order to respond to customer pressure. Satisfaction in these cases might be delayed, and perhaps not even practically possible in the short term. The indirect demand from consumers of textile products, at one remove from engineering, contributed to a lag between the trade cycles of the two industries.[2]

So the forces at work were complex and circular. Some of the tension arose from fears of being outstripped by other branches of textiles, or by new products. There was the fear that 'putting out', the reliance upon spinners and weavers far from the textile centres, was a system overextended to the point of being unsustainable. Whatever the strains, textiles and engineering had much in common, not least the context in which they operated. Here, these and other industrial activities did more than co-exist, developing a mutually supportive and reinforcing purpose.

Mechanizing the textile industry

Making woollens and worsteds was a widespread activity in medieval and early modern England, and the source of great prosperity in regions where it concentrated: East Anglia, a centre of worsted manufacture, and the West Country, for woollens. Northern England was associated with coarser types of woollen cloth.[3] The northern counties' growing dominance in textiles, predominantly in Lancashire and Yorkshire, was a phenomenon of the eighteenth century.

Mechanization crept into the woollen industry over the course of centuries, starting in the Middle Ages. The first radical change came in the fulling process. Fulling – or walking, after the traditional foot-powered method – involved pounding woollen cloth in soapy water to matt, felt and soften it. From the thirteenth century, when the force of water was first applied to the process, walking became milling, though the old term endured. Fulling stocks, giant hammers driven by water-wheels, often sat in or alongside existing corn-mills.[4]

Converting this arduous procedure into a mechanical process removed a bottleneck. But to improve any stage in woollen-cloth making – Baines

2   See below, pp. 239–40.
3   Kerridge, *Textile Manufactures in Early-Modern England*, 2–24; Jenkins and Ponting, *British Wool Textile Industry*, 4–7.
4   Buchanan, *Industrial Archaeology*, 131–3.

estimated there were 34 – or modify the numerous other tasks in different branches of textiles, knocked on to an entire sequence of production.[5] Up or down the chain, another process would be exposed as a new obstruction. As innovative activity escalated in the eighteenth century, this would be a constant force driving further improvement and reorganization.

Powered fulling was certainly a breakthrough, and a relief from a tedious and unrewarding chore. Its arrival impacted considerably upon the location of cloth-making. From being a largely urban industry, woollen manufacture spread towards the hills, where fast-flowing streams drove fulling mills. In Yorkshire, this meant the decline of old cloth-making centres, the medieval corporate towns of York and Beverley, and their influential guilds. The trade now concentrated in the Pennine valleys of the West Riding, and in eastern Lancashire.[6]

The upheaval had a further long-term effect. Fulling, in moving from what had been a domestic or small workshop setting, entered a public realm.[7] To the fulling mill, merchants and weavers carried their cloth. Over the following centuries, this became a natural site for other devices introduced to the industry, perhaps jennies and handlooms, and then, very commonly, incorporating machinery for scribbling, carding and slubbing which needed a power source.[8] Outside the mills, too, the woollen industry was public, and visible. Wool and yarn were carried around the district to be worked, cloth tentered (dried on a frame) on open ground, and taken to market. The public mill, where clothiers met each other and encountered other tradesmen, was an information exchange, and a place where social and industrial interests overlapped.[9] But more than this, it set a cultural tone for the industry, establishing it as communal and conspicuous.

Textile technologies, which evolved steadily over the centuries, saw a gathering change in pace in the early eighteenth century. After that, the speed of change was remarkable. Significant new concepts developed from the 1730s, though not all of them were immediately convertible into practical

---

5 For the stages of woollen-cloth making, see Baines, *Account of the Woollen Manufacture*, 71–3; for imbalances in cotton manufacturing systems, see for instance Guest, *Compendious History*, ch. VI; Fairbairn, 'Rise and Progress of Manufactures', clxxii.

6 Cossons, *Industrial Archaeology*, 185; for monastic fulling mills in north Yorkshire, Harrison, *Eight Centuries of Milling*, 48–54; for Lancashire, Lowe, *Lancashire Textile Industry*, 81, also 36–7.

7 Crump (ed.), *Leeds Woollen Industry*, 3–4, distinguishes between mill (public, part of the domestic system, at the service of clothiers who had always carried cloth to a water-powered mill) and factory (working the owner's yarn and cloth, entirely excluding the domestic clothier).

8 Jenkins and Ponting, *British Wool Textile Industry*, 28–9; Jenkins, *West Riding Wool Textile Industry*, 134.

9 Crump (ed.), *Leeds Woollen Industry*, 6, and especially Joseph Rogerson's diary, 59–166; Smail (ed.), *Woollen Manufacturing in Yorkshire*; Davies *et al.* (eds), *Diaries of Cornelius Ashworth*.

mechanisms. From the mid-century, some of these ideas were successfully applied to one branch of textiles, while taking longer to utilize in others. In general, wool proved most difficult to mechanize. Cotton was robust and more suited to working by machinery, which could then – sooner or later – be adapted to worsted.[10] Flax was durable but had very different processing needs from the rest, and here mechanization proceeded alongside, but somewhat apart from, other branches.

Certain machines were adopted and spread very rapidly; others did not catch on at all, or took much longer. Often they needed adapting to be practical, or the chain of production, the tasks preceding and following, must be adjusted to accommodate the new machinery. Thus new stages of manufacture would appear within the sequence, and further machinery developed to deliver them. Arkwright's water frame did not work effectively unless fed by his lantern drawing frame; a new process, slubbing, was introduced to prepare for spinning the fibres issuing from carding engines.[11] This progression was described in 1783.

> The improvements kept increasing till the capital engines for twist were perfected; and it is amazing to see what thousands of spindles may be put in motion by a water wheel, and managed mostly by children, without confusion, and with less waste of cotton than the former methods: but the carding and slubbing, preparatory to twisting, required a greater range of invention than the twisting engines, and there were sufficient motives to acourage the attempt; for while carding was performed by common cards, and slubbing by the hand, these operations took half the price of spinning … The first attempts were in carding engines, which are very curious, and now brought to great perfection, though they are still improving; and an engine has now been contrived, for converting the carded wool to slubbing.[12]

Not every stage of production lent itself easily to mechanization, and knotty problems endured. These remaining obstacles caused great practical difficulties. A campaign to develop a machine wool-comb for worsteds, started in the 1780s by Edmund Cartwright, was the most epic. The longer it took to achieve, the more valuable this last great glittering prize. It was only in the 1850s, amidst great acrimony, that a workable method was finally achieved.[13] Efficient power looms came to the woollen industry as late as the 1830s, and practical difficulties 'rendered it undesirable' to introduce them entirely before

---

10   Fairbairn, 'Rise and Progress of Manufactures', clxvii.
11   Rees, *Cyclopaedia*, II, 176; Jenkins and Ponting, *British Wool Textile Industry*, 109, 48.
12   Ogden, *Description of Manchester*, 55–6.
13   Jenkins and Ponting, *British Wool Textile Industry*, 106–9; Burnley, *Wool and Wool-Combing*; Honeyman and Goodman, *Technology and Enterprise*.

about 1850.[14] There were sometimes good technical reasons to retain old machinery, perhaps for specialist work, in the way that mules were preferred to ring-spinning for certain grades of cotton later in the nineteenth century.[15] Handlooms continued to be used for speciality and sample work after 1900, particularly in the Huddersfield fancy trade.[16] To achieve a best possible finish, old and new cloth-finishing methods were used alongside each other, on the same piece of cloth, in a Kirkstall woollen mill in 1825: 'Old fashioned blades were used to make the first cut, and the last sort of knives [a new kind of spiral blade] to finish the face'.[17] Card-clothing, an ancillary product used in vast quantities to cover the rollers on carding and other preparatory machines, was still hand-set in the 1840s.[18]

Production processes differed markedly between cotton, flax and woollen branches. Within woollens, there was wide variation between treating the longer worsted staples, which made suiting and finer cloths, and the shorter woollen fibres used for blankets and rough fabrics. In terms of applying early and rudimentary machines, worsted proved more robust than short-staple wool, displaying greater similarity to cotton. Though the specifics varied, in the initial stages of any textile production, raw materials were cleaned and fibres straightened. Cotton, wool and worsted were carded, worsted combed, wool scribbled, cotton and wool willeyed, and flax retted and heckled.[19] Rotary carding machines, appearing in 1748, were first taken up by the Lancashire cotton trade, before finding their way into Yorkshire woollens. Nowhere were they widely adopted until improved by Lees and Arkwright in the 1770s. By the century's end most scribbling and carding of wool was mechanized and water-powered.[20] The slubbing billy, said to have been developed in Stockport in c. 1783–86 by John Swindell, closely resembled the spinning jenny but was installed in mills rather than domestic settings. It proved to work better with wool than cotton, and was swiftly adopted by West Riding woollen manufacturers.[21] Arkwright's lantern drawing frame, like his water frame, used roller

14   Heaton, *Yorkshire Woollen and Worsted Industries*, 283; Jenkins and Ponting, *British Wool Textile Industry*, 49.

15   Saxonhouse and Wright, 'Stubborn English Mule', 514.

16   Jenkins and Ponting, *British Wool Textile Industry*, 116–17. A handloom in the Colne Valley Museum collection had been rebuilt in Huddersfield in the 1930s.

17   Rhode Island Historical Society, Zachariah Allen Papers, Journal of European Trip 1825, p. 30.

18   Cookson, 'Mechanization of Yorkshire Card-Making'.

19   Giles and Goodall, *Yorkshire Textile Mills*, 6–8; Hills, *Power in the Industrial Revolution*, 73–88.

20   Baines, *Account of the Woollen Manufacture*, 32; Heaton, *Yorkshire Woollen and Worsted Industries*, 333; Rees, *Cyclopaedia*, II, 176; V, 487.

21   Crump (ed.), *Leeds Woollen Industry*, 8, 22–3; Jenkins and Ponting, *British Wool Textile Industry*, 48; Baines, *Account of the Woollen Manufacture*, 122; Rees, *Cyclopaedia*, V, 484–5.

drafting, and spread into the worsted industry as early as 1780.[22] Developing machinery to heckle and spin flax was the subject of concerted attempts by John Kendrew, followed by Murray and Marshall in Leeds (with calculated borrowings from the cotton and worsted branches), and yielded to this onslaught in 1790.[23]

The next stage was spinning. The Saxony wheel was in use in Germany by the late-fifteenth century, improved by the addition of flyers and treadles. With a flyer, thread could be twisted and wound simultaneously. A treadle enabled the spinner to use both hands for drafting.[24] This wheel appears to have been little adopted in Britain during the seventeenth century, though it increased in popularity some time into the eighteenth. It had been developed for flax, and proved slow and inconsistent for woollen textiles, more suitable for drafting worsteds than for shorter staples.[25] Despite the significant innovations in spinning technology after 1750, until the 1790s much of Yorkshire's woollen yarn was still spun on traditional one-thread wheels turned by hand, known as the big wheel, and in Lancashire called Jersey wheels.[26] After 1790, the switch to slubbing and spinning by machine was rapid.[27] Descended from the one-thread wheel, James Hargreaves' jenny of 1767, first intended for cotton, was quickly adopted in parts of the woollen industry, and was in widespread use around Leeds by 1780. Simple, unpatented, easily driven by hand and suitable for children to work, it was popular in the cottage industry, proving especially suitable for coarser yarns. Later – the date is not certain – the jenny was enlarged and powered.[28]

Lewis Paul and John Wyatt had been the first to patent roller spinning, in 1738, but bringing the design into operation proved more challenging.[29] Arkwright's water frame of 1769 at last showed that drafting by this method, using the differing speeds of a series of rollers, could be commercially viable, particularly for fine cotton threads. His patent envisaged a machine driven by horse-power, but from it Arkwright produced the first system of water-powered, factory-based, spinning. The water frame was also key to

22 Jenkins and Ponting, *British Wool Textile Industry*, 109; Rees, *Cyclopaedia*, II, 176.
23 Thompson, *Matthew Murray*, 24; and see below.
24 Ponting, *Leonardo da Vinci*, 2–3.
25 Jenkins and Ponting, *British Wool Textile Industry*, 21; Lemon, 'Early History of Spinning', 486–8.
26 James, *History of the Worsted Manufacture*, 253, 324; Crump and Ghorbal, *Huddersfield Woollen Industry*, 35.
27 Heaton, *Yorkshire Woollen and Worsted Industries*, 336, 352; Jenkins and Ponting, *British Wool Textile Industry*, 48.
28 Crump (ed.), *Leeds Woollen Industry*, 7; Heaton, *Yorkshire Woollen and Worsted Industries*, 352; Jenkins and Ponting, *British Wool Textile Industry*, 48–9; Lemon, 'Early History of Spinning', 499; Cossons, *Industrial Archaeology*, 177–9.
29 Hills, *Power in the Industrial Revolution*, 32–53; R. B. Prosser, rev. G. Cookson, 'Lewis Paul, d. 1759', *DNB*.

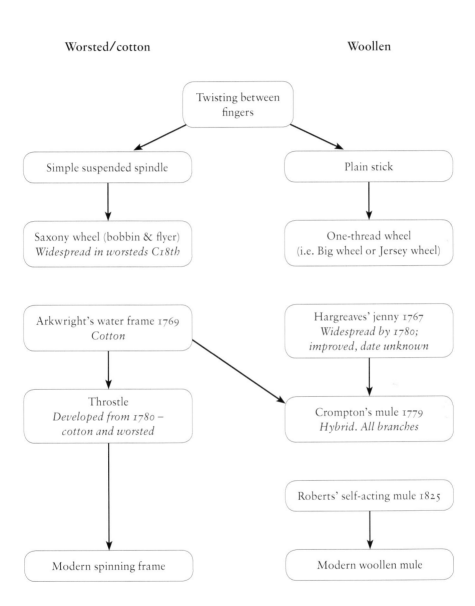

Figure 1. Early spinning methods
Source: After Lemon, 'Early History of Spinning', 499.

mechanizing worsted spinning, although this was not achieved satisfactorily until the early years of the nineteenth century.[30]

The worsted industry, which had a chequered history in Yorkshire, began to revitalize from the late-seventeenth century. Halifax was its most important centre, with significant activity in and around Keighley, and a spread eastwards into Leeds and Wakefield. Bradford, a depopulated and declining woollen town, revived in the mid-eighteenth century, reinventing itself as a centre of worsteds. Here a market hall for worsted pieces opened in 1773. A waterway link in 1774 connected Bradford to the Leeds and Liverpool canal, and thus to the Aire and Calder navigation in Leeds in 1777. James Garnett experimented with some kind of hand-driven worsted spinning frame, perhaps a throstle, at Paper Hall, Bradford, in the early 1790s. The town was quick to adopt and adapt worsted machinery, and the arrival of steam power accelerated and completed its transformation.[31] 'Bradford is particularly indebted to the steam engine for the colossal greatness to which it has in such a short time reached', said John James, Victorian chronicler of the worsted industry.[32] Several worsted-spinning factories had been built there as early as 1800, and the growth of worsteds between 1810 and 1820 was 'extraordinary'. At this point Bradford took from Halifax the mantle of 'chief seat of the worsted trade'. Ready to develop factories on a great scale, and to focus purely on worsteds, it soon acquired a reputation for excellent machine-spun yarn.[33] The new and concentrated market for machinery proved a magnet for established textile engineers from elsewhere, Hattersley of Keighley among them, who opened satellite plants in Bradford's thriving centre.

By 1820, preparing and spinning wool and worsted, cotton and flax, was largely carried out by machinery, and within factories. Handlooms were still the means of weaving yarn into cloth. So while advances in carding and spinning vastly increased yarn output, the system fell out of balance. The power looms which would restore equilibrium were long in development. It took much longer to produce them in sufficient quantities to make them universal. For as long as the technical remedy was out of sight, interim measures were taken. One was to recruit more handloom weavers to the trade, so that handlooms enjoyed a brief swansong which continued even after the number of power looms had risen beyond 100,000. 'The handlooms employed in the cotton manufacture are believed not to have diminished between 1820 and 1834, but rather to have increased'. They numbered perhaps 240,000 in

---

30   Jenkins and Ponting, *British Wool Textile Industry*, 49; Rees, *Cyclopaedia*, II, 176–7.
31   Heaton, *Yorkshire Woollen and Worsted Industries*, 264–74; James, *History of Bradford*, ii, 223; Jenkins and Ponting, *British Wool Textile Industry*, 51; Hodgson, *Textile Manufacture*, 19.
32   James, *History of the Worsted Manufacture*, 350.
33   Cookson, 'City in Search of Yarn', 43–4.

1820, rising to as many as 250,000 in 1833.[34] In the Nidderdale linen industry, even after 1850 handlooms far outnumbered power looms.[35] Handlooms also persisted in Ulster linen manufacturing.[36]

Handloom-weaving had undergone one significant change, with John Kay's flying shuttle eliminating the need for an assistant weaver on broadcloths, markedly improving its efficiency and speed.[37] Though patented in 1733, the shuttle was adopted only gradually. It first needed improvement, and Kay then imposed heavy charges on its use. Nonetheless it was soon pirated, taken up by Rochdale and Rossendale manufacturers of baize (heavy woollen cloth) from 1735, and then by the cotton fustian trade in Bolton, in the 1750s, and more generally in Lancashire by 1780.[38] The woollen industry took longer to absorb the shuttle, and it appears to have reached Yorkshire only in about 1763.[39]

Edmund Cartwright's power loom, patented in 1785, was promising enough that he built a factory in Doncaster, in 1788–89.[40] This was neither a commercial nor a technological success. In fact, Cartwright was the most high profile of a number of innovators working on such schemes, in France as well as Britain.[41] The real breakthrough, it seems, came in Stockport soon after 1800, when Marsland, Horrocks and Radcliffe borrowed a variety of adaptations from earlier innovators.[42] Improved power looms were adopted first in cotton, then in the 1820s in worsteds, and afterwards for woollens, which were too fragile to be woven at speed on early looms.[43]

It was estimated that in the whole of Great Britain in 1813, there were no more than 2,400 power looms at work. The number rose to about 14,150 in 1820, 55,500 in 1829, and perhaps 100,000 in 1833, by which time 'the machine-makers of Lancashire are making power looms with the greatest rapidity, and they cannot be made sufficiently fast to meet the demands of the manufacturers'.[44] While most of those numbers worked in the Lancashire cotton industry, power looms were then appearing in worsted manufacture. In the West Riding there were perhaps 2,768 worsted power looms in 1836,

---

34   Baines, *History of the Cotton Manufacture*, 237.

35   Jennings (ed.), *History of Nidderdale*, 207.

36   K. J. James, 'The Hand-Loom in Ulster's Post-Famine Linen Industry: The Limits of Mechanization in Textiles' "Factory Age"', *Textile History*, 35/2 (2004), 178–91.

37   Jenkins and Ponting, *British Wool Textile Industry*, 22, 25–6; Hills, *Power in the Industrial Revolution*, 22–4.

38   D. A. Farnie, 'John Kay (1704–80/1)', *DNB*.

39   Farnie, 'John Kay'; Heaton, *Yorkshire Woollen and Worsted Industries*, 340–1.

40   Hills, *Power in the Industrial Revolution*, 213–20.

41   Rees, *Cyclopaedia*, II, 183; V, 383–4; James, *History of the Worsted Manufacture*, 350–3.

42   Baines, *Account of the Woollen Manufacture*, 128; *History of the Cotton Manufacture*, 231–5; Hills, *Power in the Industrial Revolution*, 224–7.

43   Jenkins and Ponting, *British Wool Textile Industry*, 49.

44   Baines, *History of the Cotton Manufacture*, 235–7.

rapidly rising to 11,458 in 1841, 16,870 in 1843, and 19,121 in 1845.[45] The total in Yorkshire in 1850 was 30,856, of the 32,617 total counted that year in England, Wales and Scotland.[46] Power looms arrived later to the woollen industry: overall in England there were 9,168 in 1850, almost 20,000 in 1861, and more than 35,000 in 1871, increasingly concentrated in Yorkshire.[47]

The finishing stages of cloth-making were similar in cotton and linen, which were bleached or dyed, and sometimes printed. Woollen cloth and worsted were scoured (washed), then tentered to hold their shape while drying, and afterwards sheared. Both were usually dyed in the piece, if dyeing were needed. For worsted, the purpose of shearing was to expose the pattern in the weave. Woollens went through more robust procedures, to produce a dense felted finish by prolonged pounding in the fulling stocks, then teazeling the dry cloth, raising a nap cropped to an even finish with hand shears.[48] The gig-mill, a frame on which teazels were fixed, had been used for centuries in Gloucestershire, but not in the north. Shearing frames came as a complete innovation in about 1800. Although they famously incited resistance from croppers, or cloth-dressers, early versions designed to work with hand shears were unsatisfactory.[49] Several major breakthroughs in woollen-cloth finishing, notably Lewis's rotary cutter and Dyer's milling machine, emerged from the long-established West Country industry.[50] A great advance in the Leeds industry was enabled in about 1815 by William Hirst, working out how best to prepare cloth to make it suitable for gig-finishing. This was against the opposition of cloth-dressers, and after even Benjamin Gott had despaired of bringing shearing frames into practical use.[51]

Impetus for change

Consider these near contemporaneous events in Leeds around 1791: a small cluster of steam-powered cotton-spinning factories, the first within the town, were built on the Aire, 1790–92;[52] woollen-cloth factories – perhaps four in number – were established during 1791–93, of which Benjamin Gott's

45   Heaton, *Yorkshire Woollen and Worsted Industries*, 357.
46   Jenkins and Ponting, *British Wool Textile Industry*, 112.
47   Jenkins and Ponting, *British Wool Textile Industry*, 112; Heaton, *Yorkshire Woollen and Worsted Industries*, 358.
48   Giles and Goodall, *Yorkshire Textile Mills*, 11–13.
49   Jenkins and Ponting, *British Wool Textile Industry*, 49–50.
50   Baines, *Account of the Woollen Manufacture*, 47–50.
51   Crump (ed.), *Leeds Woollen Industry*, 43–51; see below, pp. 228–9.
52   Aspin, *Water-Spinners*, 462, 464, 466; Beresford, *East End, West End*, 243. See also Ingle, *Yorkshire Cotton*, 42–3 and 106–11. Changes of mill names and ownership confuse the sequence.

Bean Ing was far and away the most significant;[53] close by, in Holbeck, John Marshall opened a four-storey flax-spinning works in 1791, the first phase of a great complex dominating the neighbourhood of Water Lane over the next decades.[54]

Representing three different branches of textiles, these virtually simultaneous, proximate, ground-breaking enterprises marked significant digressions, for Leeds and for manufacturing overall. They suggest a spirit of improvement, innovation, risk-embracing, backed by an availability of expertise and resources, which found particular focus in Leeds, the marketing centre of Yorkshire woollens, at a time when the cloth trade was experiencing great prosperity. Here, factory sites were available by navigable water which was also a power source; coal was cheap and plentiful; and on the south bank of the Aire, in Hunslet and Holbeck, local rates were low. 'Coals and water made this town', as a contemporary remarked.[55] It was in these districts, at this time, that workshops specializing in textile engineering began to emerge. And yet, while the various Leeds ventures of c. 1791 were (to some degree) pioneering and significant, mechanical inventiveness was only a part of the novelty. The true interest of these coincidental ventures lies in their disparity, and what is to be read from this about the complexity of innovation.

Water-powered cotton-factories on the Arkwright model were not new: around 100 had been established in Yorkshire, and the same number in Lancashire, by the end of 1792. Most were rural, their location dictated by power source, their purpose to capitalize on Arkwright-type water-driven spinning technology after the fall of Arkwright's patent. Indeed several of these were in villages close to Leeds, set on the Churwell, Adel and Balme becks.[56] Why, then, did two or three much larger cotton-factories appear in central Leeds at this time? The answer is mechanical, but concerning power rather than textile processes. The technique of using auxiliary steam pumping engines to enhance and govern water-wheels was applied here on a grand scale, harnessing the power of the river Aire to drive a large cotton-factory. This transitional technology was soon overtaken when rotary steam-engines made water-wheels obsolete.[57] For a time, though, it had made the Leeds and Hunslet riverside sufficiently attractive that several groups of investors took their opportunity.

53   Crump (ed.), *Leeds Woollen Industry*, 5; Brotherton SC, MS193/22–31.

54   Brotherton SC, MS200/26, pp. 37–8, historical notes by S. A. M. [John Marshall's grandson, Stephen]; Rimmer, *Marshalls of Leeds*, 34–6, 45; M. W. Beresford, 'John Marshall (1765–1845)', *DNB*.

55   Beresford, *East End, West End*, 5, and *passim*.

56   Aspin, *Water-Spinners*, 452–67; Ingle, *Yorkshire Cotton*, ch. 2 and Part 2, especially pp. 21–5, 105–12. The Yorkshire factories were on average rather smaller than those in Lancashire: Aspin, *Water-Spinners*, 18.

57   Giles and Goodall, *Yorkshire Textile Mills*, 133–5.

Plate 1. The great mill yard at Bean Ing, drawn by F. C. Jones
Source: Crump (ed.), *Leeds Woollen Industry*, 264–5.

Benjamin Gott's revolution was entirely different, delivering an organizational transformation to the staple trade of Leeds. By happy chance, at an early age Gott gained control of the firm of woollen merchants where he had been apprentice and junior partner. He was a commercial man, conversant in marketing and finishing woollen cloth, and his bold move into Bean Ing was designed to support his merchanting firm. The new factory was urban, steam-powered, and the largest structure in the woollen industry of its time. Manufacture was subcontracted to several tenants, managers whose role was to supply Gott with woven cloth.[58] Under one roof, raw wool was transformed into the finished product. Installing a rotary engine from the start might then have appeared radical, but in fact Gott's steam power was applied only to processes already routinely powered, albeit by water-wheel: scribbling, carding, fulling and grinding dyestuffs. The assemblage of machinery at work in Bean Ing's closed interior was very much the status quo. The novelty was in that word 'assemblage'. Gott's jennies, looms and finishing apparatus were indeed the latest technology available, but all of these were already well-assimilated into the small workshop and domestic sector outside his factory walls. Bean Ing remained primarily a *manu*factory where a sequence of tasks was executed using domestic-type machines driven by hand or treadle. In 1800 this enterprise was one of the half-dozen largest employers of labour in the country, with 1,000 workers, far more than any other woollen or worsted factory. Yet even in 1820, three quarters of Bean Ing's workforce were still employed on hand processes, old or new. Every piece of high-quality broadcloth produced there before 1830 was woven on one of the scores of handlooms at work in Gott's vast premises.[59]

John Marshall, son of a linen draper, shared with Gott a merchanting background in Leeds. He too had the good fortune to inherit autonomy and wealth while in his twenties, and like Gott risked all on a new venture. Marshall's ambitions, though, were mechanical, chasing workable methods to prepare and spin flax by machine. Between 1788 and 1791, under licence from Kendrew and Porthouse of Darlington, he embarked on trials to improve an imperfect machine they had patented. The thread was good, but the unreliable mechanism not viable. Success eluded Marshall until he employed Matthew Murray, after which great advances were made on Kendrew's prototype. A first patent was registered in 1790, and on the strength of them Marshall invested in the new factory in Holbeck.[60]

58 R. G. Wilson, 'Benjamin Gott (1762–1840)', *DNB*; Offer in Crump (ed.), *Leeds Woollen Industry*, 167–86; Giles and Goodall, *Yorkshire Textile Mills*, 85–8, 90; Beresford, *East End, West End*, 275–7, 285–95.

59 Wilson, 'Benjamin Gott'; Crump (ed.), vii; Baines, *Account of the Woollen Manufacture*, 52–3.

60 Brotherton SC, MS200/57; /26; Cookson (ed.), *Durham VCH. Darlington*, 154–6; Aspin, *The Decoy*, 24–6; Rimmer, *Marshalls of Leeds*, 34–6, 45; G. Cookson, 'Matthew Murray, 1765–1826', *DNB*.

Gott, Marshall, and the Leeds cotton-spinners embarked on brave, costly and potentially ruinous ventures. No doubt the woollen industry's expansion and successes of the late 1780s and early 1790s gave them confidence to experiment. In this era of great change, Gott's was less of a technological breakthrough than many, and he was by no means the only person to launch a woollen factory. Nonetheless, his ambition was extraordinary in scale and he identified a path for his own trade, soon followed by others, at a time when the integrated woollen factory was not necessarily an obvious solution to its problems. Benjamin Gott was an organizer, applying system and order to textile manufacture. His brilliance lay in his overview, the planning and layout of a factory and the readiness to continue fine-tuning procedures in pursuit of further improvement.

Crump, who brought Gott's accomplishments to wider notice, saw the pioneer as part of a progression of innovation.

> It is not the inventor who dominates the story, but the user of the new inventions, the scribbling miller and the manufacturer. The group of men gathered around Watt at Soho play their part, but so do the domestic clothier and the slubber, the Yorkshire millwright and cardmaker, the dry-salter and wool-dealer, the carrier and shipping agent, merchants and agents and travellers at home and abroad.[61]

And he underlined the scale of Gott's organizational achievement:

> The outstanding figure is Benjamin Gott, the merchant-manufacturer, far-sighted and receptive of new ideas, adventurous and a born organizer. The selling organization, in a sense, he inherited, but the manufacturing organization he created, though without the former he could not have launched out on the scale that he did.[62]

But Gott was never really a manufacturer, for he remained where he had started, a merchandiser, a specialist in finishing and selling cloth, at the peak of his profession as a highly successful export merchant. Bean Ing's purpose was to supply the merchant house which made the profits that built it.[63]

Mechanizing the woollen industry had not proceeded far by 1790. Partial automation introduced new imbalances into the manufacturing process. To meet growing demand for woollens, capacity must somehow grow in those stages of production still defying mechanization. This meant expanding hand-processing: extending geographically, recruiting inexperienced (so less skilled and steady) outworkers, and maintaining an expensive and unproductive

---

61   Crump (ed.), *Leeds Woollen Industry*, vii.
62   Crump (ed.), *Leeds Woollen Industry*, vii.
63   Brotherton SC, MS193/20; Wilson, *Gentlemen Merchants*, 248.

network of fetchers and carriers. Gott's blueprint attempted to rationalize some of this and brought partial relief. The integrated system at Bean Ing, even when the factory relied so heavily on hand-working, gave his business a regional and national edge. This is apparent in Gott's phenomenal success, for instance in his ability to win large military contracts at the expense of Witney blanket weavers.[64]

The marketing of Yorkshire cloth had started to change, if subtly so, before 1790. Yorkshire's growing supremacy at the expense of previously unassailable London merchants came, as Smail shows, because the trade proved itself willing and able to adapt to new markets. Overseas customers expected cloth to be produced to order, with an emphasis on quality.[65] Northern cloth-makers were not well-situated in the mid-eighteenth century to respond quickly or precisely to specific demands. With a shift into buying ready-made yarn, from about 1780, worsted manufacturers who had previously struggled to maintain complicated systems of outworkers saw their fortunes transform.[66]

But the dispersed system of woollen and worsted production was onerous, unreliable, and ultimately reached a limit where it could not be sustained. While some small clothiers still operated within a well-established web of local spinners and weavers, others, especially larger worsted manufacturers, struggled with the logistics of moving wool, yarn, and cloth between workers and markets, sometimes between regions – 'a waste of time almost inconceivable'.[67] The networks stretched across an ever larger and less manageable area. Robert Heaton in the 1750s and 1760s sent out yarn to be spun in Lancashire and upper Wharfedale, up to 20 miles from his base at Ponden.[68] The Pease business, an isolated outpost of worsted spinning in Darlington, bought wool across the northern counties and sold yarn to manufacturers in Scotland and the North Riding. Edward Pease's fleece-buying journeys of many weeks in central Scotland and Cumberland, detailed from the 1780s, included taking oiled tops for spinning around Bannockburn.[69] A market hall for serge cloth opened in Colne in 1775, patronized by worsted manufacturers from Wharfedale and Airedale. One manufacturer near Otley was noted buying wool in York or Wakefield, transporting it by pack-horse 'on the worst of roads'; once combed it was sent similarly for spinning in Cheshire or the Derbyshire dales, the yarn returned for weaving, the pieces

64   Simon Townley provided the Witney reference: *VCH Oxford*, XIV (2004), 90; Crump (ed.), *Leeds Woollen Industry*, 246–7, 249, 251, 279.
65   Smail, *Merchants, Markets and Manufacture*, 2–3, 5–6.
66   Smail, *Merchants, Markets and Manufacture*, 142–3.
67   Heaton, *Yorkshire Woollen and Worsted Industries*, 336.
68   Jenkins and Ponting, *British Wool Textile Industry*, 8–10.
69   Cookson (ed.), *Durham VCH. Darlington*, 157.

sold in Colne.[70] Thomas Crosley of Bradford put out wool to spin as far as Lancashire, Swaledale and other parts of the North Riding, paying shopkeeper agents a halfpenny a pound commission.[71] William Jennings of Windhill, Shipley, ran a similarly complex system involving shopkeepers as middlemen.[72] After retaining six agents in the Yorkshire dales to manage his worsted-spinning operation, Jonathan Ackroyd of Ovenden abandoned this arrangement in the 1780s and bought ready-spun yarn.[73] In time, 'the whole range of Yorkshire, and some parts of Lancashire, Derbyshire and Westmorland were more or less engaged' in worsted spinning.[74]

For larger businesses, the expense was great, and generally unrecorded. The Pease worsted business in Darlington spent as much as £800 a year putting out worsted tops to Scotland.[75] Transaction costs in time and energy hit even those working on a small local scale. Cornelius Ashworth wove 30 pieces a year, losing a day's work each time he carried one to Halifax market.[76] John Aikin recorded a common routine in the Calder valley, with the head of a family engaged in domestic textiles losing one day a week to attending market, and another to the mill, so a third of his working week.[77] Carrying cloth to be milled was a tribulation: one apprentice told of fetching cloth from Pudsey to Harewood for fulling in the late 1790s; Bramley clothiers too went to the Wharfe, to Arthington, Harewood or Poole.[78] Fustian weavers in Lancashire were at times obliged to walk three or four miles, around five or six spinning households, before they had yarn to start the day's work.[79]

With demand for worsted yarn fast growing, various expedients were tried to boost supplies. The system, though, had become so unwieldy that supervising it was nigh on impossible and rested on the goodwill of domestic spinners.[80] Shopkeepers acting as middlemen in distant locations were not qualified to judge yarn quality, and feared rejecting work lest they offend customers. Family members, including children, were drawn into spinning despite a lack of aptitude, so quality was uneven, sometimes within the same hank. Thomas Crosley recalled that, c. 1800, 'much difficulty was experienced with the yarn; we had to sort it, and from the same top there would be yarn as thick as sixteens and as small as twenty-fours, shewing the difference

70   James, *History of the Worsted Manufacture*, 292.
71   James, *History of the Worsted Manufacture*, 324.
72   James, *History of the Worsted Manufacture*, 324.
73   Smail, *Merchants, Markets and Manufacture*, 142–3.
74   James, *History of the Worsted Manufacture*, 326.
75   Longstaffe, *History and Antiquities of Darlington*, 318.
76   Davies *et al.* (eds), *Diaries of Cornelius Ashworth*.
77   Aikin, *Description of the Country*, 565.
78   Crump (ed.), *Leeds Woollen Industry*, 9.
79   Guest, *Compendious History*, 12.
80   James, *History of the Worsted Manufacture*, 254; Cookson, 'City in Search of Yarn'.

in the spinners'.[81] Embezzlement, the theft of material, was a centuries-old problem in putting out, particularly rife among hand spinners of worsteds, and more difficult to check as the industry spread outwards. The first of the Worsted Acts, of 1777, covering Yorkshire, Lancashire and Cheshire, aimed to clamp down on false and short reeling by hand spinners, a fraud against the manufacturers whose raw wool was pilfered.[82]

The transaction costs in all this, including fraud as well as paid and unpaid time to administer and work the system, were immeasurable, but recognized as insupportable. Also, clearly, not only was further expansion entirely imprac-tical, but the structure was collapsing. Without radical change, producing acceptable quality in sufficient quantities was becoming impossible.

So the collapse of putting-out networks was a significant driver of innovation. The system's costs and inadequacies injected further energy into the textile revolution. Over-extension of out-working had come out of a multiplying market for cloth – the increased demand stimulated by supply-side advances in merchanting. That demand, though, had not immediately, not even rapidly, delivered widespread change to the way textiles worked, either mechanically or organizationally. This delayed response is evident from the chronology: the dates when machines and ideas first occurred, and the dates at which they were widely embraced. There are signs that individuals were earlier picking at the edges of the failing structure, investigating alter-natives to out-working in order to cut costs, improve quality and make their businesses more manageable. It was not, though, until putting out began to collapse under the weight of its own limitations that the new expedients, machines and organizational solutions, were adopted with urgency.[83]

Is there evidence here supporting Allen's contention that a high wage economy inspired eighteenth-century mechanization?[84] It is difficult to square his position with the status of domestic spinning. Humphries and Schneider have shown not only that spinners' pay was low, but that it was falling in the run-up to the 1760s and 1770s spinning innovations. Their opinion is that poor productivity and inconsistent quality drove innovation, a response to low rather than high wages.[85] In this dynamic, the critical condition of putting-out networks is a key element.

Humphries and Schneider overstate the proficiency of spinners. True, this was originally skilled work, but desperation for yarn meant that many engaged in spinning after 1750 were neither trained nor equipped to do it well. The more this industry grew, the lower the overall ability. Yarn shortages did

81   James, *History of the Worsted Manufacture*, 311–12, 324.
82   Styles, 'Spinners and the Law', 145–70, especially 146.
83   Cf. Marglin, 'What Do Bosses Do?'.
84   Allen, *British Industrial Revolution in Global Perspective*, especially ch. 6.
85   Humphries and Schneider, 'Spinning the Industrial Revolution', 32–3, 38.

not bring spinners a pay increase; rather they kindled a drive to the bottom, a tendency to sacrifice quality for quantity. Yet demand was not satisfied. Employing spinners was an enormous expense, but not because individual wages were high. The large bill came from transaction costs, and because aggregate pay – very many people each receiving a small sum – was excessive for the meagre return achieved. Thousands of low-skilled spinners were being employed to very little effect.

Machinery was therefore seized upon, not so much for its labour-saving potential, but in order to improve quality and quantity. And opportunities to bring processes into workshops, or to reorganize them more radically within factories, were seen to offer better management of resources, and so increasingly explored. Shifts towards machinery and factories were features of a growth in production, and of desires to improve productivity.

Making change

So there was motivation for change. How did this translate into action? Woollen businesses, generally smaller-scale than those in worsteds, were nevertheless stretched by the growing demand.[86] Some larger clothiers around Leeds gathered operatives into workshops, with perhaps as many as a dozen looms. This reduced opportunities to embezzle, improved quality, economized in time and carriage, and enabled a more effective reaction to market needs.[87] Gott's initiative was motivated by the same concerns. Visiting Halifax in 1795, Aikin noted widespread changes: 'As machinery is now brought to great perfection, numbers of the small manufacturers, who made perhaps a piece a week, find it more advantageous to work at those factories, where their ingenuity is well-rewarded'.[88] The machinery was imperfect, but streamlining the manufacturing system potentially transformed productivity. Even with the same unimproved domestic handloom, a factory or workshop weaver giving six days a week instead of four achieved a 50 per cent higher output. The gain was larger still if seasonal farming were abandoned.

Such expedients underpinned an impressive expansion in West Riding woollens from 1750. Measured by cloth milled, production rose from about 58,700 pieces of broadcloth and 73,700 narrow, in 1750–54, to 276,100 and 146,600 in 1800–04.[89] This amounts to an increase of 370 per cent in broadcloth production over 50 years, and an approximate doubling of narrow cloth. Worsted manufacture in the West Riding, an industry barely present in 1700,

---

86   Jenkins and Ponting, *British Wool Textile Industry*, 10.
87   Heaton, *Yorkshire Woollen and Worsted Industries*, 351–3.
88   Aikin, *Description of the Country*, 565.
89   Jenkins and Ponting, *British Wool Textile Industry*, 3; also Rees, *Cyclopaedia*, V, 461.

started slowly, but by 1770 was 'a most formidable rival' challenging East Anglia. The value of its output, and numbers employed, overtook Norwich in about 1770.[90] The West Riding's main worsted centre during the eighteenth century, Halifax, was deposed by Bradford once spinning was successfully mechanized.[91] The fate of the Norwich worsted industry was an ominous reminder of how an apparently insuperable force can fall, how fragile was the domestic system, and how, once dispersed in a downturn, a putting-out network was impossible to reconstruct.[92]

The coincident events in Leeds c. 1791 demonstrated the possibilities open to manufacturers looking to extend business in a time of unprecedented change. These Yorkshire textile producers, facing critical issues in their industries, succeeded in finding viable yet distinctly different ways forward. Marshall saw a solution in a highly focused quest to develop specific technologies. The impetus driving Gott was to bring order to his corner of a thriving trade which, if not exactly in crisis, verged upon becoming totally unmanageable. In propelling change, local pressures generated by a visibly rising market for textiles should not be underestimated. This energy was applied to process just as much as to new textile products, and internally generated, within textile communities themselves. The fledgling engineering industry added to the impetus of a dynamic search for improvement across the board.

For these same years, around 1790, are noteworthy for a first flowering of specialist machine-making, most obvious in Leeds and Keighley, later to be hubs of textile engineering in Yorkshire. John Jubb moved into Leeds, to Holbeck, before the end of 1788. In that year too, Matthew Murray arrived in Leeds to work for John Marshall.[93] Richard Hattersley (1789) and William Carr (1789–90) settled in Keighley at this time. William Smith, a Keighley native newly out of apprenticeship, launched his business in 1795.[94] The new textile ventures made work for machine-makers, and drew engineers towards these centres, with very real prospects of success.

---

90   Heaton, *Yorkshire Woollen and Worsted Industries*, 264, 275.
91   Heaton, *Yorkshire Woollen and Worsted Industries*, 269.
92   When the Suffolk outwork system collapsed, Norfolk merchants relied entirely on Yorkshire: Cookson, 'City in Search of Yarn', especially 39–40. See also Styles, 'Spinners and the Law', 155.
93   See app. 2.
94   See app. 1.

2

The Age of Machinery

It is the Age of Machinery, in every outward and inward sense of that word; the age which, with its whole undivided might, forwards, teaches and practises the great art of adapting means to ends.

Thomas Carlyle, *Signs of the Times* (1829)

The first machines

Through centuries when textiles were produced in domestic workshops, machinery was widely used and accepted. Much of this apparatus was simple, even crude, in construction, and wood was its chief material. Heavy mechanisms of the public mill – fulling stocks, water-wheels and transmission gear – inhabited another realm, defined as the province of millwrights.[1] Handlooms, spinning wheels, carding engines and other domestic machines were basic devices, hand-powered, produced even into the twentieth century. Frames and certain of the components were made of wood, while moving parts, gears and fittings were generally metallic, usually of iron. Little is documented about who made them, and how.

Oak, beech or ash, though rarely soft wood, were recorded in handlooms in southern English and Midland textile districts. Screws, nuts and bolts might be made of elm or iron, with shuttles and spools carved from solid timber. The tools most commonly used were the lathe and the graver's knife. Tradesmen engaged on this work included turners and wheelwrights (for spinning wheels), carpenters, joiners and locksmiths; and a less clear term, 'framesmith', a worker in metal, 'manufacturer of weaving frames', apparently associated with the complicated business of building knitting frames.[2] This branch of engineering was sufficiently organized to generate a small yet significant export market during the seventeenth century. More traditional pieces were made by carpenters, turners in wood. Mentioned in the sixteenth century were a 'turnour or maker of loomes' in London, and

---

1 Tann, 'Textile Millwright', 80–1.
2 OED.

in Canterbury weavers using a 'turner for framyng of ther lomes'.[3] Weavers, or their masters, might commission or assemble their own loom. It is hard to know how specialized the machine-makers of the sixteenth and seventeenth centuries might have been, even in centres of cloth-making.

Evidence of users building their own machinery, in whole or part, is sketchy. The will of a Darlington weaver in 1597 mentioned 'my own linen loom which I wrought myself'.[4] In Canterbury, Flemish drapers supposedly had their own turners' shops to produce spindles and bobbin blanks. In Norfolk, weavers made loom-frames, fitting them with parts bought ready-made from specialists. This practice was followed too by English framework knitters in Avignon in 1658, who inserted metal parts made to order by local clock-makers and locksmiths into frames they had built themselves.[5] In northern England, where the handloom was ubiquitous, it is feasible that those using machines could have commissioned or fashioned a frame and obtained components – spindles, metal fittings, wheels – from local smiths or joiners. Most likely, wood workers and smiths in textile districts accepted the construction of looms and spinning wheels, or parts thereof, as an occasional part of their work, and had the limited skills required to make them.

With the shortfall in weaving capacity resulting from the mechanization of carding and spinning, the only immediate possibility was to speedily expand production by handloom. So alongside the new engineering, a boost in demand for traditional machines brought additional producers into the trade. Directories from 1772–73 show Manchester wood workers advertising themselves as loom-makers.[6] The Leeds millwright John Jubb, who had produced improved machines for scribbling and carding wool and 'engines &c both for cotton and fleece wool' for several years before 1784, sold four handlooms to John Marshall in 1788, presumably for the Adel linen-weaving experiments.[7] Benjamin Gott bought handlooms for Bean Ing from small makers in neighbouring villages, c. 1810–16: five at £9 each from Nathan Carlton of Armley, four at £8 from Bentley of Birstall and two at seven guineas from Thomas Taylor of Armley.[8] In 1822, loom- and shuttle-makers were listed in Barnsley, Dewsbury and Batley.[9] Domestic textile manufacture was still being catered for in 1838, when White's directory marked out several joiners as 'jenny and loom makers' in Pudsey. The trade was omitted from

3 Kerridge, *Textile Manufactures*, 174.
4 Cookson, *VCH Durham* IV, 150.
5 Kerridge, *Textile Manufactures*, 175.
6 Musson and Robinson, *Science and Technology*, 431–2.
7 *Leeds Mercury*, 23 Nov. 1784; Turner, 'Fenton, Murray and Wood', 1.10.
8 Crump (ed.), *Leeds Woollen Industry*, 293. See below for Gott's purchases when first establishing Bean Ing.
9 Baines, *Dir.* (1822), 138, 165, 456.

lists in neighbouring places where they certainly did still exist.[10] Mainly there was no need to advertise, as makers of wooden machinery served a very local market.

A quarter of a million handlooms were still at work in United Kingdom cotton-weaving in 1836,[11] and thousands more in woollen and worsted branches.[12] Hand-woven worsteds had virtually disappeared by the mid-1850s.[13] Handlooms survived rather longer for woollens, with a few still featuring in rural districts after 1900. But this was a niche market. The last known maker of handlooms was recorded in 1875 in Huddersfield. Here, handlooms conveniently and economically produced twentieth-century samples and speciality weaves.[14] Into modern times, small pockets of weaver-powered production survive where old-fashioned technology suits local circumstances. The cottage industry in Harris tweed was served by treadle looms produced by Hattersley until the early 1990s. Then, the Bonas-Griffiths broadloom transformed the Harris product for modern markets. In essence, even this recent technology is an improved version of the treadle loom, and still powered by the weaver.[15]

The impact of Arkwright

> A circular machine, of new design,
> In conic shape; it draws and spins a thread
> Without the tedious toil of needless hands.
> A wheel, invisible, beneath the floor.
> To every member of th' harmonious frame
> Gives necessary motion.[16]

For several years before his roller-spinning patent of 1738, Lewis Paul experimented in Birmingham with John Wyatt, a carpenter, to find a method of cotton-spinning 'without the intervention of the human fingers'. Wyatt and Paul's machine worked, in that it could spin good thread, so it aroused considerable interest and was trialled under licence. The system proved too fragile, however, to be viable commercially.[17]

10   White, *Dir.* II (1838), 455–6.
11   Compared with 100,000 power looms: Ure, *Cotton Manufacture*, xxix.
12   Sigsworth, *Black Dyke Mills*, 35.
13   Jenkins and Ponting, *British Wool Textile Industry*, 115.
14   Jenkins and Ponting, *British Wool Textile Industry*, 116–17.
15   *Guardian*, 22 July 1993; http://www.harristweed.org, accessed 6 Oct. 2017; *Peats and Tweed* (DVD, Garenin Blackhouse Village museum, Lewis).
16   John Dyer, 'The Fleece', written in 1757, lines 292–7.
17   Prosser, rev. Cookson, 'Lewis Paul', *DNB*; Aspin, *Water-Spinners*, 129–30; Hills, *Power in the Industrial Revolution*, 47–9.

The idea of spinning by roller was a breakthrough concept. How to apportion credit for it remained contentious. But as James Watt is supposed to have remarked, 'Whoever invented the spinning machine, Arkwright certainly had the most difficult part, which was making it useful'.[18] And that, 'making it useful', was at the core of all early efforts to apply machinery to textile processes. Paul's carding patent of 1748 was likewise a promising principle, but little adopted before Lees and Arkwright improved it in the 1770s.[19] As the flying shuttle increased handloom weavers' productivity, demand for yarn grew. A bounty of £50, offered by the Society of Arts in 1761 for a frame capable of simultaneously spinning six threads, gave further incentive to innovate, if incentive were needed.[20]

A spinning frame has two tasks: drafting, that is drawing out the fibre into an ever finer thread; and inserting twist before winding the yarn on to a bobbin or other package.[21] There were two ways to draft: either by roller, as patented by Paul and Wyatt in 1738; or by stretching the thread while twist was being inserted. This second technique was the basis of Hargreaves' spinning jenny of 1767. Crompton combined the two methods into his mule in 1779.[22]

Ultimately it was Richard Arkwright who picked up drafting by roller and combined it with modified preparatory machinery within a water-powered factory. His spinning machine differed in important detail from earlier attempts at roller spinning, and he patented it in 1769 for making 'weft or yarn from cotton, flax and wool'.[23] He then adapted Bourne and Paul's roller carding engine of 1748, clothing rollers with card and adding a feeding cloth at the start and a doffer comb at the end. Patented in 1775, this machine was readily converted to work wool as well as cotton. At first it was envisaged that a horse gin would power the 1769 spinning machine, but Arkwright employed water – hence 'water frame' – for this and his carding engines. Steam power, in the shape of a Boulton and Watt engine, was first applied to an Arkwright mill in Nottingham in 1790. Arkwright also picked up the idea of adapting a jenny to make a slubbing engine, which condensed carded slivers to a suitable size for spinning.[24] The slubbing billy was introduced to the cotton industry by 1788. The date it was first powered by water or steam is less certain.[25]

18   Aspin, *Water-Spinners*, 17.
19   Heaton, *Yorkshire Woollen and Worsted Industries*, 333.
20   Hills, *Power in the Industrial Revolution*, 54–5.
21   For a succinct yet detailed description of the process and its development, see Dakin, 'Development of Cotton-Spinning Machinery', 457–78.
22   Dakin, 'Development of Cotton-Spinning Machinery', 461; see Table 1.1.
23   British Patent GB931 (1769); Hills, *Power in the Industrial Revolution*, 61–3; see Rees, *Cyclopaedia*, II, 176–7.
24   Crump (ed.), *Leeds Woollen Industry*, 7–8; Aspin, *Water-Spinners*, 24–5.
25   Jenkins and Ponting, *British Wool Textile Industry*, 48–9.

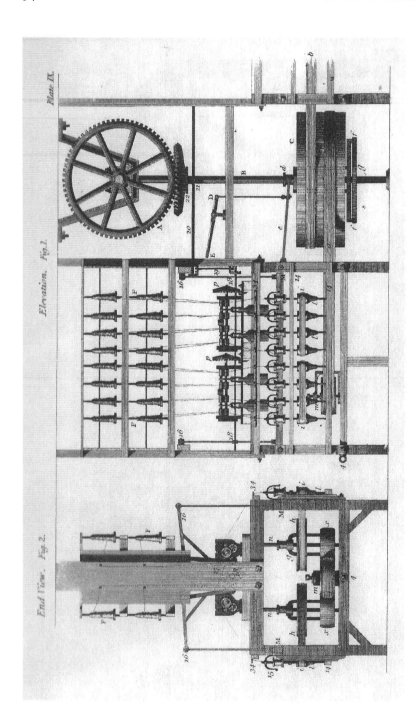

Plate 2. The water frame

Source: Rees, *Cyclopaedia*, X, I (1808), 'Cotton Manufacture', Plate IX.

Arkwright developed his own factories in Cromford and elsewhere in Derbyshire, and in Nottingham and Staffordshire.[26] He began to license out the scheme, from 1778, calculating royalties on each spindle and as a percentage of production. Very soon, Arkwright-system factories spread across the Lancashire and Yorkshire Pennine valleys, wherever there were suitable watercourses.[27] Arkwright fiercely protected his patent rights, but they were widely breached, and quashed altogether in 1785. The patents were faulty: innovation rested in his whole system, rather than being embodied in any one machine.[28] More, the drawings did not match the models submitted to the Patent Office, and too many separate initiatives had been rolled into one patent, evidently to save costs. Opponents appeared at his appeal hearing to claim credit for various features Arkwright had incorporated into his machinery.[29] Several witnesses disputed that the machines could be built from the published specifications – essential for a valid patent – and while Arkwright supporters argued that the detail was adequate, the man himself was quoted by the Crown as stating that

> he had purposely avoided describing his invention by his specification, out of public spirit, because the French should not steal it. 'The reason', says he, 'I did not disclose it fully, is, because foreigners would have understood it'; which is the same thing as if he had said, 'I meant it should not be understood'.[30]

At the time the patent was voided, there were already 60 to 70 water-powered Arkwright-type factories in Lancashire and Yorkshire. The first in Lancashire had opened at Birkacre, near Chorley, in 1778, with Arkwright himself among the partners; and in Yorkshire, in 1780, at Keighley.[31]

Low Mill's significance rests not merely on the fact that it established cotton-spinning in Yorkshire. It was also a spur to developing textile engineering in the county. An early Keighley historian told of its origins.

> The large cotton mill, called Low Mill, begun by the Ramsdens of Halifax, and completed by Messrs Clayton and Walshman, gentlemen from Lancashire, first commenced running [in] June, 1780. The machinery was made under the directions of Sir Richard Arkwright, and as it was the first cotton-mill ever erected in this county, the proprietors found themselves

26   Aspin, *Water-Spinners*, 470–1.
27   Aspin, *Water-Spinners*, 64–5; 452–68.
28   Tann and Burton, *Matthew Boulton*, 165–6.
29   Carpmael (ed.), *Law Reports*, I, especially 41, 46, 49, 53, 58–9.
30   Carpmael (ed.), *Law Reports*, I, 58; also 79–81, 86–7, 91–2, 94–7.
31   Aspin, *Water-Spinners*, 55, 452, 460; Rees, *Cyclopaedia*, II, 178–9.

under the necessity of sending a number of children and young persons to Sir Richard's works, at Cromford in Derbyshire, to learn the business.[32]

This account was reiterated almost verbatim by Hodgson, who added detail garnered from former child workers. Two of these were sent as girls to Cromford for training in 'minding and tending the carding, preparing and spinning machinery'. Back in Keighley, they 'were set to learn [teach] the new mill hands who applied for work' at Low Mill.[33] William Smith, a founding father of the Keighley worsted machinery trade, worked at Low Mill as a child of nine, c. 1783, and (presumably later) was apprenticed there as mechanic.[34]

Thomas Walshman, Arkwright associate and a co-partner at Birkacre, entered the Low Mill company despite serious losses at Chorley, for Arkwright's first Lancashire factory had been destroyed by rioters in 1779. Walshman joined members of the Clayton family of Bamber Bridge, near Preston, whose father had established a first calico printing works in Lancashire during the 1750s. The Claytons intended that Low Mill would secure yarn supplies for their older business, perhaps hoping in the relative backwater of Keighley to avoid the violent opposition generated at Birkacre. Walshman eventually retired, and the Clayton family, two of whom became his sons-in-law, managed Low Mill into the nineteenth century.[35]

How to build a factory

The air of proficiency evident in the Arkwright projects was unusual for its time. Arkwright's success certainly encouraged many imitators. Translating ambition into profitable enterprise, though, was not straightforward. Expertise, whether in practical skills or technological knowledge, was in short supply.

A few individuals already styled themselves machine-makers, but a developed, specialist textile-engineering trade was not recognizable before 1800. This 'Arkwright' phase was therefore one of transition, and factory promoters looking for technical advice about buildings and machinery had to seek out what was available and assess its reliability. The guidance on offer might be vague, second-hand, opportunistic, inaccurate or positively misleading, but knowledge and understanding were growing. The

32 Keighley, *Keighley, Past and Present*, 108.
33 Hodgson, *Textile Manufacture*, 212–13.
34 See app. 1.
35 Aspin, *Water-Spinners*, 68–71, 76–82; Hodgson, *Textile Manufacture*, 212–13; Ingle, *Yorkshire Cotton*, 66–7.

environment, fluid and uncertain, was increasingly underpinned by a strand of measured experience.

In the early years, factory promoters must gather their own resources. The investors came as individuals or in partnership, from varied backgrounds, some purely speculators, others looking to complement and extend older textile interests. Arkwright's patents had not stopped the emulators, and once his rights were lost, still more rushed into the cotton-spinning gold mine. Cotton mills were built across the northern countryside wherever there was the weight of water to drive them and a possibility of recruiting or importing labour.[36] Many projectors had textile experience, though probably not sufficient to manage a powered factory, and most were ill-equipped for the mechanical demands. The worsted manufacturer Robert Heaton applied experience from another textile branch in the hope of success with cotton. In woollen-cloth making, new sites were developed by experienced textile manufacturers looking to rationalize and further mechanize their operation – as with Benjamin Gott at Bean Ing, and John Taylor at Hunsworth. John Marshall's confidence in launching a flax-spinning factory at Holbeck rested on the success of his and Matthew Murray's systematic mechanical experiments. There are also instances of landowners, presumably quite innocent of the technicalities, building textile mills as speculative ventures.

What these men had in common, whatever their background, was that all needed help. Buying into Arkwright's package brought support in the shape of a millwright to advise on mill design, power and machinery. Usually, Arkwright favoured his own Thomas Lowe of Nottingham, or he employed the leading Yorkshire millwright John Sutcliffe. These millwrights oversaw construction, though usually at a distance, delegating day-to-day supervision to associates. Specialist tradesmen might be brought in, reinforced by local joiners and smiths.[37] This arrangement resembled Boulton and Watt's approach to installing steam-engines. And like theirs, Arkwright's method doubtless leaked expertise to local workers, who discovered new skills and prized technological information.[38]

Many intending cotton-spinners resisted paying Arkwright for a licence, even before the patents were finally quashed. His charges were daunting: the proprietors of Low Mill, Clayton and Walshman, paid £4,200 to use 2,000 spindles, more than double the £2,000 insurance value of the new factory itself. Arkwright issued licences only for 500 or more spindles.[39] Unsurprisingly, new ventures often proceeded without reference to him.

36   Ingle, *Yorkshire Cotton*, 6–11. Weight, not speed, of water was the essential factor: *Water-Spinners*, 25.
37   Aspin, *Water-Spinners*, 24–6; Tann, 'The Textile Millwright', 83–5; see below, pp. 71–6.
38   Tann and Burton, *Matthew Boulton*, 30–1, 112–13.
39   Aspin, *Water-Spinners*, 25.

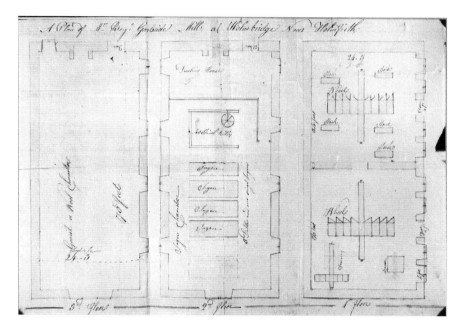

Plate 3. Benjamin Gartside's mill at Holmbridge, late 1790s. The middle floor has a 40-spindle billy, four scribbling or carding engines with space for two more, and a small dwelling. Below are two water-wheels, five fulling stocks, a dressing machine and teazer; above, a loft for storing wool.

Source: Historic England BB88/04571.

The cotton-spinning novices had before them not just Arkwright's example, but also that of the energized woollen trade. The heroic scale of Gott's factory at Bean Ing perhaps overshadows his industry's prior advances. In northern England's clothing districts there is still physical evidence of this ambition.[40] To a contemporary, the expansion of a centuries-old fulling mill to incorporate other woollen processes, however modest this appears to modern eyes, might have seemed an industrial revolution in itself.[41] But not all woollen factories under development were converted or extended from older fulling or corn-mills. A proportion were entirely new builds. John Taylor, head of a long-established Gomersal family of cloth merchants and manufacturers, created a fulling, scribbling, carding and cloth-finishing mill at Hunsworth in 1788.[42] Gomersal was a thriving centre of woollen-cloth

40   Giles and Goodall, *Yorkshire Textile Mills.*
41   See below, pp. 73–4.
42   WYAS Leeds, MD292/59.

making, where another leading manufacturer, William Burnley, had in 1751 erected a proto-factory of textile workshops. A cloth hall was also launched in Gomersal, in 1775, but this attempt to challenge Leeds failed soon after the older market centre countered with a new one of its own.[43] The village, on the ridge of a hill, had no access to water-power, so Taylor's new venture was about two miles away on the Savile estate near Hunsworth. He leased two acres of ground, enough for a fulling mill with two stocks, a miller's house, dams and leats, and a wash and floodgates to control the water supply. The mill was also intended for 'making, fixing and using any number of engines for scribbling or carding of wool; gigs for raising of cloth, or any other engines …' It would be surprising had Taylor not employed a millwright, and indeed such a man, Thomas Rushforth, is mentioned, though whether he built Hunsworth mill is not specified. It was evidently a success, as Taylor bought the property, with additional land, when the lease was up in 1800.[44] The merchant and manufacturer Charles Hudson of Skircoat, Halifax, took a similar path. He introduced scribbling and possibly spinning machinery to an existing fulling mill in the early 1780s, employing waged operatives for non-powered processes. A slubbing billy and spinning jenny were ordered from William Cockerell of Haslingden, north of Bury, Lancashire, in 1787, intended for a new mill Hudson planned. He enquired of the ironfounders Bateman and Sherratt of Salford, in 1788, the price of a steam-engine big enough to drive eight carding engines.[45]

There was some advantage in an owner-occupier with textile experience projecting a new factory. For them it was a measured risk, the basics understood. Most likely, too, they would know something about the pool of millwrights, advisors and suppliers. Speculative factory-building generally, though, seems more random in its outcomes. The Leeds dyer James Whiteley, who in the mid-1780s built a water-driven factory presumably intended for woollen processing in an isolated valley in Adel, five miles north of Leeds, may have been surprised when it was taken for flax-spinning experimentation by a linen merchant, John Marshall, with famous results.[46] After Marshall left, Scotland Mill was divided, used for both cotton-spinning and wool-scribbling.[47]

In building factories, woollen as well as cotton, landowners looked to increase their estate's value. They often needed specialist guidance. William Robinson of Pudsey offered his services to Walter Stanhope of Horsforth Hall in 1784: 'Thomas Marsden tells me that you intend building a scribbling mill

43   Cookson and Cookson, *Gomersal*, 112–15.
44   WYAS Leeds, MD292/59; /62–3.
45   Smail, *Merchants, Markets and Manufacture*, 133–4; 145–8.
46   Rimmer, *Marshalls of Leeds*, 26–7.
47   Ingle, *Yorkshire Cotton*, 106.

at Horsforth and that he had recommended to you to employ me as being a proper person to superintend the works.'

Robinson's proposal did not include millwrights' work – the mill building and power sources. Rather, he wanted to oversee the construction of machinery and afterwards act as factory manager, citing previous experience at a mill in Hunslet. He offered detailed estimates for making three scribbling machines – costs of wood, forged ironwork, cast ironwork, cards and workmanship – calculated the running costs of these and a willey, and (excluding any building and power costs, not mentioned) projected a likely annual profit of £522 with the mill on 'half work' – 12-hour days.[48]

The wealthy Beaumont estate of Bretton built Castle Hill mill in Gomersal, evidently speculative, and unusual for its time and location in being steam-driven. It was advertised in 1794 as 'a large new-erected scribbling mill and corn-mill wrought by a steam engine' and with eight engines for scribbling and carding wool. Evidently it stood empty for six years, and never worked as a corn-mill. The eventual tenant was a wool-stapler.[49] Before he moved in, substantial refurbishment was carried out by the estate in 1799–1800, involving a millwright, David Popplewell, a machine-maker named Samuel Holdsworth, and Benjamin Ross, a local blacksmith and publican. Wood and castings were brought in separately and machinery erected at the mill. On completion, the Leeds millwright and machine-maker John Jubb was among valuers of scribbling, carding and spinning machinery and transmission gear, while Edward Smalley, engineer at the Low Moor Co., listed and valued parts of the steam-engine.[50] Despite the well-qualified advisors employed by the estate – perhaps the initial advice which Beaumont commissioned had been less solid – the enterprise probably suffered from bad timing, an inconvenient situation, and maybe most importantly, a lack of purpose.

Across the woollen districts of northern England, by the early 1790s these many small factory developments collectively represented a significant shift in the cloth industry's organization. And then there came Benjamin Gott and Bean Ing. Gott took the best of what others were already doing and transported it as a package into a new dimension. Bean Ing was without doubt a brave endeavour – a factory on a scale not seen, an immense financial speculation. Brick-built on a 16-acre site on the western fringe of Leeds in 1792–93, it was arranged around a closed courtyard. Together with the main mill building of the first phase, burnt down in 1799, were an engine house and dyeworks, weaving, pressing and finishing shops.[51] Gott's ambition was

48   WYAS Bradford, Sp.St./14/39.
49   Cookson and Cookson, *Gomersal*, 117–18.
50   WYAS Wakefield, BEA/C3/B16/6.
51   Crump (ed.), *Leeds Woollen Industry*, 257; Giles and Goodall, *Yorkshire Textile Mills*, 85, 87–90, 212.

tempered by intelligence. He sought out the technology most useful for his purposes, adopting new machines and methods once satisfied that they could serve his aims. He had confidence enough to order a Boulton and Watt rotary engine at the outset, the first time one had been used to drive the entire fulling and scribbling plant of a woollen mill.[52] He brought fulling stocks from the West Country, from Wheeler of Rode, near Trowbridge, who continued to supply and advise him for at least 20 years.[53] But though Gott's factory was innovative in so many ways, technologically this was a conservative revolution.[54] In no sense was he a mechanical pioneer; indeed, he was hardly a manufacturer. His talent was in organizing a system of work, defining and managing processes, eliminating transaction costs and the associated time and trouble, in order to maximize profit. By doing this, his organization – and perhaps he was the first who can accurately be said to have had an organization – was empowered to respond to the woollen cloth market's increasingly specific demands. The record of mill practice at Bean Ing shows Gott's system at work, the division of labour, the regulation of all stages of manufacture – rules for working scribbling machines, finishing routines for various kinds of cloths, and so on.[55]

How Bean Ing was designed and built is not exactly known, though Gott oversaw construction.[56] Gott's father, John, and half-brother, William, both civil engineers, may have advised, though the father died in 1793.[57] As part of their own package, Boulton and Watt would guide arrangements for the steam-engine and see to its installation. Gott himself ordered engine castings from Joshua Walker of Rotherham, in consultation with Boulton and Watt.[58] The millwright engaged by Gott in 1792, John Sutcliffe of Halifax (fl. 1780–1816), was dismissed after the two fell out, and replaced by Thomas Lowe. Afterwards, in 1793–94, Gott commissioned the eminent engineer John Rennie, with whom he developed a close friendship.[59] George Augustus Lee, a Salford cotton-spinner known for experiments on his own Boulton and Watt engine, and later a factory designer, was another advisor

52   Crump (ed.), *Leeds Woollen Industry*, 13–14.
53   Crump (ed.), *Leeds Woollen Industry*, 36–7, 282.
54   See above, pp. 23–4.
55   Brotherton SC, MS193/117a; Crump (ed.), *Leeds Woollen Industry*, 272–312. See also Smail, *Merchants, Markets and Manufacture*, 133–5.
56   Brotherton SC, MS193/22–31, 33; Crump (ed.), *Leeds Woollen Industry*, 256.
57   Crump (ed.), *Leeds Woollen Industry*, 170; Brotherton SC, handlist 22 to MS194.
58   Brotherton SC, MS193/34–5; Crump (ed.), *Leeds Woollen Industry*, 196–9.
59   Tann, *Development of the Factory*, 99–101; Crump (ed.), *Leeds Woollen Industry*, 205–6, 208; M. Chrimes, 'Thomas Lowe, fl. 1760–90', in Skempton (ed.), *Biographical Dictionary*, 414; Jenkins, *West Riding Wool Textile Industry*, 108–9. Payments to Lowe are recorded in Brotherton SC, MS193/29–30.

turned friend.[60] Sutcliffe's reputation as the region's best practical millwright had been recognized by other factory developers in central Leeds in 1791–92, John Marshall, and also Markland, Cookson and Fawcett. But he fell out of favour, was considered very expensive, and his advice on steam-engines was soon revealed as outmoded.[61]

Watt made very significant patented improvements to the steam-engine in 1782, which were quickly embodied in a rotary engine, the first of which were sold in 1783. Yet as 1792 dawned, not a single Boulton and Watt 'sun and planet' engine had been supplied to the West Riding. Marshall, in the belief that a steam-engine alone could not produce a sufficiently even motion, powered his first flax-spinning factory on Water Lane using the transitional system in which an atmospheric engine – 'on Savery's principle' – raised water to drive a wheel. This did not work well, and in May 1792 Boulton and Watt installed a 20-hp model at Water Lane. Within three months both Gott and the Markland partnership had theirs, of 40 hp and 30 hp respectively.[62] Subsequent relations between Boulton and Watt and certain northern engineers, especially Matthew Murray, were strained. While recognizing the benefits of Watt's concept, Murray wanted to modernize the design. He improved it and was the first to make the engine entirely of iron, replacing sizeable quantities of wood used by the Birmingham firm. By selling engines and condensers separately, Murray managed to avoid being sued for breaching Watt's patent.[63] He was not alone in angering Boulton and Watt, who suspected several Lancashire engineers of pirating their technology. Among these were James Bateman and William Sherratt of Salford, a partnership established in the late 1780s to make atmospheric engines. These partners began to supply rotary engines partially imitating Watt's patent. Such was the scale of their market – Bateman and Sherratt engines probably outnumbered Watt's in and around Manchester – that Boulton and Watt obtained an injunction in 1796 against these and other Lancashire pirates. Bateman and Sherratt reverted to making the older style of pumping engine, which still found many buyers, for it was compact, quiet and efficient, 'with a quickness and ease not to be conceived'. They then impatiently stockpiled rotary models ahead of Boulton and Watt's patent expiring in 1800.[64]

The least known of the early Boulton and Watt customers in Leeds,

60   M. Chrimes, 'George Augustus Lee', in Skempton (ed.), *Biographical Dictionary*, 400–1.
61   Jenkins, *West Riding Wool Textile Industry*, 108–9; M. Chrimes, 'John Sutcliffe', in Skempton (ed.), *Biographical Dictionary*, 675.
62   Brotherton SC, MS200/26, pp. 37–8; Crump (ed.), *Leeds Woollen Industry*, 191–2, 196, 225; Giles and Goodall, *Yorkshire Textile Mills*, 134–5.
63   Ron Fitzgerald contributed ideas on this point.
64   Musson and Robinson, *Science and Technology*, 406–8, 413–23, 449–50; Tann and Burton, *Matthew Boulton*, 120; Tupling, 'Early Metal Trades', 26; Aikin, *Description of the Country*, 176–7.

Markland, Cookson and Fawcett, built Bank Mill on the Aire, east of the town, to the design of John Sutcliffe. John Cookson of Kirkgate represented a long-established and prominent family of Leeds woollen cloth merchants; Edward Markland of Park Lane was also a merchant. Cookson was partner in a carpet workshop with Joseph Fawcett, about whom little is known. Built for cotton-spinning, Bank Mill too was conceived with a water-wheel and pumping engine to lift water into the mill-dam. Like Marshall, the partners quickly replaced it with a rotary engine, fitted in 1792. Bank Mill, already a large and ambitious undertaking, was extended in 1796, at which time the water-wheel was removed. The factory was soon spinning worsteds as well as cotton, and by 1797 cotton had been abandoned.[65]

These Leeds enterprises of 1791–92 – Marshall in flax, Gott in woollens, and Markland in cotton and then worsted – present a snapshot of the most sophisticated elements of the region's textile industry, as it then was. But for all of them, the engineering influences were somewhat detached, external, at arm's length, and not fully reflecting innovation's cutting edge. Sutcliffe's guidance on power systems doubtless played some part in this, perhaps delaying the adoption of Boulton and Watt's latest technology into Yorkshire textiles. The adherence to atmospheric engines is understandable, as Sutcliffe's career had focused upon water systems, on major northern canal projects, about which he wrote a treatise.[66]

Easily overlooked, against the drama of novelty, are the other woollen factories established in Leeds in those same years which were designed on older models. Holbeck Mill, on the south side of Holbeck Lane, was started by William Fisher of Meadow Lane, Hunslet, in partnership with one Nixon, in 1792–93. The main value of the mill, insured in 1795 for £1,650, lay in its workshops, warehouse and stock. Its steam-engine was an old model, value only £100.[67] Brookfield Mill was situated on Hunslet Lane, south of the merchant houses near Leeds bridge. It was founded by two brothers from one of those merchant families, John and Edward Brooke, in 1791. The Brookes' main works included a dry house, press shops, burling house and cropping shop, but was evidently without benefit of any power, other than human, and so was a real manufactory.[68] More Boulton and Watt engines soon followed those of Gott, Marshall and the Markland partners. The first was for a

65   Crump (ed.), *Leeds Woollen Industry*, 319; Beresford, *East End, West End*, 197, 242, 244; Barfoot and Wilkes, *Dir.*, III, 537–9; Giles and Goodall, *Yorkshire Textile Mills*, 212; Ingle, *Yorkshire Cotton*, 106, 109.

66   Mike Chrimes supplied information about John Sutcliffe and ideas about millwrights.

67   Crump (ed.), *Leeds Woollen Industry*, 5, 319; Connell, 'Industrial development', II, no. 15; Barfoot and Wilkes, *Dir.*, III, 538. For prices of Boulton and Watt engines supplied to Leeds in the 1790s see Jenkins, *West Riding Wool Textile Industry*, 162.

68   Crump (ed.), *Leeds Woollen Industry*, 5, 319; Connell, 'Industrial development', II, no. 147; Barfoot and Wilkes, *Dir.*, III, 537.

cotton mill in Hunslet, in September 1792, and another 10 arrived in and
around Leeds during the following three years, in all branches of textiles.[69]
But against the whole sum of the West Riding industry, the level of rotary
engine purchases was low.

One of those new engines, installed by Boulton and Watt in 1794, was for
Mill B, Marshall's second factory in Holbeck, built by the new partnership
Marshall and Benyon.[70] Marshall's experiments at Adel had concentrated
first, in 1788, on carding and tow-spinning, and shifted to power-loom
weaving in 1788–89. Then, probably late in 1788, Marshall brought in
Matthew Murray and the tide turned.[71] Marshall's rigorous trials and patents
were then unusual among factory-builders. Investing in his first factory,
Marshall must have been satisfied that his patented technology would work in
mass production, and he retained Murray's support. Commercially, Marshall
had more in common with Arkwright than Cartwright, with his enterprise
soon a resounding success – evidenced by the building of Mill B within two
years. But despite many advantages and an obvious confidence and audacity,
Marshall nonetheless pursued a route similar to people less expert in the
technology but more skilled in textile production, in the way he commissioned his first factory.

In addition to 80 or more woollen and worsted mills built in the West
Riding before the end of 1792, there were approximately 100 cotton-factories
in Lancashire, and a similar number in Yorkshire. Some of these also engaged
in, or later converted entirely to, worsted spinning.[72] Many were sited in
out-of-the-way locations, with little or no technical expertise on hand,
adding to the practical difficulties. A millwright may advise on plans, carry
out structural work, and commission power and transmission systems. But
commonly, factory projectors were themselves central to the process, even
formulating a scheme grounded in their own investigations. B. F. Lister visited
several textile factories in 1791, including the worsted mill at Addingham,
and saw cotton machines running in Hebden Bridge. Recording sizes of
water-wheels, numbers and sizes of machines and running costs, he drew up
budgets and requirements for his own new factory.[73] Potentially useful data
was noted, its value well-recognized. Fulling and scribbling premises like
Joseph Rogerson's in Bramley were a social hub and information exchange.[74]
Besides his clothier clients, almost every week came tradesmen to nail cards,

69   Crump (ed.), *Leeds Woollen Industry*, 191–2; Jenkins, *West Riding Wool Textile Industry*,
97–8.
70   Crump (ed.), *Leeds Woollen Industry*, 191–2; Rimmer, *Marshalls of Leeds*, 44–5.
71   Rimmer, *Marshalls of Leeds*, 26–7, 29–38.
72   Jenkins, *West Riding Wool Textile Industry*, 208–12; Aspin, *Water-Spinners*, 451–67.
73   Brotherton SC, BUS/Marriner, Box 16. Whether the plan came to fruition, perhaps in
Frizinghall (Bradford) or Keighley, is not made clear.
74   Crump (ed.), *Leeds Woollen Industry*, 60; see below, pp. 162–3.

or millwrights to adjust the machinery, and Rogerson recorded some of what had been shared:

> A patent steam-engine of 16¼ Inches Cylinder will not carry 3 scribblers 3 Carders pulley & Willy & 3 Fallers & a Driver, for so it was told me by a Slubber from Yeadon.[75]

A journal kept from about 1789 by the worsted manufacturer Robert Heaton chronicled the progress of two factories under construction: his own cotton mill at Ponden, six miles from Keighley, and that of his son, also Robert, at Royd House, Oxenhope, about three miles from Ponden.[76] A series of agents and advisers came to help. John Weatherhead of Keighley, a joiner who made spinning frames, pointed out sources of metal components in Bradford and Lancashire. Though not a supplier, Weatherhead was paid expenses to visit Haworth in 1791, presumably to comment on work at Ponden.[77] A Lancashire machine-maker offered Heaton basic advice about factory layout:

> Richard Sagar, Burnley, and his brother at Blackburn, makes mules and jennys. He says a room six yards square will hold two mules of about 144 or 150 spindles. A room five yards square will hold two jenneys, a jenny with 100 spindles will cost 7£ and will spin 1 lb an hour from 24 to 30 hanks in a lb.[78]

Heaton collected names of several other machine-makers in Bolton and Manchester.[79] Seemingly Ponden's machinery was built on site, the parts delivered by tradesmen or agents. Heaton covered several pages of his journal with specifications for wood to construct two cotton frames, each nine feet in length; and three pairs of cards, binders for two spinning frames, and a roving frame.[80] Suppliers included James Greenwood, for brass work, oak planks, and 'two pairs of cards [&] iron wheels'.[81] Joshua Smith built at least four spinning frames, Peter Milner dealt with the Bradford ironfounder John Sturges on Heaton's behalf, and John Brigg was employed to cut brass for a roving frame.[82]

At Royd House the approach differed. The millwright Joseph Tempest of

75 Crump (ed.), *Leeds Woollen Industry*, 77; and Rogerson made similar enquiries about gas-lighting in 1813: 156.
76 WYAS Bradford, DB2/6/3; Hodgson, *Textile Manufacture*, 232–3; Aspin, *Water-Spinners*, 106–10; Ingle, *Yorkshire Cotton*, 97–9.
77 WYAS Bradford, DB2/6/3, pp. 36–7, 106; see app. 1.
78 WYAS Bradford, DB2/6/3, p. 27.
79 WYAS Bradford, DB2/6/3, p. 10.
80 WYAS Bradford, DB2/6/3, pp. 114–18.
81 WYAS Bradford, DB2/6/3, pp. 104–5, 107, 118.
82 WYAS Bradford, DB2/6/3, p. 107; see app. 1.

Keighley was first engaged. Afterwards the younger Heaton and his partner, his father-in-law John Murgatroyd, employed John Brigg for a year from September 1791 for £40 plus his meat, drink and lodging, 'to come and work for them at Roydhouse, brass, iron and wood turning and to act as engineer for the cotton mill erected there'.[83] Joseph Tempest was contracted as millwright at Walk Mill, Keighley, in 1783, with a secrecy clause relating to the machinery there.[84] In Oxenhope he advised on a water-wheel and gearing.

> Mr Joseph Tempest's plan for a mill to spin cotton at Roydhouse – Suppose the water wheel be 30 feet in diameter, the pitt wheel must be 23 feet 9 inches and contain 324 teeth in 18 segments, 18 teeth each. The crown wheel must be 3 feet 1 inch in diameter and contain 41 teeth.[85]

Tempest placed orders for transmission parts at Sowerby Bridge, though there is no hint that he made machinery.[86] By 1793, when he bought rollers from Richard Hattersley, he presumably produced spinning frames or oversaw their construction. But at Royd House, it was the engineer, John Brigg, who built machines. He turned brass, iron and wood, brought components including bobbins, brass wheels, an 'engine' (meaning a machine) and other parts from Keighley, and travelled to Halifax and Leeds for tools and engineering equipment.[87]

The Heaton mills were not commercially successful. The family would better have stayed with the trade they knew best, for spinning worsteds in a factory was then approaching viability. Low Mill, on the Wharfe at Addingham, though planned as a cotton-factory, instead spun worsteds from its opening in 1787. This was only the second instance of a worsted-spinning factory after Dolphinholme, near Lancaster, in 1784.[88] While Low Mill was being constructed as an extension of an older mill, the lord of Addingham, Richard Smith, evicted the miller from the manorial corn-mill upstream. He intended leasing the site to cotton-manufacturers, Henry Lister and John Cockshott, to produce weft yarn, and was himself instrumental in building the Arkwright-type High Mill adjacent to the old corn-mill. At first, it did spin cotton, but switched within a year or two mainly or wholly to worsteds. Richard Smith and his son were among the consortium running this worsted business, with some of the Quaker Birkbecks of Settle, bankers and woollen manufacturers; two Lancaster merchants; and Robert Hargreaves. On the strength of his mechanical skills,

83   WYAS Bradford, DB2/6/3, p. 121.
84   Hodgson, *Textile Manufacture*, 36.
85   WYAS Bradford, DB2/6/3, p. 100.
86   WYAS Bradford, DB2/6/3, p. 116.
87   WYAS Bradford, DB2/6/3, pp. 123, 127; see app. 1.
88   Aspin, *Water-Spinners*, 446–7; Ingle, *Yorkshire Dales Textile Mills*, 82–3. Chris Aspin and George Ingle added information here.

credited with significantly adapting roller-spinning to worsteds, Hargreaves convinced the Birkbecks to back a much larger worsted factory in Linton, inviting builders' tenders perhaps as early as April 1787.[89] Subsequently the various Addingham businesses suffered change and setback, including the bankruptcies in 1793 of Cockshott, a partner in both High and Low mills, and in 1797 of Robert Pearson, a local draper who evidently ran the jenny shop. That may have marked the end of cotton-spinning there. The death of Richard Smith and ensuing sale of the manor followed, in 1794.[90] That year Addingham had corn, worsted and tow mills, almost all newly built, the worsted section leased to Robert Hargreaves & Co. Part of High Mill, with four flax-spinning frames, was advertised to let in 1804.[91]

These complicated and fast-changing developments in Addingham show the fluctuating course of textiles in one decade. Note the range of textile manufacturers and merchants, landowners, financiers and innovators involved in promoting new ventures; the old buildings reused and new ones constructed and rapidly converted; the spread of powered factories into new territories. Alongside the suggestion of successes and technological break-through, there are more than hints of failure. But like Heaton of Ponden, Richard Smith was learning as he went along with the High Mill project. He jotted specifications for the building in the back of an account book, and of the parts brought in – tow spindles and other items from Edward Thompson of Skipton, and cast iron wheels from Salt and Gothard in Hunslet.[92] A local blacksmith called John Fawcett turned spindles and carried out other unspec-ified work. Edward Brumfitt, a Skipton cabinet-maker and haulier, acted as conduit of parts and information to Smith, delivering, besides iron wheels for the machines, a rough sketch on a scrap of paper showing how to set up machinery for roller-spinning. For his own part, Smith was able to estimate and compare expected profits from cotton and worsted spinning.[93]

If it could be secured, technical expertise was clearly advantageous, at least for as long as it took to plan, build and equip a factory. In 1784 the partners at

89   Mason, *Woolcombers, Worsteds and Watermills*, 17–23; Aspin, *Water-Spinners*, 447–8, 462; Ingle, *Yorkshire Dales Textile Mills*, 16, 89–91, 104–5; Keighley, *Keighley, Past and Present*, 110; Guildhall Lib., Sun 552473 1789; RE 118521A 1790; *Leeds Intelligencer*, 22 Apr. 1788. There is confusion about whether Richard or Robert Hargreaves was the innovator.

90   *Leeds Intelligencer*, 17 June 1793; 14 Aug. 1797; 16 Oct. 1797; 25 Aug. 1794; Ingle, *Yorkshire Dales Textile Mills*, 90.

91   *Leeds Intelligencer*, 25 Aug. 1794; 7 May 1804.

92   YAHS, DD61, Account book of Richard Smith of Addingham, 1777. The late Kate Mason helped greatly, with this reference and information on Smith and High Mill.

93   YAHS, DD61; Aspin, *Water-Spinners*, 447; Mason, *Woolcombers, Worsteds and Watermills*, 17–23; Cookson, 'Millwrights, Clock-Makers'. The drawing style is very similar to sketches made c. 1760 in John Brearley's memorandum books, of power sources connecting to cloth-finishing machinery: Smail (ed.), *Woollen Manufacturing in Yorkshire*, 59, 89, 93, 108, 115, 116, 119.

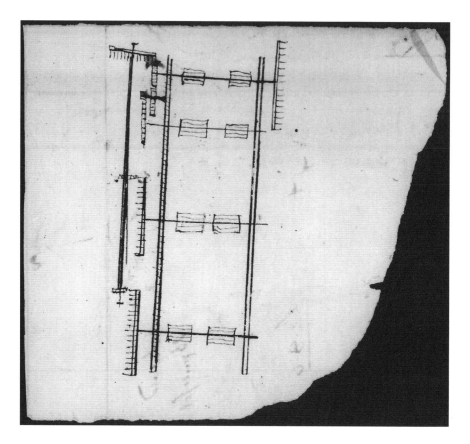

Plate 4. Sketch assisting Richard Smith in construction of High Mill, Addingham, c. 1786

Source: Brotherton SC, YAS/DD61.

West Greengate Mill, Keighley, employed an engineer called James Greenwood with 'a genius well adapted for constructing the machines and other works'. This was offered as a route into partnership, despite Greenwood's lack of capital. That did not materialize, but he stayed long enough to oversee the construction of mill and machinery.[94]

The first cotton-factory in Leeds was built on Balm Beck, Hunslet, by a merchant, John Storey.[95] Its earliest record is an insurance policy of 1787, by which time Storey had died and his son-in-law, Ard Walker, was in control. Noted as an oil and cotton mill, it had a 'fire engine for raising water' and a 24-ft wheel.[96] Though evidently without textile experience, Walker, a distiller and spirit merchant in Briggate, did well enough that the site was further developed during the 1790s and 1800s. He bought spinning shafts and other parts from Hattersley of Keighley in 1794, and then, 1800–04, completed a new five-storey factory and re-equipped at a cost of over £4,000.[97] This included a 30-hp steam-engine made by Fenton, Murray and Wood. Like other factory-builders, Walker personally supervised many of the arrangements and controlled the accounts. The master millwright, John Nicholls, was paid weekly in cash and with large quantities of ale for his men, during various periods of construction, on both the building and 'machinery' accounts. 'Machinery' here included engine, boiler and transmission gear. Payments were made to Richard Pullan for a boiler, and to Joseph Shaw, Martin Cawood, and Salt and Gothard, all of these founders in Hunslet or Leeds, for castings and other metal parts.[98]

Early in proceedings, in 1800, 10 spinning frames and other machines were ordered from one Longbottom, presumably a machine-maker, 'near Halifax'.[99] There is an unsubstantiated suggestion that these were bought as models to be copied.[100] Certainly textile machinery was constructed within Walker's mill. William Farmery and others delivered rollers and spindles, and many varieties of wooden planks and metal parts came from a host of suppliers. Walker brought in joiners, plumbers and painters to work on machinery. The most significant were apparently Farmery; a whitesmith called William Milner, retained for many weeks; and in 1803–04 'Samuel Lawson, clock-maker', in fact a machine-maker newly out of his apprenticeship, who received £4 4s. od for four weeks' work. One of the last payments Walker recorded was to a wood worker: 'Iveson, joiner, at sundry times for inspecting the make of all the new machinery £7 7s. od'.[101]

From the documented examples of late-eighteenth-century factory-building in Yorkshire, certain common features emerge. Generally, a factory owner or agent directed proceedings, monitored costs and collected technical information, as far as that was feasible. A power system, whether water, steam, or the two in combination, required a millwright to produce plans, build, supervise earthworks, and install transmission systems and perhaps an atmospheric engine. Rotary engines, less usual, were supplied and fitted by their maker, often with castings and other parts from local foundries. Where, though, did machines come from?

96 Aspin, *Water-Spinners*, 238; Connell, 'Industrial development', II, no. 199, later called Waterloo Mill. Ard Walker was the son of Richard Walker of Bank: Leeds St Peter, bap. 15 May 1754.
97 Barfoot and Wilkes, *Dir.*, III, 541; Aspin, *Water-Spinners*, 238; WYAS Bradford, 32D83/5/1.
98 WYAS Leeds, DB23.
99 WYAS Leeds, DB23.
100 Connell, 'Industrial development', 162–3.
101 WYAS Leeds, DB23.

How to make machines

Included in the 'knowledge' that Arkwright sold under licence were technical support and training.[102] The Arkwright system was popular, though his licence was not, mainly on grounds of cost. How many industrialists took up formal permits from Arkwright is not known, but they were certainly outnumbered by those attempting to work the method unsanctioned. Arkwright's first licences were issued in 1778, and he began to take action against unlicensed infringements in 1781. From then until 1785 and the final demise of his patents, he was embroiled in legal action.[103] Meanwhile dozens of imitators flourished, including those trying to adapt the principle to worsted spinning. In 1782, the tiny North Brook Mill, 'about the size of four cottage houses', bore the distinction of being the second cotton-factory in Keighley, and in Yorkshire. Here, the stuff-maker John Greenwood attempted to work out for himself how to build spinning frames, with only the closely protected Low Mill as a model. He could not make the bobbins draw. Help came from a passing Low Mill employee, who innocently pointed to a lack of washers, and cut out for him a sample. The small size of his works may have kept Greenwood beyond the notice of Arkwright's lawyers. Later he enjoyed great commercial success.[104]

In the late-eighteenth century there were two potential sources of textile machinery. The first option was to make your own. Mill-builders often bought in rollers, spindles and flyers from specialist makers, with frames assembled *in situ* by joiners (for as long as wood comprised a major element of machinery), and by smiths or other metalworkers. The second possibility was to buy from a machine-maker, some of whom advertised as early as the 1780s. Carriage was difficult, as Gott found when ordering a steam-engine from the Midlands and fulling stocks from Somerset. Transport of boilers from Birmingham or Wrexham, said Boulton and Watt, 'especially such large ones as yours, is attended with much danger of breaking the joints'. Consequently they sent drawings so that the boilers at least could be made in Leeds.[105]

Movement of bulky merchandise around the region was transformed by the opening of sections of the Leeds and Liverpool canal, though not connected to Manchester until 1822. Starting in 1770, the stretch from Leeds to Gargrave, along with its branch into Bradford, was fully navigable from 1777 and ran from Leeds to Burnley in 1796.[106] The traveller John Aikin described in 1795 how the canal had dramatically changed Bradford's prospects:

102   Aspin, *Water-Spinners*, 77.
103   Aspin, *Water-Spinners*, 24–5.
104   Hodgson, *Textile Manufacture*, 217–19; Aspin, *Water-Spinners*, 460.
105   Crump (ed.), *Leeds Woollen Industry*, 36–7, 200–1.
106   Priestley, *Historical Account of the Navigable Rivers*, 385–97.

In the parish a very capital iron foundry and forge has lately been established, which has the advantage of coal and iron ore got on the spot, and
is a very profitable concern. Coals abound in this neighbourhood, and
large quantities are sent by means of the canal into Craven, from whence
limestone is brought in return.[107]

These materials and facilities, and the vacant factory sites by the waterway,
underpinned Bradford's re-creation twenty years later as a centre of worsted
spinning – and of engineering. In established industrial towns, including
Manchester, Keighley and Leeds, machine-making and many new textile
factories clustered alongside the canal. Peter Fairbairn in 1841 dismissed
any concern about the cost of sending machinery from Leeds to Ireland:
'We have a canal'.[108] Likewise coal moved cheaply across the region, from
long-established collieries on the south side of Leeds, in Beeston, Hunslet
and nearby.[109] The canal, 'one of the boldest and most magnificent projects
hitherto attempted in Great Britain',[110] proved its worth in developing
northern England, some decades before reaching completion.

Where transport was by road, the process was more difficult, and the
machines probably assembled in the factory.

> We sent the iron wheel of[f] on Saturday by Jonathan Willson carr[i]er of
> Stanningley and we shall send billey and plucker and the willy on Thursday
> and cume with them to set them up. As we do not cast for our self we shall
> put wood bends to carrey the roulers.[111]

This was Samuel Fortune of Halifax, supplying carding engines and other
machinery to Benjamin Gott in 1794. Gott bought a 30-spindle billy from
Thomas Leeming of Salford at the same time, 'forwarded with speeds' by a
carrier. The previous year he had ordered three carding engines from Leeming.
Wright and White, Manchester machine-makers and cotton-spinners, were
also early suppliers to Bean Ing.[112] This company, one of whose partners,
William Wright, had been an Arkwright apprentice, established a branch in
Leeds in 1792.

> To Worsted, Woollen and Cotton manufacturers. Wright and White, of
> Lever Street, Manchester, have opened a warehouse at the Far Bank, Leeds,

107   Aikin, *Description of the Country*, 569.
108   PP Exportation of Machinery, 220.
109   See Newton, 'Early Coal Mining'.
110   Priestley, *Historical Account of the Navigable Rivers*, 386.
111   Crump (ed.), *Leeds Woollen Industry*, 215. Fortune was perhaps a millwright: see below,
p. 173.
112   Brotherton SC, MS193/29–30; Crump (ed.), *Leeds Woollen Industry*, 215, 211.

where they make machinery for spinning worsted, upon a new and expeditious plan, either by hand or water; also, for scribbling, carding and spinning wool; likewise for cotton of all kinds. Joiners and a Billy-maker wanted.[113]

A Preston agent had advertised worsted spinning frames for sale in the Leeds newspapers in 1789.[114] The proprietors of Pildacre Mill in Ossett bought machinery from Manchester in 1792 and 1793,[115] while Robert Heaton's investigations, c. 1786–91, led him too towards several Lancashire engineers. As well as the mule- and jenny-making Sagar brothers of Burnley and Blackburn, there were three nearer Bolton – Grime and Grisdale, Thomas Johnson, and Cannan and Smith – the latter two firms in Chowbent (Atherton). Heaton also noted Mr Marshall, a Manchester mule spinner, as a possible source of machines, and that 'Mr Weatherd' – John Weatherhead of Keighley – 'has his iron rollers from John Lee of Parks Brooke near the New Mill near Ashton under Line'.[116]

John Marshall's 'Names of Mechanicks &c' – undated but probably compiled c. 1790 while planning his first factory – listed several Manchester men: Joshua Wrigley, erector of steam-engines and cotton machinery; and two cotton machinery makers, Joseph Taylor and one Appleton, 'late servant of Wrigley's'.[117] Joshua Wrigley (d. 1810), 'a common pump-maker' associated with the process of raising water by steam to drive a water-wheel, became known as an innovator prepared to share expertise with clients. Primarily a millwright working in wood, Wrigley had abandoned an earlier interest in Arkwright-style frames.[118] Wrigley did not impress James Watt, but Marshall must have approved, choosing him to supply a Savery-type engine and install the millwork for Mill A in Holbeck.[119] Marshall, like Heaton, heard of component-makers in Ashton-under-Lyne, the fluted-roller maker Samuel Lees, and John Ogden, spindle-maker; and other spindle-makers in Colne, James Oddie and Thomas Whitacre. He noted Wake and Green of Liverpool as makers of 'cuttings engines etc.'[120] This was John Wyke (1720?–87) and Thomas Green, of Prescot and Liverpool, continuing in

113 Crump (ed.), *Leeds Woollen Industry*, 327, citing *Leeds Mercury*, 24 Nov. 1792. For Wright and White see Musson and Robinson, *Science and Technology*, 435–6, 443. The Lever Street factory turned to mule spinning before 1799: Butler (ed.), *Diary of Thomas Butler*, 268.
114 *Leeds Intelligencer*, 1 Sept. 1789.
115 Goodchild, 'Pildacre Mill', 340–1.
116 WYAS Bradford, DB2/6/3, pp. 10, 27, 36–7.
117 Brotherton SC, MS200/57, p. 6.
118 See below, p. 53.
119 Aikin, *Description of the Country*, 175; Musson and Robinson, *Science and Technology*, 396–406, 443–5; M. Chrimes, 'Joshua Wrigley', in Skempton (ed.), *Biographical Dictionary*, 803–4; Thompson, *Matthew Murray*, 27–8.
120 Brotherton SC, MS200/57, p. 6. Samuel Lees (1759–1804) was a whitesmith who from the 1780s became a renowned manufacturer of fluted and special rollers, at Park Bridge,

Green's sole ownership after Wyke died. They were known as makers of tools for clock- and watch-makers, and Wyke published a catalogue in the 1760s offering instruments as well to 'jewellers, braziers and other mechanics'. He is said to have made a wheel-cutting engine and various tools for textile-machine making, and supplied tools to James Watt from about 1760.[121] Marshall also logged Timothy Bates, a prominent millwright of Sowerby Bridge; in Sheffield, Love and Spear, steel-burners, and a roller- and spindle-maker called John Dewsnap, with some of Dewsnap's prices; and also Joshua Morris, 'fitter of spinning frames', from Doncaster. He mentioned as well spindle-makers in Nidderdale, a long-established linen manufacturing centre, James Brown of Pateley Bridge and James Wildon of Dacre Bank.[122]

Manchester was a common reference point for these early factory projectors. It might be expected that mechanical expertise would grow where it was most immediately needed, in the hinterland of the rapidly growing cotton industry. And more of the earliest cotton-factories were built in Lancashire than in Yorkshire: before the end of 1785, the year that Arkwright's patents fell, there were 47 in Lancashire and 21 in Yorkshire. Also, impressionistically, it seems early Yorkshire mills were overall smaller than those of Lancashire.[123]

But did the mechanics collect around the mills, or the mills around the mechanics who were replacing Arkwright's technologies? Certain of these, noted by Gott and Marshall c. 1790 as potential consultants, had testified against Arkwright in 1785. John Lees had constructed previous versions of Arkwright's feeder, but told the court that the new one could not be made from the patent specification.[124] Joshua Wrigley, then a machine-maker of four years' standing, and Thomas Leeming, in the business for more than 10 years, concurred. Leeming could have made a machine according to Arkwright's drawing, 'but if he had, that machine would be of no use at all'. Wrigley revealed his unsuccessful attempt to build one from the plan some time earlier, 'before there was any objection made to the specification'.[125] The proceedings did not specify these men's paths into machine-making. In a Manchester directory of 1781 only one textile engineer, Adam Harrison, cotton-engine maker of Salford, was clearly identified as such. Most likely among the many ironfounders and whitesmiths listed were producers of components or machines.[126]

Ashton-under-Lyne: Tupling, 'Early Metal Trades', 26; Musson and Robinson, *Science and Technology*, 444, fn. 5.

121   Smith (ed.), *Catalogue of Tools*, introduction, and *passim*; Musson and Robinson, *Science and Technology*, 437.
122   Brotherton SC, MS200/57, p. 6.
123   Aspin, *Water-Spinners*, 452–6; 460–2.
124   Carpmael (ed.), *Law Reports*, I, 79.
125   Carpmael (ed.), *Law Reports*, I, 80.
126   Bailey, *Northern Dir.* (1781), 244–64.

So it seems the expert witnesses of 1785, some widely known as textile engineers by 1790, did not have that profile earlier in the 1780s, or at least not in Manchester. Perhaps they worked for Arkwright, or in one of the Arkwright-licensed factories. Maybe they were following an older trade such as whitesmith, founder, or spindle maker, picking up knowledge of the new textile technologies, and tending increasingly in that direction. Their evidence suggests that, like John Greenwood in Keighley and many others, these men attempted to copy Arkwright frames still under patent. As a Quaker, Lees should not have been involved in such a breach of ethics, and maybe he was not. Perhaps he made feeder frames legitimately under licence, or justified his actions as being for the greater good.

These are speculations, the evidence only hinting at the shape and style of an infant machine-making industry. Lancashire, particularly Manchester, represented to Yorkshire textile manufacturers a fertile source of know-how, though Yorkshire engineering would soon respond. Wright and White's movement into Yorkshire shows that Lancastrians detected a potentially valuable market there. Their Leeds warehouse, though, was short-lived, replaced by a local industry better attuned to indigenous needs.

Textile manufacturers as machine-makers

Did textile manufacturers make machinery for their own use? The practice was unusual after 1800, certainly east of the Pennines. Generally speaking, before then, while a body of engineers and others held specialist knowledge and skills, organizing the contents of a factory was a piecemeal exercise. The onus fell on factory promoters or textile manufacturers. Machines, often supplied as sets of components, were built or assembled *in situ*, for practicality.

These early arrangements could explain why a received wisdom grew up, that textile manufacturers made their own machines. It was not so, though there were important exceptions. The most notable were M'Connel and Kennedy and their circle of engineers and cotton-spinners. James M'Connel (1762–1830) and John Kennedy (1769–1855), young men from Kirkcudbrightshire, were apprenticed as mechanics at Chowbent to William Cannan, originally a joiner, uncle of M'Connel and former neighbour of Kennedy in Scotland. Robert Heaton knew of Cannan's partnership with James Smith while planning Ponden Mill. M'Connel and Kennedy trained as makers of carding engines, jennies, and water frames. Immediately Kennedy, the more talented engineer, served out his time, they started business in Manchester, by 1791. Kennedy took charge of the machine shop, significantly improving and enlarging versions of Crompton's mule, so enabling fine cotton yarns to be machine-spun. It is said that M'Connel and Kennedy began spinning with two mules left on their hands when a customer could not pay. Whether or not this is true, certainly they briefly sold machinery before turning to produce purely for their own use. Soon they became hugely successful fine-cotton spinners.[127]

M'Connel and Kennedy's network embraced both cotton textiles and engineering, their influence extending into subsequent machine-making ventures far beyond Manchester. In 1799, M'Connel married Margaret Houldsworth, whose brothers were fine-cotton spinners in Manchester and Glasgow, suppliers to the Nottingham lace trade, and also machine-makers.[128] Thomas Houldsworth, later an MP, evidently took over Wright and White's mule-spinning factory in Lever Street, Manchester, in the late 1790s.[129] Henry Houldsworth (1774–1853) started out in Manchester, moving in 1799 to Glasgow where he found the cotton trade 'very inferior to that of … Manchester … not in a more forward state in Scotland than they had attained in Manchester at least 10 years before'. Reluctantly he tried to make machines for himself, but without good workmen, and deterred by the high price of tools, he instead found a young mechanic to do the work. By 1803 the arrangement broke down: his machine-maker was busy copying Houldsworth's specifications for other people, and nor would he update them as Houldsworth asked. So Houldsworth bought improved rollers and spindles, and models of machines, from Manchester, and found workmen with sufficient skill to fabricate machinery using Glasgow-made frames. Without other options, this practice continued as late as 1824.[130] One of Houldsworth's best workmen, in turn foreman, travelling salesman and partner, was Peter Fairbairn, who left for Leeds in 1826.[131]

Select Committees investigating the machinery trade, in 1824 and 1841, heard evidence of textile manufacturers making machines for themselves.[132] These witnesses mainly represented large Lancashire cotton-manufacturers, their experience at odds with the situation in Yorkshire woollens and worsteds

127   Lee, *Cotton Enterprise*, 10–13; C. H. Lee, 'John Kennedy (1769–1855), textile manufacturer', *DNB*; John Rylands Univ. Lib., Manchester, GB 133 MCK, administrative and biographical history; *London Gazette* (1827), 18320, 32; (1830), 18881, 2549; Catling, *Spinning Mule*, 42–3; Musson and Robinson, *Science and Technology*, 440–1. Robert Owen of New Lanark fame also emerged from machine-making, and was briefly a partner in their spinning business.

128   Lee, *Cotton Enterprise*, 85–6, 152.

129   'Thomas Houldsworth (1771–1852)', in Fisher (ed.), *History of Parliament*; Butler (ed.), *Diary of Thomas Butler*, 268.

130   PP Artisans and Machinery, 378–9.

131   G. Cookson, 'Sir Peter Fairbairn (1799–1861), mechanical engineer', *DNB*; *London Gazette*, 1 Feb. 1831, 18772, 200.

132   PP Artisans and Machinery; PP Exportation of Machinery.

(especially before Samuel Lister's rather unusual entry into machine-making in the 1840s), where users rarely made machines. But in the 1824 inquiry the millwright and engineer Thomas Cheek Hewes confirmed that 'a great many' Manchester cotton-manufacturers made machines for themselves.[133] Thomas Ashton of Hyde, a spinner and power-loom manufacturer who brought that technology into his own neighbourhood, was one such: 'It is the general rule with us now, to make our own machinery ... solely for my own use; I do not make any for sale.'[134] Like Henry Houldsworth, Ashton had experienced 'very great difficulty indeed' in obtaining machinery.[135] In these cases, the textile manufacturers appear reluctant machine-makers, pressed into it because they saw no real alternative. Once invested in a machine shop, it was more likely they would continue producing at least some of their own.

M'Connel and Kennedy were better placed than most cotton-manufacturers to weigh the economics as well as the engineering. In the 1790s, they offered metal components for mules with a warning to customers contemplating building their own frames that 'making machinery is generally very expensive to those who are not in the habit of it'.[136] To the 1841 Select Committee, Grenville Withers, an engineer conversant with machine-making in both Belgium and England, could not see how textile manufacturers could cost-effectively make machinery. For a Belgian machine-user to produce his own 'it must necessarily cost very dear made in that way' and would have been cheaper to buy ready-made from either an English or a Belgian specialist.[137] If Withers were correct, the only reason for users to build their own machinery would be that it was otherwise difficult to source. Thomas Ashton said in 1841 that 'a very great increase [in machine-making] took place in consequence of the demand ... many manufacturers now make their own machinery', suggesting a further squeeze on the supply of cotton machines.[138] Still, these seem out of the ordinary. As new and improved products came to the market, high demand was normal, but could usually be satisfied by specialist makers. And as technology moved on quickly and grew in complexity, textile manufac-turers were less likely to consider making their own machines.

In the flax industry, John Marshall's son and successor James Garth Marshall was clear in 1841 that English spinners ordered machines 'almost entirely from parties who are machine-makers ... I understand it to be the same on the continent'.[139] A transition from machine-making into textile

133   PP Artisans and Machinery, 347.
134   PP Artisans and Machinery, 304.
135   PP Artisans and Machinery, 299.
136   Catling, Spinning Mule, 46.
137   PP Exportation of Machinery, 46.
138   PP Exportation of Machinery, 22.
139   PP Exportation of Machinery, 194.

manufacturing, as with M'Connel and Kennedy, was more common than the reverse. In Keighley, Lodge Calvert abandoned machine-making for textiles soon after 1800. Berry Smith, a significant textile engineer in the town, moved into commission spinning in 1810, this new enterprise quickly eclipsing the old. Several of Richard Hattersley's and William Smith's many sons and grandsons founded substantial textile businesses, in a familiar industry where the family connections were useful, and because they saw good profits there. These never overshadowed the families' core engineering activities.[140]

Certainly, large numbers of mechanics worked in textile factories. They were there to repair and maintain plant, looking after engines, boilers and transmission gear as well as process machinery. 'I suppose there are as many employed in repairing, as there are in making [machines]', said Ashton.[141] And Peter Ewart, engineer and cotton-spinner: 'In cotton mills in general, there are as many persons employed in keeping the machinery in order, as there are employed in the making of it'.[142] In 1841, William Jenkinson of Salford, representing the machine-makers' committee, referred to 'immense numbers of mechanics employed in mills, not only in the making of machinery, but in the repairing of it; almost every mill has its mechanics, more or less'.[143] The Leeds flax-spinner Marshall had 70 or 80 mechanics among his 1,200 employees in 1833. As all machinery was bought in, these men worked wholly on repair and maintenance.[144]

There were a few exceptions in Yorkshire. During a power-loom shortage in the 1840s, John Foster's Black Dyke Mills at Queensbury, which despite its detached location had acquired a repair shop only in 1838, started building looms for fine worsteds. Having equipped for this in 1844, they continued, and in 1887 Foster's own machines accounted for 459 looms out of the 785 then in use at Black Dyke.[145] But Foster never made spinning machinery, and produced few wool-combs. Making looms for themselves was seemingly a last resort, and once invested in a machine-making shop, they chose to carry on.

For Lancashire, figures confirm that most textile manufacturers did not routinely make machines. Using official data, based on returns submitted by businesses, Andrew Ure in 1833 calculated that 151 cotton-manufacturers in the county employed in total 31,444 in preparing and spinning, and 16,040 in weaving, yet the numbers of 'engineers, mechanics, firemen, roller coverers etc.' came to only 1,161. That is an average of fewer than eight a firm.[146]

---

140   See app. 1.
141   PP Artisans and Machinery, 303.
142   PP Artisans and Machinery, 256.
143   PP Exportation of Machinery, 107.
144   Morris, Class, Sect and Party, 89.
145   Sigsworth, Black Dyke Mills, 184–5.
146   Ure, Cotton Manufacture, 334–42.

These 151 companies averaged over 300 employees, and each factory needed mechanics to attend to steam-engines, boilers and power systems besides carrying out routine maintenance and repair. So no more than a handful of these Lancashire factories could have had sufficient numbers of engineers and mechanics to operate a viable machine-making department.

3

Shaping an Industry

Products mould industries. The demands of machines shaped textile engineering, just as engineers fashioned the machines. The technology, constantly in flux, required acceptance of new constituents and techniques. This was only a part of the industry's character and culture. Other matters, real and substantial, determined which trades would be drawn in, and which sidelined; and also influenced the form of workplaces and how the industry was organized. One concern was how to ensure supplies of precision components, particularly spindles and rollers. There was also a question – in fact a series of increasingly demanding questions, as technology developed – of adapting manufacturing processes to accommodate new materials and products. Among many new machines, the throstle was especially challenging and formative.

The throstle

Early in the nineteenth century, the throstle and the mule (a hybrid created by combining elements of jenny and water frame) had come to dominate spinning.[1] The models worked alongside each other, with the throstle producing medium and coarser counts of yarn, in which it had a speed advantage.[2]

Emerging from a breakthrough in Stockport, c. 1779, after a drive led by John Milne and John Swindell to improve Arkwright's spinning frame, the throstle employed a 'tin' roller to increase spindle capacity.[3] Because of the thrush-like singing when several worked together, the wooden-framed

---

[1] Jeremy and Darnell, *Visual Mechanic Knowledge*, 48.

[2] Hills, *Power in the Industrial Revolution*, 245.

[3] Aspin, *Water-Spinners*, 120. For drawings of these various spinning frames see Rees, *Cyclopaedia*, II, Cotton Manufacture, plates IX–XI; and for the throstle ('throzle') in the United States, Jeremy and Darnell, *Visual Mechanic Knowledge*, 246, 248–59. Tin is defined below. John Ford of Smithy Brow, Manchester, advertised 'tin rollers for spinning jennies' as early as 1780: *Manchester Mercury*, 16 May 1780 (reference from Chris Aspin). For John Ford see also Musson and Robinson, *Science and Technology*, 457.

machine had by 1800 become widely known as the throstle.[4] The roller was hollow, formed from a beaten sheet of iron, possibly (though not essentially) tin-plated. It ran the full length of the machine and powered all the spindles, and so replaced the Arkwright-system pulleys which each drove only four. As the tin-roller principle was refined over following years, the number of spindles per machine multiplied.[5] Throstle frames of 72 spindles were recorded in 1793, and of 144 spindles in 1805.[6] The millwright John Sutcliffe wrote in 1816 that throstles were 'made with half the expense, work much lighter and require little power compared with water frames'.[7]

In the water frame, Arkwright's 'mechanical spinning fingers' consisted of three pairs of drafting rollers (reduced from four on the original 1769 patent), weighted increasingly heavily towards the front.[8] The speed differential between the second (intermediate) and third (front) rollers was by far the highest. Setting the machine was critical, for the distance between each pair of drafting rollers must be a shade more than the maximum staple length of the fibre to be spun. The level of twist inserted on the water frame, or indeed the throstle, is unlimited, and here Arkwright's system potentially outperformed the mule. But Arkwright's flat leather belts driving sets of four spindles did not cope with high speeds. The 'tin' driving roller represented a major advance.

Driving by roller was not new: early forms of spinning jenny included a large wooden drum to run the spindles.[9] But these were difficult to manufacture and impractical for more than about 20 spindles. The water frame needed to run fast (the throstle faster still) in order to insert the necessary twist into the yarn. For optimum performance, a roller-type pulley of large diameter (perhaps 5 to 7 in., 12 to 18 cm) was needed, and long enough to drive a considerable number of spindles. Weight ruled out a roller made from iron or wood. Wood had another disadvantage, that it must be jointed if it were to be used on a long, many-spindled, frame.

The solution was found in cast-iron discs (or small-spoked 'pulleys'), which could be machined accurately and include a concentric hole for a central shaft. Wrapping thin sheets of wrought iron around these discs or pulleys resulted in a long, hollow, lightweight, roller-type 'pulley'. At intervals, these 'tin rollers' had small gaps where their slim central shafts were joined to the

---

4 It is said that after conversion to steam power Arkwright's water frame too was called a throstle: English, *Textile Industry*, 227.

5 Benson, *Textile Machines*, 15, 20; Aspin, *Water-Spinners*, 125–7, 188; Jeremy and Darnell, *Visual Mechanic Knowledge*, 246–9; Hodgson, *Textile Manufacture*, 240–1.

6 Aspin, *Water-Spinners*, 126–7.

7 Aspin, *Water-Spinners*, 127–8.

8 James, *Worsted Manufacture*, 337, 344. For substantial sections of what follows, I am greatly indebted to Ian Gibson, formerly of Lancashire County Museums.

9 For the difference between drums and rollers, see Catling, *Spinning Mule*, 71–3.

next such roller and supported on a bearing. The driving rollers, used on throstles and mules and later on ring frames, may have been coated with tin, as proof against rusting. But tin was expensive and not essential.[10]

Producing these rollers drew on techniques developed by smiths over centuries. Circular iron tyres made by blacksmiths to reinforce cart-wheels required a fair degree of accuracy. There were established methods of bending metal into a cylinder, using pairs of rollers. To make the hollow 'tin rollers' to drive throstle and mule spindles, smiths developed skills in bending the thinnest wrought-iron plate made at that time. This they accomplished, 'a most impressive example of the tinsmith's craft', by building up rollers in 6ft to 8ft lengths 'from small sheets of thin tinplate soldered together to form a very light, but surprisingly rigid roller ...' and succeeded in delivering true cylinders and a dynamic balance of the sections.[11] Although this was a highly skilled operation, it seems not to have generated specialist firms. From Richard Hattersley's recorded transactions in Keighley, it appears that tinsmiths and braziers such as Phineas Smith supplied sheet metal, and this was fabricated elsewhere by whitesmiths like William Carr.[12]

The throstle's long driving rollers worked in tandem with a second critical development, cast-iron gears. Arkwright's frame used multiple sets of brass gear-wheels, so weak that they could power a set of drafting rollers only about 10 in. (25 cm) in length and producing four strands of yarn. With the throstle, there was just one set on the headstock, so it could be driven from one end. The far stronger (and noisier) iron gears could, by 1790, be cut from cast-iron blanks using a machine based on a clock-makers' gear-cutter.[13] And so, with one set of gearing and drafting rollers coupled together, the tin cylinder gave 'motion to the spindles and twist to the thread'.[14] The limitation was in the length of drafting roller which could be accurately machined. Joining short lengths of roller to rotate concentrically along the whole length was tricky, demanding high precision.[15]

From the 1790s, and as late as the 1850s, the throstle was ubiquitous in northern textile factories,[16] and the main thrust of Keighley's emergent engineering trade. The moving parts were simpler and fewer than in the water

10   Information from Ian Gibson.

11   Catling, *Spinning Mule*, 73. The point applies to the throstle as well as the mule: information from Ian Gibson.

12   Information from Ian Gibson; WYAS Bradford, 32D83/2/1, p. 76 etc.

13   Hills, *Power in the Industrial Revolution*, 243–4, 69, and plate 12 facing 242; Benson, *Textile Machines*, 15, 20.

14   Keighley, *Keighley*, 110; Hodgson, *Textile Manufacture*, 240.

15   Ian Gibson points out that on twentieth-century mules, drafting rollers were made in roughly 18-in. lengths, each uniquely stamped to guide an exact assembly procedure in the factory.

16   English, *Textile Industry*, 152–3.

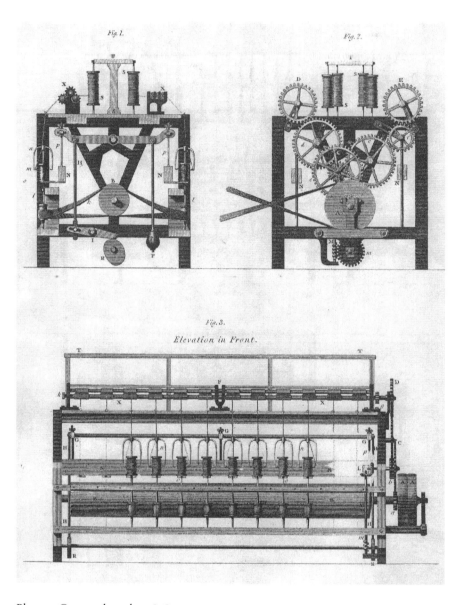

Plate 5. Cotton throstle, 1808
Source: Rees, *Cyclopaedia*, X, 1 (1808), 'Cotton Manufacture', Plate X.

frame, lighter, cheaper, and needing less power. It had disadvantages: unlike Arkwright's frame, which could be repaired or adjusted by removing the power from just four spindles, the throstle must be stopped entirely in order to be fixed. Furthermore, the yarn it produced was at first erratic, with 'great inconsistency in the twist' and variations in the count.[17] But this machine was transformational in its time, and its advance was rapid. It supplanted the mule in worsted spinning, in Britain at least.[18] Although once so common and so important, no British-made example of a throstle is known to have survived.[19] Two throstles displayed in museums in the United States are American and of later date, both probably built at Lowell in the 1830s.[20]

Before 1800, the throstle was subjected to many innovations – and inevitably, claims and counter-claims – as it developed from a single hand-powered cotton-spinning frame, to be doubled, converted to drive by water or steam, and adapted for worsteds. After the fall of Arkwright's patent in 1785, a free-for-all ensued in improving the spinning process. In the Midlands, one Brookhouse reportedly modified the throstle to spin worsteds in 1788, this technology soon afterwards arriving in Yorkshire.[21] In Preston, Benjamin Shaw recorded a great uptake in factory-based powered spinning in 1796, with 'the throstle spinning frame … much improved about this time'.[22] Keighley

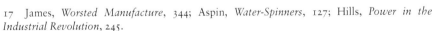

also played some part. In 1787 or soon after that, it is claimed, 'the hand throstle was invented by two individuals of this town, John Weatherhead, a joiner, and John Nicholson, afterwards a printer in Bradford'.[23] The evidence is sketchy. If true, it must be that the pair, before Weatherhead's death in 1798, furthered the task of adapting the throstle to worsted spinning. With Weatherhead the technician, Nicholson may have financed

17 James, *Worsted Manufacture*, 344; Aspin, *Water-Spinners*, 127; Hills, *Power in the Industrial Revolution*, 245.

18 Controversially, for in France mules continued to be used, to excellent effect: James, *Worsted Manufacture*, 347, 578, and app. p. 24.

19 The Science Museum has a partial jute throstle (1951–592), and Manchester Museum of Science and Industry a mid-nineteenth-century model of a throstle, from Wigan (Y1967.8). For drawings and specifications, see Rees, *Cyclopaedia*, II, 194; III, 391; Aspin, *Water-Spinners*, 126; Jeremy and Darnell, *Visual Mechanic Knowledge*, 248–9; W. S. Bright McLaren, *Spinning Woollen and Worsted* (Cassell and Co., 1899), 150–76.

20 They are at Slater Mill museum, Rhode Island, and the American Textile Museum in Lowell, Mass. A machine of similar design, though for flax-spinning, is at MIAT, Ghent. For information and ideas about throstles, thanks to Chris Aspin, George Ingle, David Jeremy; Derek Bird (Calderdale Industrial Museum); Daniel Martin (ex-Leeds Industrial Museum); Andrian Paquette (Slater Mill); Pieter Neirinckx (MIAT); Philip Butler (Lancashire County Council Museum Service).

21 Felkin, *Machine-wrought Hosiery and Lace*, 229.

22 Crosby (ed.), *Benjamin Shaw*, 36, 88.

23 Keighley, *Keighley*, 110.

this before launching a worsted business.[24] Cotton throstles were produced, and doubtless improved, by several machine-makers in Keighley, employing Hattersley rollers and spindles. William Carr, reportedly the first to produce such machines from 1798, was followed by Joseph Hindle, William Lawson, John Longbottom, and others. Berry Smith, who had been Carr's apprentice, led a move into worsted throstles in about 1800.[25] Lodge Calvert, by trade a joiner, launched into worsted spinning in 1801 with his throstle fabricated from Hattersley spindles, flyers, rollers and other parts. Within a few years he was worth thousands.[26] The mills at New Lanark had 540 throstle spindles at work by 1801.[27] Bradford worsted spinners took up the throstle only in about 1805, after which the town 'quickly became noted for the excellence of [its] yarn'.[28]

Components

The essence of an efficient spinning frame lay in the balance and precision of key components, the drafting rollers, spindles and flyers. Spindles were long and slender, finely balanced to run true at high speed. So too with the flyer, an inverted U-shape with ends curled like rams' horns, which sat above the spindle and fed yarn to a lower-placed bobbin. Spindles and flyers needed strength to resist the friction of the yarn, so were hardened and tempered – a difficult process if balance were to be maintained.[29]

Before machines could mass-produce interchangeable parts, engineering relied heavily upon very specific craft skills. For certain vital textile-machine components, even into the 1840s, there was no real alternative but manual skill – highly proficient, accuracy honed by specialization and repetition. As the number of spindles at work multiplied, so the demand for such workers grew.

The surrounding machine was described almost as an afterthought:

> The parts of machines are made to fit the rollers and spindles, and not the rollers and spindles to fit the parts; for it is chiefly in the rollers and spindles that nicety and accuracy are required.[30]

24   See app. 1.
25   Hodgson, *Textile Manufacture*, 250–1; app. 1.
26   Hodgson, *Textile Manufacture*, 20.
27   Hills, *Power in the Industrial Revolution*, 245.
28   James, *Worsted Manufacture*, 593.
29   South Yorkshire Industrial History Society, report on Damstead Works, Dronfield, by Derek Bayliss (1998), quoting Edgar Tillotson, former spindle-maker, in Embsay parish magazine, 1976.
30   PP Artisans and Machinery, 381; information from John Iredale c. 1992.

Rollers and spindles were 'those parts which a stranger would be most desirable of getting' in order to emulate the technology.[31] In Manchester specialization produced 'two or three classes of spindle-makers, separate and distinct trades, masters and men'.[32] Likewise roller-making employed 'a distinct set [of mechanics]; it has been a business in itself'.[33] As in other engineering branches late to mechanize – card-making is another example – production was streamlined to maximize efficiency, precision and output. Work was broken into smaller tasks, hand-craft married with basic labour-saving, precision-enhancing devices. Despite all this, the sector struggled to meet demand. Rollers and spindles continued to rise in price, by as much as 30 per cent over a few months in 1824. Together they made up about one fifth of the value of a machine.[34] Samuel Lees of Oldham was held responsible for some of the difficulty, having taken advantage of a lull to extend his works at Oldham, recruit specialist workers and corner the market.[35] These manufacturers were overwhelmed by orders – 'the persons of whom I have rollers and spindles are anxious to keep out of our sight, for they have promised more than they can perform'.[36] Even when demand for new machinery slackened, business was still brisk for component-makers, in repairs and replacements.[37] Eventually, inevitably, these processes were themselves mechanized, decisively in the shape of a spindle-forging machine patented by William Ryder of Bolton in 1840.[38]

Spindles were made in hubs across the northern textile districts and in south Yorkshire. The trade, centred on Sheffield, flourished in settlements between Sheffield and Penistone, including Oughtibridge, Wharncliffe Side and Grenoside. Spinning wheels had used hardwood spindles, with iron or steel tips applied by the early phases of machine-spinning.[39] Cort's malleable iron technique perhaps accelerated the adoption of iron spindles. Site investigations have revealed that Grenoside spindle manufacturers, long thought to have been wood-turners, in fact worked in steel.[40] Steel was also used in

31 PP Artisans and Machinery, 344.
32 PP Artisans and Machinery, 253, evidence of Peter Ewart.
33 PP Artisans and Machinery, 301.
34 PP Artisans and Machinery, 299, 301–2, 341, 381.
35 PP Artisans and Machinery, 341–2, evidence of Thomas Cheek Hewes.
36 PP Artisans and Machinery, 343, evidence of Thomas Cheek Hewes.
37 PP Artisans and Machinery, 301.
38 *Proc. Inst. Mech. Eng.*, obituaries (1868), 1–17; *Mechanics' Magazine*, 27 Feb. 1841; D. Farnie, 'Cotton, 1780–1914', in Jenkins (ed.), *Cambridge History of Western Textiles*, I, 730.
39 Rees, *Cyclopaedia*, V, 24–6; Kerridge, *Textile Manufactures*, 175. Derek Bayliss generously shared information about spindle manufacture, including sources referring to grinding tips and to purchases of alder poles for spindles in the early nineteenth century.
40 By the South Yorkshire Industrial History Society field recording group.

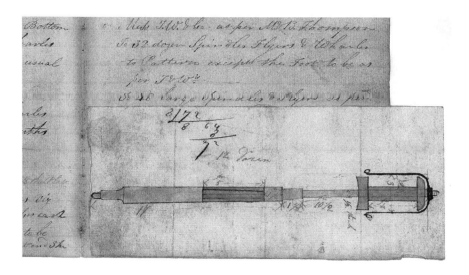

Plate 6. Spindle and flyer ordered by Taylor and Wordsworth from Richard Hattersley, 1820.

Source: WYAS Bradford, 32D83/15/1.

Manchester by 1792, when Daniel Mackay, a Manchester spindle- and flyer-maker, ordered files suitable for working on steel spindles in lathes.[41]

In 1841, spindle manufacture remained largely unmechanized. It required accurate forging, precise grinding, then setting 'and I should say that there is not one man in a thousand that could set a spindle, unless he had given his time to that particular part of the art'.[42] In such a long and slender component, to achieve the requisite hardness, and the balance to run at high speed, took considerable skill in working and treating crucible steel. Hardly surprising, then, that in Hallamshire was an important cluster of spindle-makers, and that men brought up in that district's metal trades moved into textile engineering in Leeds and Keighley.[43] Spindles were at first forged by hand, or with Oliver hammers; Ryder's powered spring hammer was increasingly embraced in the 1840s. The spindle trade maintained a significant base in Sheffield throughout the nineteenth century, and firms operating there also made flyers, loom springs and other textile machine parts.[44]

41   Ashton, *Peter Stubs*, 62.
42   PP Exportation of Machinery, 99, evidence of William Jenkinson. For detail about spindle- and flyer-making methods, see PP (HC) 1843 XIV [431], B44, b47–8.
43   Information from Peter Kelley, formerly of Leeds Industrial Museum, supplied to Derek Bayliss; for historical background see Hey, *Fiery Blades*.
44   D. Bayliss, unpublished paper (2007). Bradford Industrial Museum has a spindle forge.

The flyer inserts twist into yarn before winding it on a bobbin. Wooden flyers, in use in Germany by about 1480, were linked closely to the Saxony wheel's development during the sixteenth century.[45] Arkwright absorbed the concept into his 1769 frame, and then substantially improved the flyer in 1775. A Mansfield cotton-spinner called Matthew Etchells is credited with devising the first flyer with a hollow arm, in 1793, adapting a length of piping and mounting it on a wooden frame. Arkwright's 1769 patent stipulated 'flyes [sic] made of wood with small wires on the side which lead the thread to the bobbins'.[46] It seems flyers were not made wholly of iron until after 1800.[47]

Arkwright's frame applied power to the spindles, and bobbins were driven by being dragged around by the yarn. Because this restricted spindle speed – and in general, higher speed produces finer yarns – the water frame and throstle were able to spin only yarns coarser than about 40s count. This limitation eventually, from 1828, brought in cap-spinning, and the demise of flyers in their earlier form.[48]

Drafting rollers presented a different kind of challenge. Arkwright's 1769 patent specified:

> four pair of rollers ... which act by tooth and pinion, made of brass and steel nutts, fixt in two iron plates. That part of the roller which the cotton runs through is covered with wood, the top roller with leather, and the bottom one fluted, which lets the cotton &c. through it, and by one pair of rollers moving quicker than the other, draws it finer for twisting, which is performed by the spindles.[49]

Thomas Highs, a rival of Arkwright, described how both men made rollers of wood upon an iron core, the lower ones fluted while upper rollers were covered with calf or other leather. Arkwright's method used more rollers than Highs' – three pairs rather than two – and by paying closer attention to their spacing and weighting, his proved the more workable system.[50] The roller's centre was an iron axle, top rollers then covered with leather (sometimes with felt beneath), and bottom rollers fluted. At times, bottom rollers were made from iron with brass cast on to them, and the brass, a softer metal to

45 Dakin, 'Development of Cotton-Spinning Machinery', 463–4; Ponting, *Leonardo da Vinci*, 2–3. See above, pp. 16–17.

46 Hills, *Power in the Industrial Revolution*, 61; British Patents GB931 (1769) and GB1111 (1775).

47 Dakin, 'Development of Cotton-Spinning Machinery', 464–5.

48 Dakin, 'Development of Cotton-Spinning Machinery', 464–6; Lemon, 'Early History of Spinning', 483. Yarn was measured in counts, the number of hanks making a pound-weight, so the smaller the count, the coarser the thread.

49 British Patent GB931 (1769).

50 Hills, *Power in the Industrial Revolution*, 62–5; Carpmael, *Law Reports*, I, 79.

work, then fluted. Some drafting rollers were formed from just a solid rod of wood.[51] Leather did not work well in this process, as its unevenness made the rollers run eccentrically, causing irregularities in the yarn. Over time, many substitutes were tried, yet it was almost 200 years before a better, synthetic, option was discovered.[52]

After machine-building was largely absorbed into factories, many firms of specialist makers of rollers, spindles, flyers and other parts carried on business, particularly where textile engineering concentrated. So, for instance, in Keighley component-makers included John Crosley of Walk Mill, Shelagh Haggas of Ingrow, a roller-maker called Henry Keighley, and Thomas Smith, who also made machinery.[53] Benjamin Shaw found employment in a former smithy in Preston in 1817 with John Welch, roller-maker, when work was plentiful.[54] But this degree of specialism had been evident a generation earlier. Aaron Ogden, whitesmith, of Ashton-under-Lyne, advertised in 1775 for journeyman whitesmiths accustomed to, among other things, 'engine work', but also for an apprentice who would specialize in 'jenny spindle making'. Among the 'smith and clock-makers tools' in a cotton-factory at Chorley in 1788 was a 'cutting and fluting engine'. In 1792, an advertisement appeared for two or three 'spindle and fly forgers'. The effects of John Howard, whitesmith and machine-maker of Little Hayfield, included a roller-making machine and fluting engines in 1792.[55]

The technical ancestry of machine-making

With a new industry, indeed any major innovation, comes new language. Before a vocabulary is tacitly agreed, one best encapsulating the technology and the people who design and deliver it, terms are fluid and imprecise. Textile engineering tagged its innovations with words already in common usage. Notably, installations were categorized as millwrights' or clock-makers' work. These expressions were soon enshrined in insurance policies, conveniently differentiating 'millwrights' work' – including fulling stocks, transmission and 'going gear' – from the machinery itself, 'clock-makers' work'. This terminology, like the word 'engineer', served its purpose at the

---

51   Andrian Paquette, Curator, Slater Mill, Pawtucket, Rhode Island (20 Nov. 2013) supplied useful insights, also about the throstle.
52   Dakin, 'Development of Cotton-Spinning Machinery', 459.
53   White, *Dir.* I (1837), 685–90.
54   Crosby (ed.), *Benjamin Shaw*, 55–6.
55   Musson and Robinson, *Science and Technology*, 453–8, citing *Manchester Mercury*, 26 Sept. 1775; 1 July 1788; 17 Jan. 1792; 17 Sept. 1793.

time. But even then, it did not quite hit the spot, and it has subsequently proved misleading.[56]

The terms do not clarify the nature of trades and activities involved, and so limit an understanding of the early industry. Alternative routes into the young trade are required: exploring localities where textile engineering emerged, deconstructing (metaphorically) the products themselves, pinpointing the skills their making demanded. In this, materials are key. To contemporaries, an eighteenth-century machine may have appeared very original in concept, but its fabrics were of more familiar stamp. As there was no template showing how to produce the device, nor a ready-made workforce, skill in working these specific materials must have been paramount. The commission demanded craft techniques, in wood, iron, leather, or other metals, and perhaps a higher specialism within these broad categories, such as wheelwright, founder or screw-maker.

John Aikin, keenly observing Manchester in 1795, identified some of the more significant skills. Foundries had increased in number – half a dozen in and around the town – using pig iron shipped in by canal from Shropshire. Most produced general household and industrial cast iron goods, but one, Bateman and Sherratt, already specialized in new technologies, 'large cast wheels for the cotton machines; cylinders, boilers and pipes for steam engines'. Aikin saw numbers of ironmongers' shops with smithies attached, 'where many articles are made, even to nails'. Other occupations were carving niches in machine-making:

> The tin-plate workers have found additional employment in furnishing many articles for spinning machines; as have also the braziers in casting wheels for the motion-work of the rollers used in them; and the clock-makers in cutting them. Harness-makers have been much employed in making bands for carding engines, and large wheels for the first operation of drawing out the cardings, whereby the consumption of strong curried leather has been much increased.[57]

Also in demand was a range of woodworking skills, from the more traditional heavy work involved in building machine frames, to finer tasks such as covering and fluting rollers, and producing wooden elements for spindles and flyers.[58] By weight and volume, wood still comprised an overwhelming proportion of almost any eighteenth-century machine. Arkwright's wooden-framed spinning machines were driven by wooden pulleys. Even large gear-wheels in factories and in all industrial machinery were timber-made, with

56   See Cookson, 'Millwrights, Clock-makers'.
57   Aikin, *Description of the Country*, 176–9.
58   See for instance Arkwright's patents 931 (1769) and 1111 (1775).

applewood preferred for cogs. A textile machine's metal parts may have
amounted to as little as hooks, nails and bolts, along with parts of the rollers,
spindles and flyers. Isaac Dobson and Peter Rothwell made mules in Bolton
from 1790, chiefly of wood, most of their 20 employees joiners. The sole
metal parts were wrought iron spindles and shafts, and pinions and wheels
made of cast iron and brass.[59]

But iron brackets and ties were coming in to strengthen machine frames,
and iron and brass were increasingly used for bearings and for cylinders and
pipes in engines and pumps. The turning point was the 1790s, when new
technologies demanded something more robust than timber. Use of cast
iron then increased rapidly, for all kinds of machine framing, and for engine-
beams, bridges and other structures.[60] The Leeds brass- and iron-founder
Martin Cawood, who dabbled in making scribbling and carding machines, set
out the advantages of making the 'framing, bends &c' entirely of cast iron.

> These are gaining universal approbation, not being subject, as wood
> machines are, to give way with the varied temperature of the atmosphere,
> and stand in less room, besides greatly lessening the danger from fire.[61]

By the 1820s, the trades 'employed in the construction of a water-spinning
machine' were defined as 'the spindle-maker, the roller-maker, the turner or
bobbin-maker, the founder, the tinman, flyer-maker, and others', the whole
assembled by a machine-maker.[62] All but the bobbins had turned to metal.

Early domestic machines were of simple design and relatively easy for a
wood worker to produce. The same principles applied to the structural
elements of that generation of frames developed before 1800. It required only
basic handicraft skills to build a replica jenny for Colne Valley Museum.[63] A
handloom in the same museum was rebuilt, perhaps as late as the 1930s, by
an Almondbury joiner, J. Stansfield and Son, for Josiah France of Honley. The
superiority of the 1930s carpentry over that of the original loom-maker is
clear to see.

While the proportion of their contribution to engineering diminished
after 1800, wood workers continued to be employed. Carpenters produced
domestic machinery into recent times, for a small but persisting market. In
the United States, where timber was more plentiful than iron and was used
wherever possible, wood workers early in the nineteenth century acquired

---

59 Tupling, 'Early Metal Trades', 27.
60 Pacey, *Maze of Ingenuity*, 226–9.
61 *Leeds Intelligencer*, 20 Jan. 1806.
62 PP Artisans and Machinery, 545.
63 Sykes, *Spinning Jenny*.

considerable skill and precision in building carding machinery.[64] Such skills remained useful to the modern industry. A Gomersal textile engineer interviewed in 1992 still employed a full-time joiner-cum-coach-builder who made wooden covers for carding machines, and timber carriages for mules.[65]

Millwrights' work

Millwrights were a significant presence in the eighteenth-century textile transformation, strongly associated with woodworking, and with a long history of service to cloth-millers in the woollen districts. The extent to which they improved and constructed textile machinery, though, is ill-defined.

The earliest recorded 'milnewright', in 1387, was a freeman of York.[66] Medieval millwrights were specialist carpenters who worked on fulling and corn-mills. Because they understood circular measure, their status stood higher than most wooden crafts.[67] The eighteenth-century millwright was a developed version of this, generally of above-average education, intelligent, adaptable to new technologies, understanding a range of industries and power sources.

> Their trade is a branch of carpentry (with some assistance from the smith) but rather heavier work, yet very ingenious, to understand and perform which well a person ought to have a good turn of mind for mechanics, at least to have some knowledge in arithmetic, in which a lad ought to be instructed before he goes to learn this art; for there is a great variety in mills, as well as in the structure and workmanship of them; some being worked by horses, some by wind; others by water shooting over and others by its running under: And why not in time by fire too, as well as engines?[68]

Sir William Fairbairn, trained as a millwright in a Tyneside colliery early in the nineteenth century, looked back with nostalgia to an earlier era.

> The millwright of the [eighteenth] century was an itinerant engineer and mechanic of high reputation. In the practice of his profession he had mainly to depend on his own resources ... [he] was a kind of jack-of-all-trades,

---

64 Gross, 'Wool-Carding', 808–9.

65 John Briggs, of Alfred Briggs & Sons.

66 OED.

67 Harrison, *Eight Centuries of Milling*, 42, defines this as 'involved in marking out the cog mortises in the felloes of the cog wheel and the centres of the rungs in the lantern gears'. For a revealing account of early-modern and later northern millwrights, see Ball, 'Millwrights in Sheffield and South Yorkshire'.

68 Waller, *General Description of All Trades*, 151.

who could with equal facility work at the lathe, the anvil or the carpenter's
bench ... he could handle the axe, the hammer and the plane with equal
skill and precision; he could turn, bore or forge.[69]

The common view of the millwright, said Fairbairn, was of one of 'superior
attainments and intellectual power'.[70]

Generally he was a fair arithmetician, knew something of geometry,
levelling and mensuration and in some cases possessed a very competent
knowledge of practical mechanics. He could calculate the velocities,
strength and power of machines; could draw in plan and in section ... and
could construct buildings, conduits or watercourses.[71]

William Fairbairn did more than any other to reinvent the millwright, most
notably through understanding the properties of cast iron and rethinking
the design of structural ironwork. But his obituarist in *The Engineer* in 1874,
in suggesting that Fairbairn 'abolished the millwright, and introduced the
mechanical engineer',[72] presented an absurdity, not least because millwrighting
was, and is still, a distinct activity. That suggestion, much repeated, has
further confused definitions.[73] Yet when Fairbairn himself questioned the
demarcation, 'unable to state where the millwright ends and the engineer and
mechanist begin',[74] he meant in practical working terms, within factories.
There was no doubt, to Fairbairn or anyone else, that millwrights and
mechanical trades were separate and distinct occupations.

For millwrighting rose higher than a trade. The consulting engineers or
millwrights used by Arkwright belonged to a profession.[75] Few in number,
their role was analogous to that of a colliery viewer: a planner of new ventures,
who understood economics, assessed financial as well as technical viability,
and was indeed 'vital consultant' in any major factory-building venture.[76] Of
significant northern millwrights working before 1800, names are known, but
little about their careers.[77] Status is reflected in the title 'Mr', or perhaps the

69   Pole (ed.), *Sir William Fairbairn*, 27; Jefferys, *Story of the Engineers*, 9.
70   Pole (ed.), *Sir William Fairbairn*, ix.
71   Pole (ed.), *Sir William Fairbairn*, ix.
72   Pole (ed.), *Sir William Fairbairn*, 436.
73   Scott (ed.), *Matthew Murray*, 20; and for instance Musson and Robinson, *Science and Technology*, 429; Morris, *Class, Sect and Party*, 33.
74   Fairbairn, *Treatise on Mills*, II, 225.
75   See above, p. 37.
76   Tann, 'Textile Millwright', 85. For the role of millwrights in factory-building, see above, pp. 39–40.
77   Jenkins, *West Riding Wool Textile Industry*, 101–9; see Skempton, *Biographical Dictionary of Civil Engineers*, passim.

description 'yeoman'; both of these applied to John Jubb of Leeds.[78] Jubb was extremely versatile, had a high reputation, was knowledgeable about textile production and did in fact build textile machinery at an early date. But elsewhere, among the higher circles of northern millwrighting, which embraced Arkwright's favourites Lowe and Sutcliffe, questions were raised about specific capabilities in the new textile era. Lowe was a timber merchant, carpenter and general millwright, Sutcliffe a civil engineer who specialized in watercourses. In the dynamic context of textile factory development around 1790, it seems that neither much impressed.[79]

The work of extending and remodelling a fulling mill would more likely be undertaken by a local millwright, probably an accomplished craftsman who had specific understanding of water-powered textile sites. The work was partly civil engineering, with elements of landscaping and construction in stone, wood, and iron. It required competence in repairing, maintaining, and from time to time rebuilding, older-style mills, stocks, transmission and prime movers.[80]

To become apprentice to a London millwright in the mid-eighteenth century, a premium of £5 or £10 was expected, and to set up in business cost £100 to £150.[81] These sums are comparable with other trades in the capital. In northern England, the costs are less clear. An acute shortage of millwrights from the 1770s may have reduced premiums. In William Fairbairn's own case, it seems that none was paid, though his father's influence as estate steward probably assisted in that. Fairbairn trained as millwright at Percy Main, working under the colliery engineer on, among other things, pumps and cranes.[82]

New and complex areas of work led millwrights to concentrate more specifically in certain industries, technologies, constructions, and types of power system – whether using water, wind, animals or, increasingly, steam. Forges, for instance, would have very different technical needs from textile plant.[83] Whatever the case, the range of a millwright's skill and knowledge remained impressive. William Fairbairn described some he had known in early life, 'proud of their calling, fertile in resources and aware of their value ... the millwright in his character of "jack-of-all-trades" was in his element'. No wonder, said Fairbairn, that with 'the new movements in practical science, occasioned by the inventions of Watt and Arkwright, the millwright should

78   YAHS, YAS/MS1415, 24 Nov. 1791.
79   M. Chrimes, 'Thomas Lowe, fl. 1760–90', in Skempton, *Biographical Dictionary of Civil Engineers*, 414; Tann, *Development of the Factory*, 99.
80   Harrison, *Eight Centuries of Milling*, 150; Moher, 'London Millwrights'; Tann, *Development of the Factory*; 'Textile Millwright'.
81   Moher, 'London Millwrights', 116, 253.
82   Byrom, 'William Fairbairn', ch. 2–3.
83   Ball, 'Millwrights in Sheffield and South Yorkshire', *passim*; Tann, *Development of the Factory*, 98.

assume a position of importance'.[84] Yet still, Moher discovered of the London millwrights, they practised with 'traditional "rule of thumb" methods and a general level of technique … increasingly found inadequate for the advanced tasks facing the new industry'.[85] There, with armies of millwrights employed in breweries, waterworks, flour mills, distilleries, docks, and many other industrial processes, the journeymen (employees) were well-organized into trade societies. At least one of these, a friendly society of 1799, was forced to disband in consequence of the 1800 Combination Act. The masters too had a combination, from 1777, which set prices for millwork across London.[86] The demands of a millwrights' society in Manchester, in existence from the 1820s, particularly irritated Fairbairn, but such groupings were then exceptional in the north.[87]

So how exactly were millwrights involved in transforming textiles? Certainly they were engaged to construct factories, often acting as main contractor. In this role, at least in the early years, they hired joiners, turners and smiths to build equipment and machinery. However, a journeyman millwright – before wage and apprenticeship regulations were relaxed in 1813–14 – expected a weekly wage of two guineas, perhaps more than double a smith's wage;[88] and also millwrights' specialist skills were then in great demand in textile districts.[89] So any advantage in using trained millwrights to fit out a factory, after the gearing and transmission had been installed, is difficult to see. A promoter or textile manufacturer could equally carry the responsibility of organizing this, and skills of local smiths and joiners were probably better suited to machine-making at that time.

The aloofness and *hauteur* perceived in millwrights would come back to haunt them. So said Alexander Galloway in 1824.

> We make our machines so much better, and so much cheaper, that [the millwrights'] trade, that used to scoff and spurn at the name of an engineer, are obliged to take up the name of an engineer, and conduct their business by the engineer's economy, and that change in the short progress of 15 or 20 years.[90]

Once de-regulated, millwrights' wages did not sustain their high level. In Leeds, journeymen were paid about 26s. a week in 1839. They remained

---

84   Fairbairn, *Useful Information*, 212–13.
85   Moher, 'London Millwrights', 31.
86   See Moher, 'London Millwrights', 68, 70–1, and *passim*.
87   Byrom, 'William Fairbairn'; Musson and Robinson, *Science and Technology*, 485–6 fn.
88   Two guineas was 42 shillings (£2.10). Burnett (ed.), *Useful Toil*, 265; Musson and Robinson, *Science and Technology*, 485–6 fn.
89   Tann, 'Textile Millwright', 81.
90   Evidence of Alexander Galloway, PP Artisans and Machinery, 28; also 39–41.

among the best rewarded and fullest employed of the workforce, but lost a degree of status.[91] In certain sectors, millwrights maintained customary pay and conditions, and nowhere did they fall on hard times. The trade's own technical prowess and development is reflected in published manuals, from John Banks in the 1790s to Nicholson's *Operative Mechanic* of 1825 – works which substantiate the distinction between millwrights and machine-makers.[92] John Sutcliffe wrote about civil engineering, factory-building and power, and setting up and gearing cotton machinery, but he did not talk of building it.[93]

Thomas Cheek Hewes, 'extensively employed in erecting mills, and filling them with machinery' in Manchester in the 1820s, straddled the two spheres.[94] Hewes' business employed 140 to 150 men. Of these, about 40 were engaged on heavy millwork, which he closely defined as:

> water-wheels and shafting, and mill wheels of different descriptions, and the framing, and all the appendages till it comes to machinery, which is detached from the heavy millwork generally by a belt or rope; that distinguishes the millwright work from the machinery.[95]

For Hewes, machine-making was the bread-and-butter activity allowing him to pursue interests in power supply. Later the machinery side was allowed to decline and the firm concentrated on building water-wheels and fireproof mills.[96]

So Hewes, like most millwrights, eventually reverted to type. His textile machinery phase was serious, continued longer than others had, and was turned to good strategic advantage. But usually, millwrights stayed within their trade's traditional zone within textiles, making heavy equipment associated with finishing processes such as fulling stocks, washing machines, and later, tentering machinery. The picture in Somerset and Wiltshire woollens was similar: there, millwrights were involved only in the earliest machinery trials while continuing to produce heavy finishing apparatus.[97] Likewise in Leeds, William Kilburn of Holbeck produced stocks and accessories, and washing and teazling machinery.[98] The modern trade of millwright,

91   Morris, *Class, Sect and Party*, 105.
92   See below, p. 180.
93   Sutcliffe, *Treatise on Canals*, 1 *et seq.*
94   PP (HC) 1824 (51) V, 340. For Hewes, see Smith, 'Thomas Cheek Hewes'; Musson and Robinson, *Science and Technology*, 69–71, 445–7.
95   PP Artisans and Machinery, 341.
96   Smith, 'Thomas Cheek Hewes', 35. Hewes was in partnership with Henry Wren during the 1820s, until his death in 1832. Afterwards the firm continued as Wren and Bennett, then Wren and Hopkinson. Benjamin Gott was a client.
97   Tann, 'Textile Millwright', 82.
98   Scott, 'Early Cloth Fulling', 39–42.

no longer identified with constructing factories or transmission systems, is now understood within textiles as a manufacturer of milling or finishing equipment.[99]

Defining an engineer

Millwrights are a reminder that occupational tags conveyed social status as well as skill. To self-identify by trade was routine, and more than just a mark of employability: it carried, for instance, rights to a Poor Law settlement in the parish where apprenticed. Later, even famed textile engineers continued to define themselves by their original trade.

Of all the ambiguous terms in this new industry, 'engineer' is most problematic. Alexander Galloway, who made tools and machines, called himself an engineer, while suggesting that before 1800 it denoted something low in the occupational hierarchy, at least through the eyes of a millwright.[100] Henry Maudslay had a similar view of (presumably) London, where the Millwrights' Society was powerfully influential.

> There is a distinction between the millwrights and engineers: the millwrights' men would not work with an engineer, they thought it rather a disgrace, and they did strike in some manufactories.[101]

'Engineer', then as now, was a portmanteau label embracing a range of activity; 'engineering' an industry synthesizing a number of trades.[102] It suggests a professional standing, though the terms applies also to classes of shop-floor worker. By the 1820s, 'engineer' was widely used and devalued. No longer can it be assumed to indicate a middle-class professional engineer, one trained by pupillage. With the possible exception of Charles Gascoigne Maclea, there is no suggestion of any Yorkshire textile-machine maker emerging from such origins.

'Engineer' applied to a military man, a sapper, before Smeaton coined 'civil' engineer for all non-military activity. Mechanical, and new branches following on, fell within civil engineering until new engineering institutions recategorized them.[103] As Rees explained it, 'engineer ... in its general sense, is applied to a contriver or maker of any kind of useful engines or machines. In its more proper

---

99   Information from John Briggs of Gomersal.
100 PP Artisans and Machinery, 5.
101 PP Artisans and Machinery, 39. For London millwrights, see Moher, 'London Millwrights'; Dobson, *Masters and Journeymen*, 138–40.
102 More, *Skill and the English Working Class*, 196.
103 Rae, 'Engineers are People', 411.

sense, it denotes an officer in an army or fortified place.' Civil engineers Rees associated with canals, docks, harbours and lighthouses, suggesting they came together as a profession c. 1760.[104] The Smeatonian Society of Civil Engineers was established as a London dining club in 1771, and the more formal professional Institution of Civil Engineers followed in 1818. 'Civil' and 'mechanical' were not clearly demarcated as a profession until the Institution of Mechanical Engineers formed in 1847, in Birmingham.[105]

In the 'mechanical' branch, sometimes 'engineer' assumed a connection with steam-engines. Entering this career demanded capital and connections.

> The engineer makes engines for raising water by fire, either for supplying reservoirs or draining mines ... An engineer requires a very mechanically turned head, and should be versed in all the laws and principles of mechanics ... He employs smiths of various sorts, founders for his brass work, plumbers for his leadwork, and a class of shoemakers for making his leather pipes. He requires a large stock to set up with, and a considerable acquaintance among the gentry.[106]

So 'engineer' was just one fluid and indistinct label applied to early textile-machine makers. Uncommonly, 'machine-maker' was used as early as the 1780s, but it was inappropriate for the numerous textile engineers who never, or only much later, produced entire machines. 'Mechanic' suggested a journeyman and was later associated with maintenance and repair within textile factories. 'Millwright' had gravitas but was misplaced for most machine-makers. The nomenclature was unsettled for a long time, and meanwhile textile engineers habitually labelled themselves, in parish registers, wills, deeds and other official documents, by their earliest trade.

This transitional period produced some curious rebranding, especially for men rising in society. Matthew Murray used 'whitesmith', the trade to which he had been apprenticed, when registering his first patent in 1790.[107] Later he was sometimes said to be an ironfounder, for a foundry formed part of his business. 'Ironfounder' became something of a catch-all, a blanket word for anyone producing and working the raw material. It carried a hint of status, being long-established and, like coal-mining, associated with land ownership and higher levels of capital investment. In 1807 Murray was the only man in Holbeck's list of voters to be styled 'engineer',[108] appropriately as he then produced steam-engines. The problem of terminology followed both Murray and his partner David Wood to their graves. Murray's cast iron obelisk calls

104 Rees, *Cyclopaedia*, II, 345–6.
105 Musson, 'Engineering Industry', 87; websites of the institutions' libraries and archives.
106 Campbell, *London Tradesman*, 248–9.
107 Turner, 'Fenton, Murray and Wood', 1.3.
108 Scott (ed.), *Matthew Murray*, 80.

him 'civil engineer', which differentiates him from the military but is barely
adequate to his achievement.[109] 'Mechanician' is written on the memorial to
David Wood, originally a blacksmith.[110] It signified that he had moved far
from his first occupation, but says little of his career, while his own son was
already styled gentleman.[111] Murray's sons in law were described as 'engineer'
when they married, though one had been apprenticed to Murray as a founder,
another as machine-maker.[112] Similarly Richard Hattersley, notwithstanding
his indisputable achievements in textile engineering, continued up to his death
in 1829 to call himself a whitesmith, and occasionally machine-maker, though
he made few actual machines.[113]

Clock-makers' work

What exactly did clock-makers give to machine-making?[114] 'Clock-makers'
work' noted in factory insurance policies was certainly textile machinery;
and the term 'clock-maker' gained a particular association with Arkwright's
system. Beyond this, matters are less clear.

Rees saw no particular affinity between textile engineering and clock
manufacture, though great change was then apparent in both. Clocks
were mass-produced with 'expedition, and consequently … cheapness'.
Manufacture had been divided into 17 different operations, and machine
tools widely used.

> If we were to define the word clock-maker agreeably to the derivation of
> the term, we should simply say that it means a man who makes clocks, and
> this definition, at one period of the art, would have been sufficient for our
> purpose; but since clocks have become so common … the art of making
> them has not been confined, as at first, to one department of mechanics, but
> has gradually ramified into various branches so distinct from one another,
> that the maker of one part is frequently unacquainted with the operations
> requisite for the manipulations of another, equally essential.[115]

---

109   Holbeck St Matthew, now Holbeck Green.
110   YAHS Monumental Inscriptions now in Leeds Central Lib., Balm Lane Wesleyan
Methodists, Holbeck.
111   Borthwick, Exch. Dec. 1820.
112   WYAS Wakefield, P68/4/12; Turner, 'Fenton, Murray and Wood', 7.2; see Taylor (ed.),
Biographia Leodiensis, 517–18.
113   For example WYAS Wakefield, Deeds, GO, 13 Feb. 1817; HN, 24 June 1821.
114   Cookson, 'Millwrights, Clockmakers', 49–54, presents further detail, but a less developed
view.
115   In the original edition of Rees, *Cyclopaedia*, volume VIII (1807), 507.

In fact this process was well advanced in 1747, when there was concern about lost expertise: 'Of late years the watchmaker ... scarce makes anything belonging to a watch; he only employs the different tradesmen among whom the art is divided, and puts the several pieces of the movement together, and adjusts and finishes it.'[116] Developments in machine tools had made this system possible. Aikin wrote in 1795 that:

> The watch-tools made [in Prescot] have been excellent beyond the memory of the oldest watchmakers; and the manufacture has been much extended by improvements in making new tools of all sorts, and the inventions for first cutting teeth in wheels, and afterwards for finishing them with exactness and expedition.[117]

Prescot, and nearby Liverpool, formed a national hub of watchmaking and a nucleus of watch-tool innovation. 'The chief trade of this place is in the watch line' – when Aikin visited, a directory listed around 28 firms making watches, clocks, or parts for them, along with eight watch-tool makers.[118] With several cotton-factories close by, perhaps there was potential for cross-fertilization.[119] The Prescot watch and clock industry – its organized workplaces, advanced machine tools, and attention to precision – might have presented textile engineering with a model.[120] Except that scale and materials, and therefore technique, differed markedly.[121]

But for a few specialized tasks, clock-makers were ill-equipped for machine-making. James Lawson, Boulton and Watt's northern agent in the 1790s, reported the Lancashire watch-movement makers, who 'had only been used to small work', unsuited to heavier engineering.[122] Later, in 1824, the Manchester engineer Peter Ewart, while defending local standards of clock-making, insisted that the skills did not adapt to machine-making. Ewart, an educated and well-connected Scot, trained as a millwright under Rennie, was agent to Boulton and Watt and partner in several cotton-spinning concerns. In his view:

> the clock and watch tool and movement makers in Lancashire ... are considered the best workmen ... their workmanship is excellent; they use the same sort of tools that the cotton-machine makers use, but they are

116   Campbell, *London Tradesman*, 250–3.
117   Aikin, *Description of the Country*, 311.
118   A factory for watchmakers' tools was described by Angerstein in 1754: *Illustrated Travel Diary*, 313–14; and see Morrison-Low, *Making Scientific Instruments*, 70.
119   Tupling, 'Early Metal Trades', 22; Aikin, *Description of the Country*, 311–12; Barfoot and Wilkes *Universal British Dir*. IV, 247–9; Angerstein, *Illustrated Travel Diary*, 313–14.
120   So too, though further afield, might Birmingham hardwares and Sheffield cutlery: Berg, *Age of Manufactures*, 262–9.
121   Woodbury, *History of Machine Tools*, 4–5, 66.
122   Musson and Robinson, *Science and Technology*, 439.

brought up to no employment but making those clock and watch tools and movements; and when those men come to be employed in making cotton machines, we find that they have almost as much to learn as if they had never learnt any working in metal at all ... We have found them quite insufficient to do any ordinary filing and turning, when they have been taken from the work at which they have been exclusively employed.[123]

By then, British watch- and clock-making had suffered further setbacks, including Pitt's tax on timepieces in 1797, and foreign markets lost to the Swiss after 1815.[124]

Midlands clock-making was hit especially hard. Coventry journeymen once noted for their expertise accepted labouring jobs in order to survive.[125] With several lace-making patents expiring around 1823, they had a fresh opportunity. Clock-makers from Birmingham almost doubled their incomes making the 'insides' for bobbin-net frames in Nottingham, while their former masters won lucrative contracts to produce outer parts.[126]

All were very highly paid and the profits of the masters were great in proportion. During several years the demand was so great that it could not be supplied: the news of such wonderful wages, independence, and jollity, spread like wildfire; so that speedily machine-smiths, lock-smiths and blacksmiths, together with every watchmaker who had a wandering or adventurous spirit within 50 or 80 miles, came together in the garret workshops, extemporised in every quarter of Nottingham.[127]

Yet, as Babbage explains, these small bobbin-net frames were mainly to meet a sudden domestic demand; master clock-makers subcontracted with machine-makers to supply just one small precision element, the bobbin-carrier, and only during the boom. Finishing and forging smiths, and 'setters-up', were responsible for producing and assembling the bobbin-net frame.[128] So here is encapsulated the extent of clock-makers' experience in textile engineering: brief, and limited in scope.

In northern England, the involvement of clock-makers (that is, men trained in making timepieces) in machine-making ended before 1800. Aikin's intelligent description of Arkwright's frame identifies the 'clock-work' elements: 'the cardings of three cans put together are passed through rollers moved

---

123   PP Artisans and Machinery, 251; D. Cardwell, 'Peter Ewart (1767–1842), engineer', DNB; Pacey, Maze of Ingenuity, 235–8.
124   Landes, Revolution in Time, 274–5.
125   Landes, Revolution in Time, 280.
126   Babbage, Economy of Machinery and Manufactures, 349–52.
127   Felkin, Machine-wrought Hosiery and Lace, 285.
128   Babbage, Economy of Machinery and Manufactures, 349–52.

by clock-work, which also puts in motion small circular brushes to clear the loose flying hairs of cotton from the rollers'. So gearing was the 'clock-work', and specifically the numerous sets of brass gear-wheels used purely on Arkwright's model.

> These machines exhibit in their construction an aggregate of clock-maker's work and machinery most wonderful to behold. The cotton to be spun is introduced through three sets of rollers, so governed by the clock-work, that the set which first receives the cotton makes so many more revolutions than the next in order, and these more than the last which feed the spindles, that it is drawn out considerably in passing through the rollers.[129]

The throstle, successor to Arkwright's frame, contained just one set of gears, and those were made of iron. A clock-makers' gear-cutter was adapted for this purpose in the 1790s.[130]

This, then, was clock-makers' main contribution to machine-making. It explains why Arkwright needed them, and then how rapidly their skills lost consequence to machine-making. Arkwright's first associate, John Kay of Warrington, was a clock-maker who could make brass wheels. Kay had worked to design a spinning frame with Thomas Highs before joining Arkwright in Leigh in 1768, with famous results.[131] Arkwright then adopted the title of 'clock-maker' for himself.[132]

In Arkwright's heyday, this term referred very specifically in machine-making to makers of brass gears, at first clock-makers in the traditional sense. Then the usage slipped, to mean a range of tasks involved in machine-making. So Arkwright and Strutt in 1771 sought 'two journeymen clock-makers or others that understands tooth and pinion well' at Cromford.[133] 'Clock-makers' continued to be employed at Quarry Bank Mill, Styal, from the start of construction in 1784, until 1793.[134] Later, relevant industrial experience was called for, and a wider set of engineering skills was assumed in a 'clock-maker'. In Manchester in 1782 there was advertised 'employment for clock-makers ... would be more agreeable if they have been before employed in cotton works' and in 1789 a machine-maker wanted 'clock-makers and turners'.[135] A missing employee, 'by trade a clock-smith' but lately a 'filer

129 Aikin, *Description of the Country*, 172–3.
130 Hills, *Power in the Industrial Revolution*, 243–4, 69, and plate 12 opp. 242; Benson, *Textile Machines*, 15, 20; and see throstle, pp. 59–64 above.
131 Hills, *Power in the Industrial Revolution*, 63–6; Rees, *Cyclopaedia*, I, 109; Usher, *Mechanical Inventions*, 298–9; Musson and Robinson, *Science and Technology*, 438.
132 Musson and Robinson, *Science and Technology*, 438.
133 Tann, *Development of the Factory*, 100.
134 Hills, *Power in the Industrial Revolution*, 192.
135 Musson and Robinson, *Science and Technology*, 456.

and turner' was pursued by cotton-mill owners in 1785.[136] A clock-maker's apprentice had deserted his master in Kendal in 1785 to 'mak[e] machinery for cotton mills for 12 months past'.[137]

James M'Connel and John Kennedy, among the first apprentices to the emerging machine making trade in the 1780s, were trained in (amongst other pursuits) 'clock-making', in its new meaning.[138] As a prominent cotton-spinner, in 1815 Kennedy offered a retrospective to the Manchester Literary and Philosophical Society.

> By degrees, a higher class of mechanics such as watch and clock-makers, whitesmiths, and mathematical instrument makers, began to be wanted; and in a short time a wide field was opened for the application of their more accurate and scientific mechanism. Those workmen were first chiefly employed in constructing the valuable machines invented by Mr Arkwright.[139]

Objecting to Pitt's tax in 1798, Prescot and Carlisle clock-makers claimed that cotton and woollen factories, in bringing machinery to a 'state of perfection', were 'entirely indebted' to the clock trade. But however the clock-makers' contribution is weighed, by then it lay largely in the past.[140] And the numbers do not support any significant crossover from clock-making into textile engineering, whether among those hundreds of clock-makers active in Yorkshire from the seventeenth to the early nineteenth centuries;[141] or from an exhaustive list of Wigan clock-makers, 1650–1850.[142] Nor is there evidence that Swiss clock-making skills were used when Britons built machines there.[143] The greatest impact of the older trade upon the new was perhaps in supplying tools to make Arkwright-type gearing. Certain of Prescot's advanced and specialist machine tools, including lathes, drills, rests and gear-cutters for instrument-, watch- and clock-makers, were modified for machine-making tasks, illustrated by John Wyke's catalogue, and his clientele.[144] Again, this was limited to an early period and to finer metal components.

Aspin suggests calling producers of delicate elements for textile machines 'clock-work maker'.[145] For the eighteenth century, this may be appropriate,

136   Musson and Robinson, *Science and Technology*, 456.
137   Aspin, *Water-Spinners*, 14.
138   Lee, *Cotton Enterprise*, 17.
139   Musson and Robinson, *Science and Technology*, 435.
140   Aspin, *Water-Spinners*, 17.
141   Loomes, *Yorkshire Clockmakers*.
142   Hawkes, *Clockmakers and Watchmakers of Wigan*.
143   Henderson, *Britain and Industrial Europe*, 203 et seq.
144   Dane, *Peter Stubs*, 51; Smith (ed.), *Catalogue of Tools*, 16, and *passim*; Rees, *Cyclopaedia*, II, 231–46; Hills, *Power in the Industrial Revolution*, 241–3; for Wyke, see above, pp. 52–3.
145   Aspin, *Water-Spinners*, 44.

for then 'clock-work' described such mechanisms. Models 'moved by clock-work', and the metaphor persisted – 'as to spinning frames, they are now made with all the nicety of clock-work'[146] – even after the term had lost its association with machine-making.

Yet there was another, tantalizing, association between clock- and machine-making in northern textile communities. Clock-making came into vogue as a pastime, a natural diversion for the mechanically minded. Some prominent machine-makers cultivated a serious interest in producing clocks, instruments and models. It was a hobby, but also an exercise in mechanical aptitude, and the practical skill of model-making had direct relevance to the day job. Indeed, scale models of machines were produced as apprentice pieces, marking a graduation to full proficiency.

Early in the Keighley industry, a clock-maker called John Brigg cut brass gears and worked on Heaton's Arkwright-type factory projects before vanishing from notice c. 1794.[147] Around 1800, Richard Hattersley referred to two customers, both called William Smith, as 'clock-maker'. The older, William Smith of Braithwaite, was elsewhere called a filer and turner, and perhaps made neither clocks nor machines.[148] The other William Smith was an important early textile engineer, and 'clock-maker' reflected his early training in the Arkwright system. This man also had a serious and enduring interest in making clocks, and one of his many sons became a professional clock-maker as conventionally understood.[149] Smith's interest in precision engineering fed into worsted-spinning innovations, though he was primarily a component-maker until 1810 or later.

This William Smith also had a remarkable relationship with an accomplished clock-making family, Potts of Darlington. Evenings were spent making and repairing clocks at his home in Waggon Fold, alongside Robert Potts, formerly bound with a £20 premium to a Darlington clock-maker of high repute. Potts moved to Keighley in about 1814 to work for Smith. Their relationship was very close, to the point that Potts's motherless son William was welcomed to Smith's household in c. 1821, living as a family member until 1830. A £40 premium later placed him in the same Darlington firm where his father had trained. Robert Potts went on to work for Lawrence Smith, a younger son of William and clock-maker in Low Street, Keighley.[150] William

146 James, *History of the Worsted Manufacture*, 535, quoting Nasmyth.
147 See app. 1.
148 WYAS Bradford, 32D83/1, p. 40. See also *Craven Muster Roll*; UGLE, Samaritan Lodge, Keighley, joined 1792.
149 See app. 1.
150 Potts, 'William Potts of Leeds', 25–6. Here, clocks were certainly made: Loomes, *Yorkshire Clockmakers*.

Potts emerged as a famous maker of large public clocks, the mechanisms of which bore some similarity to textile machinery.[151]

Most interestingly, Robert Potts, not remotely typical of Smith's employees, arrived at the time Smith was working on improved worsted-spinning frames. The unusual details – Potts's high level of skill, his intimacy with the Smiths, his later return to clock-making – imply that he was engaged for a specific purpose. It cannot be that Potts saw no future in clock-making – for if so, why invest a large sum to indenture his own son back in Darlington? The best clock-makers were skilled and valued, and conceivably offered tools, techniques and insights relevant to the more polished end of textile engineering.[152] So while the case of Smith and Potts is instructive, it was exceptional.

A well-established dynasty of watch- and clock-makers, the highly regarded Lawson family, had worked in Keighley from 1740 or before.[153] But the William Lawson styled 'clock-maker' in Richard Hattersley's daybook when he bought large numbers of throstle parts, from 1797, did not belong to that family, nor was he a clock-maker. Hattersley commonly applied the term to customers who made throstles.[154] William Lawson was a tin-plate worker unconnected with clock-making, whose son William Platerous Lawson (b. 1783) built a successful business as a tinsmith and brazier on the periphery of machine-making.[155]

But some of the clock-making Lawsons did find success in textile engineering. Samuel Lawson (b. 1728), renowned for his timepieces, brought up his son Thomas (b. 1754) in the same trade. Thomas Lawson, once again it seems through the Arkwright brass gear route, became well-known for his 'considerable skill as a mechanical engineer', and 'in request among those who established textile manufactories'.[156] He was apparently involved in a frustrated attempt to adapt Arkwright's frame to worsteds at Bridgehouse, Haworth, in 1781.[157] In 1792 Lawson left Keighley for Burley-in-Wharfedale, to supervise the building and fitting out of a large cotton-spinning factory, Greenholme Mill, staying on as mill engineer.[158] He moved in 1803 to join J. and J. Holroyd's cotton enterprise in Sheepscar, Leeds. Lawson's textile-engineering successes were later eclipsed by those of his son, Samuel, himself a fine hobbyist instrument-maker.[159]

---

151   Potts, 'William Potts of Leeds', 36. Ron Fitzgerald pointed out the similarity between a factory clock mechanism at Armley Mills, and parts of a textile machine. See also, for instance, the medieval clock at Salisbury cathedral.
152   Dane, *Peter Stubs*, 51.
153   Loomes, *Yorkshire Clockmakers*.
154   WYAS Bradford, 32D83/5/1; /2/1.
155   See app. 1.
156   WYAS Leeds, Acc. 2371, box 80/2.
157   Aspin, *Water-Spinners*, 78, 306.
158   WYAS Leeds, Acc. 2371, box 80/2; Aspin, *Water-Spinners*, 436, 466.
159   WYAS Leeds, Acc. 2371, box 80/2; box 76; see app. 2, also for David Wood as an instrument-maker.

Meanwhile, the term 'clock-maker' broadened to embrace shopkeepers selling clocks; blacksmiths or locksmiths repairing public clocks; and carpenters and cabinet-makers producing clock cases.[160] Some clocks produced were less precise than elements of machine-making. Keighley's local historian William Keighley, by trade a patten[clog]-maker, was involved on the margins of these trades, and also as a retailer.[161] Employed by his brother-in-law Thomas Smith, a time-served machine-maker, from 1815, they made wooden products using basic methods. In 1820 Keighley set up as a retail clock-maker in Nelson Street.[162] William Keighley's career, a progression through different branches of carpentry – clogs to wooden machine frames, and then clock cases – demanded few mechanical skills. Across the spectrum, acquired metalworking skills were a route into working on Arkwright-style technology. Joseph Shaw of Dent, by trade a weaver, found a new livelihood after teaching himself to mend clocks, guns and locks using a vice, lathe and files. From c. 1784, he turned these skills to producing frames and parts for cotton-factories, working from 1791 as mill mechanic at Dolphinholme, before falling out with the owner and returning to clock-making.[163]

With such diverse examples, the clock-maker's place in textile engineering is hard to summarize. Certainly clock-makers had some brief consequence as brass-gear makers in the Arkwright system, and this brought 'clock-maker' into regular use, for a little time, to mean machine-maker. But to see them, even then, as central to the industry is overstretching a point.

The rise of the whitesmith

Millwrights were associated with wood, clock-makers with brass. Once iron, and to an extent tin, came to the fore, then so did founders and smiths. From the 1780s, demand increased for blacksmiths and tinsmiths, and in particular for whitesmiths, the trades skilled in working wrought iron and those lighter metals demanded for throstles, mules and the improved jenny. Wrought iron became the essential material of mechanical engineering for most of the following century.[164]

A typical smith's workshop in 1747 contained several grades of smith, the 'vice-man' being the most precise:

In all Smith's Shops they are divided into three Classes; the Fire-Man, or he that forges the work; the Vice-Man, or he who files and finishes it; and

160 Loomes, *Yorkshire Clockmakers*, 8–10.
161 *Craven Muster Roll.* Pattens, made of wood and iron, protected shoe soles.
162 Hodgson, *Textile Manufacture*, 263.
163 Crosby (ed.), *Benjamin Shaw*, 5–7, 24, 26.
164 Cressy, *Hundred Years*, 163.

the Hammer-Man, who strikes with the great hammer by the direction of the Fire-Man, who uses only a small hammer ... the Vice-Man requires the nicest Hand and the most mechanic Head, especially if concerned in Movements; and in such Shops where Works of that kind are chiefly carried on, he has the highest Wages ... Smiths of all kinds would be the better Workmen if they understood Drawing so much as to plan their own Works.[165]

Then there was a separate tradesman, the 'tin-man'. The 'tin' produced was:

a Composition of Iron and Block-Tin, not melted together, but the Iron in Bars is covered over with Tin and flatted in Mills to the Thinness we see it. It is but of late we have had any of it made in England; it mostly comes from Sweden, and is properly called Latine [latten], and in some Parts of this Island White-Iron. The Tin-Man receives it in Sheets; it is his Business, by beating it on a polished Anvil, to give it Smoothness and Lustre.

These tin-plated iron sheets were used to make lamps, pans and other household items. The tinsmith was 'a Branch that stands single by itself', requiring 'not over-and-above much Ingenuity' but judgement resting 'chiefly in the Use of his Hammer'.[166]

According to Rees in the 1810s, tin-plate, by then common, was 'vulgarly called tin'. The process had come from Bohemia in the 1680s, waned, and then revived with great success from 1740. 'It is iron plated over with tin. The French call it *fer blanc*, white iron, as we sometimes do in England. It was once known under a distinct name, *lattin*.'[167] In fact Major John Hanbury had succeeded in producing tin-plate commercially at Pontypool from 1728. The Swedish traveller Angerstein reported that tin-plate technology used at Wortley in 1754 had been stolen from Pontypool.[168]

Angerstein clearly described seeing tin used in this process in the 1750s. No doubt its cost encouraged other metals to be substituted, especially on large objects such as machinery. Latten came to be defined as 'iron tinned over, tin-plate; more explicitly *white latten*. Also, any metal made in thin sheets'.[169] And so too the whitesmith, a worker in 'white iron', a tinsmith, was also more broadly 'one who polishes or finishes metal goods, as distinguished from one

---

165 Campbell, *London Tradesman*, 180.
166 Campbell, *London Tradesman*, 183–4. Note the 'tin mill' at Wortley Top Forge, a rolling mill flanked and driven by two water-wheels. This worked special quality charcoal iron from ½ in. to ⅝ in. thick, down to fine gauges of sheet iron. But later proprietors found no evidence that tin had been plated there: Andrews, *Story of Wortley Ironworks*, 65–6.
167 Rees, *Cyclopaedia*, V, 265, 266–7.
168 Marilyn Palmer, introduction to Angerstein, *Illustrated Travel Diary*, xvii–xviii; and *Diary*, 219. For further detail of the process, see *Diary*, 54, 57, 134–5, 182.
169 OED.

who forges them; also, more widely, a worker in metals'.[170] A whitesmith may be a tinsmith, or could be the 'vice-man' of 1747, a finisher of metal pieces. These enhanced skills accruing in sheet-metal work and plating could be applied across a range of materials.

This is why the trade of prime significance in Keighley, as the town blossomed into a textile-engineering centre in the 1790s and 1800s, was the smith, and specifically the whitesmith. There were wood- and metalworkers in numbers, but in skill most were subsidiary to the whitesmith. It is ironical that 'tinker', once synonymous with tinsmith, the producer of high standard industrial metalwork, came to signify amateurism and incompetence, 'clumsy, bungling, or imperfect' work; and 'tinny', now implying poor quality, was once an appreciation of the fineness of this plated sheet metal.[171]

---

170   OED.
171   OED. See below, p. 229, for an example of 'tinker' as a slight.

1

The Machine-Makers

The new engineering

We have a number of men who have risen from being common mechanics to being men of great eminence.[1]

Northern machine-makers generally came from modest beginnings. James Watt jun. in 1802 labelled Leeds engineers as 'men without character and without means', prevented by social background from becoming 'eligible connections' for Boulton and Watt.[2] The time when humble origins were worn with pride by the wealthy and successful was still a generation or more away. Relative to other manufacturing industries,[3] textile engineering raised many former artisans to success, prosperity and social advancement. To call this 'rags to riches', though, may be stretching a point.

Machine-making originated in a largely artisanal world of small workshops, where in the early years basic tools and equipment largely sufficed, and external capital was not always needed for expansion. The skill was the thing. As in other craft industry, there was an expectation that most or all sons would follow the trade and join the family business.[4] In places where this new engineering sector was located, there were few or no guilds, nor other restrictions. Apprenticeship within certain crafts was a respected qualification. In other industries where entry costs were low, over-capacity could bring the weakest firms to failure.[5] Here, with the market for machinery fast expanding, it often bucked the trend during economic downturns. This would not have happened unless this most technical – and increasingly so – of industries produced machines which were of good quality and economically viable. So evidently the trade satisfied customers, attracted plenty of orders, and returned

---

1 PP Exportation of Machinery, 106, evidence of William Jenkinson.
2 Scott (ed.), *Matthew Murray*, 42.
3 Honeyman, *Origins of Enterprise*, 160, 170.
4 Rowlands, *Masters and Men*, 40; Rose, 'Beyond Buddenbrooks: the Family Firm and the Management of Succession in nineteenth century Britain', in Brown and Rose (eds) *Entrepreneurship, Networks and Modern Business*, 135.
5 Honeyman, *Origins of Enterprise*, 168.

profits sufficient to finance much of its own expansion. Yet there was a high dropout rate: many early participants quit textile engineering altogether.

This chapter explores the origins and experiences of textile engineers from the first generations, those building businesses in Keighley and Leeds from around 1780 until c. 1830. Most likely to succeed in the longer term were those with mechanical aptitude and perspective. This view of course benefits from historical hindsight. But mechanical skills did not guarantee continuity, and in fact the initial range of participants was wide. So where did they emerge from, which trades, industrial background, and district? And what does the calibre of machine-makers, masters and men, reveal of the products, and about the industry's changing character through these early decades?

The Keighley trade

Keighley sits where Laycock beck joins the river Worth, close to the Aire and the Leeds and Liverpool canal, which from 1777 connected the town to Leeds – and so to the sea – and to Bradford. Northern Lancashire's textile districts were close and accessible even before the canal reached Burnley in 1796. Between 1780 and 1800, 26 cotton-spinning factories sprang up alongside the Worth and its tributaries.[6] This fast-growing town doubled its population in the half century to 1780, when estimated at 4,100. In 1801 it stood at 5,700, in 1821 at over 9,200, almost doubling again by 1851, to 18,200.[7]

Three influential individuals, key to Keighley's transformation into a great centre of textile engineering, launched in business there c. 1790. William Carr and William Smith emerged from the Arkwright system, while Richard Hattersley's background lay in the ironworking districts north of Sheffield. Their careers illuminate the new trade's progression.

William Carr

William Carr's first introduction to Arkwright's system probably came in 1781, when the Blackburn merchants Cardwell, Feilden and Birley opened a factory in his home parish of Scorton, north Lancashire.[8] Carr was then a whitesmith aged about 30. He went on to oversee construction of Kirk Mill, Chipping – an Arkwright-type cotton-twist factory – in 1785, and remained there as manager and partner. It was a Catholic business, owned by Hugh Stirrup and John Shakeshaft, London merchants and linen drapers; Richard Salisbury of Chorley, cotton-manufacturer; and William Barrow of Lancaster, merchant.[9]

6   Aspin, *Water-Spinners*, 237.
7   Dewhirst, *History of Keighley*, 6, 10, 14.
8   Aspin, *Water-Spinners*, 320–5. See app. 1.
9   Aspin, *Water-Spinners*, 134–5; *Manchester Mercury*, 15 Apr. 1788.

Most likely Carr was employed for his technical talents and did not invest.[10] The purpose of Kirk Mill, like Scorton, was to provide a reliable supply of yarn for the dispersed handloom weavers working for its owners. Shakeshaft, Stirrup and Salisbury was a merchant partnership separate from the mill, manufacturing calico, muslins and other cotton goods around Chorley, for sale in London.[11] As with Scorton, Kirk Mill's output was supplemented with twist bought elsewhere. There was heavy reliance on Keighley for this, including the West Greengate and Low mills.[12]

Keighley spinners were major creditors when the merchant house failed in 1787, and Shakeshaft, Stirrup and Salisbury was made bankrupt.[13] This immediately hit Kirk Mill, though Carr was never personally insolvent.[14] The Kirk Mill company somehow accommodated its creditors and continued for a time.[15] Shakeshaft, Stirrup and Salisbury's affairs took much longer to resolve – Shakeshaft died during the process – ending with sales of property in London and Lancaster.[16]

William Carr remained in the mill house through 1788, while the Kirk Mill property was offered for sale. It was advertised as a going concern with 20 spinning frames at work – altogether 1,032 spindles – and machinery for six more frames of 48 spindles, along with carding, roving, drawing and other plant. Carr was probably paid by the assignees to keep the mill working while demand for cotton thread was high.[17] Kirk Mill sold at auction in 1789, and before it restarted in April 1790, Carr had opened his own workshop in Keighley and recruited an apprentice, Berry Smith.[18]

The move to Keighley was logical: he had many contacts among the cotton-spinners there, Keighley and Haworth alone had at least 10 cotton-factories, and a competent smith well-versed in Arkwright frames must be in high demand.[19] Carr was soon known as the 'cleverest mechanist in the town', initially a jobbing blacksmith and whitesmith repairing flyers and

---

10   This was becoming a standard practice: see above, p. 48

11   TNA, B 1/80, p. 8.

12   Aspin, *Water-Spinners*, 134–5, 323.

13   TNA, B 1/82 pp. 229–33; *London Gazette*, 12 June 1787, 12894, 287; 4 Aug. 1787, 12909, 371; 23 Oct. 1787, 12932, 503.

14   *London Gazette*, 31 July 1787, 12908, 366; 11 Aug. 1787, 12911, 383; 6 Nov. 1787, 12936, 527.

15   *London Gazette*, 12 Apr. 1788, 12981, 178. Hoppit, *Risk and Failure*, 36, discusses the complex bankruptcy laws of this period.

16   TNA, B 1/80, pp. 3–7; Aspin, *Water-Spinners*, 135; *London Gazette*, 9 Dec. 1788, 13050, 592; 12 May 1789, 13096, 375; 1 Jan. 1789, 13058, 13; 24 Apr. 1790, 13195, 252.

17   *Manchester Mercury*, 15 Apr. 1788; 14 Oct. 1788.

18   Aspin, *Water-Spinners*, 135; Hodgson, *Textile Manufacture*, 249–53. Peter Atherton, textile engineer and factory designer, was among the company taking over Kirk Mill: Aspin, *Water-Spinners*, 137; Davies, 'Peter Atherton'.

19   Aspin, *Water-Spinners*, 460–3.

guides. By 1793–94 he was also in business as Richardson, Hodgson and Carr, brass-founders and engine [machine] makers. This loose but convenient association with George Richardson, a brass-founder, and Hodgson, of whom nothing is known, was short-lived.[20] Carr was a prolific customer of Richard Hattersley's new business, from 1794, buying all kinds of ironwork – screws, studs, rollers, and later spindles and flyers – to mend or build machinery for, for example, Jonathan Bracken of Luddenden Dean (Midgley), and Baynes of Embsay (Skipton).[21]

Carr and Hattersley had much in common, as whitesmiths newly arrived in Keighley in c. 1789–91. But their paths into textile engineering had differed. Hattersley's expertise, gained in south Yorkshire and at Kirkstall, lay in precision components, screws, roller-fluting and spindles. Carr, building on his Arkwright knowledge, made machines. From c. 1798, he was one of several Keighley machine-makers using Hattersley rollers and spindles to develop the throstle. From new premises in Low Street, he produced spinning frames in a workshop above the house, the smithy set behind, the whole hand-powered.[22] His son Edward later continued as a throstle-maker, reportedly making 'the first with iron ends'.[23]

Richard Hattersley

Hattersley was born in 1761 in Ecclesfield, a nail-making centre between Sheffield and Penistone.[24] This and the neighbouring rural parishes of Silkstone and Tankersley were served by Wortley forge, then a hub of spindle manufacture.[25] From this district came Samuel and Aaron Walker, the north's leading ironmasters from the 1760s, from Grenoside;[26] Joshua Wordsworth, later prominent in Leeds machine-making; and Joseph Bramah (1749–1814), of national renown. Wordsworth and Bramah were both Silkstone-born carpenters.[27]

Richard Hattersley identified himself as a whitesmith.[28]

---

20 Barfoot and Wilkes, *Dir.*, III, 482–4.
21 WYAS Bradford, 32D83/2/1 and /5/1, *passim*; Ingle, *Yorkshire Cotton*, 145; Aspin, *Water-Spinners*, 413.
22 Hodgson, *Textile Manufacture*, 250–1.
23 Hodgson, *Textile Manufacture*, 251.
24 For biographical information and relationships, app. 1.
25 For Wortley forge, see below, pp. 163–5.
26 Hey, *Fiery Blades*, 96–7, 305; D. G. Hey, 'Walker family (*per.* 1741–1833), iron, steel, and lead manufacturers', *DNB*; additional information from David Hey.
27 C. F. Lindsey, 'Joseph Bramah (1749–1814), engineer and inventor of locks', *DNB*; McNeil, *Joseph Bramah*; for Bramah's enduring influence, see Cookson and Cantrell (eds), *Henry Maudslay*, 18–19, 21–3; Wordsworth, 'Joshua Wordsworth'.
28 For instance WYAS Wakefield, Deeds, FI, 16 Sept. 1809; GO, 13 Feb. 1817; HN, 24 June 1821.

> [Hattersley] ... was a blacksmith made nails and hired as a striker at
> Sheffield. He afterwards worked in the screw business at Kirkstall Forge
> afterwards in the screw mill near Keighley as master of the screw forges
> and lastly at Keighley where [he] took a small spinning mill which he used
> as a blacksmith shop & afterwards enlarged it and built an house adjoining
> and became a spindle, flyer and roller maker, and mill shafts of all sorts.[29]

While not fully verified, this is consistent with other evidence, and more
plausible than the idea of a direct move from Ecclesfield straight to Keighley
in 1789.[30] Hattersley married in Sheffield in 1784, where three children were
baptized, 1785–89.[31] Presumably then he was a journeyman 'improver',
broadening skills and experience for four or five years, 1784 to 1788/89. He
was certainly in Keighley by 1791, when his fourth child was baptized. In
between, Hattersley apparently worked at Kirkstall, where a new screw forge
opened in 1788.[32] News of this opportunity would pass on the grapevine,
between the forges, or via Wortley exiles already in Leeds, John Jubb, John
Pollard or the Drabbles.

Screws were important in mechanical construction, used in great quantities
to fix together (for example) steam-engines. But cutting them by hand caused
problems.

> [T]he solidity and permanence of most mechanical structures mainly
> depend[ed] on the employment of the screw, at the same time that the parts
> can be readily separated for renewal or repair ... the tools used for making
> screws were of the most rude and inexact kind. The screws were for the
> most part cut by hand: the small by filing, the larger by chipping and filing
> ... There was an utter want of uniformity.[33]

Screw-cutting lathes designed by Jesse Ramsden, an instrument-maker,
worked well on screws of delicate pitch for fine mechanisms, from 1770.
Screw-cutting at that level remained highly skilled. The same precision was
not required for screws and nuts to secure machine parts. Kirkstall's screw
forge would have employed smiths experienced in using stocks and dies to
make larger-sized screws.[34]

Richard Hattersley's name is not to be found among Kirkstall records.[35]
But they show dealings with Cawood, Wright and Binns of Stubbing House

29   C. Smith, family bible. These notes were transcribed into the bible c. 1900, source unspecified.
30   Hodgson, *Textile Manufacture*, 241, who mistakenly refers to Eccleshall.
31   Sheffield St Peter: mar. 11 Apr. 1784; bap. 25 May 1785; 7 Sept. 1787; 13 Apr. 1789.
32   WYAS Leeds, KF 4/4, notes re new forge, back of ledger.
33   Smiles, *Industrial Biography*, 225–6.
34   Derry and Williams, *Short History of Technology*, 347–8. For screw-cutting and
die-making, see Angerstein, *Illustrated Travel Diary*, 51–2; also 264, 297.
35   These are piecemeal: WYAS Leeds, 6755/4.

(Screw) Mill, Keighley, from 1787.[36] Thomas Binns conducted business in person at Kirkstall, and it was most likely here he first encountered Hattersley. Cawood, the partner with engineering capability, left Screw Mill in 1789, coinciding with Binns offering Hattersley the supervisor's job and perhaps a prospect of partnership.[37] Probably Hattersley did arrive in Keighley in 1789, but as an employee, and perhaps proceeding there ahead of his young family.

Thomas Binns (1756–1810) had joined the new screw- and bolt-making venture in Keighley in 1787. Stubbing House, a small factory with a powerful fall of water, was built as a speculative room-and-power venture. Soon it was known as Screw Mill, and Binns called himself screw-maker.[38] He had other interests, in cotton-spinning: at Stubbing House with John Greenwood from c. 1790, and then jointly with Rowland Watson in 1799, insured for £400; and in a cotton-twist and calico factory with his brother Abraham, and later his own son Thomas, in their home village of Ickornshaw, Cowling, recorded in 1791.[39] In about 1800, the Binns and Hattersley enterprise quit Screw Mill for North Brook, where Hattersleys would remain.[40]

The other screw-making partners were James Cawood, nail-maker and dealer in iron, and Joseph Wright, shoemaker. The company had a 20-year lease on the premises, but soon fragmented.[41] Cawood's bankruptcy in 1789 forced his withdrawal.[42] Wright became minister at the Swedenborgian church, established in the town in 1787–89. In November 1791, he baptized Elizabeth, the first Hattersley child born in Keighley, at the New Church at Beck Side.[43]

Wright stayed a partner, though inactive. The company remained Wright and Binns until 1791, when a Keighley attorney, Rowland Watson (?1740–1806), joined. Watson was a financier, holding a sixth share in Marriner's cotton-spinners from their foundation in 1784.[44] Watson, Wright and Binns insured premises and equipment at Screw Mill in 1792 for £1,000, £820 of this unspecified 'utensils and machinery', so probably more than just Binns' small engineering firm.[45] Binns and partners made regular purchases from Kirkstall Forge, 1787–93, mainly rod and bar iron and screws, and at times selling back

36   WYAS Leeds, KF 4/4; 6257/2, p. 145.
37   WYAS Leeds, 6257/2, p. 216; Hodgson, *Textile Manufacture*, 85–6.
38   Thomas Binns, age 31, screw-maker, in 1788 joining Royal Yorkshire Lodge of freemasons, Keighley: UGLE lists.
39   Ingle, *Yorkshire Cotton*, 179; Guildhall Lib., RE 170160, 21 Oct. 1799.
40   Hodgson, *Textile Manufacture*, 19, 53, 218–19, 241–3; Aspin, *Water-Spinners*, 463.
41   Hodgson, *Textile Manufacture*, 85–6.
42   *London Gazette*, 18 Aug. 1789, 13124, 562; *Leeds Intelligencer*, 28 July 1789; WYAS Leeds, 6257/2, p. 216; Barfoot and Wilkes, *Dir.*, III, 483.
43   Bottomley, 'Keighley New Church', 1, 3, 5, 14, 17; Barfoot and Wilkes, *Dir.*, III, 482–4; Hattersley family bibles.
44   Ingle, *Marriner's Yarns*, 13–14; Whitaker, *Deanery of Craven*, 203.
45   Ingle, *Yorkshire Cotton*, 170–1, citing Guildhall Lib., RE23/131587/1792.

screws to Kirkstall. When Cawood became bankrupt, Binns personally settled the account as reassurance of his company's solvency.[46]

Recruiting Hattersley filled the technical vacuum left by Cawood. He stepped up to partner only in 1793, when Watson and Wright retired and the old company dissolved. Wright retained financial ties with both Binns and Hattersley as late as 1803.[47] Hattersley and Binns continued to buy iron from Kirkstall Forge, occasionally part-paying with spindles.[48] On Binns' death in 1810, Hattersley bought out his share, but the debt, eventually £2,463 including interest, took years to clear. This was perhaps arranged formally, to maintain working capital. It gave Thomas Binns jun., who never worked in the business, an income – £349 in 1814, £207 in 1817. Only after Hattersley died in 1829 was settlement finalized with Binns' executors.[49] Clearing this debt perhaps added to the difficulties inherited by the three Hattersley sons who were then partners.[50]

Richard Hattersley was hugely influential in Keighley engineering, and far beyond. Starting out, he would take any kind of smith's work – mending spades, clog irons or the church gates[51] – but his talents were already extensive, from screws and bolts to rollers, spindles and flyers. While never really producing machines for sale, he was at the hub of Keighley machine-making, supplying every would-be producer of textile machinery with precision parts and acting as middleman for sheet metal, steel and other specialities. His expertise enabled non-specialists to build machines in the years before 1805, and the skills taught to a new generation underpinned the industry's growing proficiency.[52] Throughout Hattersley's lifetime, the firm's main products remained rollers, spindles and flyers. Tentative orders for power looms were placed from 1827,[53] and under George Hattersley the Keighley business became primarily a power-loom manufacturer by the mid-1840s.

From about 1800 Hattersley cultivated a significant market with Leeds worsted- and flax-machine makers, including Taylor and Wordsworth, Samuel Lawson, and Peter Fairbairn. He met this growth in business, and increased flexibility, by employing subcontractors. A new building was added in 1811, and c. 1816–20 the company's workshops remodelled into factory premises, with a new site opening in Bradford in response to its worsted-spinning boom.[54]

46   WYAS Leeds, 6257/2, pp. 145, 216; 6257/1, pp. 135, 251.
47   WYAS Wakefield, Deeds, EN, 12 Feb. 1803.
48   WYAS Leeds, 6257/1, p. 251.
49   Keighley St Andrew, memorial inscription; WYAS Bradford, 32D83/6/1; /2/2, loose paper.
50   Borthwick, Craven, Feb. 1830, for Hattersley's will; WYAS Bradford, 32D83/2/5, p. 509.
51   WYAS Bradford, 32D83/2/1.
52   WYAS Bradford, 32D83/2/1 and /5/1, etc.; Hodgson, *Textile Manufacture*; *Craven Muster Roll*.
53   WYAS Bradford, 32D83/15/2.
54   Hodgson, *Textile Manufacture*, 217–18, 275; WYAS Bradford, 32D83/2/4; /5/3; /6/2.

William Smith

Low Mill, the first Arkwright-style factory in Yorkshire, was built in 1780 for Clayton and Walshman on the lower reaches of the Worth.[55] Here, it is said, William Smith started work at the age of nine, so in 1783–84. Later he was apprenticed to Adam Pearson, the foreman and mechanic.[56] Completing his training in 1795, Smith promptly launched into business at Waggon Fold.[57] Early records are lost, but he seems initially to have made flyers, guides and mechanisms, becoming interested in building throstles late in the 1790s. Smith is first found in Hattersley's surviving accounts in January 1799. Then and later he bought spindles and flyers, and ironwork intended for various 'ingeons', some of these machine tools.[58]

Later came the association with Robert Potts, the clock-maker, as Smith worked to improve a worsted-spinning frame.[59] His firm was a front-runner in marketing these machines, from about 1820, and progressed to world leader. Smith made rollers, spindles and flyers alongside worsted machinery, and was also a worsted spinner.[60] The transition to machine-making was, as with Hattersley, a gradual process. While improvements to his Waggon Fold premises were constant, Smith did not have a foundry until 1830 or later, instead commissioning machine frames from Thomas Mills and others, who held his patterns.[61]

The Keighley machine-makers

Keighley's early engineering enterprises were largely synonymous with their proprietors. The business, in this artisan environment, *c'est moi*.

Even boosting the numbers with outlying figures – such as Adam Pearson, who may only ever have made machinery for his employers, and John Nicholson, perhaps no more than financier of Weatherhead's experimentation, and others of whom virtually nothing is known – only 18 engineers or engineering businesses have been identified as working in Keighley before 1815.[62] A few generalizations can be made. All the firms before 1815 were small, at peak times employing at most a handful of journeymen and one or two

55   Aspin, *Water-Spinners*, 76–82; Hodgson, *Textile Manufacture*, 212–14, 244.

56   Hodgson, *Textile Manufacture*, 244; for Pearson, see app. 1.

57   Later Market Street, and leased from the Burlington estate: Hodgson, *Textile Manufacture*, 244–5; Keighley Lib., rate books.

58   WYAS Bradford, 32D83/2/1, p. 101; Hodgson, *Textile Manufacture*, 245.

59   See above, pp. 83–4.

60   Hodgson, *Textile Manufacture*, 245–6; PP (HC) 1834 (167) C1, 221; Baines, *Dir.* (1822), 220; White, *Dir.* (1853), 544.

61   Hodgson, *Textile Manufacture*, 246; Keighley Lib., poor rate books, 1830–35.

62   See app. 1; for Nicholson, see above, pp. 63–4.

Table 1. Careers and affiliations of early textile engineers in Keighley

	Original trade	Dates noted as textile engineer	Later career	Born	Religion	Freemason?
John Brigg	?Turner	1791–94	n/k			
Lodge Calvert (1776–1859)	Joiner	1799–c. 1805	Mainly worsted & cotton-spinner from c. 1801	Upper Wharfedale	Methodist from 1797	
William Carr (c. 1750–1834)	Whitesmith	c. 1790–c. 1817	Retired. Sons continued to c. 1840	Scorton, Lancs	Roman Catholic	Y
Thomas Corlass	Joiner/cabinet-maker	1799–c. 1804	Primarily cotton-twist, then worsted, spinner.		Swedenborgian	Y
James Greenwood	Textiles	1784–c. 1791	Cotton & worsted spinner			
Richard Hattersley (1761–1829)	Whitesmith	By 1793–1829	Business continued	Ecclesfield, near Sheffield	C. of E. then Swedenborgian	Y As was early partner Binns
Joseph Hindle	Joiner	1799–c. 1804	Reverted to joinery?			
John Inman sen. & jun.	Joiners	1793–c. 1805	Joinery		Methodist	
William and William Platerous Lawson	Tin-plate workers	1797–1830s?	WPL emigrated, c. 1830s			
Titus Longbottom (1775–1831)	Joiner/machinist	(father) 1793; TL 1808–31	Died; no successor	Steeton		

	Original trade	Dates noted as textile engineer	Later career	Born	Religion	Freemason?
Michael Merrall (1775–1819)	Blacksmith	?1808–19	Died; no successor	?Keighley		
John Nicholson	?Printer	1793–1802	Bookseller			
Adam Pearson	?	c. 1780–96	?Twist-spinner			
George Richardson	Brass-founder	c. 1800–02	Founder			Y
Berry Smith (1772–1836)	Machine-maker	1800–c. 1830–35	Mainly textiles after 1810	Bingley parish	Swedenborgian	
Thomas Smith	n/k	?1793–?1804	n/k			
William Smith (1774–1850)	Mechanic?	From c. 1797–1850	Business continued	Stockbridge (Bingley par.)		
Joseph Tempest (c. 1753/6–c. 1836)	Carpenter/ millwright	?1793–?1795	Carpenter/mil wright	Sutton-in-Craven		Y
John Weatherhead	Joiner	?1789–?1798	Probably died c. 1798			His son was.

Main sources: NYCRO, *Craven Muster Roll* 1803; WYAS Bradford, 32D83/2/1; 5/1; Hodgson, *Textile Manufacture*; Keighley Parish Register. See also Appendix 1.

apprentices. Some ran only a one-man business, or barely produced machines or parts. Almost every individual had a recognized and relevant trade, as many of them wood- as metalworkers. After 1800, though, virtually all new entrants were metalworkers of some description. Perhaps six of the 18 had experience of fitting up Arkwright style cotton spinning factories. Several of the joiners, and some others, were involved in developing or producing the throstle.

Twelve of the 18 had left the industry or disappeared from the local record by about 1810. Weatherhead died, Brigg and Greenwood vanish. The joiners Hindle and Inman, and millwright Tempest, appear to have resumed their older trades once metal largely replaced wood in machinery. Others took up textile manufacture. Thomas Corlass, whose machine-making had in any case been ancillary to cotton-spinning, switched between that and worsteds, with many fluctuations in fortune.[63] Lodge Calvert, a joiner who made throstles for a few years, maybe only for his own use, did well spinning cotton, and later worsteds.[64]

The six Keighley engineers continuing in business after 1810 were of a certain stamp. All were grounded in metalworking, well-versed in the latest machine technologies, and understood the needs of textile manufacturers. Carr and Hattersley were whitesmiths, Merrall a smith introduced to textile engineering by Hattersley. William Smith had been apprenticed as a mill mechanic. Berry Smith was trained by Carr, and in his turn enabled Titus Longbottom to complete a thorough transition into the trade.[65] Longbottom was the only one of the half-dozen whose original trade lay outside metalworking.

Soon after 1810, the well-regarded Berry Smith put aside the trade in favour of textiles, in which he did well. Michael Merrall was killed in 1819 and his business closed. Titus Longbottom had financial problems, struggling along in reduced circumstances until his death in 1831. Only the firms of Carr, Hattersley and William Smith survived in some form, and these not without difficulty.

The industry in Leeds

To mechanical engineers, Leeds, a large and long-established centre of manufacture, transport and marketing, offered a broader base of customers than could be found in Keighley. Machines and iron goods were in high demand for textiles, and for other industries besides. Collieries and their

---

63   Hodgson, *Textile Manufacture*, 22–8; Keighley Lib., apprenticeship indenture 1802.
64   Hodgson, *Textile Manufacture*, 20.
65   App. 1.

waggon-ways were a particularly significant market, as were domestic goods in this booming town. Sales of cast- and wrought-iron household items reinvigorated Kirkstall Forge and attracted other foundries to central Leeds. Of the textile engineers, Murray and Stirk became known for high quality improved steam-engines; they and others also made important advances in machine-tool technology.

The Leeds textile industry specialized in woollens, and after 1790 in flax-spinning, contrasting with Keighley's cotton and worsteds. The influential Marshall, deploying his own flax-spinning technology in a series of new factories, and Gott, adaptor of hand processes within a highly organized system of woollen manufacture, presented examples for other textile manufacturers to emulate. These offered blueprints to machine-makers, too, as they looked to improve precision and efficiency in their own workshops. The leading engineering companies in Leeds were large and more integrated, ahead of their counterparts in Keighley. They were more likely to take moneyed partners or cultivate other external channels of finance, and to extend beyond machine-making into related work like iron-founding, machine tools and steam-engines. In Keighley such developments came later, after c. 1825.

Charting the textile engineers of Leeds, with its large and fluid population spread across several townships, is more complicated than in Keighley's well-defined settlement. Lesser engineering workshops tend to be inconspicuous in a big town. Keighley had its industrial chroniclers – William Keighley and John Hodgson – and sources effectively covering the whole town, notably the Craven muster roll which lists most adult men and their trades. In Leeds, small specialist engineering businesses, spindle-making workshops and so on, are easily overlooked, and the significance of not counting them hard to know. Certain engineers named in directories were perhaps employees rather than self-employed, but there is no real way to determine their status.

The 'submerged' sector is frustrating but not entirely confounding. The significance of Jubb, Murray, Wordsworth and Lawson has long been recognized, though with little detail of their companies and partners. Stirk and the Drabbles were not much more than names. In fact a mainstream of eight important businesses, all founded before 1830, constituted early machine-making in Leeds. They include Peter Fairbairn, whose background and approach, fresh and distinctive, signalled a new era in the 1820s. Around these leaders, a peripheral group of textile-engineering workshops, foundries, and component-makers flourished, a barometer of Leeds engineering, an expression of the rhythms of industrial life and inter-connections between firms.[66] The following analysis concentrates upon that mainstream, plus one or two transient early firms, 10 businesses with about 20 active partners.

66   App. 2.

The chronology runs as follows. John Jubb, a south Yorkshire millwright, joined a cotton-mill partnership in Churwell, Morley, just south of Leeds, in 1778. Independently he worked on other engineering projects and made woollen and cotton machinery. A decade later Jubb moved to Holbeck, on the south side of central Leeds, and then in 1796 to Meadow Lane, Hunslet, where he produced a range of machinery. The business was run from 1808 by his son, John, who took over the Salt and Gothard foundry, but it folded after the younger John's premature death in 1816. Meanwhile Jubb's premises in Holbeck had been taken over by his wife's nephews, William and Joseph Drabble. They came from Wortley by Penistone, where Jubb had strong connections, and were probably trained by Jubb in Leeds. The Drabble partnership split, and both subsequent businesses failed. Afterwards their Silver Street works passed to Taylor and Wordsworth, former employees of William Drabble, both of whom had married Drabble's cousins.[67] It is likely that they too trained under Jubb or Drabble. Wordsworth was also from Silkstone parish, near Penistone. Richard Cluderay and Joseph Matthews, both of whom set up in business in Holbeck making patent axle-trees, emulating William Drabble soon after Drabble failed, perhaps also emerged from this cluster.

A second strand grew from the business of Murray and Wood. On leaving the flax-spinner John Marshall, Matthew Murray established a partnership with David Wood c. 1794, moving into the Water Lane premises in 1796. The pair may have met while working for Marshall. James Fenton joined them soon afterwards as business manager. A separate company, Maclea and March, was established in 1825 by two of Murray's sons-in-law, both former employees. His own business continued under another son-in-law, Richard Jackson.

Although Fenton, Murray and Wood faded as a business after Murray's death, its legacy endured in large numbers of apprentices and improvers trained at the Round Foundry. Taylor and Wordsworth were also responsible for producing a legion of new mechanical engineers. The impact of these two early companies on the later Leeds industry is immeasurable. It is feasible, though unproven, that two significant figures of the next generation trained or advanced under Murray: Samuel Lawson and Zebulon Stirk, whose businesses launched in 1812 and c. 1813 respectively. Benjamin Hick (1790–1842), famed as a maker of steam-engines in Bolton, had also been Murray's apprentice, entrusted when very young with superintending engine erection, and said to have been offered partnership in the Round Foundry. Instead he moved to Bolton with Joshua Routledge (1773–1829), a Murray and Wood foreman, who became his brother-in-law.[68] Benjamin Cubitt, John Chester Craven,

67   Presumed cousins: app. 2.
68   Obit., *Mins Proc. ICE*, II (1843), 12–13.

Table 2. Significant machine-making businesses established in Leeds by 1830, and careers of early partners

	Trade	In business in Leeds	Born	Father	Religion
William and Joseph DRABBLE	?Machine-makers	1796/8–1813	Wortley by Penistone	Presumed metalworker	C of E
Peter FAIRBAIRN	Colliery millwright	From 1828	Kelso	Farm steward	C of E
John JUBB sen. & jun.	Millwrights	1787/8 – 1816	?Barnsley and Wortley		Independent
Samuel LAWSON	?Machine-maker	From 1812	Keighley	Clock-maker turned mill engineer	C of E
MACLEA & MARCH:					
C. G. Maclea	?Murray apprentice	From 1825	Edinburgh	Colonel, Russian Imperial Army	C of E
J. March	Murray apprentice	From 1825	Holbeck	Woollen worker	Independent
MURRAY & WOOD:					
Matthew Murray	Smith	From 1794/5	Newcastle	Smith	C of E
David Wood	Smith	From 1794/5	Tadcaster	Smith	Wesleyan Methodist
Zebulon STIRK	Whitesmith	From c. 1813	Otley		C of E
TAYLOR & WORDSWORTH					
Joseph Taylor	Mechanic	From 1812	?Leeds/?S. Yorks		Independent
Joshua Wordsworth	Carpenter	From 1812	Silkstone	Agricultural labourer	Independent

Sources: See Appendix 2.

Note: Business names are indicated in capitals.

and numerous others took forward Murray's technical legacy.[69] Murray was 'father of Leeds engineering' in the sense that he introduced several branches of engineering and pioneered factory production,[70] but the title also reflects Murray and Wood's role in nurturing a later generation of leading engineers, and training a mass workforce.

The last of the best-known Leeds engineers of this era, Peter Fairbairn, arrived in Leeds soon after Murray had died – arguably no coincidence – with a very different background from the rest, via collieries, millwrighting, machine tools, and extensive continental experience of textile machines, an altogether more strategic and targeted approach than any previously seen.

The origins of Leeds engineers

Geographically, early Leeds engineers and their active partners travelled further than their Keighley equivalents. As many (Jubb and his son, the Drabbles, Wordsworth) came from Silkstone and Wortley (by Penistone) as from Leeds (Taylor, March, Cluderay, and probably Procter and Fenton, the latter not strictly a machine-maker). Then there were Murray himself and the Scots-born Fairbairn, both of whom started out in colliery engineering on Tyneside, and Maclea from Edinburgh. David Wood's origins lay in countryside outside Tadcaster, Zebulon Stirk's in Otley, and Samuel Lawson's in Keighley.

Almost all had a background in metalworking, apprenticed as a smith or mechanic of some description. Smiths (like Stirk and Wood) or carpenters (Wordsworth) with a more general industrial background refined their mechanical skills as improvers under Jubb or Murray, both of whom were self-developed textile engineers. This equates to Richard Hattersley teaching the blacksmith Michael Merrall in Keighley. But even before 1800, boys were apprenticed as machine-makers, or in some specialist area of the work. Incomers from Silkstone and Ecclesfield proved useful in both Leeds and Keighley, for their abilities were known to their new masters, often relatives. The technology and systems to which they were introduced were, though, grounded in the textile towns.

When Leeds businesses ended, it was most likely because there was no real plan in place for the succession (by dying too young, like Jubb, or not producing or confirming suitable heirs, for which Murray and Wood were culpable); or perhaps a mix of over-ambition and lack of financial care (the Drabbles, Stirk, perhaps Procter). Of early Keighley engineers, several effected a complete shift into textiles. While this did not happen in Leeds, textile businesses were launched as a sideline to machine-making (Taylor and Wordsworth, and perhaps Lawson and Walker, as with the Hattersleys and William Smith in Keighley).

---

69 Thompson, *Matthew Murray*, 279–80.
70 Scott (ed.), *Matthew Murray*, 80.

Characterizing the new engineering

Three phases mark the route to a recognizably modern industry. The stages show most clearly in Keighley, where a fairly discrete group of engineers had a narrow focus on textile machinery. Keighley records, particularly Hattersley's early ledgers, are sufficiently comprehensive to establish the wider picture. The pattern does not exactly fit Leeds, where engineering's growth was perceptibly different. The larger town had a wider range of textile branches and processes, which succumbed to mechanization at varying paces. There is less evidence of subcontracting in Leeds, and it may have been much less used there. Local infrastructures also differed: in Leeds, access to finance was possibly easier, and the model of integrated factories in other industries more obvious.

The first phase of Keighley textile engineering, emerging from wood- and metal-working trades, featured small-scale craftsmen working for themselves, or as subcontractors or journeymen. Several – like William Carr and William Smith – had experienced at close quarters Arkwright's technology, or a pirated version of it, and could infuse this expertise into the mix. They left their employment in cotton-factories (or in Hattersley's case, in forges) to revert to a long-familiar, self-employed, artisan workshop setting.

During this phase, carpenters were indispensable.[71] Until the 1790s they made frames, parts of spindles and other components. After 1800 they were marginalized from mainstream engineering, unless (like Titus Longbottom) they had the capability for a wholehearted transition into working iron. Up to 1800, wood workers played a meaningful role, as with John Weatherhead's involvement in throstle design – though this transitional worsted-spinning frame effectively excluded most wood workers from machine-making. The new device escalated the skill levels required of machine-makers, especially the whitesmith's ability to produce a 'tin drum'. Wood had been relatively simple to work, but cast and wrought iron, refined and intractable, demanded several stages of production, new machine tools and labour skills, a larger variety of workers, and greater attention to avoiding waste.[72]

The threshold of a second phase, around 1805, was a transitional period bridged by metalworkers, men trained through apprenticeship, or converted from another trade under skilled guidance. New kinds of iron component drove the transformation,[73] cast-iron frames being the most obvious. Other metallurgical advances made enhanced skills in malleable iron essential: working sheet metal to build throstles and other new, lighter-weight

---

71 See above, pp. 30–2.
72 Brown, 'Design Plans', 201.
73 PP Artisans and Machinery, 381, 383, where it is claimed that continental machine-makers were 25 years behind the British.

machinery; producing spindles and flyers entirely of metal. Now a generation old, textile engineering advanced in other ways too, its own institutions emerging, along with a deepening understanding, a code recognizing newer skills and specialisms.

A boom in 1800–01 was followed by severe downturn,[74] and a rapid exodus from Keighley engineering. The need for higher-level skills eliminated many of those working outside their original trade. Their commitment to machine-making may have been weaker, their resilience in challenging times lower, and they had an option to bale out. Whatever their exact circumstances, a third of the 18 early participants stood down before 1800.[75] Another group – though seemingly more successful and better placed to continue, and despite the usually healthy machinery market – changed course soon after 1800. Calvert, Corlass, and perhaps others, moved into textile manufacture. Only six of the 18 continued after 1805, and of them, Berry Smith, whose dealings with Richard Hattersley demonstrate a machine-making business flourishing through the difficult years, soon afterwards switched largely to worsted spinning.[76]

Manual expertise in metalworking reached a high point in this second phase. In the first years of the century, 'the greater part of our mechanical operations were done by hand'.[77] The leaders, accomplished in working malleable iron, combined that with a sound understanding of textile technology. Braziers and tinsmiths – four listed in Keighley in 1822 – and brass- and iron-founders, of whom three were noted, had withdrawn to a supportive role.[78] Even then, while William Smith, William Carr and Titus Longbottom made spinning frames, not every engineer was actually a machine-maker. Hattersley did not start to produce entire machines, power looms, until the late 1820s, and then only tentatively. Michael Merrall made boilers and repaired steam-engines, and manufactured a range of components similar to Hattersley, his mentor.

The third phase was marked by a climactic wave of innovation in textiles. A new sub-branch of engineering products was created when worsted- and woollen-weaving were at last mechanized. At this time, engineering itself reached a watershed in its own production systems. Hitherto, there existed the glorious paradox, that the transformer had not transformed itself. Machines that revolutionized textile production were formed using manual techniques, albeit quite refined ones. The machine tools deployed often seemed less satis-factory than the repetitive hand method. This explains the rudimentary

---

74 Jenkins and Ponting, *British Wool Textile Industry*, 60–70.
75 Above, and app. 1.
76 WYAS Bradford, 32D83/5/1. Smith continued to advertise as a machine-maker: Baines, *Dir.* (1822), 220.
77 Fairbairn, 'On Metallic Constructions', 145.
78 Baines, *Dir.* (1822), 219–21.

powering of most engineering workshops, on a spectrum from a small steam-engine, down to the legendary 'muscular Irishman'.[79]

A decade before his younger brother started out in Leeds, William Fairbairn launched his millwright business in Manchester, in 'a miserable shed' costing 12s. a week. Little work came, but Fairbairn built himself a dead-centre lathe capable of turning shafts up to 6 in. diameter. Immediately, a large order for millwork arrived from a cotton-spinner. He recalled:

> At that time, 1817, even Manchester did not boast of many lathes or tools, except small ones in the machine shops ... there were no self-acting tools; and the whole stock of an engineering or machine establishment might be summed up in a few ill-constructed lathes, a few drills and boring machines of rude construction.[80]

A renaissance soon followed. Machine tools developed by Bramah, Maudslay, Nasmyth, Roberts and others revolutionized milling, planing, boring, turning, cutting, and other shop-floor operations.[81] With precision substantially improved, interchangeable machine parts became a practical option. Procedures carried out laboriously by hand, perhaps guided by templates or similar one-off custom-made devices, were replaced by the consistent action of a machine. A new branch developed, specialist machine-tool makers competent to fit out entire engineering factories.[82] The possibilities opened by machine tools were, for the larger engineers at least, impossible to ignore. Their efficiency and precision, robustness and reliability – the same features that the machines endowed upon their products – made them irresistible, especially with machinery markets so healthy. Most of these engineers had, after all, a demonstrably strong inclination to innovate. So in the 1820s and 1830s they chose the route of increasing capacity, improving quality, and specializing, fully exploiting steam-powered machine tools and interchangeable production.

The revitalization drove larger businesses towards integrating production under one roof. Specialist processes and parts, routinely bought in from subcontractors, might now be done in-house, and a foundry incorporated. Companies which until then had concentrated wholly on making components might see their market disappearing. But there was the option to re-fashion operations, and rethink product ranges. Machine tools were one possibility, or new branches of textile machinery.

---

79 Hayward, 'Fairbairns of Manchester', 1.5.
80 Hayward, 'Fairbairns of Manchester', 1.5, quoting Fairbairn, 'On Metallic Constructions', 145.
81 For the significance of tool steels, see Tweedale, *Steel City*, 13–16.
82 Gilbert, *Machine Tools*, 4–7; Woodbury, *History of Machine Tools*, 4–5, 66, 96–119; Cantrell and Cookson (eds), *Henry Maudslay*; Rolt, *Tools for the Job*, 90–144.

Even without new products, absorbing machine tools within the manufacturing process required an altered plan. As the textile industry had discovered, machinery could not always exactly substitute for the hand methods it replaced. Integrating new apparatus demanded innovation or adjustment elsewhere in the production chain. Like the textile industry a generation before, to remain successful engineers made structural changes, redesigned working systems, and solved technical problems in both product design and manufacturing process. The best available hand-skills might still be needed, to compensate for a persistent mechanical shortcoming within the chain. Skills required of textile engineers were in any case reshaped by the mass adoption of machine tools, for instance new forms of expertise in setting up machines.

Tensions from such imbalances are ever-present in a production system; 'best possible' solutions are all that is available to ease them. These may come through discussion and emulation, and exploring models in a local industrial context. Vital competencies, including how to manage novel situations and new technology, can have evolved only through trial and error. Thus was set the industry's longer-term path.

Among the Keighley machine-making contingent, certain features were pointers, perhaps predictors, of success. While manual skills are certainly no guarantee of business talent, in this instance technical ability proved to be of high importance. Enterprises were manageable, growth was gradual, costs could be controlled by contracting out some elements of work. The heart of the matter was the product, its accuracy and reliability. Yet the rate of continuity in this business was dramatically low. Of those 18 identified as early machine-makers, William Smith's was really the only company to last unscathed beyond 1850. Even Hattersley had experienced a crisis so serious that it interrupted and almost finished the firm.

There are, however, other ways to measure continuity. Here, where skill was so important to the proprietor of a business, and when enterprises struggled if their guiding light died young, or had bad luck, failed to produce an heir of his own, or simply chose a different direction, it could count as an achievement to nurture a new generation. So, Richard Hattersley employed the blacksmith Michael Merrall from 1796 or earlier until about 1808, trained him to make rollers, spindles and flyers, and the two stayed close once Merrall set up his own concern.[83] Had Merrall lived long enough to hand over to his own sons, there is no reason to think that his firm could not have carried on. Hattersley trained up several of his sons, of whom three established long-lasting businesses. His former apprentices John and Samuel Smith founded a company c. 1818 that employed 80 in 1851, and between 400 and 500 by 1866.[84] Titus Longbottom, a

83 Hodgson, *Textile Manufacture*, 262.
84 Hodgson, *Textile Manufacture*, 256–9; *Keighley News*, 1 Dec. 1866; Keighley Lib. rate book; Keighley census, 1851.

joiner-machinist, upgraded his skills while working with Berry Smith, himself an ex-apprentice of William Carr, before returning to the family business in c. 1808.[85] Despite Longbottom's later problems, his work was significant, with a legacy through his own apprentice John Midgley, later founder of a small firm of power-loom makers.[86] Charles and Allan Smith were sons of Thomas Smith, Berry Smith's first apprentice, who had entered business with William Keighley in 1815.[87] Possible, though unproven, is that George Bland and the Briggs and Banks partners worked for one of the large Keighley engineers before embarking on their own businesses.[88]

The stages through which the Leeds industry passed are less clear. Overall are many similarities, the same external phenomena influencing the techno-logical path of machine-making: improvements in metallurgy, declining use of wood as a material, and a new wave of machine tools after 1820. The same class of artisan, possessing more skill than money, populated the early engineering industry in both towns. Firms' long-term survival rates were comparably low. In both localities, new companies were often initiated by men inducted into the trade by a well-regarded earlier engineer. One obvious disparity, though, lies in engineering factories, which arrived rather more promptly to Leeds. Although much of the Leeds industry continued to be workshop-based, some factor, or factors, enabled certain engineers to venture into large and integrated works.

Expanding into business

An artisan outlook steered the early industry. In taking up machine-making, or moving to textile towns in search of work or experience, craftsmen showed ambition, perhaps imagination, but nothing unusually strategic or visionary. To have a trade was a considerable asset in a world of great insecurity. The artisan, once trained and improved, could reasonably expect to establish a business or inherit a family workshop. The older-style crafts saw a high conversion rate of skilled worker into small business owner, and this same inclination carried into the new engineering. Most, it appears, thought small-scale. A successful career was measured in avoidance of disaster, and living long enough to raise one or more sons to continue the business, thus securing the family's long-term future. Even the most successful of early textile engineers were perceptibly guided by these principles.

85   App. 1.
86   Hodgson, *Textile Manufacture*, 28; see app. 1.
87   Hodgson, *Textile Manufacture*, 263–4; White, *Dir.* (1853), 544; for William Keighley, see above, p. 85; app. 1.
88   Hodgson, *Textile Manufacture*, 269–70; app. 1.

How, then, to start out in engineering, without personal or family capital? For many of these engineers came from impoverished backgrounds.[89] Joshua Wordsworth's relatives in Thurgoland were poor.[90] David Wood was the son of a rural blacksmith. In Keighley, Berry Smith had been 'a poor lad without means', and John and Samuel Smith, sons of an overlooker, had to 'husband … their means so as to be able to go into business on their own account'.[91] Others eventually enjoying prosperity – Murray, Hattersley, Taylor, Carr – evidently started with little beyond their own earnings and talents.

The artisan mind-set translated into a feasible business framework. This scale of production, within its operating context, could create a remarkable industrial structure. Tweedale describes exactly this in Sheffield steel: a 'complex alternative manufacturing system … owner-operated, rather than corporate and bureaucratic; agglomerated, rather than monolithic; craft-based, instead of machine-oriented'. Sheffield's achievement built from 'quality, variety, added-value, and, above all, metallurgical skill'. Its steel industry had two divisions: one of them, bulk steel, pursued efficiencies of scale and speed; but the other, special steel manufacture, 'thrived on economies of flexibility and opportunism, tailoring their production to fill highly specific niches in the market'.[92] This equally summarizes the industrial culture of early textile engineering. The similarities are unsurprising, considering those strong connections between Hallamshire and the textile districts, fostered by migration before and after 1800.

At that early period, establishing a textile-engineering business required only a modest budget. Premises were rented, little or no capital investment was necessary, and suppliers offered long credit. Once there was income, plant might be built up out of profit, bankruptcy sales offering a chance to gain through others' misfortunes. Thus William Smith started in Keighley in 1795 in two rented cottages, extended enormously over the following 70 years to accommodate growth.[93] William Carr rented a house with a smithy and mechanics' shop in 1790, and in 1798 was able to have a house built for him, with a workshop on the top storey and a smithy behind, though still relying upon human power to work the lathes.[94] Berry Smith set up benches and lathes in his own small cottage chamber, employing boys to turn the machines.[95] It was common to take premises without steam- or water-power. The Smith brothers used 'a half-witted fellow' and a blind man to provide power for their

89 See app. 1 and 2.
90 Hey (ed.), 'Militia Men', Thurgoland list, 1806; app. 2.
91 Hodgson, *Textile Manufacture*, 252, 256.
92 Tweedale, *Steel City*, 11–12.
93 Hodgson, *Textile Manufacture*, 245.
94 Hodgson, *Textile Manufacture*, 249–50.
95 Hodgson, *Textile Manufacture*, 253–4.

shop, before moving to a cotton-mill basement where they tapped into the
steam-engine.[96] Thomas Smith also shifted from human power to room and
power, in 1820, while Titus Longbottom was able to start in 1809 with rented
room and power.[97] In Leeds, Peter Fairbairn began in a small room in Lady
Lane in 1828, where a 'stalwart Irishman' powered the lathe.[98] About that time
Thomas Armitage, a Cleckheaton machine-maker, used power 'supplied by a
man who turned a large wheel'.[99] Well into the nineteenth century, a figure of
£500 was routinely given as sufficient starting capital: for George Hodgson
in 1849, Peter Fairbairn in 1828, George Hattersley resuscitating his family's
business in 1832.[100] Hattersley later described taking the old firm's premises,
starting out 'with 500 borowed money ... I used to reel up every week to see
whether I lost or gained ...'.[101] In Sheffield, similar figures applied to crucible
steel-making.[102] While a sum of several hundred pounds was considerable,
locally-generated capital could be had, if not from banks, then through loans
from a supplier or customer, or finding a moneyed partner.

In 1793 Richard Hattersley's initial investment was counted as including
his tools in trade – stocks, dies, files, brace bits, a cutting engine, hammer
and vice – together valued at £10 10s. 10d. Thomas Binns contributed to the
partnership an anvil, bellows and hearth, vice and bench, iron, brass, scrap
and coals, worth £28 8s. 5½d.[103] The pair rented room and power at Screw
Mill, before building a new machine shop at North Brook works c. 1800.[104]
Hattersley's assets in 1816 were valued at about £3,600, net £3,000. His
fluting engine was worth £30, and a 6-hp steam-engine £508.[105] This engine
was retained in a new mill, built before 1820, when several houses were added.
The business's assets were then worth about £8,000, with debts of £1,125. In
1829, after Richard Hattersley's death, the firm had book debts of £2,044 and
stock-in-trade of £2,117.[106]

New engineering businesses continued to demand relatively little capital.
More important were recognized skill and connections, for they equated
to creditworthiness. Overall, the small and close-knit industry needed
constant rejuvenation, compensating for the loss of some promising

96   Hodgson, *Textile Manufacture*, 257.
97   Hodgson, *Textile Manufacture*, 260, 263.
98   Walker, *Fortunes Made in Business*, II, 261.
99   *Cleckheaton Guardian*, 15 Feb. 1884.
100 WYAS Bradford, 32D83/33/8; Ward, 'Industrial development and location in Leeds',
362–4.
101 WYAS Bradford, 32D83/33/8, letter 6 Aug. 1858 to his son Richard L. Hattersley.
102 Tweedale, *Steel City*, 35–6.
103 WYAS Bradford, 32D83/5/1, and above.
104 Hodgson, *Textile Manufacture*, 242–3.
105 WYAS Bradford, 32D83/2/2.
106 WYAS Bradford, 32D83/2/2; /2/4.

firms.[107] Subcontracting was a boon for machine-makers, reducing the need for both fixed and working capital. Buying in castings, and precision parts from suppliers like Hattersley, perhaps on extended credit, eliminated any immediate need for a foundry or other specialized plant. Well-established suppliers might be very accommodating to debtors. Even when his business was quite new, Richard Hattersley seemed unruffled by the many customers who settled only spasmodically, perhaps years late.[108] Accounts were sometimes squared with quantities of iron or engineering tools, wood, and even household items likes blankets, wool, a clock, bacon and butter. The business model worked because risk was spread across a large body of customers. Those who thrived, like Berry Smith, adopted more commercial habits, like paying promptly in cash. Among the rest, some never settled. Hattersley's acquiescence in granting credit and taking goods in lieu of cash, however reluctantly, certainly helped foster young and struggling businesses, some of which became important customers.

But even the most promising of engineering businesses had vulnerabilities. Much depended on the principal himself, his health, heirs, adaptability and cash flow. While prospects for success in the textile-engineering market appeared encouraging, no one could have predicted just how spectacularly this would take off. So Hattersley protected himself by adopting – how consciously is impossible to say – certain strategies. He was versatile, shown by his willingness at first to take any kind of smith's work, while building expertise in repairing rollers, spindles and flyers.[109] William Carr showed similar flexibility, starting in Keighley as 'a jobbing blacksmith and whitesmith' alongside producing flyers and guides for cotton mills.[110] A broad base of general and specialized work helped to weather fluctuations in orders from textile manufacturers. As the market for machines grew and stabilized, other work was abandoned. By employing subcontractors, and a very flexible pool of direct labour, Hattersley managed a varying demand while controlling his fixed costs.[111] His expansion was partly, perhaps largely, supported from business profits.

Hattersley's progress illuminates how, even with finance strictly limited, a textile-engineering business could build. How, though, to explain the appearance in Leeds of integrated, factory-based operations, rather earlier than in Keighley? But that was Matthew Murray, responsible for one of the world's first modern engineering works. He did not represent the generality of Leeds engineering, which however benefited from his example. Murray's

107 Saul (ed.), *Technological Change*, 142.
108 WYAS Bradford, 32D83/2/1, sales 1797–1809.
109 WYAS Bradford, 32D83/2/1.
110 Hodgson, *Textile Manufacture*, 249–50.
111 See below, pp. 137–41.

talent was exceptional, and he was encouraged by John Marshall's support. Murray also had grand technical ambition, extending beyond textile engineering into machine tools and steam-engines. He was the first – or at least among the first – to produce machine tools for sale.[112]

Murray's partnership with David Wood began in 1794 or 1795, as machine-makers in a mechanics' shop at Mill Green in Holbeck. Very soon they advertised for 'a number of smiths viz firemen, vicemen and iron turners; also a good wood turner', promising 'constant employment'.[113] Early in 1796 a plot was purchased near Marshall's mill,[114] and their new works announced five months later.

> Murray & Wood … have erected and opened a foundry in Water Lane, Leeds, for the purpose of casting iron viz engine work of all kinds … As they cast twice each day, any gentleman may be accommodated with castings on the shortest notice, in cases of emergency.[115]

Their extensive range included parts for textile machines, millwork, wheels and all kinds of foundry products. To this they rapidly added steam-engines and boilers, advertising in 1797 for 'two firemen, that can undertake heavy work in the steam line. Also a green sand moulder in the foundry; also a person accustomed to make iron boilers for steam-engines'. They sought apprentices to learn steam-engine making in 1799.[116] William Fairbairn judged Murray and Wood as one of only three companies capable of building steam-engines at this time, the others being Sherratt of Manchester, and Boulton and Watt themselves.[117] Marshall's misfortune in 1796, when a fire destroyed his factory, brought Murray and Wood yet more work equipping the new premises. They replaced the 900 spindles of Marshall's old works, probably all of their making, with new plant of 1,800 spindles, at 30s. a spindle.[118]

Such rapid expansion, particularly into steam-engines, required a building programme. The rotunda known as the Round Foundry – actually a fitting-up shop – was in progress in 1802. Whether John Marshall invested directly is unknown, though he was clearly well-disposed, and encouraging of Murray and Wood staying local.[119] Marshall sold and rented land to them, perhaps

112 Rolt, *Tools for the Job*, 87.
113 Taylor (ed.), *Biographia Leodiensis*, 299; Turner, 'Fenton, Murray and Wood', 2.3; Thompson, *Matthew Murray*, 55, 61; *Leeds Intelligencer*, 17 Aug. 1795, 31 Aug 1795, and *passim*.
114 Turner, 'Fenton, Murray and Wood', 2.3.
115 *Leeds Intelligencer*, 11 July 1796.
116 *Leeds Intelligencer*, 2 Oct. 1797; Turner, 'Fenton, Murray and Wood', 2.8.
117 Fairbairn, 'On Metallic Constructions', 145.
118 Turner, 'Fenton, Murray and Wood', 2.5.
119 Scott (ed.), *Matthew Murray*, 36; Turner, 'Fenton, Murray and Wood', 2.1.

Plate 7. Murray & Co.'s Round Foundry, on a letterhead of 1811
Source: Cumbria Archive and Local Studies Centre, Whitehaven, DCU 3/423.

2 acres of the 3½-acre site on which the rotunda and other buildings were at various times constructed.[120] James Watt jun. had reported back to Birmingham in 1802:

> It is generally believed that Murray and Co. are making a great deal of money & that the new works are constructing from their profits, as also a superb house which Murray is building for himself.[121]

The works in 1798 comprised the iron foundry (£150), an adjacent model warehouse (£150), utensils of trade (£200), and a mill for boring iron, with machine-makers' shops above (£400), along with a steam-engine (£100). The total valuation for insurance purposes was £1,000, the policy taken out by William and Richard Hargreave, joiners, and John Cave and James Longley, bricklayers, of Leeds, mortgagees, perhaps the builders.[122] The same parties insured extended premises in 1802: two model warehouses (£400), the boring mill with shops above and adjoining steam-engine house (£1,000). Fenton, Murray and Wood insured stock-in-trade and models in these buildings, and the engine, total value £750.[123]

In 1804 the mortgage to William Hargreave and John Cave extended to cover buildings, plant and stock-in-trade insured altogether for £6,050. This included the iron foundry with four chambers above used for storing models (£1,000), two engines and houses (£300), a four-storey building used as joiners' and machine shops (£800), a building containing four

---

120   Rimmer, *Marshalls of Leeds*, 64.
121   Scott (ed.), *Matthew Murray*, 36.
122   Guildhall Lib., RE 164622, 7 Nov. 1798.
123   Guildhall Lib., RE 37/172611 and /172612, 7 Feb. 1800.

counting-houses and some cottages (£400), and a number of foundries including one for brass.[124] Another mortgage, with Beckett's bank, covered the rotunda itself – 'a circular building ... used as workshops and heated with steam', insured for £2,000, and cottages, stables and cast-house, including some stock and tools, with an insurance valuation of £660.[125] William Lister came into the partnership in that same year, purely as financier. Unused parts of the Water Lane site had also been sold to raise additional capital. Within a decade of starting out, Murray and Wood's business employed about 160 men and exported to Sweden and Russia.[126]

Probate records, a rough and ready barometer of financial success, show Murray's personal assets valued in 1826 at £8,000, his partner Wood in 1820 at £14,000.[127] The elder John Jubb's probate valuation was £3,000 in 1808, his son's £5,000 in 1816.[128] Taylor and Wordsworth, much later, in 1848 and 1846, were valued for probate purposes at £12,000 and £25,000 respectively.[129] In contrast, Michael Merrall, his business in Keighley established for a decade before his death in 1819, employed 20 people and was apparently doing well, yet left personal estate valued at only £300.[130] But records are patchy, and all that can be said is that certain early-nineteenth-century Leeds engineers achieved much higher levels of affluence than any in the Keighley trade.

Taylor and Wordsworth, who started in business after their employer William Drabble's failure in 1812, joined with another former colleague, Nathaniel Marshall, as flax, tow and worsted machine-makers and axle-makers, in 'a commodious place in Holbeck'.[131] Two years later they took over Drabble's Silver Street premises, previously Jubb's, and embarked on a recruitment drive for iron turners, vice-men, and other mechanics.[132] James Maud, gentleman, insured the works in 1817, either as landlord or mortgagee: 'mechanics' workshop and engine house £650; going gear £50; steam engine £100... total (without contents) £800'.[133] Within their first decade in Silver Street, Taylor and Wordsworth had replaced Drabble's 6-hp engine with

---

124   Guildhall Lib., RE 50/210457, 29 Sept. 1804 (part relating to foundries is illegible).
125   Guildhall Lib., RE 50/210456, 29 Sept. 1804.
126   Scott (ed.), *Matthew Murray*, 40; Brotherton SC, MS165/23. The first connection with St Petersburg was made by Samuel Bentham and Simon Goodrich, of the Navy Board, ordering Murray engines for export there. Murray visited Stockholm in 1806 with his engine erectors, presumably to assess market potential in Sweden: Thompson, *Matthew Murray*, ch. 7.
127   Borthwick, Ainsty, 165, 225, Dec. 1820; Ainsty, June 1826.
128   Borthwick, Ainsty, Sept. 1809; Exch. Oct. 1816.
129   Borthwick, Ainsty Prog. Mar. 1848; Sept. 1846.
130   Borthwick, Craven, Aug. 1820.
131   *Leeds Mercury*, 7 Nov 1812. Nathaniel Marshall left the company in 1816: *London Gazette*, 23 March 1816, 17121, 562.
132   *Leeds Mercury*, 11 June 1814.
133   Guildhall Lib., Sun 116/920393. Maud was not a merchant, but evidently a tailor in Upper Headrow: *Leeds Dir.* (1798), 35; Wilson, *Gentlemen Merchants*.

an 8-hp model made by Murray,[134] and bought up neighbouring land for expansion.[135]

Two other significant Leeds businesses launched in 1812–13. Zebulon Stirk started up in or before 1813, and with a mortgage bought a plot off the newly laid York Street in the East End, near Timble or Sheepscar beck, where he built a factory and warehouse.[136] In 1821 the premises consisted of a 'steam engine manufactory, machine-maker's shop and engine house, with part of a room used for cutting tobacco, tenure of John Hilton', all insured for £800.[137] There were further extensions by 1824: a counting house, a room rented to a woollen cloth friezer, an adjoining foundry and smiths' shops, and other joiners' and smiths' shops close by. Without contents, the total value was given as £2,200.[138] The steam-engine was insured for £400, the stock for £1,000.[139]

The second new business was that of Samuel Lawson, blacksmith and maker of flax-spinning machinery, founded in 1812 in Mabgate.[140] His initial partners, Mark Walker, William Patrick and Jonathan Greaves, may well have been fellow artisans, former colleagues perhaps, for Greaves signed only his mark. It is conceivable that all had worked for Murray. Like Taylor and Wordsworth, the firm was reduced to two partners in 1816, when Patrick and Greaves left.[141] During Lawson's association with Mark Walker, which continued until 1831, they took out one joint patent, for machinery to prepare and dress hemp and other fibres.[142] The partners both lived in Green Row, Mabgate, close to their workshop, and in 1816 advertised as machine-makers and manufacturers of water-wheel governors.[143] Soon they had become 'iron founders, machine-makers, turners in wood and metal, & manufacturers of fancy tools &c' and acquired a 12-hp steam-engine from Zebulon Stirk.[144]

In 1812 Mabgate, north of Quarry Hill, was on the fringes of the town's built area. The Sheepscar beck had been harnessed to supply a number of mill

---

134   Brotherton, MS18.

135   WYAS Wakefield, Deeds, GZ 589 633; HM 472 440; HU 583 571.

136   WYAS Wakefield, Deeds, FW 633 659 and 634 660 (1813); Ward, 'Industrial development and location', 412.

137   WYAS Wakefield, Deeds, GC 513 606 (1815); Guildhall Lib., Sun CR 11937/130, 969376, 17 July 1821.

138   Guildhall Lib., Sun CR 11937/133 982279 (1822).

139   Guildhall Lib., Sun CR 11937/145 1018179, 17 May 1824; Ward, 'Industrial development and location', 412.

140   WYAS Leeds, Acc. 2371, box 76; box 80/2, notes by Capt. Lawson.

141   *Leeds Intelligencer*, 5 Feb. 1816; *London Gazette*, 13 Feb. 1816, 17110, 291.

142   *Leeds Times*, 17 Jan 1874; British Patent 5715 (1828). Possibly Mark Walker and the cotton-spinner Ard Walker were related, but no evidence has been found. Mark Walker's background appears less affluent.

143   Pigot, *Dir.* (1816–17), 144–5; WYAS Leeds, Acc. 2371, box 76; box 80/2, notes by Capt. Lawson.

144   Baines, *Dir.* (1822), 65; Brotherton SC, MS18.

ponds, and all around lay vacant land.[145] Lawson and Walker bought one such plot in 1824–25, Brick Garth on the west side of Mabgate, 3,000 sq. yards on which they built a factory and foundry workshops – later called the Hope Foundry – with a mortgage from the Clothiers' Union Society.[146] Here, they also began flax-spinning, and the whole engineering and textile works – as well as gasworks and gasometer – were insured for £4,100.[147] They employed altogether 140 workers and 20 hp in 1829.[148]

These engineering start-ups in Leeds, though few in number, present common features. The level of ambition behind them cannot be measured, but the initial ventures were practical and unpretentious. Only one direct sponsor is identified, the flax-spinner John Marshall, who helped two promising new firms set up: first Murray and Wood in about 1794, and then Peter Fairbairn in 1828, in both cases to secure his own supply of the latest and finest machinery.[149]

How else was finance obtained? If an initial venture, in a rented workshop and using extended credit, proved successful, then ploughed-back profits could support further, 'organic', expansion. Additional funds may have come courtesy of the textile boom, which, as well as stoking demand for machines, also enticed several engineers to open a secondary textile business before 1820. This was also a test bed for their engineering products. When a larger injection of capital was needed to build or extend premises, a lender might be found in the local money-market, via attorneys or other intermediaries. John Jubb seemingly stood alone among the new textile engineers in having his own money. His trade of millwright was a notch above the smiths and joiners who populated the early industry, and Jubb conceivably brought to Leeds a payout after withdrawing from the Churwell cotton-mill partnership.

The Leeds merchant community was unlikely to invest in engineering, for it was an instinctively conservative group, disinclined to join risky and troublesome industrial speculations.[150] The merchants were anyway in a state of flux themselves. Having enjoyed great prosperity throughout the eighteenth century, especially so in the 1780s, they bequeathed to Leeds a superb infra-structure, including a refined banking system and good transport links. The Aire and Calder navigation and Leeds and Liverpool canal proved especially useful to machine-makers, to import iron and wood, and ship products across the region and outwards. As machine-makers rose, the merchants declined.

145   Thoresby Soc., Leeds, Giles plan of Leeds, 1815; Fowler plan 1831.
146   WYAS Wakefield, Deeds, IF 37 35; 89 80.
147   Guildhall Lib., Sun 152/11937, 1036498.
148   Ward, 'Industrial development and location', 422–3.
149   Turner, 'Fenton, Murray and Wood', 2.1; Pigot, Dir. (1816–17), 144–5; Taylor (ed.), Biographia Leodiensis, 491–6; Ward, 'Industrial development and location', 362–4; Walker, Fortunes Made in Business, 261–2.
150   Wilson, Gentlemen Merchants, 136.

Once Benjamin Gott's idea of an integrated woollen factory spread, and manufacturers took hold of their own marketing, the gentlemen merchants were obsolete. Many of those families which had dominated Leeds society for generations withdrew to country estates.[151] Yet the wealth pumped into Leeds during the mercantile heyday had helped the wider economy. From this group came investors willing to lend on mortgage, key to engineering's expansion: Murray borrowed from joiners and builders, Taylor and Wordsworth from a gentleman risen from a family of tailors, Stirk from a militia officer and others, none of them part of the merchant élite, and Lawson and Walker from a clothiers' union.[152] Murray's Round Foundry development was supported by Beckett's bank.[153] Otherwise, only in the case of Stirk was there a hint of bank involvement, and that rather later, when the Leeds Commercial Banking Co. was involved in his insolvency in 1840.[154]

Partnership and succession

Partnership was the other route to propel engineering tradesmen to higher-level business. Partners offered both means and confidence to take an ambitious step fraught with risk. In this transitionary period, Leeds firms were more likely than their Keighley equivalents to be partnerships. It also happened that most of the leading Leeds engineers lacked an obvious successor, or did not groom their own sons to take over. Generally, though, the partnerships were established before the lack, or unsuitability, of heirs became fully apparent. Non-family partnerships were not unknown in Keighley – indeed, Richard Hattersley made his first move towards autonomy with the help of a partner, Binns.[155] But Hattersley and William Smith had large numbers of sons, some of them extremely competent, as later events showed. These were taken into the family business as young men, at the very time expansion was needed, slotting into technical or administrative roles.

A well-established and expanding business gave the next generation greater expectations and opportunities, and probably a better education, than their fathers had had. Thus Murray's and Wood's sons, although both had mechanical talents, chose tangential paths. Their fathers' success enabled Matthew Murray jun. to emigrate to Russia, and the younger David Wood to live the life of a gentleman and at some point move to Germany. Joshua Taylor Wordsworth, who might have had the running of the firm after his father and

---

151   Wilson, *Gentlemen Merchants*, 31–3, 137–45.
152   See above.
153   Guildhall Lib., RE 50/210456, 29 Sept. 1804.
154   *Law Journal* (Feb. 1840), 12; *Yorkshire Gazette*, 25 Apr. 1840.
155   Described above.

uncle died, soon extricated himself in favour of a leisurely life.[156] Perhaps there were good reasons for these young men to withdraw: poor health – David Wood died at 32, having outlived all his nine or more siblings; differences with their father; lack of aptitude; or the daunting prospect of taking on a famous firm, with all it entailed. In sufficiently comfortable circumstances, some felt no drive or obligation to maintain the business. Contrast this with Richard L. Hattersley, the third generation in Keighley, who had no choice to retire before he had started, for his adolescence coincided with the firm's collapse in c. 1832 and his father George's endeavours to pick up the pieces. Apprenticeship in the trade was the boy's only option.

The Hattersley misfortune is a reminder that family matters could turn out very complicated. Richard Hattersley made partners of the eldest three, not the best three. Had he lived longer, younger sons may have come in. But having many children created its own dilemmas, threatening even a substantial legacy. Was the aim to protect the future of all the family, or to maintain a thriving business? The strategy of a family firm might be moulded by these difficult personal matters.[157] If advancing the business were the priority, then technical skills must be matched by firm and competent direction, and further, a shared trust and understanding. This last did not always come easily to brothers, especially after the father was gone. Thus the legacies of Richard Hattersley and (to a lesser degree) William Smith were not immune from upheaval. With so many sons and grandsons, there could scarcely be a common vision. But if the main concern were to provide for a large family outside the firm, that was not in itself irrational, rather a perfectly appropriate economic and social response to prevailing circumstances.[158]

Several of Richard Hattersley's descendants were extravagant, insufficiently competent, or simply disagreeable. Easing them out came at some disruptive cost. Three sons tried to continue as partners after Richard died in 1829. Samuel, George and Levi re-established the firm with a new agreement in 1831, but very soon fell into difficulty. The father's will, made three days before his death, was perhaps ill-considered in the scope of its bequests, leaving them short of ready funds to run the Keighley and Bradford plants they had inherited. Hattersley's considerable real estate went to other family members, money was still owed to the Binns heirs, and the loan to rescue Titus Longbottom may still have been outstanding.[159] This need not have been insuperable, had the brothers been in accord, but there was animosity between Levi and George, with Samuel generally backing George. Levi was

156   App. 2.
157   Rose, 'Beyond Buddenbrooks', in Brown and Rose (eds), *Entrepreneurship, Networks and Modern Business*, 128.
158   Ankarloo, 'New Institutional Economics', 24.
159   Borthwick, Craven, Feb. 1830; WYAS Bradford, 32D83/2/5, p. 509.

Table 3. Legacy: the industrial and technical influence of early engineers

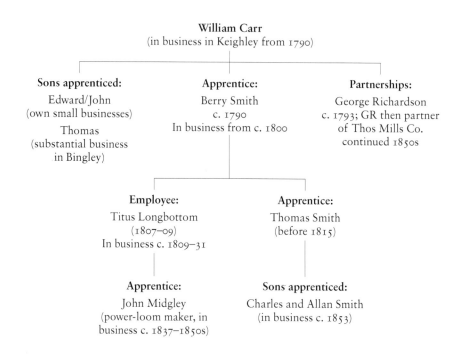

William Carr
(in business in Keighley from 1790)

Sons apprenticed:
Edward/John
(own small businesses)

Thomas
(substantial business
in Bingley)

Apprentice:
Berry Smith
c. 1790
In business from c. 1800

Partnerships:
George Richardson
c. 1793; GR then partner
of Thos Mills Co.
continued 1850s

Employee:
Titus Longbottom
(1807–09)
In business c. 1809–31

Apprentice:
Thomas Smith
(before 1815)

Apprentice:
John Midgley
(power-loom maker, in
business c. 1837–1850s)

Sons apprenticed:
Charles and Allan Smith
(in business c. 1853)

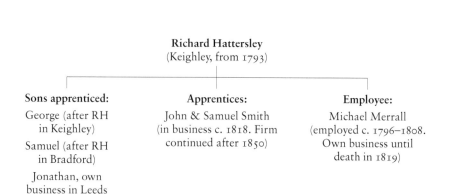

Richard Hattersley
(Keighley, from 1793)

Sons apprenticed:
George (after RH
in Keighley)

Samuel (after RH
in Bradford)

Jonathan, own
business in Leeds

Apprentices:
John & Samuel Smith
(in business c. 1818. Firm
continued after 1850)

Employee:
Michael Merrall
(employed c. 1796–1808.
Own business until
death in 1819)

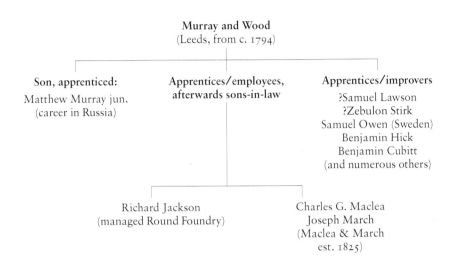

Murray and Wood
(Leeds, from c. 1794)

Son, apprenticed:
Matthew Murray jun.
(career in Russia)

**Apprentices/employees,
afterwards sons-in-law**

Apprentices/improvers
?Samuel Lawson
?Zebulon Stirk
Samuel Owen (Sweden)
Benjamin Hick
Benjamin Cubitt
(and numerous others)

Richard Jackson
(managed Round Foundry)

Charles G. Maclea
Joseph March
(Maclea & March
est. 1825)

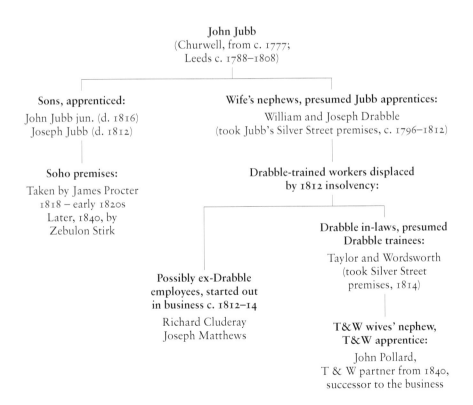

John Jubb
(Churwell, from c. 1777;
Leeds c. 1788–1808)

Sons, apprenticed:
John Jubb jun. (d. 1816)
Joseph Jubb (d. 1812)

Wife's nephews, presumed Jubb apprentices:
William and Joseph Drabble
(took Jubb's Silver Street premises, c. 1796–1812)

Soho premises:
Taken by James Procter
1818 – early 1820s
Later, 1840, by
Zebulon Stirk

**Drabble-trained workers displaced
by 1812 insolvency:**

**Drabble in-laws, presumed
Drabble trainees:**
Taylor and Wordsworth
(took Silver Street
premises, 1814)

**Possibly ex-Drabble
employees, started out
in business c. 1812–14**
Richard Cluderay
Joseph Matthews

**T&W wives' nephew,
T&W apprentice:**
John Pollard,
T & W partner from 1840,
successor to the business

thought untrustworthy with money, and indolent. In 1832 the partnership lay in ruins, the three bankrupted.[160] With borrowed money, and support from Keighley associates, George managed to buy back the Keighley premises and start again, and Samuel did the same in Bradford.[161] The Bradford works was a three-storey steam-powered mill measuring 22 yards by 11, built in 1818 on a former paddock in Silsbridge Lane. The upper floors were rented out to a succession of worsted spinners.[162] After splitting from Keighley in 1832, Samuel traded as 'Samuel Hattersley & Son, late Richard Hattersley & Son'. But his only surviving son, Samuel Longden Hattersley, a mechanical draughtsman, showed less interest in the firm than did a son-in-law, Samuel Bairstow Walmsley. After the older Samuel's death in 1852, Walmsley bought out his brother-in-law.[163]

Levi was cut adrift, never recovered, and later emigrated to the United States, where he died in poverty in Philadelphia. The fourth surviving brother, Jonathan, presumably without employment in Keighley during the family crisis, moved for a time to Accrington and Burnley, c. 1831–33, where engineering prospered, in the service of cotton-spinners. He then made his own way in Leeds, settling there by 1834 and building a solid business without help from his brothers.[164] The youngest, John, though trained as a mechanic, worked as bookkeeper for George, and then in Leeds, Bradford, and perhaps in south Wales, emigrating to Australia in the late 1850s.[165]

Events following his father's death deeply impressed George Hattersley. In 1858, history seemed to be repeating itself, with George urging his eldest son, Richard Longden, to avoid disaster by confronting the spendthrift youngest, William Henry: 'for it appears he will get thro all we have been hard working for, for upwards of 25 years, in two or three years more and we are ruined'.[166] The threat was real, and William was quickly expelled from the firm, becoming a textile salesman in Bradford.[167] Richard and Edwin, the third son, formed a partnership with their father in 1860, with Richard taking control of the engineering business while Edwin concentrated upon

160   *London Gazette*, 3 Feb. 1832, 18899, 241; 24 Aug. 1832, 18969, 1947; 15 Jan. 1833, 19013, 112; WYAS Bradford, 32D83/2/5, inside back cover.
161   WYAS Bradford, 32D83/2/2.
162   WYAS Wakefield, Deeds, GY 658 703; IO 609 599; WYAS Bradford, 32D83/12/1. Also WYAS Wakefield, Deeds, LF 583 538; RI 392 424; UP 417 449.
163   Durham RO, D/HP/18 (and see HP/74); Borthwick, Prog. June 1853, will of Samuel Hattersley of Idle, machine-maker.
164   Keighley St Andrew bap. 27 Feb. 1831; 24 May 1835; bur. 16 Jan. 1833; WYAS Bradford, 32D83/33/2; Pigot, *Dir.* (1828–29), 232–3. See app. 2.
165   Keighley St Andrew bap. 17 May 1837; 7 July 1837; bur. 14 Apr. 1839; 1851 census, Thornton Road, Bradford; White, *Dir.* (1853), 431, at St John's Street, Bradford; WYAS Bradford, 32D83/32/1, noted in 1862 in Adelaide; P. Whitcombe, Hattersley family tree (unpub.).
166   WYAS Bradford, 32D83/33/8.
167   *Bradford Observer*, 30 Dec. 1886.

the family's growing worsted-spinning interests in the Worth Valley. George's second son, John, apparently had no aptitude for business, and was excluded altogether. A much younger half-brother, James Midgley Hattersley, whom George had been keen to bring into the family firm, was pushed out by Richard after George's death. Though ruthless, Richard's policy of concentrating power upon himself paid off commercially. But he failed in that he himself produced only daughters. Without a son to take over the business, eventually a son-in-law must be groomed to succeed.

William Smith's original firm survived its founder's death in 1850, continuing under five surviving sons until some chose to retire. In 1865 it was formally dissolved, the William Smith name discontinued by agreement. Of the new Smith companies, the outstanding successor came out of a second reorganization in 1869, falling to sole control of William's fourth son, Prince, and Prince's own son, another Prince.[168] Like the Hattersleys, William Smith's sons had conflicting aspirations. Some had limited ambition and did not do well, while others opted to retreat. Prince Smith meanwhile built on his father's reputation for high quality worsted-spinning machinery, guiding his own venture to great size and renown through 'the genius, the skill, the energy and perseverance, we might almost say the natural instinct' credited by admirers.[169] Other William Smith descendants continuing as machine-makers were eclipsed.

Smooth transitions to the next generation did occur. John Jubb's important business was increasingly successful after passing to his two sons in 1808, until their untimely deaths stopped it short. Samuel Lawson brought two sons, John and Edward, into partnership in 1834, while for some reason excluding a third. The firm flourished under his descendants after the old man retired.[170] On Peter Fairbairn's death, his only son, Andrew, succeeded, later bringing in partners, a cousin and two long-term employees risen through the ranks.

Both Lawson (with Mark Walker) and Fairbairn (Greenwood and Batley) had previously taken unrelated partners. At their best, such arrangements injected new strengths, and shared the technical and managerial load. Partnership could also be a stabilizing force, a spreading of risk, the future no longer resting on a single proprietor.[171] With Murray's partners running day-to-day affairs, he had free rein to develop steam-engines and other ideas. But the significance of David Wood as works manager, and James Fenton as financial administrator, must not be understated. Did Murray's innovative urges ever threaten to cross the bounds into impractical

168   Jeremy (ed.), *Dictionary of Business Biography*, V, 213–15; Hodgson, *Textile Manufacture*, 246–8; *Keighley News*, 29 Mar. 1890.
169   Hodgson, *Textile Manufacture*, 247.
170   WYAS Leeds, Acc. 2371, box 76; app. 2.
171   WYAS Leeds, Acc. 2371, box 76.

extravagance? This cannot be known, though undoubtedly Murray fared much better commercially than certain other renowned inventors, men like Richard Roberts and Samuel Crompton. The role of Wood and Fenton was complementary, not subsidiary. It seems likely, for instance, that Fenton negotiated bank loans and other mortgages at the time the Round Foundry was built, and brought in Lister as the only known sleeping partner in Leeds engineering at that time.[172] Wood assumed responsibility for the flax-spinning machinery department, and developed a close friendship with Marshall, still his company's main customer for textile machines.[173] Murray's son-in-law, Richard Jackson, left unchecked to expand and innovate, proved to be the Round Foundry's ruin.[174] As with Murray and Wood, Wordsworth, acclaimed for his superior technical abilities, must have relied on the less heralded Taylor, for the two worked successfully in tandem for more than 30 years. And like Maclea and March, Taylor and Wordsworth was a partnership of brothers-in-law. Such contracts held the incentive of a common family interest, but without that internecine strife enjoyed by brothers.

But is this all that constitutes succession? 'Men plan, God laughs',[175] as early-nineteenth-century engineers understood only too well. Life and health were fragile, who could say how secure the new industry's future, and there was little or no help in case of failure. Worse, proprietors were personally liable, and faced the fate of William Drabble, stripped of all possessions and threatened with gaol. The upside of insolvency was that it offered assets at bargain prices to new businesses. Taylor and Wordsworth must have benefited from Drabble's sale, in the limited market for engineering plant. A sympathetic Sheffield creditor gave George and Samuel Hattersley behind-the-scenes advice (and perhaps lent cash) to retrieve premises and essential tools from their assignees in 1832.[176]

And while individual firms disappeared at a rapid rate before 1820, the industry itself was fast expanding, replenished with businesses better suited to changed times. Technological stalling was not in the spirit of this trade. The baton was passed to a new cohort, almost all trained as apprentices, or as post-apprentice 'improvers', in Yorkshire. Of the major figures, Peter Fairbairn was a lone exception, and that because he had spent his twenties upskilling with the trade's finest practitioners in Glasgow, Manchester, London and France.

---

172   Scott (ed.), *Matthew Murray*, 36, 40–1; R. L. Hills, 'Richard Roberts', in Cantrell and Cookson, *Henry Maudslay*, 54–73; French, *Samuel Crompton*, *passim*; Hills, *Power in the Industrial Revolution*, 116–33.
173   Turner, 'History of Fenton, Murray and Wood', 8.12.
174   See app. 2.
175   Supposedly a Yiddish proverb.
176   WYAS Bradford, 32D83/33/1.

Yet, returning to a question about the many family businesses, some of good reputation and high achievement, that did not last beyond one or two generations: measured against the artisan ambition to hand down a viable business, surely this amounted to failure? If, though, there were no sons or suitable heirs, or those inheriting chose to withdraw to a comfortable life elsewhere, or took up other opportunities, then the end of the firm was not a disaster. Even with insolvency, possibly there was no real underlying fault, the business perhaps caught out by circumstances hard to predict. In fact, many of those sooner or later ceasing to exist did contribute very positively to the new trade, especially in generating a legacy of skills, both technical and managerial.

This is in its way a measure of endurance, though not embodied in one surviving institution. It was a generalized inheritance rather than a direct succession. Murray did not implement a clear plan, and the firm declined under Jackson, his eldest daughter's husband, while his other sons-in-law, Maclea and March, created something more lasting. Lawson and Stirk, if indeed Murray trainees, also carried on his flame. In fact throughout the nineteenth century, Leeds engineering was populated by hundreds of shop-floor workers and small tradesmen who had trained at the Round Foundry, or under someone else who had done so. Similarly, while Jubb's own business ended disappointingly, his technical descendants were (briefly) the Drabbles, then Taylor and Wordsworth, who brought along Pollard. Procter's and Cluderay's smaller ventures perhaps also came out of Drabble. In Keighley, demonstrably, many businesses – and every one of merit and endurance – emerged from Carr, Hattersley or William Smith trainees. Thomas Carr of Bingley did not inherit his father's business, yet his own company was undoubtedly an outcome of William Carr's expertise and experience. The same is true of Jonathan Hattersley of Leeds.

There was also an element of nurturing newly-launched ventures, when former apprentices branched out while retaining supportive links to their mentors. With such trading connections, technical resources could be pooled; work shared by subcontracting; goods, materials and services sold in both directions; and new firms helped through lean periods by extended credit. Hattersley's example shows established businesses benefiting too. Some newcomers would undoubtedly fail and leave unsettled debt, but it took only one or two like Berry Smith for the favour to reap a handsome dividend. Perhaps, though, patronage was not cold calculation, but to be understood within the continuing artisan mind-set. Far into the nineteenth century, machine-makers retained some of the spirit of the class from which they had sprung. An artisan need not suddenly throw away a whole cultural tradition, even in a fast-changing world.

The closeness between enterprises is clearer in Keighley. Relationships may have been less so in Leeds, though the mutually supportive axis of

Table 4. Origins of major textile-engineering businesses in Keighley, 1853

	Number employed	Origins of the company
George Bland	12	Founded c. 1835 by Bland, a blacksmith from Addingham.
Briggs and Banks	31	Three young partners, all Keighley-born, spindle-makers and mechanics.
George Hattersley	168 (c. 70 in worsted-spinning business)	Successor to Richard Hattersley.
John Midgley	n/k	Ex-apprentice of Titus Longbottom.
Thomas Mills	22	Mainly a founder, former partner of Richardson. Not successful as a machine-maker.
Charles and Allan Smith	6	Sons of Thomas, ex-apprentice of Berry Smith. Firm established c. 1815.
John and Samuel Smith	80	Trained by Hattersley. Established c. 1818. 1866: 400–500 employees.
William Smith & Sons	n/k, large.	Established 1795. Employed c. 750 in 1878, c. 1500 in 1890s.

Sources: White, *Dir.* (1853); Keighley census, 1851. See Appendix 1.

south Yorkshire origin, Jubb-Drabble-Wordsworth, was one of two pillars of machine-making there. While the firms were small in number, the engineering centres show common patterns. Prerequisites for success were the same: technical competence, and confidence; some mutual support within the trade or with customers; flexibility, for example in finding suitable labour reinforcements when needed; commercial acumen; and luck. Lack of continuation also came down to the same, obvious, explanations.

The main difference in how the localities developed was the more rapid progression of Leeds engineering into a factory model, arranging consecutive production processes within larger premises. In Leeds, it seems, were better access to investors willing to advance capital against a mortgage; a larger pool of prospective partners; perhaps more certainty of a stream of orders, with less subcontracted work; and maybe, for some, greater family support. But while these points facilitated development, they might just as well have been the effects – of slightly different initial arrangements in the Leeds trade – as the causes of change. Without doubt John Marshall's initiative was hugely influential in shaping Leeds engineering, but it was an unintended wider consequence of his own flax-spinning ambition. Marshall's resources kick-started a campaign to mechanize flax-processing, which duly submitted to

Murray's assault, and an important sector of Leeds engineering grew out of their collaboration. Meanwhile in Keighley, the trade evolved from smaller businesses reliant on subcontracting, taking off in a big way only after the textile focus switched from cotton to worsteds. The push to expand and integrate thus followed rather later.

Reflections on entrepreneurship

Were these machine-makers 'entrepreneurs'? Applied to this era, the term 'entrepreneur' is troublesome, for it has been overlaid by modern under-standings which are anachronistic. Specifically it assumes business behaviours and motivations which were not valid in early engineering.[177]

In French, where it had been in use since the Middle Ages, the word meant a contractor or someone charged with carrying out work, especially in construction, but distinct from a promoter or architect. Later the expression came to suggest the founder of an enterprise, or a manufacturer endowed with a spirit of enterprise; and then a director, one who assembled factors of production in order to provide goods or services.[178] But 'entrepreneur' would have meant nothing to early mechanical engineers in Britain, for it was still then waiting to be borrowed from the French. The word entered English in its now familiar commercial sense only in the 1880s.[179] The current *Oxford English Dictionary* definition is sober: 'one who undertakes an enterprise; one who owns and manages a business; a person who takes the risk of profit or loss; a manager'. To the modern mind, the word probably carries more element of chance, ambition, even rapacity, than the *OED* suggests. In using 'entrepreneur' historically, there is therefore the danger of projecting inappro-priate modern values on to very different past environments.

Indeed, identifying what is 'entrepreneurial' continues to engage modern students of management. It tends towards a circular definition, in its own terms, and by intentions inferred from actions, or by trying to spot 'an explicit desire'.[180] Yet how can the motives of others be truly understood, even in contemporary situations?

While early machine-makers displayed enterprise and versatility, they were acting as any artisan would when faced with a changing world. The idea of individualistic entrepreneurs in the heroic mould has been replaced,

177 See above, p. 4.
178 *Le Petit Robert de la Langue Française.*
179 OED. Before then it meant a promoter of entertainments, a use recorded only from 1828. Thomas Carlyle used it in that sense in 1852. Only when F. A. Walker employed it in *Political Economy* (1883) did it acquire the modern meaning.
180 See for instance Jenkins and Johnson, 'Entrepreneurial Intentions', 897.

according to Smail, by entrepreneurship as 'a quality possessed by a whole host of petty producers'.[181] Yet again, this redefines entrepreneurship. Smail concludes, about his late-seventeenth- and early-eighteenth-century Halifax textile manufacturers:

> Clearly, we no longer have to see the agents behind industrialization as far-sighted, risk-taking entrepreneurs who set out with the intent of trans-forming the mode of production in the woollen industry. If the example of Halifax's early manufacturers is applicable in other contexts, and I think that it is, the initial stages of industrialization were not concep-tually difficult, for they were accomplished largely within the terms of an artisanal culture. Indeed, the evidence about the manufacturers' capital accumulation, or rather the lack of it, suggests that even some aspects of their economic practice were artisanal.[182]

But, he continues, culture did change, and 'the manufacturer became a distinct cultural type – a type with behaviours, conceptions, and values different from those of the artisan'. This emerged 'through a process of cultural formation in which the actions of the manufacturers, though artisanal in intent, created a new culture'. Smail defines his textile artisan not in any formal legal or guild sense, but by production methods – a craftsman working on his own account in a domestic setting, assisted by family members.[183]

In engineering, this would equate to a skilled individual practising a trade in a low-tech workshop, using tools and hand-power, and employing at most a few journeymen and apprentices, these likely to be relatives. Artisans aspired to security and continuity, in order to leave their heirs with a durable business to support the family in future. To this end, they might mould the succession to give the business the best chance of long-term prosperity. The earliest makers of machinery came almost wholly from this group of techni-cally proficient artisans, their background humble though not lowly, an inter-mediate social class marked out by skill.[184]

Smail's Halifax falls very much within the orbit, industrial and cultural, of Leeds and Keighley machine-makers at this time. The move towards a new culture, beyond artisanship, is evident among late-eighteenth- and early-nineteenth-century textile engineers across northern England, and it is change comparable with that described by Smail as occurring (slightly earlier) among Halifax textile manufacturers. Of course changing tack came

181   Smail, 'Manufacturer or Artisan?', 792.
182   Smail, 'Manufacturer or Artisan?', 808.
183   Smail, 'Manufacturer or Artisan?', 808, 796.
184   'Artisan' in the OED: a worker in a skilled trade, a craftsperson; (in later use) especially one utilizing traditional or non-mechanized methods. Formerly often taken as typifying a social class intermediate between property-owners and wage labourers.

with risk attached, but the greater danger could come through not adapting. Change was far less daunting when active across – and thus encouraged and supported by – a wide community. And much did remain the same. The conversion rate of skilled workers into self-employment, for instance, was little different from that in more traditional settings.

The speed of change in textile engineering was exceptional, its new materials, products and tools signalling two almost-revolutions within 20 years or so. But the nature of change more resembled an evolution, building on well-tried models, cumulative, even communal. Peter Fairbairn's move to Leeds in the late 1820s was unusual in its premeditation, a harbinger of things to come. Fairbairn came alone, fully skilled and bearing ideas. He planned to increase the speed and power of flax-spinning, simplify the process, and save waste, including using 80 spindles in place of 40 and substituting screws for 'fallers' or 'gills'. He would have known about Phillipe de Girard's flax-spinning innovations c. 1810–15, spurned in France but then rapidly adopted and developed in British centres, including Leeds.[185] Leeds was the obvious location for Fairbairn and he was advised by his brother William, who knew the local industrial scene after extending Bean Ing for Gott in 1824.[186] Peter seized the opportunity arising after Matthew Murray's death, and duly supplanted Murray's firm when his improvements found favour with John Marshall. Most unusual of all was Peter Fairbairn's period of experimentation in Lady Lane, which somehow he found the means to pay for.[187]

Is this evidence of a newly sharp-elbowed behaviour? Fairbairn was not alone in feeling that there was more to defend and that relationships must change. Once invested in machine shops fitted out with new machine-tool technology, there was far more at stake. Was this personal ambition? Circumstance delivered opportunity, and to retain a significant presence in machine-making after 1820, there was little option but an upward leap.[188]

185   Walker, *Fortunes Made in Business*, 259–62.
186   Byrom, 'William Fairbairn', 79.
187   See app. 2.
188   See below, pp. 258–9.

5

Ingenious Mechanics

By the mid-nineteenth century, a workforce of many thousands had been trained in textile engineering. The best paid and highest skilled were considered part of an aristocracy of labour. Alongside was a multitude of shop-floor engineering workers concentrated on narrowly defined duties in large factories, arguably with little independence or discretion compared with their immediate predecessors. The ways in which engineering workers were employed and trained had evolved, and the trade had changed. Whether this group was less skilled overall, and how far it might have lost touch with the industry's earlier ethos, are less certain.

It seems that chances to progress out of this rather regimented industrial proletariat had been curtailed. Many employees and employers still shared a background of apprenticeship training, an absorption in the skills and knowledge of textile technology. Yet the workers were less likely to advance. After the industry was restructured in the 1810s and 1820s, the size of capital investment needed to set up a machine shop with self-acting tools became an obstacle. The chance of building such a company from scratch was placed out of reach for most. The number of new ventures dramatically reduced in proportion to the enlarged workforce.

And there were other changes. In the large shops at least, some level of stability replaced casual employment practices. This had its attractions, compared with the uncertainties of self-employment. It came at a price, though, the loss of that relative independence to which previous generations had aspired. Capital was not the only hurdle: there was less opportunity to learn about the production process overall, about the commercial workings of the trade, and to be nurtured and supported into self-sufficiency by a former master. Yet the small-scale sector in engineering continued to be very significant, so self-employment was not an impossibility. Perhaps the real barrier was that workers classed as skilled in the larger factories were not really so. In fulfilling only a narrow range of tasks, was their lack of all-round proficiency shielded by division of labour and a range of modern machine tools? Was the trade shedding its broad-based competence?

Skill is a nebulous concept. At times, it suits sectional interests to misrepresent skill levels, what it takes to achieve them and what they actually mean.

Clearly certain types of skill were fundamental to the dynamics of early engineering. Equally obviously, much of the evidence about skill is vague, ambiguous – perhaps even deliberately misleading. But the matter is too important to be side-stepped, however improbable the idea of defining the functional skills of a workforce at two centuries' distance. So the attempt will be made, approached through analysis of the early labour force: how it arrived at this work, and acquired and developed skills and knowledge essential for machine-making; the measure of these skills; how workers were recruited and deployed. And then, later, how arrangements changed, specialization grew, and what were the routes into training, employment, and perhaps into business for the engineering journeyman.[1]

Investigating skill

As already described, the earliest textile machines were produced alongside other work by local tradesmen such as smiths and joiners, or, in the case of fulling machinery, by millwrights who worked full-time in that trade, though not exclusively in textile engineering.[2] So machine-making was largely part-time, its members elsewhere engaged, and while skilled they were not highly specialized.

From the closing years of the eighteenth century, as demand grew for increasingly complex products, so production techniques evolved and the workforce adjusted in size, location and degree of specialization. At first this meant a higher grade of skill, though after self-acting tools took over from repetitive hand processes, inevitably there was a rearrangement of expertise – re-skilling as much as de-skilling. The same had occurred in clock-making, and with the adoption into ironworking of Cort's process.[3]

Like other craft trades, machine-making around the turn of the nineteenth century was seen as an 'art and mystery'. There was a dimension beyond manual skill and formal technical knowledge, the 'inner life of workshops'. So 'the life and education of the workshop ... is twofold – technical and social'.[4] This was partly to protect the tradesman, defining and preserving the boundary of who was 'in' and who 'out'. The system offered much that was positive, including a duty to help members fallen on hard times, and pooling information about jobs and employers in other towns.[5] It chimes with an account of late-nineteenth-century wheelwrights. 'The waggon-builder's

1   A 'journeyman' has completed an apprenticeship and is paid an employee's daily rate.
2   See above, pp. 30–2, 49–53.
3   See above, pp. 79–80, and below, pp. 164–5.
4   Wright, *Habits and Customs*, 83, 107.
5   Wright, *Habits and Customs*, 100–1, 104–5.

lore' was 'a tangled network of country prejudices ... for the most part the details were but dimly understood', though 'necessity gave the law at every detail, and in scores of ways insisted on conformity'. It was essential that the waggon-builder grasped manual skills and technical details, though not in any scientific way – 'reasoned science for us did not exist' – but the trade was more than that, encompassing local custom as well as an empirically-founded technical skill, all transmitted through apprenticeship.[6]

The 'lore' of a new trade such as machine-making must have been less firmly entrenched, with fewer restrictions on those wishing to join or move within. But 'custom' might be quickly created to protect the position of those already 'in', even to the extent of confining the body of knowledge and introducing that air of mystery. In other ways the new trade developed, consciously or otherwise, its networks and a *modus operandi*. Evolving with the relationships forged between buyer and seller, engineer and subcontractor, was an understanding of what was required of these roles, who was 'in' the trade, and what kind of job they might expect to perform.

But to take a backward step, into the more traditional occupations whose skills were essential for machine-making, their own 'lore' influenced the ethos of the new industry and the trades within it. A local culture also held sway, though shaped by newcomers arriving in the northern textile districts from south Yorkshire's metal industries, from the mining districts of north-eastern England, and from Glasgow and southern Scotland.

The pull of the textile districts, their attraction to engineers, is clear. Strong engineering links were building between Glasgow and Lancashire, but into Yorkshire only limited numbers arrived from Scotland and the north east. The interchange between south and west Yorkshire was significant. Why would talented and promising individuals move from south Yorkshire? The metal trades were evidently doing well, the Walkers of Rotherham developing one of the country's largest and most successful ironworks in the late-eighteenth century, Sheffield a renowned centre of metalworking with a relatively open society.[7] These successes mask a decline in the rural villages around Penistone. Nail-making, practised in domestic workshops alongside farming within a dual economy, was in transition. The 'metropolis of the nail trade', Ecclesfield, birthplace of Richard Hattersley, also produced the Walkers, sons of a Grenoside nail-maker. But the Walkers' main business, established in 1748, was far downstream in Masbrough, where large vessels could navigate the Don.[8] The renowned Joseph Bramah, Stainborough-born

6   Sturt, *Wheelwright's Shop*, 73–4, 19.
7   Hey, *Fiery Blades*, 96–7, 197, *passim*.
8   Butterworth, 'Ecclesfield Nailers', 114; Hey, 'Walker family', *DNB*. Blacksmiths were much less engaged in agriculture: Rowlands, *Masters and Men*, 42.

and Silkstone-educated, left for London c. 1770 after apprenticeship as a carpenter.[9] Half of Ecclesfield parish's scattered population was too poor to be taxed in 1797. Nail-making paid by the piece, 6s. to 12s. a week, file-making about 10s. 6d. These were labourer's wages in Sheffield, far lower than a cutlery tradesman's 30s.[10]

Consequently communities previously thriving on nail-making, wire-drawing and other metal trades lost skilled workers. An 1806 militia list covering the Staincross parishes recorded those men (aged 18 to 45) who remained, after the loss of many others to Leeds and Keighley engineering. In Tankersley were nine nailers; in Wortley, two young men called Parkin were apprenticed to that trade. Others with surnames familiar among the west Yorkshire migrants were wire-drawers: Joseph Drabble in Wortley; George Jubb of Thurgoland; and Robert and Thomas Wordsworth of the same place. Other Jubbs were blacksmiths in Silkstone and Worsborough.[11]

Nail-making has been called 'the least skilled of the iron trades', carried on in the west Midlands by women and children with little training.[12] Yet it held some significance. Chowbent, Lancashire, known for machine-making, had been a centre of nail-making.[13] It is claimed that 'this apparently trivial and uninteresting occupation' played an important role in industrial change in the west Midlands, while similarly 'the humble nailing trade' was a key factor in developing south Yorkshire's iron industry after 1750.[14] In 1733, Ecclesfield nail-makers had sufficient power to demand a seven-year apprenticeship, although two years would have been quite enough. Thus they limited entry and prevented young men from setting up in business prematurely.[15] Even so, the trade remained overcrowded, and once nailers lost a mainstay of their incomes, their agricultural holdings, severe decline followed. The parish of Ecclesfield was enclosed in the 1780s, and a few decades later mechanization finished its nailing trade.[16] Some backyard smithies were converted to file-making,[17] which did well. Richard Hattersley bought files there, and from the Sheffield company of Hattersley and Whitham.[18]

9   C. F. Lindsey, 'Joseph Bramah (1749–1814)', *DNB*.

10   Eden, *State of the Poor*, 352, 364.

11   Hey (ed.), 'Militia Men'; added information from David Hey.

12   Rowlands, *Masters and Men*, 26; Hey, *Village of Ecclesfield*, 58.

13   Angerstein, *Illustrated Travel Diary*, 295, 303.

14   Court, *Midland Industries*, 100; Hey, 'Nail-making Background', 36; Hey, *Fiery Blades*, 305.

15   Butterworth, 'Ecclesfield Nailers', 114, 116.

16   Hey, *Village of Ecclesfield*, 31, 59; Winder (ed.), *Old Ecclesfield Diary*, 14.

17   Hey, *Village of Ecclesfield*, 59–60; guide to Hoylandswaine Nail Forge by South Yorkshire Trades Historical Trust (2010).

18   WYAS Bradford, 32D83/2/3; /2/4; /6/1. Whitham and Hattersley of Bridge Street in Pigot, *Dir.* (1818–20), 416; G. Whitham, G. Hattersley and J. Meake of Sheffield, filesmiths, in *The Tradesman* (1810), IV, 472.

Hattersley, himself a whitesmith, came from an extensive nail-making clan in Ecclesfield. Two Hattersleys were among the 39 nail-shop masters there in 1707, and five of the name signed the 1733 Ecclesfield Nailers' Agreement.[19] While for the most part Hattersley used local, Keighley, labour, he also employed family members from Ecclesfield for long and short periods from the 1790s. Similarly, John Jubb and the Drabbles imported south Yorkshire relatives, some of whom became key associates. Much, though, of the Leeds and Keighley labour force was built more locally. It was the same in the west Midlands, where the eighteenth-century transition relied largely on capital and manpower 'drawn from the community itself' with 'no evidence to suggest ... any marked recruitment of men from outside the region'.[20]

If Richard Hattersley had needed nail-makers, they were to be found in numbers four miles from Keighley. Silsden was a centre of the shoe-nail trade from about 1760 until the end of the nineteenth century, with as many as 250 forges at its peak, and over 30 nail-makers recorded in 1803.[21] But the skill of nail-making was very specific. The nail-smith needed great facility with the hammer, to carry out work both endlessly repetitive yet extremely precise:

> [I remember] as a boy, watching the making of hand-made nails ... The rod of iron was cut into the required lengths across a 'cold-sate' let into an anvil, with the cutting edge upwards, and was then deftly picked up and dropped into a hole in the anvil. A sharp blow with the hammer not only completed the head at one operation, but jumped the nail out of the hole, leaving it ready for the next nail.[22]

Silsden nail-making did not transfer into Keighley's new engineering. To be a smith, or a carpenter, was a trade with depth and breadth, involving an element of problem-solving. By contrast, nailing was wedded to a way of life on the land.

The nailers' principle, though, was applicable to producing certain engineering components. The idea was to achieve maximum accuracy through a monotonous hand process, more technique than skill, and evidently requiring little intellectual input. In machine-making, even such close refinement of tasks could not deliver interchangeable components. Every part must be adjusted to fit, and so every machine was to an extent a one-off.[23] The 'vice-man', a smith who filed and finished smith's or turner's work, is considered forerunner of the fitter.[24] His experience, manual ability,

---

19   Winder (ed.), *Old Ecclesfield Diary*, 9; R. Butterworth, 'Ecclesfield Nailers', 114.
20   Rowlands, *Masters and Men*, 147.
21   Mason, *Pennine Village*, 6; *Craven Muster Roll*.
22   Winder (ed.), *Old Ecclesfield Diary*, 8–9.
23   Mathias, *Transformation of England*, 35.
24   More, *Skill and the English Working Class*, 195–6.

and knowledge enabled this system to work. The skill level was high, very different from nail-making or spindle-forging. Boulton and Watt encountered continuing problems finding good and reliable engine erectors, and other suitable tradesmen, and were often obliged to accept indifferent results.[25] James Watt, early in his Glasgow experiments, employed a whitesmith to make his first cylinder. Though the outcome was disappointing, when this 'old white-iron man' died Watt despaired.[26] He turned to casting the cylinders, but these too proved 'next to useless' despite being stuffed with 'paper, cork, putty, pasteboard, and old hat'. In Birmingham, Watt continued to blame 'villainous bad workmanship' for his engine's inefficiencies.

> Yet better work could not be had. First-rate workmen in machinery did not as yet exist; they were only in process of education. Nearly everything had to be done by hand. The tools used were of a very imperfect kind.[27]

There were hand-driven lathes and other basic machines, templates and guides.[28] Hammers, chisels and files were vital to correct the parts, though, for measurements were taken by caliper and two-foot rule, meaning that a thirty-second of an inch was about the greatest accuracy achievable.[29] Smiles recalled in 1863 that:

> Not fifty years since it was a matter of the utmost difficulty to set an engine to work, and sometimes of equal difficulty to keep it going. Though fitted by competent workmen, it often would not go at all. Then the foreman of the factory at which it was made was sent for, and he would almost live beside the engine for a month or more; and after easing her here and screwing her up there, putting in a new part and altering an old one, packing the piston and tightening the valves, the machine would at last be got to work.

There was, said Smiles, 'the same kind of clumsiness in all kinds of mill-work before the introduction of machine tools'. He told the story of a machine which 'made such a clatter that the owner feared the engine would fall to pieces'. The fitter, 'almost in despair, at last gave it up, saying, "I think we had better leave the cogs to settle their differences with one another. They will grind themselves right in time".'[30]

---

25 Roll, *Early Experiment*, 24.

26 Smiles, *Industrial Biography*, 179–80.

27 Smiles, *Industrial Biography*, 180. Smiles 'borrowed' extensively from Fairbairn, 'On Metallic Constructions'.

28 See for instance the stiddy (anvil) featuring rough templates at Kelham Island Museum, Sheffield.

29 Tupling, 'Early Metal Trades', 30. A thirty-second of an inch is about 0.79 mm.

30 Smiles, *Industrial Biography*, 181 and fn.

Watt found some relief by:

> keeping certain sets of workmen to special classes of work, allowing them
> to do nothing else. Fathers were induced to bring up their sons at the
> same bench with themselves, and initiate them in the dexterity which they
> had acquired by experience; and at Soho it was not unusual for the same
> precise line of work to be followed by members of the same family for three
> generations.

Still, 'accuracy of fitting could not be secured so long as the manufacture
of steam engines was conducted mainly by hand'.[31] William Fairbairn's
experience, on first arriving in Manchester in 1814, was similar:

> The whole of the machinery was executed by hand. There were neither
> planing, slotting nor shaping machines; and, with the exception of very
> imperfect lathes and a few drills, the preparatory operations of construction
> were effected entirely by the hands of the workman.[32]

Fairbairn tended to hyperbole,[33] but Nasmyth made the same point.

> Up to within the last thirty years nearly every part of a machine had to be
> made and finished ... by mere manual labour; that is on the dexterity of
> the hand of the workman, and the correctness of his eye, had we entirely
> to depend for accuracy and precision in the execution of such machinery,
> as was then required.[34]

So the talents needed to produce a machine crossed quite a range, and involved
differing degrees of dexterity and technical understanding. Skills tended to be
specialized, scarce (certainly at a high level of competence), and found in only
a few centres.

But what does skill really mean? Early in textile engineering, desirable
competences were extensions of older trades. For instance, a joiner might
start to make machine frames, a smith to produce parts for a mechanism.
So here, skill was very real – the standard fell short of satisfactory in some
respects, but it was the best that could be achieved in prevailing circumstances. Nor was there any status quo to be defended, for this was not a
single trade protecting itself against incomers. In a new industry, drawing on
a *mélange* of occupations, vested interests were not far established. Skilled

---

31   Smiles, *Industrial Biography*, 180–1.
32   Pole (ed.), *Sir William Fairbairn*, vi.
33   Tann, *Development of the Factory*, 100.
34   Buchanan, *Practical Essays on Millwork*, quoted in Musson's introduction to Pole (ed.),
Sir William Fairbairn.

workers were sought out, their abilities essential if the job were to be done. So 'skill' was actual, not an artificial construct, nor a creation to protect any particular group.[35]

The most sought-after proficiencies changed as the industry evolved, and an expanding formal knowledge was asked of skilled workers.[36] An intermediate semi-skilled class would emerge in machine shops. But Hattersley had always had workers who were apparently semi-skilled, so perhaps it is most accurate to say that this group was eventually recognized as such.[37] Every workshop also had unskilled workers, for routine production processes, moving goods around the premises, or providing power. The supporting array of less expert workers thus concentrated the essential core of skill more effectively.

Flux and flexibility

The Craven muster roll, drawn up in 1803, is a route into analysing Keighley's mix of occupations at this key time.[38] Here were recorded 1,118 men potentially available for military service, the intention being to capture the parish's entire male population aged 17 to 55. As the foundations of machine-making were already laid, it includes men and boys described by a textile-engineering occupation. But many of their co-workers were listed by an earlier trade. Most of those surveyed lived in the town itself, but its fringes, including William Smith's birthplace at Stockbridge, lay across the Aire in Bingley parish, for which there is no similar roll.

The Craven roll does more than confirm who then worked in the new engineering. It exposes the bedrock of local trades underlying the industry, occupations at hand upon which to build an engineering workforce. In the town were small yet significant numbers of specialists, brass-filers and founders, tinsmiths, and many smiths working in iron; also numerous wood workers, though then of decreasing interest to machine-making. Altogether 34 metalworkers and 33 wood workers were listed. Two unspecified apprentices are known to have been textile engineers, and there would doubtless have been others. There was no millwright in the parish. Four nail- and seven comb-makers represented trades which, as far as is known, played no part in Keighley machine-making.

How were these skills drawn into the machine and component shops? The earliest textile engineers turned the 'characteristic irregularity' of

35 See More, *Skill and the English Working Class*, preface.
36 More, *Skill and the English Working Class*, 79.
37 See below, pp. 136–41.
38 *Craven Muster Roll*; Lawton, 'Economic Geography of Craven'.

Table 5. Sources of labour: engineering-related trades in Keighley parish, 1803

Brass-filer	2
Blacksmith	9
Whitesmith	8
Smith	4
Machine-maker	1
Engine Man	1
Founder	2
Brass-founder/Brazier	3
Tinworker	2
Clock-maker	2
Shuttle-maker	1
Woodturner	3
Turner	2
Joiner	20
Carpenter	7
Nail-maker	4
Comb-maker	7
All trades (men aged 17–55)	1,118

Source: NYCRO, Z787; *Craven Muster Roll.*

contemporary working habits to advantage.[39] Piecework and day rates were used flexibly to increase output or control costs, according to the state of trade. A pool of casual employees came into the workshop when needed, or worked flexibly from home. They filled, or perhaps did not fill, their working hours with casual or subcontract tasks elsewhere.[40] This 'semi-domestic' system probably faded from the industry after 1800, though the use of subcontractors, both large and small, continued to be a distinctive feature.

Payments to workers by Richard Hattersley in 1796–98 and 1808–09 provide detail.[41] During the earlier period (Table 6), altogether 19 people were employed. At the core, three skilled men were fully engaged: Hattersley

39   Rule, *Labouring Classes*, 130.
40   For example WYAS Bradford, 32D83/10/1.
41   WYAS Bradford, 32D83/6/1; /10/1.

Table 6. Employment patterns: Richard Hattersley's workforce, 1796–98

	Employment period	Weekly pay	Usual occupation
Edm. Bradley	Oct. 97 – c. Aug. 98	Casual*	?Labourer 1803
Jos. Cook	Dec. 97 – Aug. 98	Casual*	
Jos. Crossley	Apr. 96 – Oct. 97, and occasional	c. 9 shillings	Weaver 1803
Thomas Eamet (or Emmet)	every week	c. 9s. 10d	Whitesmith 1803/ Smith 1817
George Hattersley (b. 1789)	from mid-1798	apprentice rates	RH's son
John Hattersley	Dec. 1796 only	Casual*	?RH's uncle, b. 1736
N. Hattersley	four weeks in 1796	c. 13s. 8d	Likely to be RH's brother Nathaniel, of Ecclesfield
Richard Hattersley	every week	£1 1s. 0d	Whitesmith
Samuel Hattersley (b. 1785)	from mid-1796	apprentice rates	RH's son
Solomon Hattersley	every week	apprentice rates	RH's brother b. 1783; apprentice 1803
Michael Merrall	every week from c. 1795	c. 12 shillings	Smith
Robert and Wm. Morrill	Dec. 96 – Oct. 97	Casual*	Wm. Merrall: apprentice 1803
Robert Smith	6 or 8 weeks in 1796	Casual*	?Weaver 1803
Reuben Stell	Feb. 96 – June 96, and occasional.	Casual*	Weaver 1803
Jos. Sugden	Feb. 96 – Apr. 96	c. 4 shillings	Weaver 1803
Thomas and Roger Teal	occasional weeks in 1796		Thomas Teal: ?cottoner/ infirm 1803
D. Wildman	Feb. 96 to Apr. 96	c. 4 shillings	Thomas Wildman: weaver 1803

Sources: WYAS Bradford, 32D83/6/1 (Hattersley's cash book 1795–1820). Occupational data: NYCRO, Z787; *Craven Muster Roll*; parish registers, Keighley St Andrew.

* Source does not specify whether casual labourers were paid per hour or by the piece.

himself; Thomas Eamet, whitesmith/smith; and Michael Merrall, called either blacksmith or whitesmith. Next, a group of family members was apprenticed, or working prior to apprenticeship: sons Samuel, aged about 10, and George, around nine; and Solomon Hattersley (b. 1783), Richard's much younger brother. Solomon's employment had started by 1796, continuing through apprenticeship; he was the highest paid regular employee in 1808–09.

Most workers though, 13 in all, were casuals with no particular skill.[42] Some did little for Hattersley, while others appeared frequently, presumably during busy periods. This section of the workforce comprised weavers or labourers very local to the workshop, mainly youngsters, children even. Hattersley's shop was essentially a handful of accomplished metalworkers supported by, and supporting, others with no evident skills. Hattersley did not make machinery so had little need of joiners or the other generalist trades then present in the town. To him, the flexible pool of low-cost labour on his doorstep, while needing expert supervision, proved most convenient and cost-effective. Skilled workers (if they could be had) would demand steadier employment, and when trade was slow, would have to be deployed on unskilled chores. The 13 casual workers used during 1796–98 were quite dispensable, absent from the employees listed in 1808–09.

The casuals are proof that already some separation of tasks, or division of labour, applied. Though Hattersley had few machine tools, he employed a high proportion of low-skill labour. So what were these workers doing? While contemporaries found early textile machines impressive, these now appear 'modest, rudimentary, wooden contrivances'.[43] They worked as well as they did only because component-makers like Hattersley managed to achieve tolerances exceptional in their time. It seems that he did it by emulating the nail-making example familiar from his youth (though without using actual nail-makers); that is, with limited training in narrow tasks, the technique then refined through endless repetition. In supplying precision parts for others to assemble, Hattersley had picked up on a growing practice – the development of a 'best possible' system, a means to attain finer tolerances to ease the fitting process.

Before c. 1800 Boulton and Watt used a similar method, supplying plans and drawings, along with parts (some of dubious accuracy) from subcontractors such as John Wilkinson. Customers were expected to order boilers and pistons locally, and might employ a Boulton and Watt erector to supervise fitting.[44] M'Connel and Kennedy, Manchester machine-makers in the 1790s, bought in many components from small manufacturers: rollers from Matlock, Mayfield (Derbyshire) and Mosley; cards from Halifax; and

---

42 'Irregulars' included John and N[athaniel] Hattersley, visitors to Keighley: see below, p. 169.
43 Landes, *Unbound Prometheus*, 64–5.
44 Roll, *Early Experiment*, 24–5.

spindles from Stalybridge.[45] As machines increased in size and iron frames replaced wooden, often it was most convenient to supply them prefabricated. M'Connel asked a Belfast customer in 1797:

> Would it not be cheaper and more convenient for you to have all the iron and brass work made here and sent over ready to be put together, and to have a confidential and experienced journeyman machine maker or two to go from here and make the woodwork and fit up the mules with you, and to have one or two complete mules made here and sent over for a pattern, that you might see that those fitted up with you were the same.[46]

The value of certain skilled workers rose higher still. By 1802, Matthew Murray used articles to bind foundry workers whose skills were key to his technical success. The death of one green-sand moulder left him with a particular problem.[47] Fixed-term contracts cost employers some flexibility; employees gained security but could not then take up a better offer. Increasing use of contracts reveals how much importance was attached to having a stable workforce with specific skills.

Richard Hattersley had not reached a point of indenturing labour – other than apprentices – though he would later bind subcontractors. Comparing his wages records from a nine-month period in 1808–09 (Table 7) with the previous series shows the progress towards specialization that he and his workforce had made over the decade. Before and after 1800, the firm's focus was on rollers, spindles, flyers, and other textile machine parts. But the customer profile shifted. In the 1790s, many products were sold direct to textile manufacturers. Some of these were retained, but in 1808 a few machine-makers accounted for a high proportion of Hattersley's sales by value.[48] The volume of work, and pressure for accuracy from engineer customers, had forced an upgrade in skills and specialization. This kind of concentration and division of work is often identified with factories, but it was by no means confined there. It could be effective in one workshop, or spread across several units.[49] The system did not, however, satisfy Hattersley's customers, in quality or quantity. He received numerous complaints about late delivery and poor quality, such as this from Taylor and Wordsworth in 1824:

> We cannot think of sending such rubbish out of our shop … the man that made them must have been drunk … instead of improving you are getting

45   Lee, *Cotton Enterprise*, 17–18.
46   Lee, *Cotton Enterprise*, 20.
47   Scott (ed.), *Matthew Murray*, 36.
48   Analysis of WYAS Bradford, 32D83/2/1.
49   Roll, *Early Experiment*, pt 2, ch. 1 and 2; Berg, 'Small Producer Capitalism', 23.

Table 7. Employment patterns: Richard Hattersley's workforce, October 1808 – June 1809

	Employment pattern	Wage (6 days)	Occupation
John Driver	Mostly f/t, left Apr. 1809	14s. 0d	(?Weaver or ?cotton spinner in 1803)
Richard Fowler	f/t, then p/w	18s. 0d	Turning and fluting rollers (whitesmith aged 17–30 in 1803)
George Hattersley	f/t, some p/w, or laid off	14s. 0d	Still apprenticed
Richard Hattersley	f/t	£2 2s. 0d	
Samuel Hattersley	f/t or p/w or laid off	18s. 0d	
Solomon Hattersley	f/t or p/w (flyers) or laid off	£1 1s. 0d	
Nimrod Holmes	f/t	15s. 0d	(Weaver aged 17–30 in 1803)
Joseph Midgley*	f/t	8s. 0d	?Apprentice
Robert Scafe/Skaife	f/t	15s. 0d	(Smith aged over 30 in 1803)
William Smith	p/w (flyers) for 9 days only	£1 1s. 0d	Smith the machine-maker?
Occasional labour:			
James Bowskill		18s 0d	
Samuel Haggas	p/w		Flyer forger
James Holmes	p/w		Screw cutter
James Spencer		14s. 0d	
George Stell		14s. 0d or 15s. 0d	

Sources: WYAS Bradford, 32D83/10/1. 1803 descriptions are from the *Craven Muster Roll* (NYCRO).

* Presumably the same man who contracted to serve Hattersley as spindle-forger for six years from 1822, and as manager of the spindle-forging department from 1825 (WYAS Bradford, 32D83/12/1).

f/t = full-time, p/t = part-time, p/w = piecework

worse you formerly made a good spindle how it is you are fallen off so much
we cannot tell. We are not the only persons that find fault there are many
worsted spinners that have made the same remark.[50]

Hattersley, though, kept his customers, who continued to clamour for
deliveries, suggesting that his products were no worse than anyone else's.

After fifteen years in business, in 1808 Richard Hattersley himself was still
the only employee on the firm's books who consistently received a full-time
wage, even though at times as many as a dozen men were employed.[51] Other
than family members, his workforce had changed entirely over the decade.
The nucleus remained roughly four skilled men: Richard Hattersley, his wage
doubled to two guineas a week; Richard Fowler, a whitesmith specializing
in turning and fluting rollers; Robert Skaife, a smith; and Nimrod Holmes,
formerly a weaver, presumably retrained in metal-working as his pay matched
Skaife's. John Driver, another former textile worker, paid slightly less, worked
through most of the period. Flexibility was maintained in several ways. First,
casual labour was used, though no longer the young and unskilled workers of
the 1790s. Some casuals performed specific skilled tasks such as flyer-forging
or screw-cutting. At least one received the fully skilled rate. Secondly, day rates
were interchanged with piecework, and workers at times laid off. Hattersley's
sons, George – still an apprentice – and Samuel, and brother Solomon, were
often temporarily displaced so that core workers, probably men with families,
maintained a wage. At other times piece-rates boosted weekly earnings when
there was urgent work to complete. But almost every worker was laid off at
some time during these nine months.

Across the industry, piece or day rates were used as a tool to maximize
quality, and to motivate and retain those with prized skills. Thomas Cheek
Hewes, whose millwrights had been paid by the day as was traditional in their
trade, shifted to one-third, and then two-thirds, piecework in his machine-
making division to improve productivity. His pieceworkers would make
perhaps 36s. to 40s. a week, compared with 30s. paid by the day. A full switch
to piece-rates he thought undesirable, as some work could not be done to an
acceptable standard at higher speed.[52] The basic pay for 'operative machine-
makers' had risen little, at about 26s. to 30s. a week in 1841, though much
depended upon 'the cleverness of the men'. More worked for regular wages
than piece-rates, but 'the piece hands are generally first-class men, and some
of them will earn as much as £3 and £4 a week'.[53]

50   WYAS Bradford, 32D83/32/1.
51   WYAS Bradford, 32D83/10/1.
52   PP Artisans and Machinery, 345.
53   PP Exportation of Machinery, 104, William Jenkinson.

Terms of engagement

Hattersley's experiences illustrate the tests facing new engineering businesses. He was, like most of the rest, a novice at running a company, albeit a still small one. The example of the artisan workshop worked as a starting point, but clinging to the familiar was not enough. To thrive meant being sufficiently adaptable to absorb countless changes, in technology and the industrial environment. Skill and labour shortages in a fluctuating market must be managed with only limited financial resources; manufacture flexible enough to allow for product development; production systems planned in the most efficient and economical way.

This whole half-century of engineering was transitional, up to perhaps 1840, and the evolving nature of skill, every bit as much as product and process technologies, defines the change. At first, small masters must recruit men of suitable experience, and hope to train them in the specifics. Soon, apprentices came up within the trade, though as production methods changed, they too must adjust. The preferred skill in 1790s and 1800s engineering was that of whitesmith – or blacksmith, or plain smith, the labels fluid and to an extent interchangeable. Hattersley inducted several such men into specialist skills that were particularly valuable to him. Largely they continued to label themselves smiths, though en route to something more. This path was not available to a later generation. Thomas Cheek Hewes, the Manchester machine-maker, described in 1824 how his own workmen '[would] not allow a common blacksmith, that only has to forge iron into any kind of shape, to work at our trade, because he has not worked in the cotton trade'.[54] The 'corps of blacksmiths' among Peter Fairbairn's workforce in 1841 carried out mechanized and demarcated tasks.[55]

Training included a mix of manual skills and technical knowledge. At first, with new and quickly developing products, and processes improvised from other industries and also in constant flux, there could be no simple path of instruction, no clearly defined body of information. Entry was, in general, through apprenticeship in one of the wood- or metal-working trades, enhanced by familiarity with certain technologies: 'Mechanicks wanted – three or four good workmen who understand the making and fitting up of cotton or worsted machinery.'[56] This, from John Jubb in 1789, sounds precise, though the terms are actually vague. That year, George Lyster of Revolution Mill, Retford, asked for joiners, whitesmiths and turners, and a 'blacksmith who has been used to work a steam engine, or wishes to be instructed and

54 PP Artisans and Machinery, 348.
55 *Chambers's Edinburgh Journal*, 513, 27 Nov. 1841, 354.
56 *Leeds Mercury*, 6 Jan. 1789.

employed in working one of the patent engines'.[57] In 1792 Wright and White, opening a textile-machine workshop in Leeds, looked for general joiners and specifically a 'billy-maker' to construct slubbing machines.[58] John Jubb advertised his needs thus in 1794:

> John Jubb, millwright and machinery maker, Leeds, is in want of three journeymen millwrights and the same number of joiners who have been accustomed to work at scribbling and carding machines, also a whitesmith who understands the above businesses. An apprentice is also wanted.[59]

The millwrights would have been intended only for Jubb's millwright business, the others for machine-making. Smiths, after all, were paid less than half the rate of millwrights. The separate identity of millwrights was maintained, their society standing apart from the first trades unions catering for skilled and semi-skilled engineering workers.[60] Alexander Galloway told the Select Committee in 1824:

> In engineer shops, new men's wages are generally fixed after working a fortnight on trial: we give as much as we can afford to the most expert men, and then bring down the reward upon that standard; but in the business of a millwright, all the men have two guineas a week, and a man of that class formerly was employed to turn a grindstone, while one at 18s. a week would have done as well.[61]

Other witnesses reported that 'millwrights men would not work with an engineer' and that having a carding machine repaired by London millwrights had 'cost double the money that a new engine would have cost in Manchester'.[62]

Labour shortages were a recurring theme, confirmation that engineering skills were real enough. Boulton and Watt had struggled to find and retain suitable workers, initially fitters, and later founders. Watt wrote to John Smeaton in 1778: 'We wish we could join you in saying that we can easily find operative engineers who can put engines together according to plan, as clock-makers do clocks; we have yet found exceedingly few of them.'[63] That same year, Boulton complained to Watt about two smiths Watt had trained as engine erectors and sent out to a customer:

57   *Leeds Intelligencer*, 22 Sept. 1789.
58   Crump (ed.), *Leeds Woollen Industry*, 327.
59   Crump (ed.), *Leeds Woollen Industry*, 321.
60   More, *Skill and the English Working Class*, 146–7.
61   PP Artisans and Machinery, 28; see above, pp. 73–4.
62   PP Artisans and Machinery, 9, 300.
63   Roll, *Early Experiment*, 61.

> Sam Evans and young Perrins at Bedworth are two drunken, idle, stupid, careless, conceited rascals and have used the engine and their masters so ill that they wish to change them, but these two fellows say, and their masters seem to believe, that it requires the learning and knowledge of a university man to keep an engine in order.[64]

To a point, employers endured bad behaviour because skilled workers, even when unruly, could not easily be replaced. George Hattersley noted employee and apprentice absences in the 1830s, occasionally going to the length of having a magistrate order their return, but did not dismiss them.[65] The men fought around the grindstone over whose turn it was, threw gauges and other items at each other, raced round the shop, played marbles, fratched and quarrelled, were found sleeping in the privy, played practical jokes on others, were insolent, and went absent without leave. On one occasion, seven apprentices disappeared for half a day to follow a passing hunt. A cup of 'tea' given to a fellow workman turned out to be urine, provoking a fight. Many of the incidents happened when George was away from the works, and were noted by his brother, John, the bookkeeper.[66] While Thomas Wood stressed the importance of technical competence and hard work at Platt's in Oldham in the 1840s, he also thought his colleagues 'wicked and reckless', satisfied only by 'a rough and rude plenty' and given to gambling while at work.[67]

Would these men have been retained if there were better options? Reliable, qualified employees were in short supply across all iron and steel industries after 1770. The obvious solution was to recruit and train new ones. Matthew Murray was not alone in struggling to keep a full complement of foundry labour, nor in enticing men from other firms. Legislation first enacted in 1770, later extended, and repealed only in 1825, aimed to prevent skilled workers from emigrating, but despite it, many were lured to America or the continent.[68]

Elsewhere, for instance in making toys, buttons and buckles in Midland hardwares, division of labour maximized the efficiency and quality of hand processes.[69] This plan did not suit engineering, where the need was for a spread of expertise with lesser-skilled operatives in support. Furthermore, fine division of labour was feasible only in large workplaces, coming into its own for large batches of identical, or similar, items. Engineering workplaces varied dramatically, with many products small batch or one-off. Steam-engine manufacturers and foundries had no choice but to invest in large machine tools (some needing permanent bedding-in), and in plant like overhead lifting

---

64   Roll, *Early Experiment*, 62.
65   WYAS Bradford, 32D83/12/1.
66   WYAS Bradford, 32D83/32/1.
67   Burnett (ed.), *Useful Toil*, 311.
68   Ashton, *Iron and Steel*, 200; Scott (ed.), *Matthew Murray*, 38–41.
69   Court, *Midland Industries*, 239–40.

equipment. For most textile engineers such scale of investment was not yet justifiable. The shops of Boulton and Watt and Matthew Murray were in 1800 as atypical of engineering as Bean Ing was of textiles. But the organization of textile-machine making at Murray's surely benefited from the plant he had installed for his engine-building activity.

The spectrum of large and small workplaces continued into the 1830s and 1840s, and spanned methods ancient and very modern. Thomas Wood of Bingley (1822–80) was apprenticed to a power-loom maker in his hometown, leaving in 1845 for Platt Brothers of Oldham. Platt, who had started in business in 1821 making carding engines, then employed nearly 2,000 men and used mainly Whitworth machine tools.

> I, who had never worked in a shop with more than eight or ten men and with country-made tools, the very best of which Platts would have thrown away as utterly useless ... had cause to fear that I should not succeed and be found as efficient as other men in a place where no favour was shown.[70]

But Wood found that he could 'drop into place' at Platt's, despite the extreme contrasts, particularly in the narrowness of the tasks he was set.

> Men in large shops are not troubled with a variety of work, but had one class of work and special tools. The men soon became expert and turned out a large quantity of work with the requisite exactness without a little of the thought required of those who work in small shops where fresh work continually turns up, but always the same old tools. I learned quickness and accuracy, also that hard work and application were indispensable.[71]

Wood suggests not that work was more or less skilled in the larger establishment, but that procedures were entirely different. The volume of work enabled Platt to subdivide tasks finely, introduce great repetition, and consequently accomplish much greater accuracy. Laid off by Platt a year later, Wood found work in 'a small engine shop with no proper order or economical way of working' in Darlington.[72]

> At my work I was gaining confidence, of which I was sadly deficient. Of course the class of work was something new to me, but I often saw men pose as good hands, 'clever', who I was persuaded owed their all to bounce and brag ... The improved method of working and supervision has been the death of ... these windbags.[73]

---

70 Burnett (ed.), *Useful Toil*, 310; Tupling, 'Early Metal Trades', 27.
71 Burnett (ed.), *Useful Toil*, 310.
72 Burnett (ed.), *Useful Toil*, 311.
73 Burnett (ed.), *Useful Toil*, 312.

A small firm could in fact improve precision, with or without complex machine tools, by itself specializing, limiting the product range to concentrate on certain components or machines. Hattersley's forte in rollers, spindles and flyers is an example. By the 1820s even these niche trades were further subdivided.

> There are two or three classes of spindle-makers, separate and distinct trades, masters and men. Before the demand was so great as it is, one master spindle-maker would make several kinds of spindles; now since the demand has increased so much, he confines his work to one kind of spindles only; each man confines his work to a smaller variety of spindles, and by that means produces them better adapted to the purpose, and cheaper than others could do before.[74]

For there was as yet no spindle-making machine. Roller-making had also developed as a separate trade.

> Are not a distinct set of mechanics employed in making rollers? – A distinct set, it has been a business in itself.
>
> It is one of the subdivisions of labour? – Yes.[75]

Until finally mechanized, in the 1840s, spindle-making made particular demands.[76] Hattersley was obliged to enter agreements with specialist subcontractors, offering enhanced piece-rates against a commitment to guarantee supplies over a term of years.[77] In 1818 William Sharpe of Keighley, worsted spindle-maker, accepted 36s. a gross for spindles, 6s. more than previously paid, in exchange for binding himself to Hattersley for six years and 'taking the whole management of the spindle department'. Samuel Haggas and William Denton were contracted for five years from 1820 to forge flyers at 13s. a gross, with Hattersley pledging all such orders to them. Joseph Midgley was recruited in 1822 for six years, with a sliding scale of rates according to the size of spindle forged, and was also given the job of repairing tools. In 1825 management of the spindle-forging department was added to Midgley's contract. Similar agreements in the 1820s refer to forging, finishing or repairing flyers, and to roller-turning.

But these components were rather exceptional. Elsewhere in the machine-making process, perhaps self-acting tools were indeed diluting skills. One view is that machines have skill built into them, from which an inference is drawn

---

74 PP Artisans and Machinery, 253, Ewart and Kennedy.
75 PP Artisans and Machinery, 301, Ashton and Bremner.
76 See above, pp. 64–6.
77 WYAS Bradford, 32D83/12/1.

that the workforce is de-skilled. This claim is used to justify cuts in wages and in employee numbers. A study of the products of Springfield Armory (Mass., USA) in the 1840s and 1850s, though, concluded quite differently: machinery here considerably improved quality and precision, while not at all replacing artificers' skills.[78] Contemporary British opinion at times suggested otherwise, though perhaps with some wider agenda. William Jenkinson told the Select Committee on machinery in 1841 that 'by the production of tools, machinery is made by almost labourers'.[79] Jenkinson supported allowing machine exports. This, he believed, would maintain British advantage over countries which produced machinery to a good standard with machine tools and unskilled labour. But Jenkinson distinguished between inferior employees, and the far less dispensable 'best men'; and, he went on, an artificer would make 'one kind of machine his principal study ... by that means each is able to make cheaper and better than they otherwise could'.[80] If de-skilling had progressed as Jenkinson first claimed, such specialization would not have been necessary. Skills had certainly changed, but labour had not been de-skilled.[81]

Outspoken in support of a 'Free Trade in Ability', the famed Lancashire engineer James Nasmyth frequently introduced new machine tools into his works. This lessened the need for 'mere manual strength or dexterity', and had the happy (for him) result of breaking the hold of skilled workers and engineering unions.[82] Semi-skilled employees too were threatened by 'totally unskilled labourers, including young boys, who were competent to act as machine minders'.[83] Nasmyth sparked a strike in 1836 by employing labourers he had trained up without a seven-year apprenticeship. To break the strike he recruited 64 men in Scotland, and some of their relatives followed on, so that Scots made up a majority of Nasmyth's replacement workforce.[84] These men he described as skilled, from small engineering establishments, and

> accustomed to use all manner of mechanical tools. They could handle with equally good effect the saw, the plane, the file, and the chisel; and, as occasion required, they could exhibit their skill at the smith's forge with the hammer and the anvil ... The men had been bred to various branches of mechanics. Some had been blacksmiths, others carpenters, stonemasons, brass or ironfounders; but all of them were *handy* men. They merely

---

78   Gordon, 'Mechanical Ideal', especially 747, 777–8.
79   PP Exportation of Machinery, 96.
80   PP Exportation of Machinery, 98.
81   Robertson and Alston, 'Technological Choice', 331.
82   Smiles, *James Nasmyth*, 213–19; Checkland, *Rise of Industrial Society*, 134.
83   Cantrell, *James Nasmyth and the Bridgewater Foundry*, 227.
84   Cantrell, *James Nasmyth and the Bridgewater Foundry*, 240–2.

adopted the occupation of machine- and steam-engine makers because it offered a wider field for the exercise of their skill and energy.[85]

This could as well have been a profile of an earlier generation of textile engineer in northern England. Nasmyth's account is confusing. Did he consider the Scottish mechanics more or less skilled than his striking workforce? Employing these men during the strike was very much an expedient, and it seems they were not retained. Afterwards no other Lancashire engineer would employ them, because, said Nasmyth, they were considered 'nobs' or blacklegs.[86] Looking back after he retired, Nasmyth mused:

> One great feature of our modern mechanical employment has been the introduction of self-acting tools, by which brute force is completely set aside, and the eye and the intellect of the workman are called into play. All that the mechanic has to do now, and which any boy or lad of 14 or 15 is quite able to do, is to sharpen his tool, place it in the machine in connexion with the work, and set on the self-acting motion.[87]

Elsewhere he wrote:

> The machine tools when in action did not require a skilled workman to guide or watch them. All that was necessary to superintend them was a well-selected labourer ... The work merely required to be shifted from time to time, and carefully fixed for another action of the machine.[88]

Something here is not fully explained: 'eye and intellect' were still required, and machine tools could be run by one unskilled, but specifically only *when in action*. Nasmyth's belief was that 'the thinking had been embodied in [the machine tools] beforehand'. His labour policy was, though, driven by strong objection to trade unions and formal qualifications, and ever confrontational. Nasmyth's version underplays the significant numbers of men needed to oversee processes, to set up and fix machine tools, to trouble-shoot. Furthermore, he said, 'I made an extensive use of active handy boys to superintend the smaller class of self-acting machine tools', and 'observant attention' familiarized them with the basics of the trade. The most promising were then promoted into higher classes of work.[89] This suggests a range of work that, although less than skilled, was not quite as unskilled as Nasmyth held it to be.

---

85   Smiles, *Nasmyth*, 214–17.
86   Cantrell, *James Nasmyth and the Bridgewater Foundry*, 241–2. Evidently engineering unions were then stronger in Lancashire than Yorkshire.
87   Berg, *Technology and Toil*, 155.
88   Smiles, *Nasmyth*, 296–7.
89   Smiles, *Nasmyth*, 296.

Women and children under 14 were conspicuously absent from machine-making, yet within the textile industry female labour had already entered certain areas previously reserved for adult men. The new arrangement in textile factories was one of women and children as low-skill machine-minders, while a male overlooker supervised spinning or weaving sections and solved routine mechanical and operational problems. This bears similar-ities to Nasmyth's system, so why did he not employ women? The union there was powerful, but Nasmyth did not fear exerting his authority. Here was a young and dynamic industry, starting out anew without entrenched employment restrictions. Nasmyth's troublesome workers had only their skill to distinguish them, this their only bargaining counter. If no brute force or training were needed to operate machine tools, if tasks were broken down and allocated by more expert supervisors, then why should he not recruit the cheapest of labour? Women and children were more than low-cost, they were a bargain, and their manual dexterity had elsewhere been turned to good use in factories.[90] Social constraints might have weighed against women working in engineering, yet females were readily allowed into mines, and into other newly automated occupations (like weaving) traditionally male.

Later in the nineteenth century, new industries such as railways, gas and electricity categorically excluded women from most work.[91] In contrast, female labour had been of great important to the modernizing industries, like textiles, previously operating in a domestic setting. Women's experience and knowledge of textiles eased their transition into factory work. However, the workshop environment of metalworking took it outside the home, into another zone. So women were less close to tools and techniques in working metals, and presumably considered insufficiently strong or technically adept to partic-ipate. In other manufacturing trades, it was common and acceptable for young widows to carry forward a family business until sons were qualified and of an age to take over. Socially, there was nothing to stop a widow taking responsi-bility, yet this did not happen in machine-making. The wives of Michael Merrall and John Jubb could not sustain their late husbands' engineering ventures. The problem must have been technical – that 'hands-on' owners were needed, who understood industrial processes and commercial practices – a challenging enough demand at this time even for a man in sole charge. By custom, the metalworking trades were dominated by men, and this became the ethos of the new engineering factories. Yet the suspicion remains that women were excluded not merely for cultural reasons, but that more strength and expertise were required to run a machine tool than Nasmyth would admit.

Journeymen had reason to object if their skills were undermined by machines, so the lack of opposition to new process machinery is also

90   Berg, 'On the Origins of Capitalist Hierarchy', 177.
91   Jordan, 'Exclusion of Women', 274, 294.

significant. This workforce must have seen its future in innovation and improved quality, and in new products. In fact, after about 1824

> the more exacting requirements of machine production made it clear to the employers that while many of the operations previously done by hand could be done by machines, the machines must be operated by skilled men, since an unskilled operator would spoil more work on a machine than he would if engaged in handwork.[92]

Peter Fairbairn agreed that the need for skills remained high:

> In the manufactory of machinery, though more machinery has been introduced, which has greatly improved the accuracy and finish of the work, yet I am of opinion the demand for workpeople in this line is at least equal now to what it has been at any former period.[93]

In 1841 Fairbairn described how a textile works with 20,000 spindles would have 'a score of mechanics, men and boys' doing nothing but keep the machinery in repair. These workers required a more general, flexible, set of skills, while in his own factory operations were subdivided to make do with some 'inferior' men.[94] In a large factory, retaining skilled men who occasionally switched to cover lower grade tasks could be more economical than keeping low-skilled workers who lacked this flexibility. Nasmyth, if his account is accurate, had perhaps set up on the 'dilution' principle, finely dividing tasks in a way that worked only with a very limited product range.[95] But if so, why did he not introduce women and children?

In smaller workshops, repair work and one-off jobs continued to demand all-round skills. Here there might endure the close personal relationship between employer and journeyman which had typified the earlier trade, for the two were near equals 'in skill, intelligence and manners'.[96] Such mutual understanding allowed workers to plan their work, a 'discretion content' being part of the skill.[97] But this element of individual responsibility was likely to fade on the factory floor.

The social aspects of life as a tradesman, along with a sense of who was 'in' and who 'out', emphasized by Wright,[98] suggest a strong solidarity within the trade. During the early stages of mechanical engineering in these

92   More, *Skill and the English Working Class*, 155.
93   PP (HC) 1834 (167) C1, 43.
94   PP Exportation of Machinery, 211.
95   More, *Skill and the English Working Class*, 28–31.
96   Burnett, *Useful Toil*, 251.
97   More, *Skill and the English Working Class*, 22–5.
98   Wright, *Habits and Customs*, 103–7.

centres, though, nothing suggests that craft consciousness translated itself into influencing general terms and conditions, entry or training. Much of the workforce was dispersed, including employees and the self-employed, in a variety of occupations and arrangements.

Apprenticeship

'On the job' training in some kind of textile-engineering establishment became the recognized and sole practical route into the trade. Education did not end at 21, for as technology changed, new skills and knowledge must be absorbed.

> We cannot make machine-makers so quickly as any other description of persons; they require a long time to learn, though all is done and has been, for a considerable time, to increase the number of mechanics.[99]

Larger establishments bound the apprentice to a journeyman; in smaller workshops the master himself would guide.[100]

Two other types of apprenticeship existed in northern textile districts, but neither applied to machine-making. Premium apprenticeship, later called pupillage, required a payment, sometimes considerable, to a master who would instruct and introduce a young man in an occupation such as cloth merchant, millwright, or high-end clock-maker. Such trainees came from a class above the generality of machine-makers, and in the case of merchants, almost of gentry status.[101] Benjamin Gott's father paid £400 to bind his son for four years to the Leeds merchant house of Wormald and Fountaine in 1780.[102] In 1792, 16 guineas was charged to train a worsted stuff-maker.[103] John Jubb asked a premium to take an apprentice (millwright) in 1791.[104] The clock-makers Potts, who worked with William Smith in Keighley, paid to be trained in Darlington: £20 for William in 1793, and then £40 for his son Robert in 1830. Though the father might have trained the boy, the cachet and quality gained from a master craftsman must have been thought worth this cost.[105] Pauper apprenticeship occupied the farther end of the economic spectrum, a means of placing children who would otherwise be a burden on

---

99   PP Artisans and Machinery, 304, Thomas Ashton.
100   More, *Skill and the English Working Class*, 42–4.
101   Wilson, *Gentlemen Merchants*, 23–6; More, *Skill and the English Working Class*, 42, 104–5.
102   R. G. Wilson, 'Benjamin Gott (1762–1840)', *DNB*.
103   Heaton, *Yorkshire Woollen and Worsted Industries*, 303.
104   *Leeds Intelligencer*, 8 Nov. 1791.
105   Potts, 'William Potts of Leeds', 25–6.

the parish. Many became domestic servants, or increasingly were brought from London and elsewhere to work in rural textile factories.[106]

At the time textile engineering came together as an industry, the institution of trade apprenticeship appeared in disarray.[107] Yet it retained its status and, in engineering at least, was confirmed in the 1820s 'as much a passport to a job as it had ever been'.[108] The system rested on an Act of 1563, enforcing a seven-year term in named industries, then becoming customary in others. Whether seven years was appropriate and necessary across every trade was disputed, and eighteenth-century worsted manufacturers denied that the law related to them. In 1806, reportedly 19 out of 20 workers claiming skilled status in West Riding textiles had not served regular apprenticeships.[109]

The Elizabethan statute was repealed in 1813–14, along with wage regulation. After this, employers were free to employ and pay on merit, a practice that spread in the 1820s and came to be called 'the engineers' economy'.[110] Compared with the French, Britain's apprentice system proved notably flexible.[111] This more casual approach to apprenticeship and training suited the industry during its formative years when skilled labour was hard to find. Matthew Murray looked for trainees in 1799 who fell outside the usual pattern.[112]

> Wanted a number of young men from sixteen to eighteen years of age, that would engage for a term of years to work in a steam engine manufactory, where they may learn a valuable business and meet with constant employment.[113]

This, not entirely clearly, hints at management, or at least opportunity to progress. Conceivably such an offer, closer to premium than craft apprenticeship, perhaps involving draughtsmanship and commerce, attracted Charles G. Maclea, Samuel Owen, and others, to Murray's shop. Richard Hattersley too tailored a workforce, in his case centred on conventional craftsmen, largely smiths, trained alongside less skilled individuals for specific needs.[114]

In north Lancashire, Benjamin Shaw depicted a rather informal world of mainly small-scale workshops. At the age of 18 or 19, 'as I could work well at

---

106 See Honeyman, *Child Workers in England*; Heaton, *Yorkshire Woollen and Worsted Industries*, 303.
107 More, *Skill and the English Working Class*, 41–2.
108 More, *Skill and the English Working Class*, 155.
109 Heaton, *Yorkshire Woollen and Worsted Industries*, 102, 106, 301–21.
110 Burnett (ed.), *Useful Toil*, 265.
111 Ó Gráda, 'Did Science Cause the Industrial Revolution?', 231–2.
112 Pollard, *Genesis of Modern Management*, 196–7.
113 Crump (ed.), *Leeds Woollen Industry*, 322–3, quoting *Leeds Mercury*, 3 Aug. 1799.
114 As described above.

the vice', Shaw was formally indentured for three years as a filer and turner in Dolphinholme mill's machine shop. His duties stretched to millwrights' work on the dam and weir; on marrying in 1793 he called himself a whitesmith.[115] Subsequently Shaw worked in Preston, noting wage fluctuations in line with the state of trade. He complained, though:

> But these times of revival in our business is a great evil to our trade in future, for at such times all that can work any at all, can get work anywhere, this encourages many to travel to where they are not known, and pretend to be worksmen, if they can do any thing they get a place, and become old hand very soon, &c this also encourages apprentices, & such as are under agreements to run away &c – and when bad times comes then those that have regularly served an apprenticeship are ill of to get work, for the new upstarts are so many & they will often work for less wages &c.[116]

His own son Joseph (b. 1792) did more or less that very thing:

> Followed the carding business until the year 1824, when trade was good, he got to work in the machine way, he first went to Tom Parrishes shop (this was a throstle spindle and fly shop &c) & some time after to the Spittles Moss shop, under Horrockses concern &c – but trade going bad in the later end of the year 1825, he was discharged and is now tenting a steam engine in Bridge Street.[117]

After 1810, as engineering products and methods settled, the seven-year apprenticeship was re-established as main provider of skilled labour. Apprenticeship, far from an obstacle to the spread of skills, remained a necessity in skilled trades long afterwards.[118] Richard Hattersley trained many apprentices, though records survive only from a later date. In 1832 and 1833, altogether 14 apprentices were recruited, mostly 14 or 15 years of age and contracted for six or seven years. Alongside were less conventional arrangements, older trainees serving shorter terms. William Preston, 'artificer', age unspecified, was bound in 1833 'to be apprentice for two years to learn the art of making spindles, rollers, etc'. His weekly wage, 15s., suggests that Preston was already an adult with some skill, as Hattersley's final-year apprentices were then paid only 8s.[119] This contract – formal, with Hattersley, in a specialist trade – while not a standard apprenticeship, conferred a

---

115   Crosby (ed.), *Benjamin Shaw*, xvi, 7, 26, 28, 30, 33; for Dolphinholme, north of Preston, see Aspin, *Water-Spinners*, 304–12.
116   Crosby (ed.), *Benjamin Shaw*, 64.
117   Crosby (ed.), *Benjamin Shaw*, 88.
118   More, *Skill and the English Working Class*, ch. 7.
119   WYAS Bradford, 32D83/12/1.

recognizable qualification with currency in the labour market. That such an arrangement suited employers as well as workers, and that wage differentials persisted between occupations, both reinforce how real engineering skill was. This was no artificial construct.[120]

But skill was not homogeneous. While coach making was one trade, it encompassed a hierarchy of skill-sets attracting different pay grades. These competences demanded varying levels of training.[121] Was a full seven-year training always needed? Probably not. Hattersley showed that it could be done more quickly, but depending upon previous experience and the demands of the work. William Fairbairn thought that even an expert workman in other kinds of machinery would take 'a considerable time' to train as a cotton-machine maker.[122] Fairbairn spoke of knowledge and technology, while Hattersley thought rather about technique within a narrow product set. How effectively these approaches worked rested also on how the workplace was organized, including the ratio of journeymen and improvers to apprentices and lesser skilled workmen. This measure, set by the 1563 Act, became a matter for employers to try and test.[123] Taylor and Wordsworth were criticized by a political opponent who thought that more than half their employees were apprentices. He was proved wrong, but the true proportion, of 65 out of nearly 300, was evidently acceptable.[124]

Nasmyth was typically robust in opposing traditional forms of apprenticeship. 'Free Trade in Ability', he said, had been responsible for the greatest advances in mechanical invention. Brindley, Smeaton and Watt 'owed very little to the seven years' rut in which they were trained' and everything to their 'innate industry, skill and opportunity'.[125] This overlooked engineering's fundamental needs. There was a limit to how many James Watts could be accommodated in a business. The real need was for skilled workers on shop-floor duties. 'The great inventive genius' Watt, after all, had proved 'entirely unsuited for a business career'.[126] Nasmyth considered that apprenticeship, 'the fag end of the feudal system', which encouraged bad work, bad behaviour and bad example, should be abolished.[127] He allowed trainees to progress according to ability. This, though, was possible only late in the period, and because his factory was technically advanced. Platt of Oldham

120   More, *Skill and the English Working Class*, 164.
121   Burnett (ed.), *Useful Toil*, 250.
122   PP Artisans and Machinery, 569.
123   Heaton, *Yorkshire Woollen and Worsted Industries*, 106.
124   *Leeds Intelligencer*, 2 Mar. 1839; 9 Mar. 1839.
125   Cantrell, *James Nasmyth and the Bridgewater Foundry*, 237–8; Smiles, *Nasmyth*, 217. Of the three, only Brindley had served an apprenticeship, and that as millwright.
126   Roll, *Early Experiment*, 20.
127   Cantrell, *James Nasmyth and the Bridgewater Foundry*, 239.

claimed in the 1860s to have done away with apprenticeship;[128] this too was in large and modern shops. Peter Fairbairn told the Children's Employment Commission in 1834 that he did not indenture anyone, though he taught them, and every one of his employees had entered the trade at 13 or 14. If not quite a formal apprenticeship, this came very close.[129]

There was potentially an advantage in confining training to specific parts of a firm's operations. Workers whose skills were not transferable could thus be retained, and it avoided the cost of full training that enabled workers to later sell their skills elsewhere. Few engineering firms before the 1830s were large enough to consider this, though Peter Fairbairn with his 'corps of black-smiths' may have been approaching it in the 1840s.[130] Fairbairn displayed an open mind about formal qualifications, instead concentrating on specific abilities and qualities. In 1830 he advertised for 'a man who is perfectly competent to engage the grinding and polishing of machinery items. None need apply who are not well acquainted with the business.'[131] A week later Fairbairn sought three 'vice-men' who could 'bring recommendations as being good and steady workmen'.[132] Any recruit, however skilled, presumably required induction into his highly departmentalized factory.

The first apprentices were recruited to machine-making in the 1780s, to be trained by men who had converted from other trades. James M'Connel was sent from Scotland to an uncle in Lancashire in 1781 when aged about 19, and his later partner, John Kennedy, was 15 in 1784 when he joined the same master, a joiner turned maker of carding engines, jennies and water frames.[133] William Smith, son of a corn-miller, was apprenticed in Keighley in the late 1780s.[134] For the new trade to expand as it did after 1800, it must recruit outside the occupations with which it was first associated. Some apprentices were sons of men in dying sectors such as handloom weaving. In 1836, the 14-year-old Thomas Wood, hoping for relief from the 'bondage of factory life' and to become his own master, wanted to be a weaver like his father, or a wool-comber.

> Father would not hear of it, so I was put to be a mechanic. Perhaps it caused as much remark among our neighbours as it would now if I put a son to be a doctor … I wonder if anyone thought of the anomaly of sending me to a power loom maker for my trade while power looms were slowly and surely drying up industrial life. Perhaps my father accepted the inevitable, or, more likely still, I was sent there because there was no other

---

128 Rule, *Labouring Classes*, 121.
129 PP (HC) 1834 (167) C1, 43–4.
130 *Chambers's Edinburgh Journal*, 513, 27 Nov. 1841, 354.
131 *Leeds Mercury*, 8 May 1830.
132 *Leeds Mercury*, 15 May 1830.
133 Lee, *Cotton Enterprise*, 10–11.
134 Hodgson, *Textile Manufacture*, 244; Feather, 'Nineteenth-century entrepreneurs'.

opening. Mechanics, though so plentiful now [1878] were rather scarce then; I am quite sure in saying there were not twenty in Bingley either in shops or factories.[135]

Wood's father earned less than 10s. a week. Thomas, the eldest of 10 children, had been paid 4s. 9d in a mill. As an apprentice, he worked a month or two for nothing, then three months at 1s. 6d, gradually rising to 8s. in his final year, aged 20. Wood's parents accepted a financial sacrifice, short-term yet significant, to make him a mechanic, the decision perhaps taken in a more positive spirit than he had understood. In Armley, formerly a centre of handloom weaving, 20 boys were reportedly apprenticed to mechanics in 1840.[136] The detail of Keighley's 1851 census conveys an impression of the engineering workforce as very young, many of them first-generation engineers in their own families.

By then a seven-year training in machine-making had again become customary. Apprentices aged 14 or 15 generally spent the first months in running errands, familiarizing themselves with tools and materials.[137] Many recruited to engineering at 14 had other work experience, for as much as five years, often in textile factories where some basic understanding of machines and processes was absorbed. Conceivably, apprenticeship could be artificially prolonged, tying the trainee to the firm in order to recoup some of the employer's investment. A competent 19- or 20-year-old commanded less than the fully skilled rate. But in general, men newly out of apprenticeship were not considered quite fully skilled, referred to as 'improver' and routinely moving around in order to broaden their experience.[138] This practice, a mandatory period of 'journeymanship' after apprenticeship, had been a feature of older guilds elsewhere.[139]

Moving on

Tradesmen travelled frequently for work-related reasons: in the course of duties, in search of new employment, or to extend skills and knowledge. Among men newly out of apprenticeship there was a pattern of short-term jobs and relocations. These are sometimes whimsically portrayed as 'restless wanderings' – and in the case of Peter Fairbairn, taken as evidence of an impatient nature.[140] In fact there was some method in these movements,

---

135 Burnett (ed.), *Useful Toil*, 307.
136 Morris, *Class, Sect and Party*, 35, quoting PP (HC) 1840 23, 582–3.
137 More, *Skill and the English Working Class*, 78.
138 More, *Skill and the English Working Class*, 71–2; Burnett (ed.), *Useful Toil*, 309.
139 Ogilvie, 'Economics of Guilds', 181–2.
140 'Sure Foundations', *Alphomega* (1946), 2.

elements of planning and clear direction, the practice well-established and even encouraged by masters.

Thus young journeymen broadened their experience, in new shops, districts, and even countries. Millwrights, their work largely site-based, were mobile through necessity. But they also travelled to gain a first-rate experience post-apprenticeship, perhaps in industries outside their previous sphere. Through a well-planned tour, Fairbairn gained the skill and confidence to convert to machine-making. After apprenticeship with a Newcastle engineer and millwright, he moved to Henry Houldsworth's Anderston Foundry in Glasgow, as foreman and then traveller, twice worked for his famous brother in Manchester, was employed by Rennie in London for a time and passed a year in France, 1822–23, with British companies in Charenton and Paris. After three years of travel, he returned to Houldsworth as a partner, from 1824 until his move to Leeds in about 1826. On his travels, Fairbairn came into contact with 'leading mechanicians and manufacturers of the day', including Rennie, 'then at the height of his fame', and gained 'a fair knowledge of French industrial pursuits'.[141] Two decades later, one of Peter Fairbairn's own apprentices, Charles Cotton, ending his six-year training at Wellington Foundry in 1843, left to superintend machinery in a mill (presumably flax) in Leeds, for six or nine months; then returned home to work for the steam-engine manufacturer, Napier, in Glasgow; to Cocker and Higgins, Manchester flax-machine makers, for six weeks; to Nasmyth's, Patricroft, for some months; then Hick of Bolton, founded by Murray's former apprentice, for a fortnight; to Jenkinson and Bow, cotton-machine makers in Salford, for a few months. All this took less than two years, and in January 1845 Cotton was back in Leeds, working for Samuel Lawson. After less than a year he returned to Glasgow, and then in 1846 to Combe and Dunville, engineers and flax-spinners, in Belfast, where he quickly rose to foreman, leaving after 18 months.[142] In this short time Cotton gained experience with several great names of Victorian mechanical engineering.

With similar intentions the machine-tool manufacturer John Stirk (1838–1917), after an apprenticeship with Joseph Ogdin March in Leeds, moved to work for Peter Fairbairn, then Shepherd, Hill and Co.; Smith, Beacock and Tannett of Leeds; Francis Berry of Sowerby Bridge; Darling and Sellers of Keighley; then Buck and Watkin, and Scott Bros, of Halifax, where he set up in business in 1866.[143] Self-employment was not the only possibility, and former masters might hope for the eventual return of their journeyman,

141 'Death of Sir Peter Fairbairn', *The Engineer* XI (1861), 29; Walker, *Fortunes Made in Business*, 252–4.
142 *The Repertory of Patent Inventions*, XVIII (July–Dec. 1851), 240–4.
143 Calderdale Ref. Lib., P621.

bringing new knowledge and experience.[144] With fast-advancing technology, and resources such as technical books little available, well-planned 'restless wanderings' made sense for young men with ambition.

This was Thomas Wood's idea in 1845. He gave notice to leave the small shop where he had served his time.

> I thought I was deficient in my trade, though I learned, and long practised, all I could learn there. But I heard about new tools, new machines, and new ways of working. I could never hope to see them in our shop, and if I was to learn, and improve, I would do so now before I either married or thought of it.[145]

Attracted, like many engineering workers, to experiencing a large and modern shop, Wood aimed straight for Platt Bros of Oldham. A workshop grapevine, based on 'the travellers' tales of those who have been on tramp', circulated information about employment possibilities.[146] Improving skills enhanced job prospects, for versatility still had a price.[147] But the end of apprenticeship was also the end of job security, so that a youth who could not prove his worth, or whose master was short of work, would leave, even though the wage at 21 was as little as 70 per cent of the top rate.[148] Mobility then became a necessity.

From the time that Benjamin Shaw arrived in Preston in 1795, working at first for the cotton-spinner John Horrocks, and then for a succession of small engineering firms, he entered a world of relatively unstable ventures that made and repaired machinery in rented sheds and workshops close to the factories they served.[149] Shaw did not move far – severe disability limited him – but every so often an employer's precarious circumstances forced him to seek new work.

Though the industry was expanding, and greatly so, still there came episodes of stagnation that interrupted trainee recruitment. Recovery was therefore likely to bring skills shortages – of clerks and draughtsmen besides shop-floor engineers. The long lead-in time and expense of training were reasons to poach labour from other companies.[150] In places, it seems, employers made local agreements to limit this.[151] The 'slow process of breeding' was probably

---

144   More, *Skill and the English Working Class*, 141–2.
145   Burnett (ed.), *Useful Toil*, 309.
146   Wright, *Habits and Customs*, 100.
147   More, *Skill and the English Working Class*, 71–2.
148   Sturt, *Wheelwright's Shop*, 175; Burnett (ed.), *Useful Toil*, 309.
149   Crosby (ed.), *Benjamin Shaw*, xv–xvi, 26, 33; 37–8, editor's fn. 217; and see above, pp. 152–3.
150   Roll, *Early Experiment*, 63.
151   Pollard, *Genesis of Modern Management*, 199.

behind most attempted enticement,[152] though companies had other motives. The feud between Murray and Wood and Boulton and Watt descended from technological rivalry into a desire to irritate and inconvenience by spying and poaching. Skilled men commonly signed for a term of three years, but might be persuaded to abscond. While Kirkstall Forge advertised for skilled workers in Birmingham (and elsewhere), Murray made a more direct approach, his 'emissary' Brennard visiting pubs near the Soho works to buy beer and offer 8s. to 10s. over their weekly rate, with other inducements, to Watt employees. It seems that all but one 'resisted these tempting offers though powerfully seconded by a copious distribution of ale', and duly tipped off Watt. Murray had tried to entice a contracted engine-erector, Gavin McMurdo, who worked frequently in Leeds. Boulton and Watt's response was a three-year extension of McMurdo's bond, and a pay increase from 20s. to 25s. a week with added bonuses. The firm also paid loyal staff a Christmas gratuity.[153] Meanwhile, Watt persuaded former employees back to Soho, while milking them of information about the Round Foundry's workings.[154]

These episodes were exceptional, and relationships generally more cordial. This was especially so with former employees, journeymen entering business for themselves. As with masters and men in the West of England clothing industry, rather than being viewed with hostility as 'nascent competitors', the start-ups received support and credit.[155] There were mutual benefits. Subcontracting was not itself a stage of industrial development, but a technical and commercial convenience for all concerned.[156] It spread production costs, and enabled component production with a maximum of precision while the customer avoided the potentially heavy commitment of taking on additional employees. Contracts guaranteeing a level of work and pay also offered security to the component manufacturer.

So there was a range of possibilities. Distinguishing between employed and employer, supplier and customer, was not always clear-cut in textile engineering. Putting out to subcontractors, switching methods of payment between day rates and piecework, carrying out freelance work in various premises, using casual, otherwise-employed, labour, or laying off regular workers, all blurred relationships. Added to this, component-makers might move from exclusive contracts to develop a broader customer base, becoming

152   Pollard, *Genesis of Modern Management*, 206.
153   Turner, 'Fenton, Murray and Wood', 2.8, 2.14–19. Scott (ed.), *Matthew Murray*, 33–41, omits letters reflecting badly on Murray's conduct.
154   Turner, 'Fenton, Murray and Wood', 3.6–8; Scott (ed.), *Matthew Murray*, 34–41. Boulton and Watt had earlier tried to entice David Wood from the partnership: Thompson, *Matthew Murray*, 109.
155   Randall, *Before the Luddites*, 92.
156   Pollard, *Genesis of Modern Management*, 39–47.

a much larger concern, like that of Jonathan Hattersley, the Leeds spindle- and flyer-maker, a younger son of Richard.[157]

The close links with former employees show up in Richard Hattersley's records. Michael Merrall, the smith trained up by Hattersley, left him in c. 1808 after more than a decade, but the two continued to supply each other with parts and materials until Merrall's death in 1819.[158] Hattersley's key employees of 1808–09, Richard Fowler and Robert Skaife, seemingly took the well-trodden and logical path into self-employment.[159] In 1829, spindles, flyers and other parts were supplied to 'Skaife and Co., Banks Mill'.[160] Fowler, having gradually moved from day to piece-rates by 1809, received payments from Hattersley during the 1820s as 'Richard Fowler, Son and Co.', presumably for subcontracted rollers.[161]

For a while it is true that subcontracting continued to be significant to the workings of engineering; the subcontractors themselves were growing in size, no doubt reflecting investments needed to achieve new expectations of quality. Small-scale self-employment was still possible, perhaps in repairs or making specialist components, but opportunities for journeymen to set up like this were much diminished. New paths opened, though: moving between firms to increase experience, finding a niche to improve earnings potential through piecework.

The industry's immense expansion from the 1820s entailed returning to a traditional style of apprenticeship, though skill shortages recurred during the 1820s and 1830s. Then, most entrants joined as apprentices, many of them local and attracted from dying trades like hand-weaving by the employment opportunities and relatively high pay and status of textile engineering. Even the growing regimentation of the industry may have appealed, offering a measure of stability attractive to those who had seen the insecurity of other trades.

157 See app. 2.
158 WYAS Bradford, 32D83/2/2.
159 WYAS Bradford, 32D83/10/1.
160 WYAS Bradford, 32D83/15/2.
161 WYAS Bradford, 32D83/10/4.

6

The Social Life of the Engineer

Any snapshot of a northern manufacturing centre between 1770 and 1850 will reveal a wide assortment of ventures, comfortably out of step with one another. Manual worked alongside mechanical, large and coordinated workplaces neighboured upon small and traditional shops, goods were shipped around the world and also served very local consumption, production systems were quite at odds.

Because change was not linear, nor did it move in discrete stages, each and every industrial district accommodated many points of difference. Disparate environments co-existed successfully because commercial and individual connections allowed them to do so. If knowledge and resources were not immediately on hand, then within the circle of acquaintance would be a means to locate what was needed. Local economies whose component parts were fascinatingly variable contained many elements of mutual dependence, constant transaction between ancient and modern.

From this, certain localities emerged so strongly, so closely identified with a particular occupation, that their specialism was almost impenetrable by others. Peter Fairbairn, employer of 550 workers and £50,000 to £60,000 in capital, explained in 1841 that making cotton machines was so 'thoroughly localized' in Manchester, and likewise flax-machinery in Leeds, that 'It is very difficult to obtrude any other places afterwards, from their possessing all the requisite information, which puts them in a superior position as compared with almost any other place.' Flax-preparing centres in Scotland and Belfast, like Leeds itself, were almost wholly served by Leeds machinery.[1]

Defined by their contrasting products and customers, specialized almost from the start, each engineering centre was unique and distinct. There were also significant common features, with many mutual and overlapping interests and affairs. At such points, where textile engineers met and mixed – formally and otherwise – with each other and the wider world, rested the soul of the trade. How did social exchanges connect into industrial life? And does this social context enable the trade's ethos to be in any way re-captured? In this of all industries, the culture, its levels of collaboration and mutual support (or

---

[1]   PP Exportation of Machinery, 208, 210, 220.

otherwise), is weighted with great significance. The answers to why machine-making advanced as it did are rooted in social relations and individual aspirations, in a world of increasing complexity.[2]

Meeting places

Outside working hours, blacksmiths' shops, warm and bright, were an enticing place to congregate: 'This was one of the great gathering places of the village gossips, especially on cold winter nights, when the glowing forge shed its cheerful light across the deserted market place.'[3] Here – and also at inns and barbers' shops – newspapers were shared and read aloud.[4] To other workplaces, too, people were drawn, to discuss politics, scandal, and business. Textiles had its formal venues in cloth halls and markets, and the offshoot inns where visiting merchants had their base in town. Many public mills had opened – around Pudsey and Farnley there were about 10 scribbling mills by 1815 – giving plentiful opportunity to share information, find work or workers, strike deals. The diary kept by Joseph Rogerson, 1808–14, profiles the social and business callers to his Bramley scribbling and fulling mill, friends and neighbours as well as suppliers, customers, and carriers. In 1808, 'Mr Wetnell from Low Moor Foundry din'd at our house today', and Rogerson visited Low Moor a number of times. He and his associates journeyed frequently to collect debts and call on customers, and to fairs, markets and races, at some far distance.[5]

Travel was onerous and time-consuming, especially from the rural outposts. Robert Heaton of Ponden delegated and shared errands where he could.[6] But not every interchange could be entrusted to others, and riding through the textile districts meant staying in touch, commercially and technically, with industrial life. Equally important was to learn of fluctuating fortunes, and about ventures in different trades and places. In these exchanges commercial practices evolved, and so too a business ethos.

For both textile manufacturers and engineers, many roads led to Kirkstall Forge. Developed by the Butler family from 1778, the forge's wide influence across northern textile districts is apparent from Thomas Butler's late-eighteenth-century diary. The forge kept very busy, with customers, suppliers and contractors constantly filing to its doors. Butler also travelled frequently into Lancashire, via Otley and Keighley to Burnley and beyond, sometimes

---

2   Nowotny, *Cunning of Uncertainty*, especially 8, 15.
3   Peel, *Spen Valley*, 297–8.
4   Lawson, *Progress in Pudsey*, 60.
5   'Diary of Joseph Rogerson', in Crump (ed.), *Leeds Woollen Industry*, especially 90, 94, 72.
6   WYAS Bradford, DB2/6/3.

returning through Manchester and Halifax, collecting money and orders, dealing with insolvencies, helping friends, breakfasting and drunkenly dining with contacts in the towns where he stayed.[7] Additional to this were Kirkstall Forge's longstanding links to ironworks further south, particularly Wortley.

The social life of the forge

Ironworks proved to be a melting pot of people as well as metal. Their customers came from many industries and from the public at large, for the forges supplied cast and malleable iron, and finished goods as well as metal for reworking. The engineering trades, very consequential as customers, had particularly close working relationships here.

Larger forges worked for engineers just as public fulling mills did for textile manufacturers, places of business where acquaintances were made and information shared. The ironworks held customized patterns for cast-iron machine parts, and supplied wrought iron in forms suitable for nail-making, wire-drawing, and other metal trades.[8] Their status in machine-production was essentially that of subcontractor, though geographically more stretched than most. Ironworks, and ironmasters, bridged Yorkshire's textile and metalworking regions. The connection was as much social and familial as it was industrial, and was of long standing. A main hub of this network since the late-seventeenth century had been the district around Wortley, between Sheffield, Barnsley and Penistone. Wortley Top Forge sits on the Don, site of a bloomery from early in the 1600s, and probably a Cistercian ironworks before then.[9] Later, a market into the woollen districts was well-established: iron (presumably forged in Sheffield) was supplied for shear-making; Wortley produced iron for wire-drawers in the immediate locality and further afield, which was used in card-clothing; and the Top Forge slitting mills sent rods to nailers in Ecclesfield and Tankersley.[10]

This industrial activity was based upon Tankersley ironstone, the neighbourhood also rich with coal outcropping on a line running south from Huddersfield to Sheffield. From about 1660, various forges and furnaces were gradually absorbed into combines owned by two gentry ironmaster families,

7   Butler (ed.), *Diary of Thomas Butler*, 3 and *passim*; Butler, *History of Kirkstall Forge*, 45–6.

8   See Hayman, *Ironmaking*, 9–11, 29–33.

9   Johnson and Worrall, *Top Forge, Wortley*. Barry and Margaret Tylee and Ted Young gave insights into Wortley Top Forge and other south Yorkshire industries.

10 Raistrick and Allen, 'South Yorkshire Ironmasters', 174; Andrews, *Story of Wortley Ironworks*, 32. For nail-making, see above, pp. 131–3; for localized specialisms, Hey (ed.), 'Militia Men'.

the Spencers and Cottons, and their associates.[11] The centre of operations fell within the southernmost point of the West Riding, but two important works lay in the textile districts: at Colne Bridge, Huddersfield, and near the former Cistercian forge in Kirkstall, Leeds.[12] Grouping forges into syndicates smoothed individual profits and losses. While not intended to integrate production, this may have occurred to a degree. And while relations within the grouped forges and furnaces were close, they were not always cordial.[13]

This earlier history of ironworking in south Yorkshire, describing a strategy which peaked some time before 1750, is relevant to engineering in the Yorkshire textile districts a generation later. The older industry sowed seeds of connection, underpinning the transfer of skills, knowledge and other resources. Especially striking is the association of Wortley, Colne Bridge and Kirkstall forges. William Cotton and Thomas Dickin, cousins in partnership managing the forge and slitting mill at Colne Bridge, took over the Kirkstall lease in 1676, and brought in John Spencer of Cannon Hall, Barnsley, a cousin of Cotton, as financier of a new slitting mill there.[14] Another Cotton, perhaps William's father, ran Wortley Top Forge at this time. Around 1700, a syndicate including first Thomas Dickin, and soon John Spencer, absorbed the Top Forge.[15] Management linkages continued to the mid-century. Matthew Wilson and James Oates, of the Wortley forge, joined a Mr Burley as partners in Kirkstall and Colne Bridge in 1722.[16] John Watts (1683–1751) of Barnes Hall, Ecclesfield, was the dominant figure and managing partner at Kirkstall from 1720 until his death.[17]

The Spencers and their associates lost ground by not embracing the new technology of coke-made pig iron, and withdrew from the iron industry c. 1750.[18] After Matthew Wilson died in 1739, his nephew John Cockshutt assumed management of Wortley. Cockshutt's sons proved to be great innovators, early adopters of Cort's puddling process, in 1787. The method,

---

11   Raistrick and Allen, 'South Yorkshire Ironmasters', 168–9, 172–3; Hayman, *Ironmaking*, 21, 32.

12   Sellars, 'Iron and Hardware', 395; Raistrick and Allen, 'South Yorkshire Ironmasters', 170; Cruickshank, *Headingley-cum-Burley*, 225–6.

13   Butler, *History of Kirkstall Forge*, 2–8.

14   Cruickshank, *Headingley-cum-Burley*, 231–5 and *passim*; Butler, *History of Kirkstall Forge*, 5, 2–8. For interrelationships of Yorkshire ironmasters (though mainly non-Quaker) see Raistrick, *Quakers in Science and Industry*, 152–60; Hayman, *Ironmaking, passim*.

15   Andrews, *Story of Wortley Ironworks*, 27, 29, 40–3.

16   Andrews, *Story of Wortley Ironworks*, 46.

17   Butler, *History of Kirkstall Forge*, 2–8; also information from commemorative stone found at Kirkstall, 1937: Leodis collection of Leeds images, http://www.leodis.net, accessed 10 Oct. 2017.

18   Raistrick and Allen, 'South Yorkshire Ironmasters', 177; Cruickshank, *Headingley-cum-Burley*, 232–3. For this innovation's adoption, see Rydén, *Production and Work in the British Iron Trade*, 27–32.

refining cast iron into good wrought-iron bars on a large and economical scale, demanded high skills of the workforce.[19]

At this time Kirkstall came under new management, when John Butler took over the lease in 1778.[20] Butler rebuilt the slitting mill as a plate mill, renewed the water-wheels, and added a screw mill. A decade later much of the plant was converted to workshops to make finished items, primarily domestic goods. Puddling started at Kirkstall in 1797. The unprofitable screw mill, with a 'great stock of screws we have on hand', almost closed in 1798, though enduring until 1807.[21] Thomas Butler thought that his father offered too many products: 'Our business upon the whole is tolerably brisk – save the screw trade which [is] going to decline. It is a trade that requires more attention than we can possibly bestow upon it.'[22] Ten days later, though, salvation arrived: 'Rhodes came after dinner. He wants a very large quantity of screws making to fasten down an iron waggon-way – of near four miles in length; it will be a good job for us.'[23] A printed price list, undated, shows that Kirkstall supplied standard sizes of screws, ½ in. to 3 in., and customized to other specifications.[24]

Butler's comment implies that the forge lacked specialist skills to take screw-making further. It was a niche, a sought-after expertise, and retaining workers was doubtless difficult. Richard Hattersley worked there only briefly, c. 1788–89, before (it seems) being poached to manage a similar works in Keighley.[25] Two important advances in screw-cutting lathes and techniques were made during this period, first that by Jesse Ramsden in about 1770. Then came a major breakthrough in 1800, by Henry Maudslay, who had trained in London under Joseph Bramah, the brilliant engineer whose early education was at Silkstone – at the town school endowed in part by John Cockshutt of Wortley Top Forge.[26]

Losing their screw business did not overly concern the Butlers. 'Tolerably brisk' was the usual state of the iron trade at this time, demand booming during years of war, of which there were very many between 1750 and 1815.[27] Post-war, many smaller foundries and forges in Leeds – the likes of Cawood,

19 Andrews, *Story of Wortley Ironworks*, 44; Johnson and Worrall, *Top Forge, Wortley*, 5; Sellars, 'Iron and Hardware'; Hayman, *Ironmaking*, 46; Marilyn Palmer, intro. to Angerstein, *Illustrated Travel Diary*, xvii.

20 Cruickshank, *Headingley-cum-Burley*, 235.

21 Butler, *History of Kirkstall Forge*, 15–16, 46, 32; WYAS Leeds, KF 4/4, scrap iron ledger containing accounts for new forge, 1780s; 6755/10, inventories, 1783–84.

22 Butler (ed.), *Diary of Thomas Butler*, 198, 6 Feb. 1798.

23 Butler (ed.), *Diary of Thomas Butler*, 200, 16 Feb. 1798.

24 WYAS Leeds, 6755/4, scrapbook 1779–1951.

25 Hattersley bible; see app. 1.

26 Cossons, *Industrial Archaeology*, 133–4; McNeil, *Joseph Bramah*, 14.

27 Hayman, *Ironmaking*, 9–10.

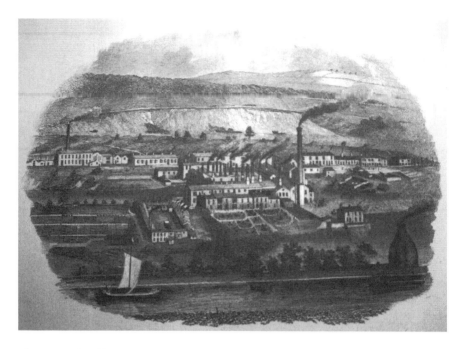

Plate 8. Kirkstall Forge in 1830, with Leeds and Liverpool canal in the foreground
Source: Butler (ed.), *Diary of Thomas Butler*, facing p. 70.

Pullan and Shaw – found new direction, into structural castings, kitchen and other domestic ware, gas or railway plant.[28] Starting with Matthew Murray in 1796, the leading textile and machine-tool engineers moved to integrate operations, with foundries alongside machine shops. Indeed, larger machine-making factories adopted the name of foundry to describe their whole operation – Round, Union, Wellington, Midland Junction.

In Bradford, after the Bradford Canal Co. in 1774 linked its town centre basin to the Leeds and Liverpool canal at Shipley, in 1780 a gravitational waggon-way was constructed from the south to connect Low Moor, Wibsey and Horton collieries with the waterway. Several new ironworks took advantage, transporting limestone economically into Bradford, and exporting processed iron by the same route.[29] The first, established at Bowling in 1788 by a group headed by John Sturges of Sandal, John Elwell of Wakefield, and the Leeds financier Richard Paley, was technologically advanced. The partners

28 See app. 2.
29 Dodsworth, 'Low Moor Ironworks', 122–3.

were soon called to account for a pirated Boulton and Watt-style engine.[30] Elwell left to set up Shelf ironworks in 1794, with Samuel Aydon, a Wakefield ironfounder, and John Crawshaw.[31] Aydon and Elwell supplied cast-iron rails for early colliery waggon-ways and after 1815 became noted for their iron bridges. Their works were taken over in 1824 by the Low Moor Co.[32]

Low Moor is the best known of the south Bradford group. Its partners, Richard Hird, John Jarratt and Joseph Dawson, bought the manors of Royds Hall and Wibsey in 1789. The ironworks opened on Wibsey Low Moor in 1791, Dawson having resigned his Unitarian church ministry to manage the venture. He was the only partner with technical knowledge, as a practical scientist with a particular expertise in chemistry, and also industrial experience from mining coal near his chapel in Idle.[33]

The original blowing engines were designed by Edward Smalley, Low Moor's resident engineer, and made at Emmett's foundry, Birkenshaw. Plates came from Kirkstall, and so, it seems, did iron, until the coal and iron measures on the company's own property were fully explored. There was another link back to Silkstone, where mining rights were acquired in 1803. Between 1795 and 1798, Low Moor produced 2,000 tons of iron a year.[34] Wrought-iron production began in 1801, when the first forge was installed.[35] Company output included domestic items, iron for textiles and engineering, and from 1795, munitions.[36] In fact the first hydraulic press deployed in the Yorkshire textile industry was made here, for Benjamin Gott and constructed under the eye of Joseph Bramah.[37]

The Bowling Iron Co. maintained an agent and office in Leeds, promoting sales of its goods to engineers, especially to smaller businesses.[38] Like the Leeds foundries, the Bowling company was from time to time a significant creditor when engineering businesses collapsed. Few insolvencies were as complicated as that of Zebulon Stirk, in which Bowling first rescued the machine-maker, then acted as his main assignee, only to have its former Leeds agent sued by Stirk. Such proceedings confirm where engineers obtained their

---

30 Long, 'Bowling Ironworks'.

31 John Crawshaw (1746–1819), gentleman, of Button Hill, Sheffield, a distant relative of Walkers, Masbrough ironfounders, may have been their partner: D. Hey, 'Walker family', *DNB*. John Suter added information on south Bradford ironworks.

32 Parker, *Illustrated History*, 159–60; Dodsworth, 'Low Moor Ironworks', 136; information from J. Suter.

33 Dodsworth, 'Low Moor Ironworks', 124–8; Sellars, 'Iron and Hardware', 399.

34 Dodsworth, 'Low Moor Ironworks', 124–6, 131; Parker, *Illustrated History*, 15–17.

35 Dodsworth, 'Low Moor Ironworks', 129; Sellars, 'Iron and Hardware', 399.

36 Sellars, 'Iron and Hardware', 399–400; Dodsworth, 'Low Moor Ironworks', 128.

37 Crump (ed.), *Leeds Woollen Industry*, 225–7, Gott to Bramah, 1802; McNeil, *Joseph Bramah*, ch. 7. The press was not a success.

38 Baines, *Dir.* (1822), 115; Baines and Newsome, *Dir.* (1834).

castings and wrought-iron supplies. Cawood and Gothard handled Drabble's bankruptcy, and in 1837 Bierley Ironworks and J. O. March of Union Foundry were assignees in the collapse of Brook, Raper and Brook, ironfounders and machine-makers at The Bank.[39]

Industrial families

The south Yorkshire ironmasters set a tone. They had robust commercial links into west Yorkshire, they intermarried and promoted family members within the combines, and their forges were a focus of intermingling.[40] Socially and financially they stood relatively high. Later ironworks in Leeds and Bradford, from c. 1780, lacked the sense of empire. For the artisan founders of machine-making, iron foundries and larger forges served as founts of information as well as iron. This familiar model yielded its influences on the new engineering, if subliminally.

Connections between Wortley and Leeds, Kirkstall and Keighley, have been described.[41] So have complex intermarriages between engineering families such as the Drabbles, Jubbs and Hattersleys.[42] Even a generation later, all four of Joshua Wordsworth's children married into a group of wool-comb innovators. Wool-combing, the holy grail, was the final major textile process to defy mechanization. The Noble principle was not new but was impracticable before the 1850s, when a feed system was devised by Tavernier, Donisthorpe and Crofts. This, 'admirabl[y] construct[ed] by the firm of Taylor, Wordsworth and Co.' later delivered great profit to the company.[43] In 1844, Elizabeth Wordsworth, the eldest daughter, married George Edmund Donisthorpe, wool-comb innovator in Leicester and, from 1836, holder of patents taken in 1842 and 1843 in Yorkshire.[44] In 1848 Joshua Taylor Wordsworth married Donisthorpe's niece and, after she died, her sister. Mary Ann Wordsworth, Joshua's second daughter, married Ferdinand Raphael Tavernier, a French machine-maker 20 years her senior, who was involved with patenting wool-combing technology; the youngest daughter, Ellen, was married to John Crofts, woollen and worsted spinner and collaborator of Donisthorpe.[45]

This Wordsworth example is remarkably intense, but there are multiple

39 See app. 2, Drabble and Stirk; *Leeds Mercury*, 22 July 1837.
40 Butler, *History of Kirkstall Forge*; Raistrick and Allen, 'South Yorkshire Ironmasters', *passim*.
41 See above, pp. 91–3.
42 See app. 1 and 2.
43 Burnley, *History of Wool and Wool-Combing*, 379.
44 *Leeds Mercury*, 13 July 1844; Burnley, *History of Wool and Wool-Combing*, 156–8.
45 *Leeds Intelligencer*, 29 Jan. 1848; information from Stephen Wordsworth.

instances of partnership and intermarriage, and strong bonds through training and trading, subcontracting and other employment. This is unsurprising in an artisan-initiated industry which retained an impetus for family-based security. The drive was still for a viable business to bequeath, useful training for sons (even if they were not ultimately absorbed into the family firm), and advantageous marriages for daughters – the advantage sometimes benefiting the business as much as the daughter. And alongside, opportunities arose to offer good turns, to brothers and the wider family, to former apprentices, or other acquaintances or distant relatives from a home village. The favour might help all parties. Knowing the person's abilities and character, the master saw potential to fill a particular role. As success grew, both Wordsworth and Hattersley brought relatives from south Yorkshire, while also supporting family members who had chosen to remain.

There is an intriguing entry in Richard Hattersley's wage books. Briefly, John and N[athaniel] Hattersley, probably his uncle and younger brother from Ecclesfield, were paid to work in Keighley. Most likely they were nailsmiths, or some other type of metalworker. On one reading, they came to assist for a few weeks when Hattersley's workshop was busy; but this was late in 1796, coinciding with the launch of south Yorkshire's first known spindle-making ventures, in Ecclesfield and Grenoside. Could it be that the pair were trained as spindle-makers in Keighley, returning home to build a new trade and supply spindles back to Hattersley?[46] If so, here is further cross-pollination of technical skill within extended family networks.

Social mixing

To list the places in which people came together with some purpose – that is, in a way that was more than casual – is a simple task. More difficult is to establish with any clarity how their exchanges impacted upon working relationships within machine-making. Commercial networks, including customers, suppliers, financiers and workforce, are most obvious. Beyond these, other forces were at work. Transactions were underpinned by priorities, values and beliefs which at a distance of two centuries are unfamiliar and less easily appreciated. In particular, family responsibilities and religious affiliations weighed heavily and could prevail over other business considerations. This was not necessarily detrimental to industrial progress – indeed it might have the reverse effect, by strengthening bonds, developing trust and stabilizing the trade, thus enabling advance and growth. The social and

46 WYAS Bradford, 32D83/6/1, and Table 5.2; Bayliss, 'Damstead Works, Dronfield'.

belief systems which informed their own perceptions and priorities were not marginal. They lay at the heart of how the new engineering worked.[47]

These northern innovating communities were rooted in such values. The culture of the village and small town, and of the artisan, took in matters of religion, education, clubs within trades, and social groups such as freemasonry. It may be too much to claim a more fundamental influence at work among the engineers, generating great vision and confidence, but the achievement seems more than a matter of shared beliefs breeding some measure of loyalty and trust. Pacey suggests that the 'work ethic' held to explain the industrious drive of certain cultures cannot account for success in invention. For innovation requires an ability to visualize, to imagine, and to search for practical means to accomplish an idea.

> Even today, in the most technical of contexts, innovation is an imaginative act. One reason why thirteenth-century Europeans proved to be so good at it was simply that they were very imaginative people. There was plenty to stimulate the imagination – in … symbolism … in the religious mysticism of the time.[48]

This idea transfers into what we know of late-eighteenth-century textile districts. More was at work than commerce's limited considerations. Diverse aspirations, a wider context, moved, inspired and motivated. It was something other than the tribal narrowness of having education, religion or locality in common. If loyalties and liabilities did prompt certain courses of action, any allegiance to co-religionists did not constrain them. But in any case, within machine-making there were no dominant sects, no groups of Huguenots or Quakers, on which to build such an explanation.[49] Fraternity lay elsewhere.

Without doubt, to many within these communities, religion was a profound matter. Church was a large part of social life and education, particularly for nonconformists. Joseph Rogerson, though an Anglican, would go some long distance to hear nonconformist sermons.[50] Cornelius Ashworth, a convert from Independent to Baptist, was an assiduous chapelgoer in Halifax and on occasion travelled great distances, to Bradford and beyond, to catch a famous preacher.[51]

---

47   See Brown and Rose (ed.), *Entrepreneurship, Networks and Modern Business*, introduction; also Caunce and Cookson chapters in Wilson and Popp, *Industrial Clusters and Regional Business Networks*; Cookson, 'Quaker Families and Business Networks'.
48   Pacey, *Maze of Ingenuity*, 85.
49   The Huguenot textile innovator Lewis Paul has no known northern equivalent. The Leeds merchants Busck/Busk and Bischoff were not Huguenots, nor apparently was the ironfounder Timothy Gothard. See 'Busk, William (1769–1849)', in Thorne (ed.), *History of Parliament*; Clay (ed.), *Familiae Minorum Gentium*, 10–11; app. 2.
50   'Diary of Joseph Rogerson', in Crump (ed.), *Leeds Woollen Industry*, 70.
51   Davies *et al.* (eds), *Cornelius Ashworth*, 36–40, 166, *passim*.

The new engineers belonged to a range of established and nonconformist churches. Leeds machine-makers were mainly Anglican or Congregationalist (Independent).[52] In Keighley, several were Methodist, and William Carr a recusant Catholic, with the remainder mostly Anglican. Unusually, some adhered to the New Jerusalem church, known as Swedenborgians.[53] Religious groups associated with a better-educated middle-class were not represented in machine-making, though found among ironfounders: the Unitarian minister and chemist Joseph Dawson at the Low Moor Co.;[54] and prominent Quaker ironmasters and merchants such as Lees of Oldham, Darby of Coalbrookdale, Lloyd of Birmingham, and Benjamin Huntsman, son of German immigrants, who developed crucible steel in Sheffield in the mid-eighteenth century.[55]

Swedenborgism was a brief craze, explored (and rejected) by William Blake, studied by John Wesley and Anglican thinkers interested in radical ideas. Emanuel Swedenborg (1688–1772), a Swedish scientist with mechanical interests, was concerned with the relationship between the physical and spiritual worlds. While connected to the Moravian church, he did not himself found a sect, though one grew from groups studying his philosophy. The New Jerusalem church started in 1783, its creed free will, morality and divine humanity; one of its British co-founders, William Sharp, was among numbers of engineers attracted to Swedenborg's beliefs. Swedenborg's influence on the rituals of Swedish freemasonry was marked, although he himself appears not to have been a freemason.[56]

Swedenborgian churches started up in Embsay, near Skipton; in Leeds (Albion chapel); in Keighley; and near Huddersfield, though seemingly not in south Yorkshire.[57] In Bolton, Samuel Crompton, of mule-spinning fame, became a Swedenborgian in c. 1796.[58] Keighley's New Jerusalem church was an early and important one, with Joseph Wright, partner in Screw Mill, a co-founder and its first minister. Richard Hattersley, then in Wright's employment, had a child baptized at the church in 1791, and was himself

---

52   See Table 4.2.

53   See Table 4.1.

54   Dodsworth, 'Low Moor Ironworks', 124.

55   See occupation index in Milligan, *British Quakers*, 487–516; Smiles, *Lives of the Engineers*, ch. 6; Ashton, *Iron and Steel*, 213–20.

56   Prickett (ed.), *The Romantics*, 131–2, 224; Uglow, *Elizabeth Gaskell*, 170, 508; Nicholas Goodrick-Clarke, review of M. K. Schuchard, *Emanuel Swedenborg, Secret Agent on Earth and in Heaven* (Leiden, Brill, 2011), at http://www.history.ac.uk/reviews/review/1236, accessed 10 Oct. 2017; *John Rylands Research Institute Newsletter*, 13 (1996–97), 9–10. Thanks to Harriet Sandvall for many Swedenborg references. See also http://www.swedenborg.com/emanuel-swedenborg/about-life/, accessed 10 Oct. 2017.

57   J. Wolffe (ed.), *Yorkshire Returns of Religious Worship*, 31 (2005), 29, 95, 172; 32 (2002), 21, 39.

58   Bolton Archives and Local Studies, ZCR, introduction.

initiated the following year. He became a committee member and perhaps introduced Berry Smith, later the church treasurer. The Swedenborgians had a Sunday school from 1791, and opened Keighley's first library; this, a circulating one, started in 1823 with 500 to 600 volumes, most on political and religious themes. The church president in 1820, an artist called John Bradley, was founding secretary of the Keighley Mechanics' Institute, opened in 1834.[59] There is no suggestion that Swedenborgism drew engineers to settle in Keighley, but once there, Hattersley, and maybe others, discovered the church and the related fraternity of freemasonry.

The Leeds Swedenborgian chapel does not appear to have had machine-makers among its congregation.[60] Nor, it seems, had the nearby Unitarians at Mill Hill, other than James Fenton, partner and business manager of Matthew Murray from c. 1796, a linen merchant altogether more genteel than the general run of engineering proprietors. As with their Manchester equivalents, the Leeds Unitarians represented a higher plane of civic and industrial life.[61] Joseph Priestley, polymath, scientist, and towering enlightenment figure, served as minister to the liberal Mill Hill congregation, 1767–73. Here he embarked on celebrated electrical and chemical experiments. Priestley had some acquaintance with industrialists – his wife was sister to the ironmaster John Wilkinson – and after moving to Birmingham joined the Lunar Society alongside Boulton and Watt.[62] Priestley's research, though, had little if any immediate application to industry, and the later Unitarians of Mill Hill, with inquiring and educated minds and progressive views, had no discernible connection with the machine-makers who set up in Leeds a few years after Priestley left.

Keighley's masonic lodges certainly attracted engineers. Richard Hattersley joined the Royal Yorkshire Lodge in 1801, alongside his partner Thomas Binns, member since 1788. Earlier members included the millwright Joseph Tempest, and several braziers and tinsmiths – some (William Taylor, Robert Lawson, Phineas Smith) with connections to Halifax, which shared strong trading links with Keighley. Hattersley's brother Solomon became a freemason at 21, in 1804, and others associated with machine-making followed: Joseph Midgley, a whitesmith aged 21 in 1813, later in charge of Hattersley's spindle-making; Samuel Clapham, mechanic; and John Fowler, machine-maker. William Carr joined Keighley's other lodge, the Samaritan, in 1792, soon after his arrival. William Smith of Braithwaite, the turner and filer, was already a member there, and others joining included George Richardson,

59   Bottomley, 'Keighley New Church'; *Keighley News*, 21 Aug. 1970; Hodgson, *Textile Manufacture*, 86.
60   Table 4.2.
61   Uglow, *Elizabeth Gaskell*, 86–8.
62   R. E. Schofield, 'Joseph Priestley (1733–1804)', *DNB*.

the brass-founder (1794); Carr's son Edward (1801); and a Bingley machine-maker called Samuel Driver (1806).[63]

The lodges drew from neighbouring towns and entertained other visitors, the masonic hospitality reciprocated. Halifax lodges received guests, and perhaps resettlers, from Keighley. There, the Lodge of Probity listed Thomas Binns, a Keighley comb-maker, as a member in 1783. Also admitted to this lodge were two Bradford engineers, Edward Smalley (1792), resident engineer for the Low Moor ironworks, and John Brown (1793).[64] The Halifax Lodge of Harmony had various metalworkers, including wire-drawers and card-makers, among its members. There were several millwrights: James Farrer and Samuel Whiteley, masons from 1791; Mordecai Fortune of Hebden Bridge (1800), presumably a relative of the Halifax man, Samuel Fortune, who supplied slubbing billies to Bean Ing in 1794; and Joshua Bates of Ripponden (1804), likely a brother or other relative of Timothy Bates of Sowerby Bridge, who established Bank Foundry there in c. 1786 and was later a famed builder of stationary steam-engines. Other Lodge of Harmony members were braziers, tinplate workers and smiths.[65]

In other places, notably the United States, freemasonry is identified as an element in the social base of textile-machine making.[66] Not, though, in Leeds where several lodges around the town were well-supported, but not by machine-makers. Hugh Wright, machine-maker, briefly representing the Manchester firm of Wright and White in Leeds, joined the Lodge of Fidelity in Briggate in 1792. He was exceptional in all respects, and external to the Leeds trade.[67] The Leeds lodges attracted gentlemen, professionals and merchants, commerce rather than manufacture.

Locating education and science

When the new engineering came into being, a social divide separated even the most affluent artisan from the merchant and professional class. Status decided access to education, and to scientific circles. Accordingly, much that was novel in machine-making was initiated by artisans whose technical education had gone no further than a workshop training. In an industry so central to the process of industrialization, this is no mere detail. It is a significant finding.

---

63 UGLE, membership lists, Keighley lodges.
64 UGLE, membership lists, Lodge of Probity, Halifax; Banks, *Treatise on Mills*, xxiii.
65 UGLE, membership lists, Lodge of Harmony, Halifax; Crump, *Leeds Woollen Industry*, 24, 215; Bayliss, 'Sowerby Bridge, 1750–1800', 66–7. See also WYAS Calderdale, handlist to the archive of Pollitt and Wigzell, Bates's successor at Bank Foundry.
66 Jeremy and Darnell, *Visual Mechanic Knowledge*, 34–6.
67 UGLE, membership list, Lodge of Fidelity, Leeds.

Indeed, most of those engaged in machine-making before 1850, from business proprietor to journeyman, had no more than a basic education.

A few of the sons of the middle class learnt writing and arithmetic, but very few others learnt anything but reading. Large numbers never entered the door of a schoolhouse – having to work at something when they arrived at school age.[68]

Andrew Ure in 1835 recognized how far 'mechanized talent' had contributed to engineering's remarkable growth, and fully appreciated that this skilled élite had had little or no formal learning.[69] Samuel Owen, who worked for Matthew Murray before 1804 and was later lauded as 'the founder of engineering in Scandinavia', had seen for himself the limits of mathematics at the Round Foundry.

Few knew the simple rules of arithmetic save the clerk in the office. Mr Murray made his calculations with a carpenter sliding rule. I was looked up to as a light and became a companion to my principals and several workmen took lessons in arithmetic from me.[70]

Both Murray and Wood were exceptional technicians, Wood (like another Leeds machine-maker, Samuel Lawson) producing mathematical and other instruments as a spare-time pursuit.[71] Joseph March said of his father-in-law Murray that while blessed with the 'attribute of real genius' and a 'rich mechanical mind', he was 'no mathematician'. But Murray produced 'remarkably proportionate' sketches to instruct those who made his drawings, and these 'show[ed] the strengths very nearly accurate when they were reckoned out'.[72] Benjamin Hick was among his draughtsmen.[73]

Thomas Wood of Bingley, who attended a small local school where he learned to read, followed by two years from age six at grammar school where he studied Latin grammar and writing, though not mathematics, was better educated than the average journeyman of the 1820s.[74] Those schooled in the Scottish system, with its high reputation for maths and practical subjects, generally fared better still. The Fairbairn brothers, M'Connel and Kennedy,

68   Lawson, *Progress in Pudsey*, 58.
69   Ure, *Philosophy of Manufactures*, 427, *passim*.
70   Brotherton SC, MS165/23. Göran Rydén views Owen as highly significant, much written about in Swedish but with no known English biographer. See also Thompson, *Matthew Murray*, 143–4, 159–60.
71   See app. 2.
72   Scott (ed.), *Matthew Murray*, 49. Murray's schooling was presumably rudimentary: Thompson, *Matthew Murray*, 6–7.
73   Thompson, *Matthew Murray*, 178.
74   Burnett (ed.), *Useful Toil*, 305.

and Charles Gascoigne Maclea were all educated, in part at least, north of the border. The wool-comb developer Isaac Holden (1807–97) described his good fortune at having been born in Scotland: 'I should not have had the education I had otherwise … Forty years ago the Scotch were the best-educated nation in the world.'[75] Though Holden's education was spasmodic, he was taught by John Kennedy, 'a man of considerable mathematical and scientific attainments'. Holden afterwards taught mathematics and lectured in science.[76] Such proficiency was highly unusual in textile engineering during his lifetime. Compared to America, Scotland, France and Germany, England's deficit in mathematical education was pronounced, into the late-nineteenth century.[77]

Mechanics' institutes, whatever their original intention when established in the 1820s and afterwards, ranged widely in their offerings, and they educated rather than trained. In Keighley, only about a quarter of institute members belonged to metalworking trades, and most lectures covered general topics. Without doubt, occasional classes in writing, arithmetic, geography and drawing helped some workers improve basic skills. While technical drawing was to prove extremely popular, it was not taught there before the 1850s.[78] The Manchester Mechanics' Institution, founded like the Leeds institute in 1824, aimed to improve workers' general education, and particularly to teach how science might be applied to engineering and other industries. Through this, better opportunities would open for workers, benefiting employers too. But the venture, and others associated, never attracted young men in the hoped-for numbers.[79]

Contact between early mechanical engineers and universities was most exceptional. This was so even for the professional engineer, for whom premium pupillage was the usual point of entry. James Watt was exposed to theoretical science at Glasgow University, but later rebuffed a suggestion that this influenced his steam-engine designs.[80] English universities had little of use to offer: sciences were largely a postgraduate subject at Oxford and Cambridge, with mechanics taught as a branch of mathematics, by repetitive and non-experimental lectures. The first Cambridge chair of engineering – rather, of 'Mechanism and Applied Mechanics' – was created only in 1875.[81] The elder John Rennie's view in 1809 perhaps reflected wider opinion at that time. Rennie was keen on theory but did not want his own son exposed to university

75   *Bradford Daily Telegraph*, 6 May 1897.
76   *Keighley News*, 14 Aug. 1897.
77   Brown, 'Design Plans', 227–8.
78   Lumby, 'Keighley Mechanics' Institute'.
79   Byrom, 'William Fairbairn', 228–33; R. J. Morris, 'Middle-class Culture, 1700–1914', in Fraser (ed.), *History of Modern Leeds*, 213.
80   Tomory, 'Technology in the Industrial Revolution', 158, citing Donald Cardwell, *Steam Power in the Eighteenth Century* (Sheed and Ward, 1963).
81   See for instance Cardwell, *Organisation of Science*, 97, 136–41, and *passim*.

teaching, on the grounds that it would turn him from practical engineering.[82] Apprenticeship tutelage, that is, training members of engineering professions on the shop floor alongside craftsmen, was favoured, and persisted through the nineteenth century. It instilled a due respect for manual skill, but was arguably detrimental to strategic thinking in the industry.[83]

From the 1840s, the more successful machine-makers could have educated their sons in science and theoretical aspects of engineering, at some level. But they did not choose to do this. Instead the boys were brought up in commercial, practical, even linguistic subjects, and commonly served a seven- or eight-year workshop training. Samuel Lawson's son John (1805–83), 'one of the most resourceful mechanics of his day' who very successfully managed the Mabgate works, was conventionally apprenticed.[84] The next generation of Lawsons had more opportunity, but still came back to extended practical training in the works: John's son Arthur, later Sir Arthur Tredgold Lawson Bt (1844–1915), following education at St Peter's School, York, then Winchester and Cambridge; his brother Frederick (1845–1915) after Leeds Grammar School.[85] Peter Fairbairn's only son, Andrew (1828–1901), after schooling in Leeds, Switzerland and Glasgow, then Cambridge and the Inner Temple, where he was called to the Bar in 1852, abandoned legal practice in 1855 to join the family business.[86] The leading Keighley engineers did not reach such educational heights before 1850, and apprenticeship was standard for owners and journeymen alike. But once George Hattersley had recovered from insolvency, by 1844 he chose to send two younger sons to a private academy near Ripon, while another underwent commercial training in Bradford.[87]

Joseph Priestley embodied the distance between spheres of science and practical engineering. He had lived on the doorstep of places where the town's machine-making and ironworking flourished, though he left before it became properly established. But his research was experimental, abstract, of little or no immediate interest to industry. Indeed, for him the flow of practical benefits ran from industry to science, for a nearby brewery supplied a by-product, carbon dioxide, for his famous study of gases.[88]

Priestley was part of a significant Leeds scientific circle. His successor as minister at Mill Hill, William Wood, was a founder of the Linnaean Society.

82   Checkland, *Rise of Industrial Society*, 76.
83   Brown, 'Design Plans', 228–9.
84   *Yorkshire Evening News*, 24 Feb. 1915. John Lawson's deafness possibly restricted his earlier options.
85   *Yorkshire Post*, 2 June 1915; *Yorkshire Evening News*, 24 Feb. 1915; *Proc. Inst. Mech. Eng.*, 89 (1915), 481.
86   Walker, *Fortunes Made in Business*, 279; Jeremy (ed.), *Dictionary of Business Biography* II, 311.
87   WYAS Bradford, 32D83/33/4.
88   Schofield, 'Joseph Priestley', *DNB*.

The surgeon William Hey (1736–1819), distinguished in local intellectual life, was fellow of the Royal Society. These men were close to John Smeaton, to the Low Moor ironfounder Dawson, and to others interested in chemistry, medicine and philosophy.[89] Dawson, whose interests linked science and manufacturing, emerges as unique among local ironmasters in his depth of scientific under-standing. When in 1800 Dawson proposed to the Yorkshire and Derbyshire masters' friendly association that their meetings include formal discussion of metallurgical science, he was the only member prepared to present a paper.[90] As for science making any connection into machine-making – any benefit, proximity, even passing of information – there is no suggestion at all.

What of John Smeaton himself? Not only is he recognized as founder of the civil engineering profession, but he was also a talented mechanic and instrument-maker. Smeaton was born and died at Austhorpe, five miles east of Leeds, and was still alive and active as the first machine-makers gathered in the town.[91] But there is no link, no evidence that Smeaton, in the rather grand situation to which he was born, had any association with the industry embodied in the textile engineers of Holbeck and Hunslet.

Science was for the educated and moneyed, its societies clubs for a small élite. There was a wider group, including Leeds merchants and their families, of people sharing high status and altogether broader interests. They might attend philosophical lectures, but on diverse and eclectic topics, and it was this group who founded the Leeds Philosophical and Literary Society in 1783.[92] It collapsed after only three years, and was revived in 1818. Matthew Murray then became a member, which would have been unthinkable before business success had raised his social standing. So most of Murray's productive and innovative years were lived outside the town's scientific and intellectual clique.[93] Similarly, Joshua Wordsworth and Joseph Taylor were elected to the society in late middle age, in 1838.[94] The learned societies, of Manchester, Bradford and elsewhere, were launched and sustained by clergymen and surgeons. For engineers, membership signalled respectability following on from their industrial achievements. The gatherings were polite, not of practical utility.[95]

89   Morris, *Class, Sect and Party*, 203–4; Musson and Robinson, *Science and Technology*, 153–9.
90   Hayman, *Ironmaking*, 58; Dodsworth, 'Low Moor Ironworks', 129–30.
91   A. W. Skempton, 'John Smeaton (1724–92), civil engineer', *DNB*. Smeaton coined the term, and after his death the society he founded was renamed the Smeatonian Society of Civil Engineers.
92   Musson and Robinson, *Science and Technology*, 153–6.
93   Musson and Robinson, *Science and Technology*, 155–9.
94   Wordsworth, 'Joshua Wordsworth', 39; *Leeds Mercury*, 17 Nov. 1839.
95   Morrell, 'Bourgeois Scientific Societies', 316–20, 330–1. See also Cormac Ó Gráda's important critique of Jacob, *First Knowledge Economy*: Ó Gráda, 'Did Science Cause the Industrial Revolution?'.

Matthew Boulton and James Watt, occupants of a higher social rung than Murray, were connected via the Birmingham Lunar Society to an international scientific network. Yet Boulton, much the businessman, actually cautioned Watt in 1783 against losing commercial focus: 'We are not anxious about the honour of acquiring gold medals nor of making an *éclat* in philosophical societies.'[96] Watt had considered himself a natural philosopher first, and an engineer second, claiming in 1771 to have no experience of 'engineering in the vulgar manner'.[97] By implication 'pure' science, natural philosophy, stood higher than applied mechanics.

While engineering may have been vulgar, that is not to suggest that scientists always had substance to offer. This was a 'golden age of amateurs, cranks, quacks and crazy theorizing'.[98] Dr Jean Theophilus Desaguliers (d. 1744), French-born scientist, lecturer and writer, follower of Newton, and fellow of the Royal Society (and a leading figure in English freemasonry), could not fully understand the workings of the Newcomen engine. *A Course of Experimental Philosophy* (1734–44) betrays this ignorance, exposing the chasm between scientist and practical craftsman.[99] For, as Serjeant Adair pleaded on Richard Arkwright's behalf in 1785:

> It is well known that the most useful discoveries that have been made in every branch of art and manufactures have not been made by speculative philosophers in their closets, but by ingenious mechanics, conversant in the practices in use in their time, and practically acquainted with the subject-matter of their discoveries.[100]

Industry, then, tended to grant science little acknowledgement. But the process of technological innovation itself stimulated scientific enquiry. Industry offered facilities for new kinds of experimentation, and through this, science itself advanced and gained more practical uses.[101] The relationship between the two took many forms. Ironmaking, in which chemists might have taken some closer interest, was in fact 'empirical and collaborative' before Bessemer's breakthrough in 1855.[102] More than that, it is suggested that only an 'amateur' like Bessemer, a non-metallurgist with the 'splendid audacity of ignorance', could have so dramatically experimented with reverberatory furnaces.[103] The theoretical framework of electrical engineering emerged in

96   Quoted in Tann, 'Marketing Methods', 368.
97   Robinson and Musson, *James Watt*, 5.
98   Mathias, *Transformation of England*, 72–3.
99   Rolt, *The Mechanicals*, 5.
100   Quoted in Mantoux, *Industrial Revolution*, 206.
101   Cardwell, *Organisation of Science*, 100.
102   Hayman, *Ironmaking*, 10.
103   G. Tweedale, 'Sir Henry Bessemer, 1813–98, steelmaker', *DNB*.

the 1850s from ad hoc laboratories in the Mediterranean and Atlantic, where scientists laid and tested undersea telegraph cables.[104]

Before then, exceptionally, abstraction did meet practicality. The connection between William Fairbairn and the mathematician Eaton Hodgkinson laid the foundations of structural engineering. Peter Ewart had alerted Fairbairn to Hodgkinson's trials on the strength of cast-iron beams in 1822. Fairbairn then employed Hodgkinson, who managed to produce beams using 25 per cent less material with no loss of strength. This revolutionized the construction of bridges, fireproof mills, and other large structures, and was the beginning of a 20-year collaboration in Fairbairn's premises.[105] Hodgkinson's work encouraged Fairbairn to embark on his own trials on plates and joints in iron-shipbuilding.[106] Hodgkinson's research in 1822, and further work published in 1830–31, were of immediate practical service to engineering, basic to understanding the properties of cast-iron and proving its superiority to timber in many applications.[107] A second remarkable example of theory developing alongside technology involved the younger generation of the Boulton and Watt firm. Their pioneering experiments on gas-lighting from c. 1800 encouraged William Henry (1774–1836) to extend his previous study on the nature of inflammable airs. Henry's work between 1805 and 1821 was 'a hybrid between speculative and industrial inquiry' which laid down basic principles for the gas industry, just as Hodgkinson did for structural engineering.[108] In both cases, Hodgkinson and Henry, members of the Manchester Literary and Philosophical Society, were central – though neither had a direct connection to textile engineering.

In general, was science either useful to, or penetrable by, the engineering workforce? It would seem not. Only with great difficulty could scientific literature be accessed. A small international group of scientists shared ideas in learned journals, these available only to the wealthy and multilingual – men like Smeaton.[109] Relative to the French, literature in English on mechanics, engineering and drawing, from the 1790s up to about 1825, was outdated and limited. English textbooks have been described as 'belonging to an earlier century', work on mechanics and mathematics not having progressed significantly since Newton.[110] Even so, few engineering workers before 1825 would have seen such books, which were expensive, scarce, and unintelligible without

104   Cookson and Hempstead, *Victorian Scientist and Engineer*.
105   Byrom, 'William Fairbairn', 100–1; J. Sutherland, 'Eaton Hodgkinson, FRS (1789–1861)', in Cross-Rudkin and Chrimes (eds), *Biographical Dictionary of Civil Engineers*, 408–11.
106   Fairbairn, 'Experimental Inquiry'.
107   Sutherland, 'Eaton Hodgkinson', 409. John Suter supplied ideas on this point and more.
108   Tomory, 'Science and the Arts'; also 'Fostering a New Industry'.
109   Information from Ron Fitzgerald.
110   Cardwell, *Organisation of Science*, 124; on the then state of mathematics in England, see Enros, 'Cambridge University and the Adoption of Analytics'.

a certain level of education. John Nicholson's *Millwright's Guide* (1830) has a two-page bibliography of published treatises on millwork, the oldest dating from the seventeenth century. To understand all of these, the reader would need an ability to follow the science as well as knowing German, Dutch, Latin, French and English. Robert Heaton listed some of these same books when planning the machinery for his new factory in 1791. Those interesting him were entirely theoretical, on mathematics, mechanics and natural philosophy.[111] Many were over twenty years old, with two – Ditton's *Laws of Nature and Motion* (1705), and Moxon's *Mecanic Exercises* (1695) – published almost a century earlier. The 'nadir of English science' did not find its renaissance until Babbage and Herschel after 1820, so ancient theoretical works were perhaps all that Heaton could identify as even of marginal relevance.[112] Whether he acquired any of the books, or whether they would have helped him, is unknown. As a merchant, and patently an educated man, Heaton was better positioned to access them than any 'untutored mechanic' for whom mathematical theory was difficult and 'far removed from practice'.[113]

But there were new manuals, seemingly designed for engineers and bridging the divide between abstract and practical.[114] John Banks followed his *Treatise on Mills* (1795) with *On the Power of Machines* (1803). Then came Andrew Gray with *The Experienced Millwright; or, a Treatise on the Construction of some of the most Useful Machines*, published in Edinburgh in 1804; followed by the American Oliver Evans' *Young Steam Engineer's Guide* (1805); John Sutcliffe's *Treatise on Canals and Reservoirs* (1816); Robert Brunton and the *Compendium of Mechanics*, published in Glasgow in 1825 and into its fourth edition by 1828; and John Nicholson with *The Operative Mechanic and British Machinist* (1825), reissued in part as *The Millwright's Guide* in 1830.[115] Nicholson's first edition, sold in 30 weekly parts at one shilling each, was more affordable than anything previously. All the handbooks had a straightforward approach aimed at non-scientific readers. In fact, there was only a slender connection to science. The contents were generally basic mathematics and mechanics, practical calculations for the use of millwrights, and specific though simple diagrams of various machines, again primarily for millwrights. Brunton, 'a mechanic of Glasgow', ranged from weights and measures to the strength of materials, but based on experience not abstraction. In pleading for his trade to be better recognized, Brunton suggests that its achievements were not given due credit, and that science was viewed as a higher calling.

111   WYAS Bradford, DB2/6/3.
112   Cardwell, *Organisation of Science*, ch. 5.
113   Checkland, *Rise of Industrial Society*, 74.
114   Emmerson, *Engineering Education*, ch. 14, presents a wider overview.
115   Nicholson is thought to be an alter ego of John Farey: see A. P. Woolrich, 'John Farey (1791–1851), mechanical engineer', *DNB*.

That much-wished-for time appears to be at hand, when mechanics shall not only be acknowledged cunning artificers, but men of science: when the word mechanic shall convey the idea of wisdom and understanding, and the profession, highly fraught with good to man, shall be honoured and respected.[116]

Another of the authors was more in a 'Lit and Phil' mould. John Banks (1740–1805), self-styled 'lecturer in experimental philosophy', was educated at the dissenting academy in Kendal, which the ironmaster John Wilkinson also attended. For many years, Banks delivered public lectures around northern England, including several series in Leeds, a guinea to attend, or 2s. 6d per lecture. Topics included pneumatics, hydrostatics, and specifically water-wheels.[117] Introducing *A Treatise on Mills*, Banks suggested that practical mechanics could benefit from greater attention to theory.

It is true, that we have in the kingdom many intelligent engineers, and excellent mechanics; and there are others who can execute better than they can design, otherwise there would not have been so much money expended in attempting what men of science know to be impossible.[118]

But Banks acknowledged his own limitations: 'The problem concerning the lathe is accurate, but not by any means what I could wish. Some person better acquainted with science may perhaps give a much shorter and simpler solution, but it is the best I could give.'[119] Though he was at one point reproached by John Sutcliffe for inaccurate calculations on water-wheels, Banks enjoyed the respect of William Fairbairn and the elder John Rennie.[120] His approach, in a critique of claims made for the efficiency of water-wheels and other machinery, suggests that debate was carried along in technological rather than scientific forums.[121]

But little in these books relates to textile machinery, beyond the millwright's province of fulling stocks and factory design. Sutcliffe's section on 'carding, roving, drawing, stretching and spinning of cotton' was largely about installing and maintaining machinery. Nicholson, a civil engineer, offered a lengthy section on textile machines which gave a general and historical

---

116   Brunton, *Compendium of Mechanics*, preface.
117   Musson and Robinson, *Science and Technology*, 107–9; additional information and references from John Suter, including *Leeds Intelligencer* advertisements from 5 June 1787, 12, 19 and 26 May 1794.
118   Banks, *Treatise on Mills*, viii.
119   Banks, *On the Power of Machines*, iv.
120   S. Chapman, review of Musson and Robinson, *Science and Technology*, in *Textile History*, 1/3 (1968–70), 373–7; information from John Suter.
121   Banks, *On the Power of Machines*, iii.

account of processes and contained sections lifted from Rees's *Cyclopaedia*.[122]
These textile sections were omitted from his 1830 edition republished as *The
Millwright's Guide*.

Millwrights' work, wide-ranging and slow to change, was a more attractive
proposition for publishers than the new branches of mechanical engineering,
where technology evolved quickly and disparately and with close attention to
changing products. Banks's first book attracted wide interest among proprietors of ironworks, cotton- and flax-spinners, merchants, millers, and many
other industries. His subscribers, though, were overwhelmingly well-educated
and middle-class – more ministers and schoolmasters than mechanical
engineers. In a ten-page list, no Yorkshire textile engineer is identifiable. The
appeal of such books – like that of learned societies – was non-specific, aimed
at an educated readership. Like Rees's *Cyclopaedia*, itself in an eighteenth-
century mould, such books were descriptive, a matter of record not design.

The social chasm between those who practised or followed science, and
the workers in iron and wood, is demonstrable. Nor was there any obvious
bridge crossing the divide, a channel of communication conveying technical
or scientific information. This was certainly so during the decades that saw
textile engineering established as an industry. The two factions inhabited
different spheres, even within the same town. This finding is important,
for it challenges the proposition that the new engineering was a 'top-down'
process, the idea that scientific know-how was vital to this phase of industrialization, and that such knowledge must cascade into workplaces to underpin
mechanical developments. The experience of early mechanical engineering in
Yorkshire shows that this was not the case. In this trade of unique significance, pivotal to the industrializing dynamic, there seems little or no inter-
action between circles of scientists and technologists. But also, the 'science' on
offer was unreliable; early engineers knew little of it, but evidently functioned
well without it.

Science and technology are different things, and neither is superior to
the other. The same applies to education and training, and to theory and
practice. Remove the idea of a hierarchy of concepts and skills, and pay
attention to how this key trade in fact developed. Thus, fundamental flaws
are exposed in the contention that industrial change was triggered in, or even
much influenced by, some higher, external quarter. Historians claiming an
'Industrial Enlightenment' have far underestimated the weight of social class.
Evidence of supposed connections between scientists and technologists is not
found; conduits through which 'enlightenment' reached machine-makers are
not identified.[123] However 'invention' as a concept is cut, and however far its

122   Nicholson, *Operative Mechanic*, 378–415.
123   Mokyr, *Lever of Riches*; Allen, *British Industrial Revolution in Global Perspective*,
239–42.

categories are refined, it has little value if it does not reach people who could make something of it.

The reality was that relationships between scientific knowledge and technical innovations were diffuse and complex, and in flux.[124] In this instance, innovation took more from the scientific method, the experimental tradition, than from 'pure' scientific knowledge. Mechanical inventiveness was driven not by any scientific impetus, but rather stimulated by an encouraging technical and commercial milieu in which craftsmen discovered a new métier. What we see is a practical approach to problem-solving, informed by a strong commercial sense.[125] By 1800, there was some belief 'that the secrets of nature would yield to the efforts to understand them and that enhanced control ... would follow'.[126] Hence the dogged pursuit of solutions to engineering problems by certain innovators, whose methods were mechanical, practical and empirical, and could also be systematic.[127] But innovators were also invigorated by advances in associated technologies – bearings, lubricants, metals, tools – in which the debt to science is more obvious. So while science did have something to offer engineering, the practical achievements of textile engineers owed little to abstraction. The industry developed methods which suited its needs, within a commercial environment which swiftly evaluated any improvements.

The productive community

So was community strategic in shaping the new engineering? Without much deliberate and conscious planning, would this even be possible? And where does competition fit?

But competition and productive association are complementary, not mutually exclusive.[128] In the same industrial environment, Smail's 'host of petty producers' exhibited commercial initiative fully consistent with the cultural context.[129] Among West Riding woollen workers a 'community character ... both dynamic and conservative' has been observed, and it is remarked 'how deeply the social context of manufacturing production

---

124   Mathias, *Transformation of England*, 72.

125   Mathias, *Transformation of England*, 85.

126   Mathias, *Transformation of England*, 85.

127   See, for example, Marshall's early records; notes of mill practice by Gott and others, indicating frequent small improvements; and Heaton's journal of casual but detailed observation: Brotherton SC, MS200/57; Crump (ed.), *Leeds Woollen Industry*, 287–307; WYAS Bradford, DB2/6/3.

128   Sabel and Zeitlin, 'Historical Alternatives to Mass Production', 143–4, building from Proudhon.

129   Smail, 'Manufacturer or Artisan?', 792–3.

influences its potential for transformation'.[130] In machine-making, less entrenched in custom than the woollen industry, change was less painful and more readily effected.

The structures in place owed a debt to older industrial forms, and looked rather different from a business network as now understood. Textile engineering launched on a system of connections intrinsic to function and advancement.[131] It was founded upon tenets of common interest and collaboration, within which competition had its place. The new engineering rested on a stable base, of a common framework and shared knowledge, which did not inhibit individualism. Personal opportunities were grasped, private rather than collective interest served. But the dynamic collaborative environment empowered individuals, arguably in ways that a less reciprocal model could not have achieved. The atmosphere of commitment and co-operation, rather than control, was positive, and conducive to innovation, efficiency, and possibility.[132]

'Productive association' is a route into understanding the character of early machine-making. The engineer's hinterland, outside the industry but within its social context, delivered both practical inspiration and, partly through the need to build family security, motivation. Later, textile engineering lost much of this spontaneity, as technology grew more complex and a better-resourced group rose to dominate.[133] But this trade had never been composed of equals, which is why calling it a 'network' is problematic. The word says too much, but also too little.

Early textile engineering does not quite fit models of historical business networks.[134] To think of a network of commercial connections within a local ethos stops short of reaching into the heart of what occurred in this specific, remarkable, pioneering endeavour, and the extraordinary level of innovation achieved. The new engineering grew up embedded in social relations that were empowering and efficacious, though not, it appears, especially visionary. Strength came in combination, building confidence and granting opportunity to people of relatively low status and otherwise limited resources.

As with the Quakers of Darlington, famed for promoting the Stockton and Darlington railway in the 1820s, closer inspection counters the story's more mythical aspects. The Quaker example also reminds that there was more to life, and to business, than profit maximization.[135] Communities

---

130   Randall, *Before the Luddites*, 93, 285.
131   Cookson, 'Family Firms', 1.
132   Cookson, 'Family Firms', 9.
133   Sabel and Zeitlin, 'Historical Alternatives to Mass Production', 143–4; Cookson, 'Family Firms', 16–17.
134   For instance, Wilson and Popp (eds), *Industrial Clusters and Regional Business Networks*, 12–15; review of Wilson and Popp by Robin Pearson in *Business History*, 46/4 (2004), 652–3.
135   Cookson, 'Quaker Networks', 172–3.

which innovated, in engineering or other fields, were robust, resting on many linkages, including family and intermarriage, partnership, subcontracting, social life, and a fairly standard and accepted set of values. Mutuality of this kind is recognized as significant in more genteel circles, in more highly capitalized industries such as ironmaking, so why would it not work for machine-making?

While the Darlington Quakers were well-heeled and well-connected, their approach to the railway project had common features with that of early textile engineers. Both groups were dynamic and purposeful, relatively informal though not casual, and far more robust in character than merely random business exchanges. They built in contingency, a 'best possible' system producing what was practical. Both achieved far more than even they could possibly have envisaged or intended at the outset. Their paths subsequently diverged, for building stability meant shaping appropriate institutions, and in this the needs of each industry were different. But both forsook informality in order to progress further, suggesting that the possibilities of 'start-up' combinations had stalled, and the life of such ventures was finite.[136]

These Darlington Quakers, and several early textile engineers, would discover that even in a high-trust culture, family was not guaranteed to be trustworthy.[137] Productive association held traps as well as limitations. In the case of engineering, some of the strength came from understanding the skills and abilities of a host community (whether within one locality, or more widely spread). While there was openness and informality, the industry identified cases of incompetence or dishonesty, so it also set boundaries. But none of this is unusual, for there are many models of co-existence, of security built through mutuality in changing times.[138] Collaboration and a socialized security made sense among trades and artisan groups, in eighteenth-century populations perpetually on the brink. Were these in general positive, or damaging, for industrial development? It is hard to imagine that they stultified.[139]

Echoing the earlier communality, leading industrialists afterwards created formal groups to promote mutual interests. By then, instinct and spontaneity might have largely retreated behind factory walls, yet these creations testify to how useful, how expedient, some common front could be. Association, albeit with a modern slant in changed times, had industrial purpose even when

---

136   Cookson, 'Quaker Networks', 172–3; review of Wilson and Popp by Pearson.
137   See Mark Casson, 'Entrepreneurship and Business Culture', in Brown and Rose (eds.), *Entrepreneurship, Networks and Modern Business*.
138   For instance in the Western Isles, c. 1800, a communal farming system was dismantled and crofting imposed by landlords; in the twenty-first century smallholders collectively rescued and regenerated the local economy: Hunter, *Crofting Community*, especially 53–4, 309–12.
139   Nowotny, *Cunning of Uncertainty*, especially 15–17.

companies were self-contained. And yet textile engineers did not themselves much follow this trend before the mid-nineteenth century. There had not been any formal trade or mercantile structure in this industry, no guild to support or inhibit its path.[140] The framework within which machine-making operated differed from other manufacturing trades, in Birmingham, Sheffield, and Leeds itself, which were managed and controlled by merchants. Textile engineers, close and responsive to their market, had no need for the elaborate distribution arrangements required for consumer goods. Thomas Cheek Hewes in 1824 said that not only did no formal combinations of master engineers exist in Manchester, but 'so little do we know of each other, that I do not know more than two in my line, as townsmen, I do not know them personally'.[141] But if true, that certainly did not apply in Keighley's close-knit community, nor in Leeds, and probably not in Lancashire's smaller centres.

The first institutions bringing together industrial interests were chambers of commerce, and societies serving specific trades. But in ironmaking, 'friendly association' could mean a thinly disguised cartel. Kirkstall Forge matched the prices and wages of Walker of Rotherham in 1785.[142] More formally, from 1799 the Iron Masters' Association regulated prices in Leeds, Bradford and Dewsbury, including the ironworks of Kirkstall, Bowling, Low Moor, and Shaw of Hunslet.[143]

Leeds Chamber of Commerce operated between 1785 and 1793, and after that, spasmodically. Its first phase may have been in response to the Tools Acts of 1785 and 1786, which restricted exports and impacted upon many manufacturing trades.[144] The chamber revived in 1851, when seven of its 85 members were machine-makers. While the chamber was interested in new machines, for instance inspecting a gig and shearing frame in 1854, and a cloth-raising machine in 1855, there was criticism that it spoke for textiles at the expense of engineering. The ever-vocal Peter Fairbairn complained in 1854:

> We all know that there are other important Leeds trades besides woollens and flax: for example there are locomotives, machine-making and iron forges. I never see any reports of these in the reports of the state of trade. I know that some American buyers have remained ignorant that we make flax-machinery here, and they have gone elsewhere.[145]

---

140   For a discussion of the influence of guilds on economic growth, for better or worse, see Ogilvie, 'Economics of Guilds', especially 170, 173–4, 181–4.
141   PP Artisans and Machinery, 346.
142   WYAS Leeds, 6755/4, scrapbook 1779–1951, p. 2.
143   Dodsworth, 'Low Moor Ironworks', 130; Butler, *History of Kirkstall Forge*, 58.
144   Beresford, *Leeds Chambers of Commerce*, 31; Harris, *Industrial Espionage*, 460–1, 466–70.
145   Beresford, *Leeds Chambers of Commerce*, 31, 54, 56.

So it appears that no group solely represented local engineers, while they felt their economic importance undervalued in the general trade associations.

The 'privatization' of forges and factories, their closure to public inter-action, added to the need for more formal commercial exchanges, societies, newsrooms and libraries. Filling the gap left when informal meeting places were lost, the club-like exchanges typically appeared late in the Georgian period: Leeds in 1806, Halifax before 1822, and Bradford Exchange Buildings, 1827–29.[146] So times had changed, and the industrial context – in which engineering was then very significant – had modernized. Social association was no longer quite the bedrock of development that it had formerly been.

To determine exactly what these relationships had meant in industrial terms is difficult. In many cases, engineers' actions suggest that immediate profit maximization was not their only, perhaps not even their main, intention. They had other concerns and responsibilities, preoccupations that continued through their careers, and these might override manoeuvring purely for quick profit.[147] What is more, 'co-operation', as now defined, is rather more formal than these earlier arrangements. While accepting co-operation and compe-tition as 'intimately related', in modern terms co-operation is characterized as something achieved only with difficulty, through 'will and effort'; altruism is a gift, better if presented discreetly; technical change is likely to unsettle social relations.[148] The modern view tends to formalize, to play down possibility and spontaneity, to expect change to be resisted. As such, it is a poor fit for this historical environment. The bonds within early engineering are perhaps best seen not as co-operation, but as a form of collaboration, a mutually advanta-geous co-working.

And of course there were vivid differences between places, between industries, and even between parts of industries. Community might be liberating and supportive, but there are alternative interpretations, one being that it has a deadening and inhibiting effect. Long overlaps between tradi-tional and modern working systems explain how, like Randall's woollen workers, textile engineers and others quite sensibly combined dynamism and conservatism. There were sound, pragmatic, reasons for this, not so much institutional constraint, but to make the best of processes and systems not fully developed to their purpose.[149] Where industries were young, and work culture elastic, new models were there for the making.

---

146 Grady, *Georgian Public Buildings*, 19, 22, 154, 157, 164.
147 A different matter from an already wealthy person engaging in philanthropy. Their wealth may derive from profit maximization, whatever any subsequent choices about charitable giving; cf. M. and C. Casson, *Entrepreneur in History*, 44.
148 Sennett, *Together*, 64, 73–6, 115.
149 Randall, *Before the Luddites*, 292.

Resisting machinery

Having described communities in which innovation was generally welcomed
and encouraged, how then to explain Luddites and others who resisted textile
mechanization? Stories of violent attacks and threats against machines and
people underpin traditional views of how new technology was greeted in
textile districts across England. Without doubt, dramatic and violent episodes
occurred. Physical conflicts and serious threats were, though, few, and their
effects limited. Protesters' motivations are still not fully explained, contemporary evidence often unclear and its meaning contested. Through research
that takes account of the culture and communities surrounding machine-
breaking, there has come a fresh understanding of why people reacted as they
did.[150] These incidents occurred in the same places where machine-making
flourished. The story of textile engineering adds context to the debate about
resistance to technology, and gives perspective to the narrative of protest.

So to the riots of 1779. Arkwright's first Lancashire factory, Birkacre,
near Chorley, drew the anger of a mob and was wrecked in 1779, a year after
opening. Yet the county had another water-frame factory, Halsall, which
was threatened but escaped damage. Arkwright was hostile to Halsall's
owner, Col. Mordaunt, for allegedly stealing his technology. The attack on
Birkacre, it is suggested, was inflamed by Arkwright's personal unpopu-
larity. Also noteworthy is that within a year, Thomas Walshman, a Birkacre
promoter, had opened Low Mill in Keighley without challenge.[151] Nor was
there difficulty at Arkwright's own new factory, at Shude Hill, Manchester,
in 1781.[152]

Water frames stole the headlines in 1779, Arkwright and partners blaming
the loss of their factory on drunken Wigan weavers inciting a riot.[153] In the
aftermath, older tales of frustrated invention were recast: spinning innovations of c. 1753–54, by Laurence Earnshaw of Cheshire, said to have heroically
abandoned his scheme as he feared its effects on the poor; and James Taylor of
Ashton-under-Lyne, persecuted by 'the working classes' for his patent. In both
these instances it seems more probable that neither had the capital to proceed.[154]

But certainly some attempts to mechanize were stopped in their tracks,
or interrupted, by protests. The arsonists attacking Grimshaw's Manchester
factory in 1792 also destroyed any prospect of developing Edmund
Cartwright's powered loom. His one large customer ruined, Cartwright's

---

150   See Randall, *Before the Luddites*, 3–4.
151   Aspin, *Water-Spinners*, 63–4, 68–73, 452, 460; Berg, *Age of Manufactures*, 192, 254;
Aikin, *Description of the Country*, 168. For Walshman and Low Mill, see above, pp. 35–6.
152   Aspin, *Water-Spinners*, 452–3.
153   Aspin, *Water-Spinners*, 69.
154   MacLeod, *Heroes of Invention*, 43–4.

Plate 9. The improved jenny, by James Hargreaves of Blackburn, c. 1767

Source: Guest, *Compendious History*, plate 7.

own business failed with great losses.[155] Also well-known is James Hargreaves'
retreat from Blackburn to Nottingham after a mob attacked his first jennies in
1767.[156] This interrupted his work, but not the jenny's absorption by domestic
textile workshops across northern England, which was rapid.[157] Arriving in
the Holme Valley in about 1776, the 18-spindle jenny had been 'hailed as a
prodigy' and 'rapidly multiplied in numbers, as well as in spindles'.[158] The
domestic clothier 'speedily adapted himself to the new order' within public
mills or in his own workshop, and 'nor did the introduction of the steam-
engine, in place of the waterwheel, disturb him at all'.[159]

This very adaptability to frequent low-tech advances carried a paradox.
Many workers threatened with displacement from 'traditional' occupations
were themselves recent recruits to 'best possible' systems. They represented
previous re-balancings, pragmatic reconfigurations allowing a degree of mechanization into production processes. Here, machinery created new areas of work,

155 Strickland, *Edmund Cartwright*, 107–9; Aspin, *The Decoy*, 22–3; Woodcroft, *Brief
Biographies*, xiii.
156 Baines, *History of the Cotton Manufacture*, 158–9; Berg, *Age of Manufactures*, 253–4.
157 See above, p. 16.
158 Morehouse, *Parish of Kirkburton*, 31.
159 Crump (ed.), *Leeds Woollen Industry*, 4.

or greatly increased existing ones. So, many more hand spinners were needed to serve the flying shuttle; armies of handloom weavers were newly engaged after yarn-spinning was powered; children were intensively employed in setting card-clothing by hand, when demand exploded after carding itself was mechanized. While card-making was a long-established trade around Halifax and the Spen Valley, occupying children in this way was no more traditional than hiring them in cotton or worsted factories, and dated back little further, to the third quarter of the eighteenth century. Once the process was mechanized and hand-setting became obsolete, it disappeared immediately, no doubt with relief rather than resistance. No 'rump' clutched at outmoded methods, as in some adult trades.[160] Child workers readily adapted to other factory work, and if there were losers, it was the owners of lucrative card-clothing 'schools'.

So where the status quo was a recent confection, new technology was likely to be positively welcomed. Few would mourn the end of hand-spinning, nor the 'great deal of drudgery' involved in making card-clothing by hand.[161] As for the jenny, Ogden's very contemporary view describes their appeal.

> [Jennies] were first used by the country people on a confined scale, twelve spindles being thought a great affair at first, and the aukward posture required to spin on them, was discouraging to grown up people, while they saw with a degree of surprize, children, from nine to twelve years of age, manage them with dexterity, which brought plenty into families, that were before overburthened with children, and delivered many a poor endeavouring weaver out of bondage to which they were exposed, by the insolence of spinners, and abatement of their work, for which evils there was no remedy till spinning-jennies were invented.[162]

For a time before this, fustian weavers had bought weft 'in the cops' direct from out-spinners. Thus, without an intermediate quality check, 'no detecting the knavery of spinners' before the piece was woven, manufacturers held weavers to account for faults resulting from imperfect yarn. 'In a scarcity of spinning', weavers dared not complain, nor seek compensation from the spinner, 'lest their looms should stand unemployed'. Jennies, run by children, shifted the power relationship. 'Many who had been insolent before, were glad to be employed in carding and slubbing cotton for these engines.' Some weavers, too, were anxious, for Ogden continues: 'The plenty of weft produced by this means gave uneasiness to the country people, and the weavers were afraid lest the manufacturers should demand finer weft woven at the former prices'.[163]

160 Cookson, 'Mechanization of Yorkshire Card-Making', especially 54.
161 Cookson, 'Mechanization of Yorkshire Card-Making', 55.
162 Ogden, *Description of Manchester*, of which sections are repeated verbatim in Aikin, *Description of the Country*.
163 Ogden, *Description of Manchester*, 54–5.

And then came Arkwright's water frame, raising new fears among some who had done well from the jenny.

> When the larger [Arkwright] machines were first set to work by water, they produced such excellent twist for warps, that they soon out-rivalled the makers of warps on the larger jennies, some of whom had several at work, and had reaped a good harvest of profit by them; but as the larger machines were encouraged, they suffered abatement in proportion.[164]

By Ogden's account, the 1779 riots were ignited not by the weavers accused by Arkwright, but by those owners of shops working larger jennies.

> [A]nd one of them concerned, making his complaint to others when they were intoxicated at the ale-house, a resolution was taken to destroy the water machines, and some were demolished before the owners could be protected, or the deluded country people who joined them could reflect, that if more warps were made, there would be a greater demand for weft from their jennies, and a better price for it; which has been fully experienced in the introduction of muslins.[165]

The 1779 disturbances have sometimes been called the jenny riots. They drew in colliers and labourers as well as weavers, and targeted a fairly incoherent mix of carding engines, jennies and Arkwright frames. The rioters were concerned about rising unemployment and falling wages, their situation sufficiently serious that the Malicious Injuries Act of 1769, intended for these very circumstances and carrying the death penalty, did not deter them.[166] It seems the protesters had widespread local support, among middle-class people too, for an idle workforce and higher poor rates caused unease.[167]

If indeed the owners of large jennies instigated these protests, then they were soon the worse for it. According to Baines:

> It is said that the rioters spared the jennies which had only twenty spindles, as these were by this time admitted to be useful; but those with a greater number, being considered mischievous, were destroyed, or cut down to the prescribed dimensions.[168]

---

164   Ogden, *Description of Manchester*, 56.
165   Ogden, *Description of Manchester*, 56–7.
166   Wadsworth and Mann, *Cotton Trade and Industrial Lancashire*, 374–5; Mantoux, *Industrial Revolution*, 411–13; 9 Geo. III, c. 29.
167   Baines, *History of the Cotton Manufacture*, 160.
168   Baines, *History of the Cotton Manufacture*, 159–60. Jennies of 24 spindles or fewer were tolerated: Wadsworth and Mann, *Cotton Trade and Industrial Lancashire*, 375.

The unrest was soothed. A local magistrate reminded weavers of the misplaced objections to flying shuttles, and reassured them that jennies promised similar widespread benefit. An impression was taking hold that, notwithstanding the misfortune of displaced sectional workers, a region at the vanguard of mechanization had more to gain than lose.[169]

West Riding cloth-finishing emerged as a notorious theatre of conflict in 1811–13. With fatal shootings on both sides, and 17 Luddites executed at York, the drama inspired many reports, factual and otherwise.[170] In fact this was part of a longer story. Gig-mills (for raising the nap on woollen cloth prior to cropping) were first patented in 1787 and 1794. The technology was basic, designed to slot into a workshop setting, and from c. 1793 was widely adopted, with no recorded strife, in Huddersfield and Halifax. Because in Leeds it remained contentious, some of the town's merchants quietly put cloth out for gig-dressing elsewhere, as William Cookson confirmed to the 1806 woollen trade enquiry.[171] In Somerset, clothiers acted likewise, sending cloth to Gloucestershire where the gig-mill had been long accepted for coarse cloth, and 'custom had assimilated its presence into the work style of the community'. It is true that applying it to fine cloth proved technically more difficult.[172] An attempt to introduce the gig-mill in Beeston in 1797 met with violence, which did not stop Gott installing one at Bean Ing in 1801. Attacks on his factory and personal threats against him made him retreat for once, and his gig-mill was dismantled. After this, there was no further attempt to bring the gig-mill to Leeds for at least a decade.[173] The shearing frame was never introduced to the Leeds industry, for it was overtaken by powered cropping, which first came to Bean Ing in 1824.[174]

Gott was above all a pragmatist, and may have forced the gig-mill had it proved more efficient. A similar issue with Bramah's hydraulic press turned out to be more a technical question than a matter of labour relations. The press was 'laid aside for fifteen years', with an implication that workmen refused to use it. But a letter from Gott to Bramah in 1802 shows that after some months' efforts, the Bramah press could not be made to work any more

---

169   Ogden, *Description of Manchester*, 55; Wadsworth and Mann, *Cotton Trade and Industrial Lancashire*, 478–9. For the standpoint of a region on the losing side of this equation, see Cookson, 'City in Search of Yarn'.

170   *An Historical Account of the Luddites of 1811, 1812 and 1813, with Report of their Trials at York Castle* (Huddersfield, 1862). Charlotte Brontë's *Shirley* (1849) was informed by older friends who witnessed events in Spen Valley; Frank Peel's *Risings of the Luddites, Chartists and Plug-Drawers*, first published in 1880, is heavily fanciful.

171   Crump (ed.), *Leeds Woollen Industry*, 38–40, 46.

172   Randall, 'Philosophy of Luddism', especially 9–10; *Before the Luddites*, 119–22, 124; Berg, *Age of Manufactures*, 253–4.

173   See below, pp. 228–9.

174   Crump (ed.), *Leeds Woollen Industry*, 57–8, 327; Heaton, 'Benjamin Gott', 58.

effectively than the screw press it was intended to replace. This was agreed by both workmen and employer: '[If] we had experienced any advantage from the use of your press, we should have insisted on those men working it, or we shou'd have appointed others in their places who would have been obedient.'[175] A cloth-finisher, William Hirst, encouraged by Matthew Murray, first brought Murray's hydraulic press into operation in 1816. After this, Gott's men followed the example and finally made the Bramah press work. The idea that workmen had prevented the press's introduction in 1801–02 originated some decades later with Hirst, who had worked for Gott at that time.[176] Gott had seen things differently in 1802, when he wrote to Bramah that, as the men were paid by the piece, their own interest lay in making the process as fast and efficient as possible.

In 1811–13, protest took different shape in other regions. Nottingham Luddites picked out unpopular masters, not novel technology. They broke stocking frames; in Lancashire, 'steam loomes and all the newly invented machinery' drew the anger.[177] Everywhere, the context was poverty. Machines were easy, accessible targets, but the backdrop was bank failures, closure to British goods of their main foreign markets in the United States, high wheat prices, and the resulting extreme distress in manufacturing districts.[178]

Similar conditions applied in 1826. Relations within textiles had soured following a five-month stoppage by up to 20,000 handloom weavers and wool-combers seeking higher pay and union recognition. Earlier, in 1822, weavers smashed a cotton loom experimenting with worsteds in Shipley. But soon after that episode, worsted power looms started to take hold in the district. They were blamed retrospectively for the widespread suffering among groups of textile workers in 1826. Stoked by events in Lancashire, though never matching them in scale, localized rioting in Bradford, Addingham, Gargrave and elsewhere turned not only on looms, but on other machinery.[179] At one point 'combing machines belonging to Mr Gill' at Baildon were in the attackers' sights.[180] Mules passing though Colne on their way to Addingham were wrecked when mistaken for looms, indicating that the attackers were non-specialist. Protest itself was more important than specific targets.[181] But the purchaser, a cotton-spinner called Jeremiah Horsfall, may have been

175   Crump (ed.), *Leeds Woollen Industry*, 49, 223–7.
176   Crump (ed.), *Leeds Woollen Industry*, 49; Heaton, 'Benjamin Gott', 58.
177   Crosby (ed.), *Benjamin Shaw*, 51.
178   Mantoux, *Industrial Revolution*, 415–16; Crump (ed.), *Leeds Woollen Industry*, 45.
179   *Leeds Intelligencer*, 4 May 1826; Ingle, *Trouble At T'Mill*, 2, 6, 16–17, 28–9, 37, *passim*; Hodgson, *Textile Manufacture*, 267; Walsh, 'Lancashire "Rising"'.
180   *Leeds Intelligencer*, 4 May 1826. Presumably Thomas Gill and Sons, worsted spinners: Baines, *Dir.* (1822), 198.
181   *Leeds Intelligencer*, 4 May 1826; Ingle, *Trouble At T'Mill*, 39.

singled out for an association with the Bradford Horsfall, whose worsted power looms were purposefully targeted.[182] For it appears, as with Birkacre and Halsall, that certain uncompromising factory-owners were pursued, while other premises escaped without incident.[183] If, said Matthew Boulton in 1781, Arkwright had been less confrontational, if he 'had been quiet, he might have gone on and got £40,000 pr annum by all the works he has now erected, even if there be some interlopers'. He was talking about Arkwright's attitude to patent protection, but illustrated an approach to the world that invited hostility.[184]

What is more, factories themselves, especially in the woollen trade, were widely feared and disliked.[185] Crump, taking the domestic industry's viewpoint, explains why resistance to machinery was so patchy around Leeds:

> [The] neighbouring villages had adopted and assimilated all the current inventions. The scribbling mills had steam for their motive power to drive their willeys, their scribblers and carders; the slubbings from the mill were spun on the jenny in the weavers' cottages and the clothiers' houses, and the fly-shuttle had been fitted to the handloom. The manufacture had been speeded up, the warp and weft were more uniform, the cloth of better quality. Children had found employment in the mills as pieceners and fillers; the slubber was a new class in the industry and in the village life. But not all these changes combined had shaken the stability of the domestic industry or dislocated its organization.[186]

This is not to say that all machines had been adopted without complaint. The rapid advance of scribbling stirred opposition in 1786,[187] but within public mills was soon accepted. 'The menace of the factory' was another matter, for it segregated and excluded outsiders. Clothiers had no means to engage with the 'new competitor producing on a vast scale', the opportunity fast disappearing to set up with small capital and use public mills.[188]

By the time of the 1826 disturbances, there was no suggestion that the surge of textile innovation, nor the many factories, should or could be stemmed. Rather, the regional press, looking to explain the 'outrages', were markedly concerned by the destitution of (in particular) handloom weavers. As in 1779, ratepayers also felt the effect, for weavers' families could not survive without

182   *Leeds Intelligencer*, 4 May, 11 May, 13 July 1826. The Horsfalls' relationship, if any, is undefined.
183   Ingle, *Trouble At T'Mill*, 35; see also Uglow, *Elizabeth Gaskell*, 146.
184   Wadsworth and Mann, *Cotton Trade and Industrial Lancashire*, 490.
185   Randall, *Before the Luddites*, 43–8; Mantoux, *Industrial Revolution*, 419–20.
186   Crump (ed.), *Leeds Woollen Industry*, 6.
187   Crump (ed.), *Leeds Woollen Industry*, 315–16.
188   Crump (ed.), *Leeds Woollen Industry*, 4.

parish relief.[189] A humanitarian response was led in 1826 by clergy in the most 'miserably distressed parishes'.[190]

Impoverishment, whether or not it was somehow a consequence of the objects being attacked, was a general theme in these episodes of disorder. Another was the sense of striking out at a class seen as responsible for this plight, in particular picking upon unsympathetic powerful individuals who had made themselves obnoxious. There was often a local explanation for the upsurges. While fury might bear down on some new industrial or mechanical arrangement, this was no knee-jerk response opposing change in principle. But machines were easy to attack, and no doubt breaking them was seen as somehow justifiable. This kind of protest was not confined to textile districts. The Malicious Injuries Act is thought to have been born of alarm when a mob destroyed a mechanical sawmill in Limehouse, London.[191] Or it may have been intended to protect colliery engines, for miners customarily destroyed colliery plant during protests, entirely unrelated to any technological grudge. The list of examples involving pitmen is long, from 1731 and perhaps earlier.[192] Cutting ropes, attacking engines and horses, ensured that work must stop.[193]

In the textile districts, change was embraced if it promised general benefits. Industrial questions, especially with systems in such flux, were rarely black and white. The vested interests with most reason to object to particular new technologies might themselves be recent upstarts within a 'best possible' system: neither society and guild members in the closed shops of legend, fighting a rearguard action; nor a less regimented workforce combating unemployment. Nor were employers any more homogenous or flexible. Manufacturers as a group could be irrationally conservative in turning their back on innovation, as with British slubbers' groundless prejudice against American and Belgian condensers in the 1820s.[194] But all technological change carries with it some frustration, and a level of resistance might be expected. The most remarkable feature of this period is how rarely protesters directed their anger against machine-makers themselves.

189   Ingle, *Trouble At T'Mill*, 24–5, 28, 34, citing *Leeds Mercury*, 6 May 1828; *Morning Chronicle*, 25 Apr. 1826, drawing from the *Manchester Guardian*.
190   Ingle, *Trouble At T'Mill*, 55–8.
191   Mantoux, *Industrial Revolution*, 411–14.
192   Mason, *Pit Sinkers*, ch. 5; Colls, *Pitmen of the Northern Coalfield*, ch. 13.
193   NEIMME, 3410/For/1/18, lists outrages in 1831 during a strike of 20,000–30,000 colliers in north-east England.
194   Lawson, *Progress in Pudsey*, 54–6; Jenkins and Ponting, *British Wool Textile Industry*, 105–6.

7

Innovating

> The power of inventing mechanical contrivances, and of combining machinery, does not appear, if we may judge from the frequency of its occurrence, to be a difficult or a rare gift.
>
> Charles Babbage, *On the Economy of Machinery and Manufactures* (1833)

In his own time, Babbage's reasoning is understandable. The best machine-making shops were by then highly organized and equipped, and manifestly innovative. Even so, Babbage qualified his view: extremely rare were 'the more beautiful combinations ... found only amongst the happiest productions of genius'. And, he noted, while inventions amounted to 'a vast multitude', many failed 'from the imperfect nature of the first trials'. A larger number, while mechanically successful, proved non-viable in practice, for 'the economy of their operations was not sufficiently attended to'.[1]

A long road had been travelled towards institutionalizing mechanical innovation. Whether that made the process more efficient, how effectively creativity was managed, how sparks of brilliance and initiative channelled into something workable and economical, are questions to consider. The history of inventions, thought Mantoux, 'is not only that of inventors but that of collective experience, which gradually solves the problems set by collective needs'.[2] Finding a solution involves producing a design that can be executed into a working mechanism. Equally important is that a machine is functional and cost-effective in local circumstances. Mantoux, his focus the eighteenth-century high point of 'productive association', offers a non-specific definition, tied to neither time nor place. But what became of the innovation process after engineering was largely absorbed into factories, and apparently separated from its surrounding community?

The spurs to innovate remained broadly the same – speed, quantity, quality, efficiency.[3] Each advance tended to knock-on, requiring change to

1 Babbage, *On the Economy of Machinery and Manufactures*, 260.
2 Mantoux, *Industrial Revolution*, 211.
3 See above, pp. 20–8.

other processes. Invention indeed bred invention.[4] Engineers' customers had little choice but to keep up. Hence Benjamin Gott persisted in trying to make Joseph Bramah's press work for him in 1802:

> Those who have tried any machines and found a realized advantage from the use of them will speedily consult their own interest by generally applying such productive power & the rivalship of their neighbours will bring them into general use.[5]

Inventiveness and aspiration were in the air; there was little sign of technological fatigue or inertia; and making things work was as vital as ever to the process.

Building an idea

For some technologies, an outline ancestry can be sketched out, as William Fairbairn did with the cotton power loom.[6] But the multitudes of unrecorded improvements to textile machines make a complete account impossible, so innovation cannot be quantified.[7] Where there was a significant advance, such as perhaps with the jenny or power loom, the machine's spread can be estimated and an impression formed of its practical and economic impact. But this is as far as figures will take a debate about the pace of technological change. Nor do they explain how innovation happened.

'Invention' is a thorny matter. In the popular imagination it is a 'eureka' moment of individual, original, usually spontaneous, genius.[8] The idea of heroic inventors, associated particularly with textiles and steam power, developed as a cultural phenomenon from about the time Watt died in 1819.[9] Invention, though, does not work without context. Even the most pioneering design – even Leonardo himself – incorporated technologies already in use.[10] Samuel Smiles, writing in the 1850s and 1860s about the value of individual achievement and with some sympathy for the 'heroic' great inventor, did not promote the idea directly. Familiar with engineers and engineering, Smiles

---

4   To misquote Ralph Waldo Emerson (1803–82).

5   Crump (ed.), *Leeds Woollen Industry*, 225–6.

6   Fairbairn, 'Rise and Progress', II, lxxii; and see above, p. 17.

7   For a discussion of the difficulties in such analysis, see Rosenberg, *Perspectives on Technology*, 69–78.

8   See Gilfillan, *Sociology of Invention*, 23–4, 28, 31.

9   MacLeod, *Heroes of Invention*, 2. Tomory, 'Technology in the British Industrial Revolution', offers an excellent historiography of changing views about technological innovation.

10   How far is debatable: Ponting, *Leonardo da Vinci*, 30–2.

offered a more grounded 'inventor', who could practically execute a concept, with hard work and application always key to success.[11]

'Innovation' suffers from vagueness. Anything new, large or small, significant or not, consciously made or chanced upon, any improvement made to textile machinery, those 'age-old, multitudinous accretion[s] of little details, modifications, perfectings, minute additions',[12] falls within it. Innovation covers a spectrum from eureka events, into a lower stratum of 'continuum' improvement: the countless, unrecorded modifications to textile machinery that Mathias argued 'may yield a cumulative advance in productivity greater than the identifiable discrete innovations'.[13] If so, workplaces were of immense significance in the creative process. Here, mechanical and commercial judgements determined which practices to discard, and what could beneficially be continued. Rosenberg resists dividing invention from innovation, or indeed from diffusion. To split them risks overlooking continuities in innovation, and giving disproportionate attention to discontinuities. Furthermore, 'excessive significance' falls on early stages of invention, with crucial later events ignored; and 'pure' science's importance is exaggerated compared with 'lower' kinds of knowledge like 'mere' technological or engineering know-how.[14] The result distorts the view of technological development, for social processes of more importance than individual flashes of inspiration are underplayed, and institutional and economic contexts downgraded.[15]

Terms in this chapter are used advisedly. 'Innovator' is generally seen as more appropriate than 'inventor', even for the most self-conscious originator of technology. It embraces those who designed concepts, who captured ideas and made them real, or who had a gift to see and nurture other people's inventiveness – and instances where several of these qualities were blended within one individual, or where people united to share their talents. In such combinations creativity flourished. Lewis Paul, with a promising idea and financial resources, came together with the technical aptitude of John Wyatt.[16] James Watt, philosophical instrument maker of extraordinary versatility, and thorough student of earlier steam technology, was supported by a Glasgow merchant called John Craig before the more celebrated encounter with Matthew Boulton.[17] Matthew Murray's starry career grew out of the years of experimentation directed and financed by John Marshall. Murray and Marshall's base was the flax-spinning patent of John Kendrew of

---

11   Checkland, *Rise of Industrial Society*, 78.

12   Gilfillan, *Sociology of Invention*, 3.

13   Mathias, *Transformation of England*, 56.

14   Rosenberg, *Perspectives on Technology*, 61–2, 74–5, 77.

15   Rosenberg, *Inside the Black Box*, 35; also Gilfillan, *Sociology of Invention*, 49, 52.

16   See above, p. 32.

17   Marsden, *Watt's Perfect Engine*, 23–5, ch. IV, and *passim*; Morrison-Low, *Making Scientific Instruments*, 112–13.

Darlington. Kendrew's foundation had been the spinning jenny, his spinning frame developed in association with the watchmaker Thomas Porthouse as technician, and funded by the banker and linen merchant James Backhouse.[18]

From this point, business partnership might capture and fuse capabilities, giving them productive shape. An ideal combination was flair alongside steadiness – a Murray with a Wood, Wordsworth with Taylor. Cautionary examples, Zebulon Stirk or Richard Roberts, show what could go wrong, in a commercial sense at least, with creative powers untempered by pragmatics. The most resourceful and experienced of engineers were in demand as partners, with or without finance to invest. Thus Peter Ewart, Boulton and Watt's former millwright, was snapped up by Samuel Oldknow of Stockport in 1792, and then by Samuel Greg of Styal. George Lee's technical gifts made him a welcome associate, even without funds, and so the Salford firm of Philips and Lee was born.[19] William Carr in Chipping, Richard Hattersley in Keighley, James Greenwood at West Greengate – all were offered a share in a firm on the strength of engineering skill alone.[20]

Excepting Murray and Roberts, none of these men is well known. Their achievements are, though, to an extent recognized. Alongside these was an immense wave of largely anonymous mechanical advances, great and small, across hundreds of textile and engineering processes over many decades. Smiles noted that 'most mechanical inventions are of a very composite character, and are led up to by the labour and the study of a long succession of workers'.[21] Ideas came from everywhere, including in significant numbers from abroad, and many improvements emerged from the engineering shop floor, or from textile manufacturer customers.[22]

To a Select Committee in 1841, Peter Fairbairn acknowledged the role of machine-users:

> From your observation what is your opinion as to the persons who suggest improvements in machinery; do the improvements proceed generally from those who are connected with the working of the machines, or from those who make the machines? – From both. As a machine-maker, I am very much indebted to the spinners; if they have any improvement to bring into operation they suggest it to me, and I carry out the mechanical department.[23]

Fairbairn took several patents jointly with external collaborators. Improvements in drawing flax and other fibres were made in tandem with a Newcastle

18   Cookson, *VCH Durham IV*, 154–5; and see above, p. 23.
19   Pacey, *Maze of Ingenuity*, 239–40.
20   See above, pp. 90, 93, 48.
21   Smiles, *Industrial Biography*, 178–9.
22   See below, pp. 224–5.
23   PP *Exportation of Machinery*, 211.

flax-spinner, William Suttill.[24] Other co-patentees were the flax-spinners
Baxter Bros of Dundee, S. R. Mathers (Leeds), and J. G. Marshall (Leeds),
and an engineer, Ferdinand Kaselowsky of Berlin.[25] With a former partner,
Henry Houldsworth of Glasgow, Fairbairn registered a patent applying differential motion to the roving frame.[26] Houldsworth had earlier argued that in
fact 'cotton-spinners make all the improvements; it would not pay a machine-
maker to adopt new plans till their merits were established by practice'.[27]
Peter Ewart too saw the positive pressures from users:

> [It] is only within three years there have been any silk mills in Manchester;
> since those have been introduced, there has been a great deal of excitement
> among the machine-makers to improve the silk machinery. I have been told
> ... that considerable improvements have been made in silk machinery, even
> in the short time that it has been introduced in Manchester.[28]

Joshua Wordsworth worked with textile manufacturers to develop ideas,
sharing patents with the Bradford worsted spinner John Wood (1816 and
1830), and in 1842 with George Jarmen of Leeds, flax-spinner, and Robert
Cook of Hathersage, heckle and needle manufacturer.[29] He educated himself
by travelling around the textile districts and was 'acquainted with most of
the [flax-spinning] mills in Yorkshire and Lancashire'. With two prominent
Leeds spinners, Moses Atkinson and Mark Walker, Wordsworth undertook
a visit to Lancashire in 1825 to inspect Kay's new fine flax-spinning frame.[30]
Significant innovations in worsted spinning and preparation post-1815, it is
strongly suggested, were prompted by (unnamed) Bradford textile manufacturers demanding frames to mass-produce fine quality goods. In responding,
engineers created a great market for themselves, for the improved class of
yarn could be spun only with this 'newest and best machinery'.[31]

Ideas from the engineering shop floor were both numerically and qualita-
tively important, and bonus payments encouraged workers to share them.

> Are not many of the improvements in your machines, actually suggested by
> the workmen themselves? (Mr Taylor) Many, constantly.[32]

24   *Leeds Intelligencer*, 6 Feb. 1841.
25   *London Gazette*, 6 May 1851, 21206, 1196; 7 Jan. 1853, 21400, 49; 20 May 1853, 21441,
1426.
26   Walker, *Fortunes Made in Business*, 266; Taylor (ed.), *Biographia Leodiensis*, 493.
27   PP Artisans and Machinery, 380.
28   PP Artisans and Machinery, 255.
29   *General Index to the Repertory of Patent Inventions, 1815–45* (1846), 448; *Leeds
Intelligencer*, 11 Mar. 1830; 5 Mar. 1842; British Patent 9254, 14 Feb. 1842.
30   *Repertory of Patent Inventions*, VII, Jan.–July 1837, 151, 153.
31   James, *History of the Worsted Manufacture*, 383–4, 391–2.
32   PP Artisans and Machinery, 38, evidence of Philip Taylor, engineer.

Did you ever know the operative mechanic ... suggest any important improvement? – (Mr Jenkinson) Yes, very often.

And the probability would be, that the more practice he had the more improvements he would suggest? – Yes; and the English mechanic is noted for that which you now speak of; because there is an inducement for him to do so; he often gets very liberally rewarded for it.

How does he produce his improvement; is it upon paper or in the process of hand-labour? – It is very seldom on paper, but by hand, showing you what he can do, and what would be an improvement.[33]

The more successful engineering companies drew on such experienced employees, retaining them for long periods, in some cases with a formal technical role.[34] In the factory-based industry, with complex machinery, departmental foremen became key figures. Even if not routinely involved in product design, the foreman had a role in planning production systems. Richard L. Hattersley, George Hattersley's son and successor, was renowned for many significant power-loom improvements. The 'designing and arrangements' had been achieved jointly with his foreman John H. Wilkinson, a Hattersley employee for over 35 years.[35] Indeed, the firm's founder Richard Hattersley was essentially a foreman when first arriving at Screw Mill in Keighley.[36] Adam Pearson was a technical force at Low Mill, Keighley, c. 1785–c. 1796, as foreman for Clayton and Walshman, cotton-spinners.[37] When Martha Jubb tried to sustain the family business as a widow in 1816, she reassured customers that Jubb's foreman of more than 20 years remained as manager.[38] Samuel Lawson's foreman, William Littlewood, spent the whole of his 30-year career in the firm's service.[39]

For Murray and Wood, sustaining financial and technical success through a period of rapid growth rested on balancing many talents. Murray's brilliance was clear – 'he touched nothing that did not come out of his hands a new thing' – but Wood too was out of the ordinary, mechanically 'a man of genius'. The third partner, James Fenton, managed commercial affairs.[40] A core of specialist supervisors worked in support, including William Horsfield, foreman boiler-maker, there for 17 years; and Henry Aveson, bookkeeper and manager for over two decades.[41] Not all were directly involved in innovation, but they sustained a framework within which inventiveness thrived.

---

33 PP Exportation of Machinery, 106, William Jenkinson.
34 See MacLeod, 'Negotiating the Rewards of Invention'.
35 Hodgson, *Textile Manufacture*, 272.
36 See above, p. 93.
37 Notes of Ian E. Carr, great-great-grandson of William Carr, now with Clive Thompson, Clitheroe.
38 *Leeds Mercury*, 20 Apr. 1816.
39 *Leeds Mercury*, 19 Jan. 1856.
40 Scott (ed.) *Matthew Murray*, 49; *Leeds Intelligencer*, 9 Oct. 1820; see app. 2.
41 *Leeds Mercury*, 1 Dec. 1821; *Leeds Intelligencer*, 26 Feb. 1829; see app. 2.

Once into the factory era, drawing offices formed part of this structure. Wellington Foundry rested on Peter Fairbairn's own immense energies, his reputation for designs of 'almost classical neatness', and a constant stream of managed innovation. The drawing office was nerve centre, the chief draughtsman reporting directly to Fairbairn. Here were generated 'a great many new ideas and improvements in machinery … it is clear that the drawing office had its thinking cap on a good many times', which, roughly sketched, were passed into the works for testing.[42]

At this point, research and development (as it was later known) was formally established within some larger ventures. Before that, efforts to crack a technological problem might have been closely directed but they equated more to an individual skirmish than a concerted campaign. The 'R&D' term was not really appropriate.[43] So men with a concept but no craft skills – Paul, Marshall, Kendrew – would attack a specific problem. After 1800, it fell to inspired proprietors, skilled mechanics with technological knowledge often working in a well-balanced partnership – Murray, Wordsworth, Peter Fairbairn – to come up with solutions. Formal 'R&D' accompanied the rise of drawing offices.

Open and shut: patents and secrecy

A paradox lies at the heart of patenting. As the word conveys, a patent is the opposite of secret. Registering a design is also the means of publishing a blueprint from which the machine can be copied.[44]

How far patenting contributed to technological advancement is controversial. Did patents impede innovation, or were they 'institutional inducements for invention'?[45] Did they block technology's flow, or stimulate it by advertising new techniques? The burdensome process before 1852, the difficulties in applying for or accessing patents, was especially discouraging to the social class to which most machine-makers belonged.[46] Whether or not patenting encouraged innovation, the pre-1852 patenting system was not encouraging of patenting.

Between improvements that were patented and those that were not, no qualitative difference is clear. A patent, the fact that it existed at all, reveals as much or more about the sponsor and industry as it does about the product it protected. But the corpus of patents is convenient to measure and analyse,

---

42   *Alphomega*, 1 (3), Sept. 1946, 15–17; Taylor (ed.), *Biographia Leodiensis*, 492.
43   Cf. Allen, *British Industrial Revolution in Global Perspective*, 140–4.
44   MacLeod, 'Paradoxes of Patenting'.
45   Cooper, 'Making Inventions Patent', 838.
46   MacLeod, 'Paradoxes of Patenting', 909–10.

and so attracts attention and analysis. In contrast, the numerous unpatented devices, ideas and techniques, recorded unsystematically or not at all, do not offer much of a dataset. Individually, these innovations may or may not have been significant, but that also applies to patented products. The patented, because they are known, are elevated to a benchmark: the device is significant because patented; but whether patented because significant is questionable. A concept must have appeared promising when patented, but there could be no guarantee that it would prove viable in operation, nor that something better would not soon overtake it. So practicality is the crux.

In this most dynamic industry of textile engineering, before patent law reform in 1852 patenting was so little used that it cannot have greatly shaped technological development. Indeed, there are obvious instances where patents positively hampered progress in engineering. Certain textile innovators and other engineers – Paul, Arkwright, Cartwright, Boulton and Watt – notoriously employed the patent system, for better or worse. But the two outstanding spinning innovations – Crompton's mule and the throstle – were never patented. English patents issued for textile innovations were so few that they accounted for only a small fraction of the industry's inventive activity. Altogether there were 1,976 textile patents in England between 1711 and 1850, representing 15 per cent of the total in all industries.[47] Of these textile patents, 1,467 came after 1820. During the peak innovation period, 1760 to 1820, textile patents numbered 471, or fewer than eight a year – this for all branches of the textile industry across the whole country.[48]

In woollen textiles, the West Country had a greater inclination to patent than did Yorkshire. The west accounted for over half of English patents between 1790 and 1830: 70 compared with Yorkshire's 41 (one a year). What is more, woollen industry patents concentrated heavily in cloth-finishing, accounting for 16 of the 19 woollen patents between 1790 and 1812, 38 out of 43 between 1813 and 1824, and 31 of 46 patents issued between 1825 and 1830. In other words, where merchants dominated – in the west, in finishing processes – patenting was far more common than it was in preparing, spinning or weaving woollens in northern England. For cotton textiles, patents were spread more widely around processes, but were relatively few, the total of 168 patents from 1790 to 1830 averaging just over four a year.[49] These numbers can barely reflect total innovation.

So why were patents not more used? Perhaps because patenting was 'cumbersome and unreliable and expensive, with the result that most

47   Sullivan, 'Revolution of Ideas', 352.
48   Sullivan, 'Revolution of Ideas', 353–4, shows low patenting rates in textiles relative to numbers employed.
49   Jeremy, *Transatlantic Industrial Revolution*, 55, 57.

inventors shunned it'.[50] It was also insecure and potentially counterproductive, 'chaotic'.[51] The system did not keep pace with technological change, which could suit the Arkwrights or Boulton and Watts aiming to control a winning concept through licensing.[52] For most northern textile engineers, though, patents held no appeal. High-profile cases of innovators coming to grief despite, or because of, the patent system were not encouraging. Edmund Cartwright, educated and well-to-do, who patented power looms and a wool-comb in the 1780s, was bruised by the experience.

> A patent is a feeble protection against the rapacity, piracy and theft of too many of the manufacturing class. There is scarcely an instance, I believe, of a patent being granted for any invention of real value, against which attempts have not been made to overthrow or evade it.[53]

Arkwright's attempt to deceive the pirates by deliberately obscuring the design in his Patent Office application led to the patents being invalidated in 1785.[54]

John Marshall's flax-spinning experiments employed the jenny-inspired Kendrew and Porthouse frame, patented in 1787. Marshall held a licence, as did four Scottish companies, from 1788–92. Another party who copied it was successfully sued. In 1790 Marshall, believing that his and Murray's machine had progressed so far beyond the original that it was effectively a new model, refused to pay further royalties to the Darlington partners. They and their investor, Backhouse, brought a claim against Marshall, and in 1794 were awarded £1,100 in damages. The case turned on a point of law. Kendrew conceded privately to Boulton and Watt that Murray had 'very much altered' the Darlington machine.[55] The damages were substantial, but hardly troubled Marshall, by then reaping large profits through working his own patented machinery.

Marshall was again sued, in 1836, for infringing James Kay of Preston's fine-flax spinning patent. After a long process of development, Kay's machine had been patented in 1825 and widely licensed. Based on his own 30-year knowledge of flax and worsted machinery, Joshua Wordsworth testified

50   Ó Gráda, 'Did Science Cause the Industrial Revolution?', 228.

51   Jeremy and Darnell, *Visual Mechanic Knowledge*, xiii; MacLeod, 'Paradoxes of Patenting', 896–7, 906–7; for difficulties in taking out and enforcing patents before 1852, see MacLeod, 'Strategies for Innovation', 288–9; *Inventing the Industrial Revolution*, 89, 102.

52   Though licensing was far from straightforward: see MacLeod, 'Paradoxes of Patenting', 901–5.

53   Edmund Cartwright, c. 1820, quoted by Burnley, *History of Wool and Wool-combing*, 134.

54   See above, p. 35.

55   Aspin, *The Decoy*, 24–6, and fn. 85; Cookson (ed.), *VCH Durham IV*, 154–5; Thompson, *Matthew Murray*, 16–20, ch. 3 especially 52–3.

to Kay's originality. Taylor and Wordsworth had in fact worked with Kay to improve his machine, which they produced in large numbers. Kay had successfully defended his patent on a previous occasion, and won his first round against Marshall at the York Assizes. But he lost at a higher court, and an appeal failed. The patent was voided because parts too closely resembled another person's older patent.[56] To a rich man like Marshall, these proceedings were inconvenient but manageable; to the less wealthy they spelled ruin.

The most notorious patent battle in Leeds engineering related not to textile machines but to steam-engines, and marked the climax of animosity between Boulton and Watt and Matthew Murray. Murray had started to make steam-engines by 1797, taking his first patent in 1799. His improvements included a horizontal cylinder and self-acting damper.[57] Boulton and Watt's principles were solid, but their engines were not. The apparatus was poorly executed, and still featured wooden beams. The Soho firm did not even produce its own cylinders until forced to dismiss their subcontractor, John Wilkinson, when he was revealed as chief among the pirates of its technology. Still, Boulton and Watt thrived as their patents effectively stopped other engineers from improving Watt's designs. Murray, pioneering engines made almost entirely of iron, sold the condenser separately and managed (unlike those who bought from him and worked engine and condenser together) to avoid being sued. Murray was, it seems, stockpiling complete engines, and poised to sell them immediately Boulton and Watt's patent expired in 1800.[58] James Lawson, agent to Boulton and Watt, and long-term acquaintance of Murray, reported to Soho in 1797 that 'Murray I well know will go as near the wind as he dare'.[59]

Between the Birmingham and Leeds engine-makers there was already a mutual and well-founded suspicion, of industrial spying and enticement of workmen. Relations soured further after Boulton and Watt's engineer William Murdock and foundry manager Abraham Storey visited Holbeck in 1799. Murray 'admitted [them] into every part of the manufactory ... they were permitted to take patterns and specimens of our workmanship'.[60] 'A plentiful dose of ale' loosened Murray's tongue.[61] But when Murray accepted their invitation to Birmingham, to his fury access to Soho was refused as 'their rule was not to show them to any persons in the trade'.[62]

56 *Leeds Intelligencer*, 30 July 1836; *Repertory of Patent Inventions*, VII, Jan.–July 1837, 35–60, 107–56; Carpmael, *Law Reports*, II, 117–26.

57 British Patent 2327; Scott (ed.), *Matthew Murray*, 48–50; Rees, *Cyclopaedia*, V, 127, 130.

58 Discussion with Ron Fitzgerald; Tann and Burton, *Matthew Boulton*, 120–1; see also Marsden, *Watt's Perfect Engine*, especially ch. 7.

59 Thompson, *Matthew Murray*, 70.

60 *Leeds Intelligencer*, 25 July 1803, letter of Matthew Murray; also in Scott (ed.), *Matthew Murray*, 12. See J. C. Griffiths, 'William Murdock (1754–1839)', *DNB*.

61 Scott (ed.), *Matthew Murray*, 33.

62 Scott (ed.), *Matthew Murray*, 49.

Information gleaned from the Round Foundry visit had quickly been applied in Soho. Matthew Boulton jun. wrote of 'Murdock and Abraham ... highly delighted and full of panegyricks upon Murray's excellent work' and that a sample of his forging 'was the most beautiful and perfect piece of work I ever beheld'. Boulton and Watt immediately emulated Murray's techniques, which promised to do away altogether with filing, using the Leeds specimens as a standard for their own men to aspire to, and ordering the very same sand for their own foundry. Despite this, they could not match Murray's quality of casting.[63]

Murray took out a second steam-engine patent in 1801, with new features to increase power and fuel economy.[64] Boulton and Watt, their own patent expired, the founding partners retired, and no new technology to offer, looked for retaliation. James Watt jun. spent several weeks in Leeds in the summer of 1802, while Murray and Fenton were away. Helped by Benjamin Gott, he tracked down a former Soho employee, homesick for Birmingham and prepared to share knowledge of Murray's techniques. Watt recorded the man's observations in letters back to Soho, and also investigated buying a building with a view over the Round Foundry's yard. Murray, who 'solicits orders, superintends the erections of engines etc', Gott described to Watt as 'a great scoundrel but a very able mechanic & Gott says he has got great credit for his last patent, no one doubting that the inventions are exclusively his own'.[65]

Watt concluded that 'there are no hopes of getting at Murray's men, as all of the least consequence are engaged [under contract] and at high wages'. Murray's prices were also considerably lower than Soho's. A visit to the engine-maker Emmett at Birkenshaw showed Watt that Murray was not alone in having sophisticated modern plant and steam-engine patents.[66] So instead, Boulton and Watt tried to overturn Murray's 1801 patent, on the grounds that it was entirely their own technology, obtained by Murray from spies among their own workmen. This was untrue, but Watt had collected evidence while in Leeds (though by illegal means) that Murray was paying a workman at Soho for drawings and other information.[67] A court case could have been embarrassing for both parties. In the event, Murray withdrew his plea, and the patent was set aside in 1803.[68]

Murray's riposte came via the columns of the *Leeds Intelligencer* the following week. He had, he said, 'to vindicate my character as an engineer, against a foul insinuation'.

63   Scott (ed.), *Matthew Murray*, 33–4. Around 1800, the sons of Boulton and Watt effectively took charge of the business.
64   British Patent 2531; Rees, *Cyclopaedia*, V, 128; Scott (ed.), *Matthew Murray*, 50.
65   Scott (ed.), *Matthew Murray*, 34–43; Thompson, *Matthew Murray*, ch. 5 and 6.
66   Scott (ed.), *Matthew Murray*, 41–3.
67   Scott (ed.), *Matthew Murray*, 38–9.
68   *Leeds Intelligencer*, 18 July 1803; Rees, *Cyclopaedia*, 132, 134; Scott (ed.), *Matthew Murray*, 50.

Had they used my inventions in the manner described in that patent, prior to the date thereof, they certainly would have practised them in the engines they made ... or taken out a patent for the improvements themselves.

He had backed down 'not from any fear of losing the trial', but because of the expense against 'such rich and powerful opponents'. And then came his *coup de grâce*, that Boulton and Watt were a spent technological force.

But had I been guilty of obtaining a knowledge of their improvements, if they had any (but I do not believe they have made any worth notice since Mr Watt, senior, retired from the management) it would only have been a return in kind.

And so he went on to describe his hospitality to Storey and Murdock in 1799, and how it had been reciprocated. The world, said Murray, cared little about engineers stealing each other's ideas: 'What people want of us, are good engines, and I am confident I can make good ones.' His challenge to Boulton and Watt, to compete in making a 1-hp engine, met no response.[69]

This had the feel of a moral victory, and did no harm to the booming Holbeck business. Murray's last patent covering steam-engines, in 1802, included a method of epicyclic gearing, converting linear to circular motion. Here was an alternative to Watt's sun-and-planet and to James Pickard's crank and flywheel, though it proved immediately useful only for very small engines. The idea for hypocycloidal motion was said to have come from Theophilus Lewis Rupp (d. 1806), a Manchester cotton-spinner of German origin with serious scientific interests.[70] It was Murray, though, who faced the exceptional difficulty of designing and producing the hypocycloidal gear.[71]

In 1824, Murray would maintain that Boulton and Watt engines had shown no material improvement since the older Watt's time, except in automatic feeding.[72] Meanwhile he continued to innovate, Murray engines finding strong support in other regions, including his native Tyneside where the eminent John Buddle and other colliery viewers commissioned them.[73] But there were no further steam-engine patents after the battle with Boulton

69   *Leeds Intelligencer*, 25 July 1803.

70   Thompson, *Matthew Murray*, 175–6. Papers by Rupp on chemistry and bleaching were published by the Literary and Philosophical Society of Manchester.

71   Ernest Freeman advised on this point. Murray's hypocycloidal engine, the oldest still working, is in Birmingham Science Museum.

72   NEIMME, 3410/Wat/1/5/72.

73   NEIMME, 3410/Wat/2/2 pp. 308–9; 2/3 pp. 1, 6; 22/21; 3/19; 3410/For/1/9/132; 3410/Bud/24/15, /24, /32, /35; 13/111; 16/7; 21/106; 3410/John/5/54. See Thompson, *Matthew Murray*, 484–8, for list of steam-engine customers.

and Watt. Defending them was bruising, potentially ruinous, and a colossal diversion from what mattered: making the lucrative, high-demand products that few other companies were capable of engineering. The licensing model could be extremely profitable, as Arkwright and Boulton and Watt had shown. It was also fraught with problems, and a less well-resourced patent-holder could struggle to defend their position. Doubtless this was in Murray's mind when he backed away from further conflict with Boulton and Watt. His winning position was that he was the better engineer. He profited not through licensing, but by making machines work, and others shared this stance. That is why, relative to the volume of innovation in textile engineering, patenting was rare from the failure of Arkwright's patent in 1785 until after 1830, coming into its own only in the mid-1840s with Holden and Lister.

In Keighley, there was little (if any at all) use of patenting by textile engineers during the most innovative period. Not until the new law came in 1852 did the prolific Richard Longden Hattersley register the first of his British patents, which by 1895 amounted to around a hundred – many in joint names, mainly for looms and machine tools. Leeds engineers did patent under the old system, though not in great numbers. John Jubb patented not a textile innovation but a threshing machine, which he supplied for 25 guineas, plus extra for the associated horse wheel.[74] It was a later generation who began to register mechanical advances. Samuel Lawson took out three patents for improvements in processing hemp, flax and other fibres, in 1828, 1833 and 1840, the first with his then partner Mark Walker.[75] That of 1833 was most significant, for a screw gill for drawing, taken jointly with William King Westley, a flax merchant with other patents to his name.[76] A machine in production at the Hope Foundry in 1845 was said to have been invented there by 'young Robinson', but patented by Lawson. In fact no such patent was ever registered.[77] Peter Fairbairn's original Lady Lane experiments did not result in patents – perhaps he could not then afford them – but between 1834 and 1860 he registered 32 sole or joint patents, most relating to drawing or spinning flax or other textiles, a few for machine tools and other devices.[78] Most significant was the screw gill motion, drawing long fibres such as flax and worsted

74   *Leeds Intelligencer*, 22 Feb. 1796; 17 Oct. 1796.
75   British Patents 5715, 9 Oct. 1828; 6464, 20 Aug. 1833; 8332, 2 Jan. 1840.
76   *Alphomega*, 1 (3), June 1946, 19–21; *Industries of Yorkshire* (1888), 162.
77   *Repertory of Patent Inventions*, XVIII (July–Dec. 1851), 240–4.
78   British Patents no. 6741, 1834; 7699, 1838; 7700, 1838; 8568, 1840; 8810, 1841; 10518, 1845; 11393, 1846; 12299, 1848; 12870, 1849; 13208, 1850; 14124, 1852; 125, 1853; 1032, 1853; 1646, 1853; 1935, 1853; 2432, 1853; 645, 1852; 662, 1852; 674, 1852; 1150, 1852; 2545, 1856; 441, 1854; 634, 1854; 1855, 1854; 1877, 1854; 1248, 1857; 1600, 1858; 729, 1859; 2980, 1859; 1794, 1860; 2089, 1860; 2704, 1860; see also *Leeds Mercury*, 31 Jan. 1835; *Leeds Times*, 8 Aug. 1840; 8 Mar. 1845; and above for some of Fairbairn's collaborations.

into workable form.[79] Joshua Wordsworth also had several external patent partners, and sole patents for various flax and woollen processes.[80] Other forays into patenting did not turn out well, as in 1839 when his move to have a patent of John Sharp set aside was dismissed.[81] Wordsworth's own considerable influence was acknowledged in another case of patent infringement, one which did not directly concern him:

> [N]otwithstanding the imputations they had sought to cast on the machine which had cost Joshua Wordsworth many moments of deep thought, that machine was, for many years, a rock ahead of the plaintiff; when he rose in the morning, he murmured Joshua Wordsworth, and when he went to bed at night it was whirring about his head.[82]

Neither March and Maclea nor Zebulon Stirk, significant innovators both, ever took out a patent.[83]

At this time, patenting was far cheaper, simpler and more widespread in the United States.[84] Price and accessibility were significant deterrents to patenting in Britain. To seek and defend a patent drained other resources, too: time and effort in the application process, production of plans and models, and readiness to act against transgressors. These secondary issues were a diversion for proprietors – very central to the fortunes of engineering companies – whose attention might be far better spent on improving and upgrading products and processes. For most innovators, the best returns were achieved through increased business, not monopolizing a discovery.[85]

Engineering's inventive and dynamic spirit, in the early days at least, may even have bred aversion to the patent system. There was some moral objection to patenting. Thomas Jefferson argued that ideas were not transferable as property.

> He who receives an idea from me, receives instruction himself without lessening mine ... That ideas should freely spread from one to another over

---

79   The gill box concept perhaps originated with Charles Gill, a partner at Glasshouses Mill in Nidderdale, 1812–28: Jennings (ed.), *History of Nidderdale*, 237–8. Derek Bird suggested the possibility and reference.

80   British patents 6287, 1832; 6518, 1832; 7657, 1838; 9254, 1842; *Leeds Intelligencer*, 20 Sept. 1832; see above for Wordsworth's collaborators.

81   Carpmael, *Law Reports*, II, 461–2.

82   *Repertory of Patent Inventions*, XVIII (July–Dec. 1851), 186, comments by counsel for the plaintiff Carmichael of Dundee.

83   See app. 2.

84   Sokoloff and Khan, 'Democratization of Invention', 363; Sokoloff, 'Inventive Activity in Early Industrial America', 819.

85   MacLeod, *Inventing the Industrial Revolution*, 104.

the globe, for the moral and mutual instruction of man, and improvement of his condition, seems to have been peculiarly and benevolently designed by nature.[86]

This was not merely theoretical. When Isaac Holden conceived the Lucifer match in about 1829, he declined to patent what he saw as a fortuitous accident.[87] Later, as bookkeeper for the worsted spinner Townend of Cullingworth in the 1830s and 1840s, Holden made breakthroughs in solving the long and unyielding problem of mechanizing wool-combing. On principle, Townend himself did not patent Holden's improvements, but in this case, after such concerted effort, Holden decided that patenting was justified. On that basis he left Townend for a seven-year partnership with Samuel Lister.[88] Holden and Lister subsequently developed new and spirited paths into managing patents. Opening a factory in France to exploit their square motion comb, patented in 1847, Lister vigorously bought up competing rights. The partners intended to monopolize the spread of wool-combs in Britain, and impede competing technology in France.[89] Lister could embark on this course because, unusually among textile innovators, he had a very wealthy family. No other engineer or manufacturer, before or after the Patent Law Amendment Act passed in 1852, could have attempted such a thing. Lister paid £27,000 to Donisthorpe for a share of his wool-comb patent, £33,000 for Heilmann's patent, and £20,000 for the 1853 Noble comb patent. In the 1850s Lister's nip, an advance on the square motion comb, employed one worker to do what three had previously done. Lister achieved his monopoly:

> and the trade was well satisfied to give me what otherwise would have appeared to be an outrageous price, the sum of TWELVE HUNDRED POUNDS A MACHINE, OR A THOUSAND POUNDS PATENT RIGHT, the machine itself costing about two hundred ... and for years I sold a large number.[90]

This episode was exceptional not only in the resources at Lister's disposal: wool-combing was the final challenge, the last major process to capitulate to mechanization. Lister was perhaps unique as a textile manufacturer in systematically attacking a specific mechanical problem at whatever cost. The closest

86   Lipscomb and Bergh (eds), *Writings of Thomas Jefferson*, III, article 1, 8/8/12.
87   K. Honeyman, 'Sir Isaac Holden (1807–97)', *DNB*. Holden was perhaps not the only producer of the Lucifer match.
88   *Keighley News*, 14 Aug. 1897. Elsewhere the split has been explained by disputes over status and profits.
89   Honeyman and Goodman, *Technology and Enterprise*, 4–5, 25; S. E. Fryer, rev. D. T. Jenkins, 'Samuel Cunliffe Lister, 1815–1906', *DNB*.
90   Lister, *Lord Masham's Inventions*, 46.

comparison is with John Marshall, 50 years earlier. Lister's approach showed that patents could secure a more than compensatory return on a very great outlay. Protection had much more purpose as machinery grew increasingly complex, innovation formal and expensive, and engineers wealthy enough to defend their patent rights. The 1852 Act reflected changing attitudes during the 1840s.[91]

Before then, innovators were more likely to employ secrecy, if this were practicable. In the wake of the Boulton and Watt encounter in 1803, Murray continued to be the most inventive of engineers yet took out only one further patent.[92] When Joseph March started work at the Round Foundry in 1814, he found there an unpatented planing machine: 'like many inventions in those days, it was kept as much secret as possible, being locked up in a small room by itself to which the ordinary workmen could not obtain access'.[93] With a one-off specialized machine tool, used only within the workshop, this avoided the problems of patenting and of exposing the technology more widely. But technology made to sell, such as textile machines, could not be contained. For most engineers, neither were patents a practical option, especially in the light of Murray's and others' experiences.

Attempting secrecy in more open environments was futile. In a case in 1819, a flax dressing machine went deliberately unpatented, 'thereby keeping it as secret as it was possible to be'. Within six months identical machines were on sale in France.[94] Before the fall of his patents, Arkwright-style ventures tried to suppress information about their operations, to keep it from inquisitive locals, or (if working illicitly) to foil Arkwright's agents. Confidentiality clauses appeared in employment contracts, like that issued to James Greenwood, the mechanic involved in setting up West Greengate Mill, Keighley, in 1784.[95] Thomas Robinson, joiner, and the millwright Joseph Tempest bound themselves to cotton-spinners at Walk Mill, Keighley, in 1783, promising to 'forfeit £100 if [they] reveal or make known any secret respecting the construction or movements of any of the machines or works'.[96] But both Greenwood and Tempest soon afterwards worked for Robert Heaton of Ponden, and Tempest made spinning frames using Hattersley components.[97] Pledges of secrecy were at best a temporary block on technological flows, knowledge could not be unlearnt, and there was little restraint on an employee moving to a competitor, or setting up in business himself.

91 Dutton, *Patent System and Inventive Activity*, 63; MacLeod, 'Strategies for Innovation', 288–9.
92 Thompson, *Matthew Murray*, 483.
93 Scott (ed.), *Matthew Murray*, 49.
94 PP Artisans and Machinery, 162.
95 Baumber, *Revival to Regency*, 43–4; app. 1.
96 Hodgson, *Textile Manufacture*, 36–9.
97 WYAS Bradford, DB2/6/3; 32D83/5/1; Baumber, *Revival to Regency*, 44; app. 1.

The fabled privacy of Bean Ing lent Benjamin Gott an air of mystery within the woollen trade, yet there was no technological reason for secrecy there. Many smaller, fully visible, textile workshops were working with similar apparatus. Gott's closed approach owed more to security, protecting goods from theft or damage and closing the premises to undesirables, perhaps disgruntled outworkers.[98] Outside his walls, the culture was of transparency. In the opening years of the nineteenth century, 'the industry at Bramley and in the neighbouring villages had adopted and assimilated all the current inventions'.[99] Pudsey clothiers in the 1820s had 'no secret in the manufacturing, are not afraid of others getting their styles and patterns, all is fair and above board, as they are nearly all making similar goods'.[100]

Even James Watt, despite his company's later policies, claimed an openness with his ideas, at least in earlier days of experimentation in Glasgow.

> [Mr Watt] was without the smallest wish to appropriate knowledge to himself, and one of his greatest delights was to set others in the same road to knowledge with himself. No man could be more distant from the jealous concealment of a tradesman.[101]

Neither Boulton and Watt nor Richard Arkwright, despite their rights, wealth and power, managed to stamp out piracy. Before Boulton and Watt's patents expired in 1800, an illicit industry 'of considerable proportions' served a home market with Watt-style engines, straight copies or some parallel invention not bearing scrutiny.[102] An over-priced patented machine gave strong incentive to others to circumvent it. Arkwright, despite the costly failure to retain his patents, consolidated a fortune through using the system to spin cotton. Matthew Murray's decision in 1803, that he had better stick to engineering, suggests the same conclusion.

For machine-makers in general, secrecy was as elusive as patenting was inaccessible. Nor, for any competent machine-maker in a booming market for machines, was it necessary. Although information had currency, the greater gain accrued from a culture where ideas, including many incremental improvements, freely circulated. Textile manufacturers welcomed any advance increasing efficiency and productivity. Free exchanges of technology were a problem only for the few investing in targeted experimentation, for they must look to defend their intellectual property: Marshall and Lister were more than equipped for this, while Peter Fairbairn, who could not immediately patent,

98   Crump (ed.), *Leeds Woollen Industry*, 26, 33.
99   Crump (ed.), *Leeds Woollen Industry*, 6.
100   Lawson, *Progress in Pudsey*, 42.
101   Muirhead, *James Watt*, 49, quoting Professor John Robison on Watt in Glasgow c. 1762.
102   Tann and Breckin, 'International Diffusion of the Watt Engine', 542.

found support from Marshall, energetically produced the machines and, as soon as he could afford to do so, proactively guarded his rights. The returns were good, though Lister's 500 per cent royalty premium was probably unique, and possible only because he had batted away any possible rival by buying a monopoly, which he then uncompromisingly secured.

Channels of technology

The means by which eighteenth-century technology circulated are neatly summarized as 'men, manuals and machines'.[103] Under normal circumstances, machines were not bought to be copied, for specialist makers' products were cheaper and better. But when export restrictions were in force, machines were sent abroad clandestinely to North America and the continent, as models to reproduce and adapt to local conditions. In practice this meant delay, technical difficulty without the maker's guidance, and problems obtaining spare parts and ancillary items like card-clothing.[104] But parliamentary inquiries in 1824 and 1841 were told that smuggling was widespread, though the copy machines were not good: 'It would be a very long time before they could make them so cheap, and so well adapted to the purpose as ours'.[105]

Technology seeping overseas was a concern of governments long before textile machinery was the main issue, even when Britain probably derived net benefit from international exchanges. An Act of 1719 restricted skilled workers' movements abroad, its aim to stop metalworkers being lured to France and Russia. The disquiet surrounded iron and cutlery trades, with wool, iron, steel, brass and horology mentioned specifically.[106] From 1750 the law also covered the enticement of textile workers, and export of 'tools or utensils' for working wool and silk; and from 1774 included cotton and linen equipment, allowing intending exporters to be apprehended on suspicion rather than wait until goods reached a ship.[107]

After this, regulation struggled to match the pace of change. A 1781 Act, mainly to protect the cotton industry but referring to all textiles, broadened the range of prohibited goods to include terms like 'machine' and 'engine', and embraced models and plans. It also threatened makers of any device

103   Inkster, 'Mental Capital', 405.
104   Jeremy, *International Technology Transfer*, 15, 84–6.
105   PP Artisans and Machinery, 251, 303, 342; PP Exportation of Machinery, 44, 99, 110; see also Saul (ed.), *Technological Change*, 144.
106   5 Geo. I c. 27; Harris, *Industrial Espionage*, 8–10, 12, 456–7. Harris, ch. 18, surveys eighteenth-century legislation limiting exports and movement of workers.
107   Harris, *Industrial Espionage*, 457–8; 23 Geo. II c. 13; 14 Geo. III c. 71.

intended for illegal export.[108] Then followed the Tools Acts of 1785 and 1786, the first hastily drafted and influenced by lobbying, in particular from Birmingham, the second intended to clarify the resulting confusion after strong resistance from other manufacturer groups.[109] Metal trades now fell within this legislation, with certain tools, components and machines identified. There was baffling inconsistency: some machine tools banned from export in 1785, for instance drilling machines, were removed from the list in 1786. Grooved rollers moved in the opposite direction. Files, of utmost importance to precision engineering, were freely shipped abroad because this was a well-established export trade. The ban on skilled artisans going overseas did not apply to gentlemen, so professional engineers were at liberty to move around the continent and elsewhere.[110]

Nor were the laws in place enforced effectively or consistently, and there was always opposition. Illegality probably made spies and their accomplices more cautious, but did not stop them. Customs officials, war with France, and prospects of heavy fines and commercial losses could not stem 'technological Darwinism'.[111] There are countless examples of knowledge and expertise moving overseas.[112] Prohibited machinery could be obtained on the continent at a premium of around 30 to 40 per cent.[113] Even in times of supposed enmity, new British textile technology invariably turned up promptly in France.[114]

But smuggling an entire machine was not easy, and the penalties severe. In 1801, Francis Wheelhouse advised an associate who was joining him in Portugal on how to ship mule frames from the Isle of Man. Keeping a vessel in harbour for a few days, 'you may put your household furniture aboard in the day time and anything that cannot be exported at night'. He recommended using a Portuguese vessel as 'they would tell no tales'.[115] Models were another possibility for smugglers.[116] They were used legitimately to record machines in various ways, and 'model' had several meanings: prototype machine,[117] or simply design, as in 'they have all the models of England in

---

108   21 Geo. III c. 37; Harris, *Industrial Espionage*, 459.
109   25 Geo. III c. 67; 26 Geo. III c. 89; Harris, *Industrial Espionage*, 462–3, 470.
110   Harris, *Industrial Espionage*, 462–5; 491.
111   Mathias, *Transformation of England*, 57; also Harris, *Industrial Espionage*, 463–4.
112   See Chaloner, 'New Light on Richard Roberts'; Goodchild, 'Case of Industrial Espionage?'; Harris, 'Attempts to Transfer English Steel Techniques'; *Industrial Espionage*; Heaton, 'A Yorkshire Mechanic Abroad'; Jeremy, 'British Textile Technology Transmission'; 'Damming the Flood'; *Transatlantic Industrial Revolution*; 'Immigrant Textile Machine Makers'; Mathias, *Transformation of England*, ch. 2; Schmitt, 'Relations between England and Mulhouse'.
113   Babbage, *On the Economy of Machinery and Manufactures*, 345–6.
114   Harris, *Industrial Espionage*, 545.
115   Aspin, *The Decoy*, 20–1.
116   Rimmer, *Marshalls of Leeds*, 234.
117   See Hodgson, *Textile Manufacture*, 251.

France at present'.[118] George Hattersley kept a 'pattern flyer' and 'fluting engine moddles' in 1832.[119] Matthew Murray was awarded a Gold Medal in 1809 by the Society of Arts for a model flax-hackling machine, later exhibited in the Science Museum. He may even have entered this competition to stake his claim to the design, so heading off a competitor planning to patent something similar.[120] Murray also retained models of engines.[121] From 'patterns and specimens of our workmanship' given unsuspectingly by Murray, Boulton and Watt were able to copy elements of his steam-engine.[122] As most machine-makers did not cast for themselves before about 1820, moulds for machine frames were kept by subcontractors, further opportunity for designs to circulate.[123]

Manuals and drawings were easier to transport, but presented machine-builders with a difficulty.

> No drawing or model, except it was as large as the machine itself; not a
> model but a machine can possibly point out the parts where the best work
> is necessarily to be applied, in order to adapt a machine to its purpose.[124]

This was Peter Ewart, associate of Rennie and Watt, whose drawings were the finest of their time. By the 1820s, was building a machine from a drawing really not possible?

The problem was twofold: with the drawing, and then its translation into solid form. Eighteenth-century design came out of architectural tradition, the style of drawing adopted by other professionals including naval and civil engineers and millwrights. This was the route followed by makers of stationary steam-engines, whose clients expected individually tailored plans for their high-value purchase and associated construction work. Thus James Watt and Matthew Murray, unusually for the time, produced good quality drawings.[125] Almost the first item listed in Murray's will was 'my Mechanical Drawings and Mechanical Books', bequeathed to his son-in-law and successor Richard Jackson.[126] Most drawings emerging from Murray's shop were of steam-engines, and produced by draughtsmen.

Other machine-makers, largely ignorant of what had gone before, set

---

118 PP Artisans and Machinery, 104.
119 WYAS Bradford, 32D83/33/1.
120 Scott (ed.), *Matthew Murray*, 51; Turner, 'Fenton, Murray and Wood'.
121 Scott (ed.), *Matthew Murray*, 30, 32.
122 Scott (ed.), *Matthew Murray*, 12.
123 Sir William Swallow (1905–97), former Managing Director of Vauxhall Motors, confirmed that this still applied in the 1920s. Briggs of Gomersal used a similar system in 1992.
124 PP Artisans and Machinery, 251 (Peter Ewart), also 303.
125 Scott (ed.), *Matthew Murray*, 18, 32; see app. 2.
126 Borthwick, Exch. June 1826.

a different path in mechanical drawing. But even in the era of engineering factories, drawings were scarce. Into the 1830s, a firm as large and reputable as the Newcastle marine and locomotive engineers Hawthorn spurned formal drawings. Basic craft methods of ordering work continued until the 1860s, the foreman's discretion instructing the workforce.[127] Engineering drawings were still 'few and far between' as late as 1920.[128]

Shortage of draughtsmen may have been the reason. James Nasmyth, doubly advantaged as son of an artist and Scots educated, applied to Henry Maudslay in 1829 knowing that his technical drawing skill was a trump card.

> I executed several specimens of my ability as a mechanical draughtsman; for I knew that Maudslay would thoroughly understand my ability to work after a plan. Mechanical drawing is the alphabet of the engineer. Without this the workman is merely a "hand". With it he indicates the possession of "a head"... I knew it to be a somewhat rare and much-valued acquirement.[129]

An unusual portfolio produced by Isaac Markham of Vermont, 1814–25, shows the growing divide between British and American mechanical drawing styles. For drawings were not 'a universal culture ... comprehensible to all' but rather reflected 'unique professional cultures of mechanical engineers'. Markham's brief career coincided with a significant shift from perspective to proportional plan-and-elevation drawings in the United States.[130] By the 1940s, drawing practices in America and Britain had diverged fundamentally, but the disparity was clear more than a century before. British engineers saw drawings as a tool for designing machinery; Americans used them as instruments of production control, to organize work.[131] Markham was an early exponent of projective drawing, taking ideas from British technology which he laced with his own considerable improvements.[132] One source which fed him (and other Americans) was Rees's *Cyclopaedia*, a static and rapidly dating record of technology at work in Britain. Nonetheless, a series of Rees's clear and accurate drawings commanded a high price when republished and sold in the United States from 1806.[133]

The greatest difficulties were accurate measurement and achieving

127 Brown, 'Design Plans', 200–2, 204–5.
128 Information from Sir William Swallow.
129 Smiles, *James Nasmyth*, 122.
130 Jeremy and Darnell, *Visual Mechanic Knowledge*, especially 40–7, 58, 71–3. David Jeremy supplied additional ideas.
131 Brown, 'Design Plans', 196, 199.
132 Jeremy and Darnell, *Visual Mechanic Knowledge*, 25, 29, 86.
133 Jeremy and Darnell, *Visual Mechanic Knowledge*, 335–44; also 34–5, 75–6; and see Harte, 'On Rees's *Cyclopaedia*'.

acceptable tolerances. American workers in the 1850s used detailed drawings but were equipped only with 'boxwood rules which every man carried in his pocket', working to plus or minus one thirty-second of an inch (0.79 mm). So each machine was fitted to itself. In Britain, the Great Western Railway engineer Daniel Gooch issued workers with templates and gauges set to key dimensions of drawings, but the method had limitations.[134] Furthermore, 'tacit knowledge', the instinctive and abstract part of skill, was not easily transmitted through static means.[135] Technology was not inert, could not quite be captured, frozen and sold on. Technological problems were ones of making and working, and solving them initiated further innovation. So the engineering environment was all-important, and because innovation was generated in a space of personal communication where little was written or otherwise recorded, then the interpersonal was for a long time the main means of diffusing technology, locally or internationally.[136] Samuel Slater, the first to successfully introduce Arkwright-style machinery to America, took not a single drawing or note from England, replicating the machines from memory in 1790–91.[137] The popular imagination held foreign spies culpable in stealing technology; in reality, migrating workers were far more significant.

After Albert's success in Mulhouse, discussed below, there followed many cases of British design and technique reaching Alsace, a steady interchange of engineering and textile expertise into Alsace from northern England, and moreover some French engineering movement into Lancashire.[138] Numerous British mechanics benefited from the foreign demand for their skills and knowledge, but most migration was short-term.[139] From the mid-eighteenth century, a few went to France, including supervisors and those equipping factories, who were less restricted by law than machine-makers were.[140] Although controls on emigration continued, in 1812 more than 1,300 Britons, 185 of them textile engineers of some description, were registered as alien immigrants in US textile trades.[141]

How far these migrants did or could effectively export technology is hard to establish. As with the Arkwright system's introduction into Britain, it often needed skilled mechanics to bed in a machine and bring it into working

---

134   Brown, 'Design Plans', 213.

135   Jeremy and Darnell, *Visual Mechanic Knowledge*, 78–9.

136   See for example Jeremy, *Transatlantic Industrial Revolution*; Bruland, *British Technology and European Industrialization*, 5, 22, *passim*; MacLeod, 'Strategies for Innovation', 286.

137   White, *Samuel Slater*, 77–8.

138   Schmitt, 'Relations between England and Mulhouse'; and see below.

139   See for example Heaton, 'Yorkshire Mechanic Abroad'; Brotherton SC, MS165, notes of Samuel Owen 1844.

140   Henderson, *Britain and Industrial Europe*, ch. 2.

141   Jeremy and Darnell, *Visual Mechanic Knowledge*, 21. The emigration ban for skilled workers was lifted in 1825: see below, pp. 253–4.

order.[142] Even so, the supervising engineer must soon depart, leaving the machine in other hands. And as Boulton and Watt's man memorably wrote when accompanying a steam-engine to Italy, the locals were an 'ignorant sett of piple as ever I saw – they kno nothing of mushiniry'.[143] Nor were English émigrés always the most efficient or sober workers.[144]

Francis Wheelhouse, a Sheffield freemason who carved a career in Portugal from 1789, and almost single-handedly established that country's factory system, saw an early version of a throstle at work in Portugal in 1795. This was copied from 'one made by a man from Manchester for the French king. It is the worst thing I ever saw ... wasted as much as was spun'.[145] Industrial espionage clearly had its limits. And as Harris identified among Huguenot immigrants to Britain, the true value of workmen could lie in their skills, rather than in any novel technology they brought.[146]

Investigative tourism

The 'spies' assumed many guises. A visiting foreigner might be an esteemed potential customer; a lady or gentleman on a grand tour of new industrial marvels; a spy whose devious dealings threatened British engineering supremacy; or some permutation thereof.[147] Set against states of war with France and America, dire warnings in local newspapers provoked suspicion, perhaps hysteria. Frequently, engineers produced goods allowed for export alongside banned items, so admitting foreign customers was entirely reasonable. A distinguished caller, or any potential client, would not lightly be turned away. Some were very open to the flattery implied by a grand visitor, even without the possibility of a sale. Matthew Boulton's 'love of a lord' was noted.[148] The younger James Watt drew Johann Conrad Fischer's 'particular attention to the fact that the Grand Duchess [Catherine of Russia] had been graciously pleased to discuss with him at some length the construction and mechanism of the many steam engines which she saw [at Soho]'.[149]

Though the Grand Duchess was an unlikely mole, espionage was not a fantasy. The French government commissioned the disreputable Bonaventure

142   Harris, *Industrial Espionage*, 550.
143   Tann and Breckin, 'International Diffusion of the Watt Engine', 557.
144   Harris, *Industrial Espionage*, 549.
145   Aspin, *The Decoy*, 1, 16.
146   Harris, *Industrial Espionage*, 539.
147   For an overview of travellers' accounts and 'spies', see Woolrich, *Mechanical Arts and Merchandise*.
148   Harris, *Industrial Espionage*, 534.
149   Henderson, *Fischer and his Diary*, 133.

Joseph Le Turc to record industrial processes and recruit key workers from various trades in England in the 1780s.[150] Other suspicious foreigners were caught red-handed. In 1781, a German called George Claus, of Aix-la-Chapelle [Aachen], was apprehended after several months in Leeds as he left for London

> having in his possession a machine for spinning woollen-yarn before it is made into cloth, as practised in this neighbourhood ... The machine had been above a week at his lodgings, where he had set it up, & actually practised on it; but when seized, it was nailed up in a box ... stuffed with straw.[151]

Claus had commissioned 'a compleat spinning jenny' and 'bespoke another lately invented machine', a scribbling mill. Here is the earliest known reference to scribbling mills working in Leeds.[152] 'Wood wheels were to be made w[h]ere wood wheels are used, and iron where iron', by local workmen bribed to make 'a compleat working scribbling mill'.[153] Claus managed to avoid remand in York Castle prior to trial, through three sureties of £150, and his own guarantee of £200. The *Leeds Mercury* had less faith in Claus.

> [F]rom his being well-recommended to the merchants, having plenty of cash, and being very ingenious, there is no doubt that his sole business was to have stole patterns both of our spinning & scribbling machines, a model of the later being making at Armley; and at Hunslet he had engaged a cloth-maker and his family to go with him, on promise of £100 a year. We hope all persons concerned in managing these machines will, for the future, take care how they suffer unknown persons to make observations on them, as the consequences to this country may be very fatal.[154]

William Bouchier Leonard, a Gloucester-born Frenchman practising in Leeds as a surgeon, was brought back from London after being found in possession of

> plans of a scribbling machine, a willy and a scribbling-dick ... and ... also found, cast in brass, wheels for the greatest part of a scribbling machine, a one-handed shuttle, and several other utensils used in the woollen manufactory. By the depositions of several witnesses it also appeared that

---

150   Harris, *Industrial Espionage*, 2, and ch. 17 for Le Turc's machinations.
151   *Leeds Mercury*, 6 Feb. 1781, reproduced in Crump (ed.), *Leeds Woollen Industry*, 314.
152   *Leeds Intelligencer*, 6 Feb. 1781; Crump (ed.), *Leeds Woollen Industry*, 9–10. They were already in use in Huddersfield.
153   TNA, T1/568/281–286, 6 Mar 1781, with thanks to Chris Aspin.
154   *Leeds Mercury*, 6 Feb. 1781.

he intended to go to America, to set up a manufactory of wool, having endeavoured to inveigle them to go with him.[155]

Despite protesting innocence, Leonard was fined £200 and imprisoned for a year. In 1788 he reappeared, in the United States, in Boston, 'to introduce the manufactory of woollens ... he has no models, but drawings upon paper of different machines'.[156] After his conviction in 1784, the *Mercury* had again warned 'the in general too credulous manufacturers against permitting strangers, especially of a foreign nation, to inspect their machines and improvements'.[157] Certain suspicious callers were actually British. A West Country man with a sack of 'models in miniature of every working article used in the woollen and stuff manufactory' was released by magistrates, though his models were confiscated.[158] Henry Dobson, for 15 years an ironfounder in Rouen, was reported to authorities while visiting Ossett in 1802, by someone with a grudge, it was said, for spying in contravention of the 1781 Act, having done no more than make notes and sketches.[159]

François-Bernard Boyer-Fonfrede opened a cotton mill at Toulouse in 1791 after making drawings of machines and recruiting workers in England. He then despatched François Charles Louis Albert (1764–1853) to Manchester to gather further information. Albert was arrested and, unable to pay the £500 fine, imprisoned for five years. He went on to found a factory of his own in Mulhouse, making a name as a pioneer of English techniques in Alsace.[160]

Novel technologies and techniques drew foreign callers to all kinds of industrial sites. Usually there was transparency about their own business interests and they were readily admitted. Clearly not all were spying, though some had quite specific concerns. Many were sightseers on a new grand tour, embracing Britain's industrial marvels. Their journals note all sorts of historic and modern sights, not only factories. As for organized espionage, the French state's active encouragement branded it the main culprit. The Danish government was also involved. Other nationalities were implicated, but without obvious state sponsorship, and indeed the situation varied country by country. Strained relations with the United States, after war and independence in the 1770s, limited the movement of technology, but there was no official sponsorship of industrial spying. With Russia, commercial treaties

155   Crump (ed.), *Leeds Woollen Industry*, 10, 326; *Leeds Mercury*, 24 Feb. 1784.
156   *Leeds Intelligencer*, 25 Nov. 1788.
157   *Leeds Mercury*, 3, 24 Feb., 9 Mar. 1784; Crump (ed.), *Leeds Woollen Industry*, 10.
158   *Leeds Mercury*, 22 June 1784.
159   Goodchild, 'A Case of Industrial Espionage?', based on papers from Cusworth Hall. Around Manchester, similar alarms were sounded about foreign and British 'spies': Aspin, *Water-Spinners*, 18–22.
160   Schmitt, 'Relations between England and Mulhouse'; Henderson, *Britain and Industrial Europe*, 46.

and friendly contact throughout the eighteenth century eased the transfer of workers and technology.[161]

Casual introductions were often enough to see strangers welcomed into industrial premises. Fischer, a Swiss steel-maker carrying a recommendation to James Watt in 1814, was greeted with lavish hospitality and immediate admission to the whole of Boulton and Watt's works – far more than visitors were normally shown.[162] On such short acquaintance Watt supplied a note to Philips and Lee, the Salford cotton-spinners, who in turn introduced Fischer to Benjamin Gott in Leeds. After seeing Gott's factories, a letter of introduction from Gott took him into John Marshall's flax-mill. Though it was understood that Marshall did not admit foreigners, he personally conducted Fischer through the works.[163] While in Leeds, Fischer also inspected the Middleton railway, and a partner conducted him round the Low Moor ironworks. On a later visit, in 1825, Fischer met more engineers and iron- and steel-makers, in Lancashire and south Yorkshire, some through compatriots then working or training in Manchester.[164] His account suggests open discussion of technical information without concealment.

Less commonly, certain factories were entirely closed to visitors. This may not have been through fear of technological espionage. Despite Fischer's reception in Soho, some viewed Boulton and Watt as unreasonably secretive.

> With respect to the practice of the house of Boulton and Watt, they have always displayed an uncommon degree of mystery; and have always shut their works against any competent judge in England, and therefore foreigners have been no worse treated than everybody else; but my opinion is decidedly, that they have nothing to show beyond what is well known in other places; they continue from pride that exclusion which before was dictated by interest.[165]

So the cupboard they concealed was bare of novelty. When in 1826 Strutt of Belper declined to admit Karl Friedrich Schinkel, a wide-ranging Prussian with particular interests in architecture and design, most probably the reason was that visitors were a general nuisance, not that Schinkel appeared especially suspicious.[166]

George Brownell, superintendent of the Lowell (Mass.) machine shop sent abroad in 1839 to learn more of industrial and mechanical practices,

---

161 Harris, *Industrial Espionage*, especially ch. 15 and 16; Aspin, *Water-Spinners*, 21; Henderson, *Britain and Industrial Europe*, 18–19; Woolrich, *Mechanical Arts and Merchandise*, 19–61, especially 33–6, 51–2.
162 Henderson, *Fischer and his Diary*, 131–4.
163 Henderson, *Fischer and his Diary*, 57–60.
164 Henderson, *Fischer and his Diary*, 62–5.
165 PP Artisans and Machinery, 20, evidence of Alexander Galloway.
166 Bindman and Riemann (eds), '*English Journey*'.

was received with openness by leading northern engineers, though turned away from Seaward's London steam-engine works. His letter of introduction cut no ice: Seaward was 'very jelious of strangers'.[167] So were the owners of Manchester cotton-factories, where Brownell made several attempts: 'Have not seen any cotton mill at Manchester yet, the owners are very jelious, dubtfull whether we shall be admitted'.[168] Instead his extensive interests in engineering led Brownell to seek out machine tools, railroads, textile machinery, machine prices, card-makers and spindle works, visiting such notables as Sharp and Roberts, Whitworth, Nasmyth and William Fairbairn in Manchester, Stephenson in Newcastle, and Napier in Glasgow. Several purchases were made from these companies, with no problem or constraint evident.[169]

Textile manufacturers appeared the most reluctant to share information with outsiders. The Leeds flax-spinner James G. Marshall would not admit anyone engaged in the same work. It seems he feared losing key workers, suffering general inconvenience, and sharing production techniques. Yet Marshall did not object to these same foreigners accessing the machine shops that supplied him. He also thought that 'reciprocity of advantages is, I believe, on the whole, the most advantageous policy', and when asked about French attempts to maintain secrecy, replied that he 'should rather doubt the practicability of that being maintained'.[170] William Jenkinson of Salford offered the machine-maker's view:

> Do you give [foreign machine-makers] free access to your works, or is there any restraint imposed upon their inspection of new machinery and new inventions? – If they come properly introduced we never make any hesitation about it.

> Your object as machine-makers being to sell the articles which you produce? – Yes.[171]

More remarkably, William C. Davol of Fall River (Mass.) passed more than two months in northern England in 1839, the main attraction Sharp, Roberts & Co.'s Manchester machine-shop. Davol wanted to obtain a self-acting mule, register a US patent and share profits with Roberts. After many days at the works, he embarked on other visits. Returning to Manchester, Davol was boarded by Sharp, Roberts & Co. with one of their employees, a pattern-maker, where their principal draughtsmen, a German called Beyer, also

167   Bennett, 'Journal of George Brownell', 361–2.
168   Bennett, 'Journal of George Brownell', 349, 364.
169   Bennett, 'Journal of George Brownell', 325–6.
170   PP Exportation of Machinery, 195.
171   PP Exportation of Machinery, 107.

lodged. Davol then spent days in the company's 'experiment room' studying the motions of the self-actor, engaging in long discussion with technical staff, examining the machine tools and foundry used to produce mules, even noting factory dimensions and working conditions.[172] If this were spying, it had the blessing of Sharp and Roberts. But exporting the machinery was still illegal. Davol acquired a single model of the self-actor, but only by having a third party purchase it, saw it into small pieces, and send it via France. It was two years in reaching the United States, after which Davol rebuilt it and in 1841 obtained a patent on Roberts's behalf. Davol later pioneered the use of self-acting mules in America.[173]

In London as a young man in 1794, Johann Conrad Fischer was himself employed to produce parts for textile machines, taking home with him various steel samples. He was cautious about appearing as a foreigner in London, but this was because of an unsympathetic political climate in the 1790s. There was no industrial reason, for he was clear that any comparison between British 'mechanical arts' and those of the continent 'was entirely in England's favour. The English did not fear foreign competition in this or in other branches of industry'.[174] Fischer was the first to produce cast steel in continental Europe, from 1805 at Schaffhausen on the Swiss-German border; so on subsequent visits to Britain he carried a reputation, and came as a potential supplier of cast steel.

Zachariah Allen's journal of a northern England tour in 1825 was particularly expansive. He made small sketches of machinery, factory layouts and fireproof construction, with explanatory notes. It was, though, insufficient as a basis for machine-construction. Allen, a well-educated Rhode Island textile manufacturer and innovator, encountered little difficulty in accessing premises. Not much was held back. In just one recorded altercation, a machine-maker took him to see a new carding engine at work. The textile manufacturer 'a rough-looking Yorkshireman became very jealous & accused us of wishing to get away his trade & at last vented his choler on the machine-maker ...'.[175] The reaction was clearly unexpected, for generally Allen had been hospitably received as a prospective customer.

Allen's case shows technology transfer as a dynamic, creative process, a dialogue in know-how.[176] Viewing it as an advanced sector handing down packaged information to one less developed would be a travesty. Allen's journal

---

172   Fall River Historical Society, Wm C. Davol diary (journal of trip to England), 1838–39: see entries 5 Jan. to 20 Feb. 1839.

173   Koorey, *Fall River Revisited*, 40; Jeremy (ed.), *Technology and Power*, 104, 235 (fn. 40).

174   Henderson, *Fischer and his Diary*, 24–5; http://www.georgfischer.com, accessed 11 Oct. 2017, for a history of Georg Fischer AG Schaffhausen, founded 1802, employing 2,900 in 2016.

175   Rhode Island Historical Society, Zachariah Allen Papers, Journal of European Trip 1825, p. 72.

176   For technological dialogue see Pacey, *Technology in World Civilization*.

reveals exchanges founded in subtleties and unbounded curiosity, for like other intelligent travellers, his interests ranged far outside his trade.[177] Much that he recorded was well-established, even traditional, and as concerned with technique as with engineering novelty. His contrasting of American and British machinery did not routinely favour the British version.[178] Indeed, he hinted at British reluctance to adopt certain new technologies, for example in Benjamin Gott's opposition to an improved steam-milling method.[179] And just as Allen noted British practices, the manufacturers he met doubtless absorbed some of his thoughts, and considered adapting American methods to local conditions. There were good reasons to welcome informed foreign visitors, and the potential for a stimulating two-way, mutually beneficial, technical and commercial interchange.[180]

In fact Britain entered the eighteenth century as a 'technical debtor',[181] borrowing European ideas and techniques, with British industrialists themselves no strangers to investigative continental tourism.[182] Seventeenth- and eighteenth-century Sheffield steel-makers imported German steel and manufacturing technology, including cementation furnaces and tilt hammers.[183] Before and after the technological balance swung into Britain's favour, information passed along a two-way street with Europe, and later also America.[184]

'We have derived almost as many good inventions from foreigners, as we have originated among ourselves', John Farey told the Select Committee on Patent Laws in 1829. Farey was a well-travelled patent agent, in France as well as Britain, a writer and mechanical draughtsman who as a youth produced multiple drawings for Rees's *Cyclopaedia*.[185] Matthew Curtis, a Manchester machine-maker, testified in 1841 that 'the greatest portion of new inventions lately introduced to this country have come from abroad ... not improvements in machines, but rather entirely new inventions'. He saw the US as a source of much originality, its inventiveness stimulated by labour shortages and

---

177   Allen, *Practical Tourist*, *passim*.

178   Allen, *Practical Tourist*, 171, 196–7.

179   Rhode Island Historical Society, Zachariah Allen Papers, Journal of European Trip 1825, pp. 55–6.

180   Bruland, *British Technology and European Industrialization*, 22.

181   Harris, *Industrial Espionage*, 535.

182   Benson, *Textile Machines*, 7; Harris, 'Industrial Espionage in the Eighteenth Century', 129; Inkster, 'Mental Capital', 423–4, 434; Farnie, 'Textile Machine-making Industry', 154–6; Musson and Robinson, *Science and Technology*, 60–4; also Catling and Richards in Jenkins (ed.), *Wool Textile Industry in Great Britain*.

183   Hey, *Fiery Blades*, 115–16, 183–4.

184   See for example Woolrich, *Mechanical Arts and Merchandise*, 66–8.

185   Musson and Robinson, *Science and Technology*, 63–4; A. P. Woolrich, 'John Farey (1791–1851), mechanical engineer', *DNB*.

'untrammelled by predilections in favour of a machine already in existence'.[186] But once imported to Britain, such machines were generally improved.

> It is not the case that parties have come here to perfect the machines; they are perfect, as the foreigner imagines, when he brings them to this country; but when they come here they are placed in the hands of mechanics … [who] from the more extensive knowledge they have of the working of the various machines, are better able to perfect them, the workmen generally paying great attention to the different working parts.[187]

Peter Fairbairn informed that same inquiry that he 'had machines from the inventions of Swiss, and the workmanship of those machines was exceedingly good'.[188] Being receptive to ideas, open to adapting and assimilating technology, were the keys to continuing success, arguably 'as important as inventiveness itself'.[189]

What is more, the tenor of information-gathering was changing. Matthew Murray was despatched to Cheshire by John Marshall in 1790, clandestinely it is assumed, expressly to check spinning techniques.[190] The Leeds cotton-spinner Ard Walker appears to have bought frames from Halifax in 1800 and employed a spindle-maker to copy them.[191] These questionable activities are understandable when technological confidence was fragile, but pointless once engineering established a solid local footing. Keeping abreast of developments would become more casual and cordial, an arm of commerce. So in 1821, when Samuel Hattersley, eldest son of Richard, set out on an extended visit to clients across northern England, he gathered potentially useful information besides orders and monies owed.[192] In Preston at 'Sleddon's Place' the foreman showed him round, 'which proved a treat indeed. I saw the completest machines, for their various uses, that I ever saw'.[193] In Burnley he noted that one manufacturer 'intends to make alterations to his spinning machines soon'. In 1847 George Hattersley sought details of looms in use in the linen trade, from Edward Hattersley of Barnsley, presumably a relative. Edward offered to show him 'what is doing in Barnsley as I can have access to any of the power loom factorys in the town'.[194] George's eldest son, Richard

---

186 PP Exportation of Machinery, 111.

187 PP Exportation of Machinery, 113.

188 PP Exportation of Machinery, 212.

189 Rosenberg, *Inside the Black Box*, cited by Inkster, 'Mental Capital', 403.

190 Turner, 'Fenton, Murray and Wood', 1.12.

191 Connell, 'Industrial development', 162–3; WYAS Leeds, DB23.

192 WYAS Bradford, 32D83/2/5.

193 WYAS Bradford, 32D83/15/1. He visited Todmorden, Manchester, Ashton, Stalybridge, Oldham, Halifax and the upper Calder Valley, and then Linton, Grassington, Gisburn, Clitheroe and Whalley.

194 WYAS Bradford, 32D83/33/7.

L. Hattersley (1820–1900), recorded continental excursions from 1846 until the closing years of the century. While the main aim was loom sales, he constantly sketched and noted technical information.[195]

Making things work

[Most] mechanical inventions are of a very composite character, and are led up to by the labour and the study of a long succession of workers … But the making of the invention is not the sole difficulty. It is one thing to invent, said Sir Marc Brunel, and another thing to make the invention work.[196]

So the obstacle overcome by Arkwright, that of 'making it useful', continued to challenge mechanical innovators.[197] For Smiles wrote in the present tense, in 1863, when the main textile processes were mechanized, and machine tools were efficient and ubiquitous. Evidently these new tools had not delivered a complete solution. 'To make the invention work' took more than precise and consistent components. Bedding in new technology, settling it into the chain of processes, handling materials of varying strength and plasticity, achieving necessary economies, were other dimensions in making a viable textile machine.

From Leonardo onwards, converting a paper concept into reality was checked by the limitations of engineering, and the boundaries of social, commercial and technical context.[198] Timing was everything.[199] By the late-eighteenth century, while engineering problems still hampered Watt's quest to build engines more efficiently, the dynamics of place and time motivated him to keep trying.[200] This new environment inspired many modifications of other people's imperfect machines, or encouraged concerted efforts to make them work: Marshall with the Darlington flax-spinning machinery, and using John Jubb's looms and Cartwright's designs to advance linen-weaving; Gott and his Bramah press; James Ackroyd of Halifax with a French Jacquard loom.[201] Wyatt and Paul's roller-spinning system of 1738 did not make the grade until Arkwright applied it in the cotton industry.[202] To employ rollers in

---

195   WYAS Bradford, 32D83/42.

196   Smiles, *Industrial Biography*, 178–9.

197   See above, p. 33.

198   Mathias, *Transformation of England*, 76; see also Ponting, *Leonardo da Vinci*.

199   See Nowotny, *Cunning of Uncertainty*, 161–8.

200   See above, pp. 133–4.

201   Rimmer, *Marshalls of Leeds*, 23, 27–33; Turner, 'Fenton, Murray and Wood', 1.10; Cookson (ed.), *VCH Durham IV*, 154–5; Crump (ed.), *Leeds Woollen Industry*, 49–50; James, *History of the Worsted Manufacture*, 440.

202   Usher, *History of Mechanical Inventions*, 297–8; Cookson, 'Lewis Paul', *DNB*.

worsted spinning took yet more experimentation, and further adjustments to Arkwright's water frame.[203]

Edmund Cartwright exemplifies what could be achieved by a committed, intelligent, well-resourced gentleman. But even for him, effort, energy and money were not enough. Cartwright's achievement was as a designer of power looms (patented from 1785) and wool-combs (from 1789) – concepts well ahead of their time. Solid in theory, they were neither commercially nor technically successful. The loom, despite years of modification and efforts to run it in a purpose-built factory, frustrated the most skilled Manchester machine-makers Cartwright could hire, who 'despaired of ever making it answer the purpose it was intended for'.[204] Over the following decades, others took Cartwright's principles in hand and made something useful. By the time of his daughter's memoir in 1843, the loom had changed radically: 'The patent ... has doubtless been receiving continual additions from various hands during the last fifty years; and the beautiful machine ... differs considerably in detail, even from the most improved form of Mr Cartwright's invention.'[205] In fact it was 40 years before Cartwright's loom worked efficiently on worsteds.[206] Even then, countless refinement followed, chasing higher speeds, improving performance, adapting to new products. Richard L. Hattersley and his foreman John Wilkinson produced an impressive list of enhancements and new applications for the loom after 1850.[207]

How, then, to characterize Cartwright? His loom trials, underway at precisely the time of Marshall and Murray's flax-spinning experimentation, were far less productive, at least immediately. Cartwright had mechanics on his payroll but was himself no technician. He also lacked the imperative, the supportive and instructive context, of a local textile community. Indeed Cartwright was located in late-eighteenth-century philosophical circles, the world of Joseph Priestley and Matthew Boulton, though unusual among his *confrères* in pursuing his interests so mundanely (as they perhaps saw it). Cartwright's conceptions were outstanding, but they were blueprints, not working models.[208] He stands tall by virtue of these designs, and also because his legacy was promoted by Samuel Lister, Lord Masham. Lister's motives were less than worthy, for he sought to undermine his one-time partner Isaac Holden, another pretender to the wool-comb inventor crown.[209] In truth,

203   Hodgson, *Textile Manufacture*, 240–1.
204   Strickland, *Edmund Cartwright*, 72; Hills, *Power in the Industrial Revolution*, 213–20.
205   Strickland, *Edmund Cartwright*, 59.
206   Hodgson, *Textile Manufacture*, 267; Jenkins and Ponting, *British Wool Textile Industry*, 110–11.
207   Hodgson, *Textile Manufacture*, 272–3.
208   Cf. O'Brien, 'Micro Foundations of Macro Invention'.
209   O'Brien, 'Micro Foundations of Macro Invention', 211–12.

neither Lister nor Holden started from scratch, and both produced workable solutions. Lister's derived from Cartwright, Donisthorpe and others, while Holden 'exercis[ed] his ingenuity' upon some imperfect combing machines which he had persuaded his employer to buy in 1833.[210]

But there was no shame in being a visionary whose designs were not immediately useable, nor an adaptor of other people's work. Richard Roberts, while claiming to know nothing of cotton-spinning, responded with the self-acting mule to a direct appeal by cotton-spinners hoping to undermine striking employees. The idea of a self-actor was not original, but Roberts was the first to 'work it out into a practicable process'.[211] An early biographer described Peter Fairbairn, credited with some of the greatest mechanical breakthroughs of the nineteenth century in spinning and preparing worsteds and flax, and in designing and making machine tools, as 'an inventor and improver of machinery'.[212] His engineering skills and commercial knowledge were as impressive as his technical grounding in cotton and other machinery in Manchester, Glasgow and France.[213]

Sets of erectors and adapters despatched to help 'bed in' equipment attacked this problem of making things work.[214] Skilled erectors accompanied Matthew Murray's engines.[215] Later, ever more sophisticated sales packages were offered, including training operators and tuners to achieve maximum efficiency in working the plant. Exporters to Norway sent out technical information, ancillary kit and construction expertise along with skilled operatives and managers.[216]

William Hirst, a cropper formerly employed by Gott, made a career of bringing problematic machinery into use. By his own account, in 1816

> Fenton Murray & Co. ... told me that if I would use the hydraulic presses, they would let me have them at almost any price, as they wanted to get them into the hands of some party who could bring them into operation, so as to give them a fair chance.[217]

Hirst (who tended towards self-promotion) noted that Murray had praised his persistence.[218] Hirst also claimed to have worked out a solution enabling gig-mills to be used on Leeds cloths, by changing the prior process. This was

---

210   *Keighley News*, 14 Aug. 1897.
211   Smiles, *Industrial Biography*, 267–9.
212   Taylor (ed.), *Biographia Leodiensis*, 491–6.
213   See app. 2.
214   See above, pp. 133–4.
215   Scott (ed.), *Matthew Murray*, 24.
216   Bruland, *British Technology and European Industrialization*, 5–6.
217   Hirst, *History of the Woollen Trade*, 8.
218   Hirst, *History of the Woollen Trade*, 8.

in about 1813: 'I was not the first who introduced gigs, but I was the first who made cloth suitable for gig-raising. The ordinary fabric made at that time was always worse for being finished by machinery than if it had been done by hand'. That the quality of yarn available had improved considerably possibly assisted Hirst in this.[219] Here is another recurring theme in 'making work' – successful mechanization of one textile process pressing a review of what preceded or followed. For power-loom weaving to work well, said William Fairbairn, automatic dressing machines were essential.[220] Cartwright's loom had become easier to operate as machine-spun yarn improved in quality, and after Radcliffe devised a system of dressing the warp before it was placed upon the loom.[221] Mechanizing spinning 'compelled' innovators to turn their attention to improving preparatory processes.[222]

This reinforces the idea that environment stimulated inventiveness. Even modest improvements drew attention to a larger context, a current and informed view of textiles and mechanics. The intelligence was specialized, but it was widespread in textile communities. Actual improvement, of making work, was clearly not theoretical; but neither – even in textile engineering's earliest phases – is it adequate to characterize it as 'the rearrangement of known gadgetry by handy tinkerers'.[223] Terms like 'tweakers' condescend to and downplay essential expertise, one embracing manual ability and knowledge.[224] In reality, the task was focused, substantiated and thoughtful.

Another element in 'making things work' was adapting technology across districts and fibres. Machines working in different settings, most obviously in other branches of textiles, were not instantly transferable. But they could stimulate parallel innovation, and patented machines might have a similar effect. Precedents were widely borrowed, further indication of adaptation often being more opportune than starting from scratch. The evidence is strong that many early machines and technological ideas originated in places where cotton production concentrated, notably Manchester, and then moved into other textile branches.[225]

As noted, textile manufacturers did not usually make machinery.[226] A handful of early engineers switched to textiles and discontinued machine sales, while still (in some cases) making their own. M'Connel and Kennedy of Manchester converted entirely to fine-cotton spinning by about 1800.[227] Berry

---

219 Crump (ed.), *Leeds Woollen Industry*, 48–50.
220 Fairbairn, 'Rise and Progress of Manufactures', clxxii.
221 Strickland, *Edmund Cartwright*, 218–19.
222 Hills, *Power in the Industrial Revolution*, 73.
223 Biernacki, 'Culture and Know-How', especially 222.
224 Meisenzahl and Mokyr, 'Rate and Direction of Invention', 446 and *passim*.
225 See above, pp. 14, 52.
226 See above, pp. 54–8.
227 Lee, *Cotton Enterprise*, 10, 23; see above, p. 55.

Smith, a successful machine-maker in business in Keighley from 1801, was solely a commission worsted spinner by about 1830.[228] But there were also machine-makers who engaged in textile manufacture as a secondary string. John Jubb was a partner in Churwell cotton mill during the 1780s.[229] Joshua Wordsworth owned a business in Barnsley, spinning and manufacturing linen and mixed fabrics, during his later career.[230] Samuel Lawson, in partnership with the flax-spinner Mark Walker from 1812 until 1831, continued afterwards to run a flax-dressing and spinning concern, employing 66 people in 1834.[231] Richard Hattersley's eldest son, Samuel, took charge of their small worsted spinning business in Keighley between about 1817 and 1822, before being sent to manage a new machine-making branch in Bradford in 1824.[232] A generation later, George Hattersley's third son, Edwin, successfully managed four worsted spinning factories in the Worth Valley, c. 1850–90, while a more technical older brother, Richard Longden Hattersley, took over the machine-making business.[233]

These examples stretch over a century, and the purpose of engagement in textiles may have changed. There were commercial reasons. Machine-makers knew the profit opportunities in textiles. A textile subsidiary might balance the peaks and troughs of a more volatile capital goods market. The latest technology could be seen in action, encouraging other textile manufacturers to buy. Textile businesses absorbed family members unsuited to engineering, or surplus to engineering company requirements. This was certainly the case for two generations of Hattersleys and Smiths, with many sons to accommodate. A textile factory was also a laboratory to trial and perfect new machinery. Working the processes brought solutions to technical difficulties, within a machine or in settling it into the production chain. The engineers involved in textile manufacture were all active innovators; and so were Matthew Murray and Peter Fairbairn, both with exceptionally close links to textile manufacturers.

Managing innovation

Far from abating, the torrent of innovation increased as engineering established itself in factory bases. The keys to success were little different in new settings than in the unsteady older world of machine-making. One difference

228   Hodgson, *Textile Manufacture*, 252–6; PP (HC) 1834 XX (167) C1, 220–1.
229   *Leeds Mercury*, 23 Nov. 1784; app. 2.
230   Borthwick, Prog. Sept. 1846. Collaborations with textile manufacturers are discussed above, pp. 199–201.
231   PP (HC) 1834 XX (167) C1, 249; WYAS Leeds, Acc. 2371/Box 80/Bundle 2; Ward, 'Industrial development and location', 422–3.
232   WYAS Bradford, 32D83/9/2.
233   Keighley census 1851; WYAS Bradford, 32D83, introduction to list.

was the level of resources available, though dedicated experimentation was expensive and held no guarantee of recompense.

It was therefore sensible to spread the risks of innovation. The northern communities where inventiveness flourished minimised the uncertainties, offering opportunities to focus, appropriate industrial contexts and an encouraging milieu. There was a clear field unencumbered by problematic institutions, incompatible vested interests, or endemic inertia. The difficulties experienced when trying to transplant and 'indigenize' innovations to different cultures show just how significant this local framework might be.[234] Likewise the presence of other machine-makers and users meant that new technology could be readily assessed, practically and commercially besides mechanically.[235] So personal relationships were a highly significant element of the innovation process, these affiliations colouring attitudes about the need and desirability of restricting technology's flow.

Above all, real success came not through protectionism, nor by any theoretical means, but by making things work. Innovation could bring a loss of perspective, causing the most talented engineers to overstretch and fail spectacularly. The knack was to manage the imperfect while chasing perfection. Hence the importance of a David Wood or a Joseph Taylor to maintain a well-run business and complement a technically gifted partner. The best of the new firms managed to build a structure replicating the finest aspects of community.

234 Mathias, *Transformation of England*, 36–7.
235 Rosenberg, *Perspectives on Technology*, 36–7.

8

Reaching Maturity

The factory imperative

Fully developed factories were late to arrive in this most advanced of industries.[1] Textile engineering before 1820 was characterized by flexible specialization and an 'ever-changing assortment of semi-customized products'.[2] In this it resembled the metal trades of Sheffield or the west Midlands, which took a middle path in workshop scale, contracted out certain processes, and adopted division of labour as far as was practical.[3] In 1850, still many small establishments offered useful specialisms and extra capacity, co-existing alongside vast and sophisticated engineering factories. Large did not imply inflexible; indeed British engineers were later criticized for being over-flexible, too willing to offer tailored products rather than, more efficiently and profitably, well-defined ranges.[4]

The rise of the engineering factory followed closely upon a series of breakthroughs in machine-tool technology between 1815 and 1830.[5] From relying heavily on manual dexterity in 1800, textile engineering had by 1840 advanced to a point where machines made machines.[6] Key breakthroughs were to the lathe and planer. Particularly significant was the work of Roberts and Whitworth, who, said William Fairbairn, made 'new and more perfect tool machinery, which has given not only mathematical precision, but almost a creative power – as one machine creates another'.[7] But process mechanization did not in itself make factories inevitable. Many of the new machine tools could be accommodated in existing workshops. The systems serving machine-makers for 40 or 50 years still presented advantages, optimizing the use of

---

1 Contrast with early textile industry examples: Chapman, 'Textile Factory before Arkwright'.
2 Sabel and Zeitlin, 'Historical Alternatives to Mass Production', 134, 142–56; see above, pp. 183–4.
3 Berg, 'Small Producer Capitalism', 17–20, 22.
4 Floud, *British Machine Tool Industry*, 56.
5 Steeds, *History of Machine Tools*, 26.
6 Jefferys, *Story of the Engineers*, 12; Checkland, *Rise of Industrial Society*, 81; Steeds, *History of Machine Tools*, 26.
7 Pole (ed.), *Life of Sir William Fairbairn*, 421.

labour, with subcontractors and casual staff working intensively or otherwise, according to demand. Even after 1840, the small workshop sector employed large numbers on jobbing and repair work, or other tasks or products outside machine-making's mainstream.

By about 1820, though, the industry's leading lights were moving to factories. Economics decided it, the prospect of enhancing quality and efficiency. Engineering – unlike textiles – never required a vast, unwieldy and fragile outwork system, nor was it much troubled by labour discipline and embezzlement. For engineers, moving into a factory actually demanded more of management. They must assume quality and training responsibilities previously dealt with by subcontractors, and learn to supervise a large workforce and address skill shortages. These inconveniences were counter-balanced by improvement in quality and consistency, and potential savings in transaction costs. But still, building and equipping new plant was costly. The outlay must be justified by an expectancy of continuing growth. Expanding markets, advances in products, tools and productivity, and the economies of scale made possible in a factory, all reassured firms to invest.

Subcontract reinforced the new arrangements.[8] The economies machine tools offered were fully realized in factories, but valuable too in the small-scale sector active alongside. Generally, smaller shops concentrated upon specialist component manufacture, repair and maintenance, and peripheral tasks. Potentially, all sectors gained by introducing specialist tools, mechanized lifting equipment and organizational improvements. Indeed, advances in mechanical handling and lifting propelled the shift to factories. They were arguably as significant as machine-tool innovation in this reshaping, perhaps more so. The power to move heavy components made possible a smoother, better-integrated production system. Machines and components could then be constructed in the same place, and this reordering brought not only economies of scale, but higher quality and accuracy too.

William Carr's workshop, aloft of his house, was built in 1798 with a 'crane' door from which machinery and parts were hoisted or lowered to street level, using only human power.[9] The arrangement was typical of early workshops. Some impetus to improve lifting technologies came out of construction and servicing around dockside facilities.[10] Separately, Bramah and Murray pioneered hydraulic cranes in c. 1800, for their own use. Murray designed a crane when extending his premises to make steam-engines, and Bramah when building new works. Bramah's prototype crane was shown off, but not taken up by the civil engineers then reshaping London's waterfront, nor widely adopted before William Armstrong became interested in the

8   Pollard, *Genesis of Modern Management*, 39.
9   Hodgson, *Textile Manufacture*, 250.
10 Rees, *Cyclopaedia*, II, 199–204; Cossons, *Industrial Archaeology*, 302.

technology in 1846.[11] In 1832, Murray's works had a dozen cranes, some able to lift 10 tons, 'and a hydraulic crane capable of lifting 40 tons, for loading boilers'.[12]

Aydon and Elwell of Shelf cast several fixed and moveable dockside cranes for London's West India docks (1813 and 1817) and in 1814 for Liverpool.[13] Possibly textile engineers commissioned lifting and handling equipment from this or similar companies, but it is more likely that they fabricated their own. The local ironworks and forges, as they upgraded to embrace a widening range of activity, may have been influential. Kirkstall, Low Moor and the rest, and Murray's Holbeck premises, gave a model. The facilities in Murray's new steam-engine plant doubtless benefited his textile engineering operation. Most of those working only with textile machinery, though, being smaller scale, financially limited and with no pressing need of heavy-duty equipment, continued much as before.

A template for factory-based mechanical engineering came in 1824, with a model machine shop constructed in Bolton by Johann Georg Bodmer (1786–1864). Commercially, it was not an instant success, but the Swiss engineer's state-of-the-art machine-making plant blazed a trail in production engineering, and showed what was possible. The machines, carefully arranged in rows, included small and large lathes, planing, drilling and slotting machines, all made by Bodmer – the most inventive being his gear-cutting machinery. Remarkable, though, was the totality, the system embodied within this workshop. Small travelling cranes placed articles accurately on large lathes; planing machines were served by other cranes; trucks on rails moved the work along.[14]

While subcontracting was heavily integrated into the fabric of early machine-making, this was a system based on skill, trust and understanding. It did not equate to the 'putting out' (Verlag) system, where insuperable problems of quality and logistics had driven sections of the textile industry to distraction, and into factories.[15] But it was evident that process mechanization was only one aspect of bettering quality. Factories made closer supervision possible, while skills were enhanced by narrowing and refining tasks and specialisms. John Lee Bradbury, a Manchester calico printer, believed

---

11   Cossons, *Industrial Archaeology*, 302; McNeil, *Joseph Bramah*, 154–7.

12   Scott (ed.), *Matthew Murray*, 47.

13   Information from John Suter, drawing upon 'The West India Docks: Power and Transport', in H. Hobhouse (ed.), *Survey of London: Vols 43 and 44, Poplar, Blackwall and Isle of Dogs*, 326–35; Dupin, *Commercial Power of Great Britain*, II, 280–2.

14   Rolt, *Tools for the Job*, 134–5. When Bodmer fell ill, the project stalled. The Bodmer memoirist is ambiguous about the date of the highly polished machine-shop described by Rolt. Its completion may have been as late as c. 1839, when Bodmer patented versions of these machine tools: *Proc. Inst. Civil Eng.*, 28 (1869), 573–608, especially 580–1, 588. Thanks to Richard Byrom for the reference.

15   Cookson, 'Family Firms and Business Networks', 11.

that the way work was organized gave local engineering the edge over that of London. In Manchester 'a workman is frequently kept in a manufactory at one article, all his life, and consequently attains great skill in the production of such article'.[16] With this trend to specialization, it was unthinkable that one person could produce an entire machine. 'There is not one man that could do the blacksmith's work and casting; a man could not make a spindle and a roller, but perhaps half a dozen men could do the whole'.[17]

But that is to describe the end of a process, a well-established and factory-centred industry. Why had it taken so long? In 1815, textile engineering was still settling and defining itself. The number of firms was small – in fact, fewer than before, once the less proficient and committed had been weeded out. Those in business in 1815 had faith in their own abilities and strategy, and knew their place in relation to the textile industry. As for the breakthroughs in machine tools, from 1815–30, was the timing entirely coincidental? These tools encouraged a more general transition into factory-working, but came as a response to a perceived need for better equipment, just as textile-processing technologies answered the textile trade's needs. Who better, indeed, to produce machine tools than machine-makers themselves? They had made their own for years, because they could, but the other significance of the 1820s was that specialist makers emerged, dedicated to producing better tools for the purpose.[18]

Consolidating and specializing

Factories generated increasing levels of specialization. Manufacturing components and machines together, in one establishment, forced the firm to plan more strategically, to seek out niches and concentrate on specific categories of machine. And on the shop floor, workers' tasks became more narrowly circumscribed.

By the 1840s, three clear divisions had formed within mechanical engineering.

> I should make three classes of the mechanical arts: the manufacture of steam-engines, mill-gearing, hydraulic presses and such other heavy machinery, I should call one class; the next, and a separate branch, I should say, was tool-making; and the third I should call machine-making, with its various branches of spindle and fly-making, and roller-making.[19]

16   PP Artisans and Machinery, 547.
17   PP Exportation of Machinery, 23, Thomas Ashton.
18   See above, p. 108.
19   PP Exportation of Machinery, 95, William Jenkinson.

Textile engineering, the third of these classes, was seen then as discrete. Northern England, and centres within it, effectively monopolized the main types of machine.[20] Keighley had speedily switched from cotton machinery to worsted, and the principal engineers, William Smith and George Hattersley, developed specialisms in, respectively, worsted spinning frames and worsted power looms.[21] A large part of the Leeds industry was devoted to flax-machines, with some of the same firms also involved in worsted and silk machinery. Bradford and Bingley were smaller centres of engineering.[22] Spen Valley produced woollen machinery as well as card-clothing, and Huddersfield had substantial machine-making – wider-ranging firms sometimes serving several textile branches. In Salford, Thomas Marsden, a machine-maker of some reputation, catered to woollen and flax industries as well as cotton in 1836.[23] But specialization was far advanced in Lancashire, and was a clear trend across the north as the mid-century approached, especially in larger firms.

Scale was crucial, making specialization both possible and essential for quality and efficiency. The 'high state of the subdivision of labour' gave British machinery its superiority, said Peter Ewart, and the size of firms had enabled this to happen: 'We never had any subdivision of labour till it was carried on to a great extent, and it is impossible to have a great subdivision of labour, but in proportion to the extent of business.'[24] Richard Hattersley remodelled his workshops into a factory before 1820, but as his focus remained components, these premises did not compare with the Leeds machine-makers – Taylor and Wordsworth, Fairbairn, Maclea and March, Lawson and Walker – to whom his firm supplied spindles and other parts into the 1840s.[25] Hattersley's reorganization was doubtless in reaction to unprecedented demand for spindles, which at one point produced a 20 per cent price increase in under a year,[26] as customers sought better quality and larger quantities of components which were still, by necessity, hand-made.[27]

It was Hattersley's neighbour, William Smith, his premises constantly upgrading from 1829, who was credited with bringing system to local machine-making. Said to have been the first to apply planing machines and similar tools to the manufacture of worsted-spinning frames in about 1830, Smith gave 'a completeness, finish and beauty to the various parts of their machinery which hitherto had not been realised'.[28]

---

20   See above, p. 161.
21   Though Hattersley's path was not straightforward: see below, p. 249.
22   PP Exportation of Machinery, 393; Banks, 'Progress of Engineering in Bradford', 16.
23   *Leeds Mercury*, 4 June 1836; PP Exportation of Machinery, 83 etc.
24   PP Artisans and Machinery, 251, 258; also 303, Thomas Ashton.
25   WYAS Bradford, 32D83/15/1; /2.
26   PP Artisans and Machinery, 341.
27   See above, pp. 64–8, 146.
28   *Keighley News*, 29 March 1890, 5; Keighley Lib., Poor Rate Books 1829–35.

So to achieve an integrated factory, or indeed interchangeable parts, was a staged process even for the leading engineers. Mass-producing identical products by machine continued to be far from standard.[29] Much was still accomplished by hand-working, using emery cloths and 'go, no go' gauges.[30] The rollers and spindles produced to finer tolerances were said to be interchangeable with others made to the same specification, though not between different models of machine.[31] But 'interchangeability' is not easily definable, when considerable skill was required even to re-assemble a factory-built machine on site.[32]

Nonetheless, British engineering had made great progress. In comparison, William Fairbairn found French equivalents 'very deficient in arrangements and method ... they appeared much more confused in their operations'.[33] Fairbairn's brother had the advantage of a standing start in 1829, when he set up in Leeds at an optimum time. By 1841 Peter Fairbairn employed 550 at his Wellington Foundry.[34]

> [T]he bulk of the operatives are involved in turning small pieces of iron, adjusting them with files, or boring them for the admission of axles – all, as far as possible, aided by steam power, which is distributed by shafts with hundreds of belts throughout the various floors. Much is also done by a corps of blacksmiths, whom ... I found hammering away in first-rate style in a long apartment on the ground floor ... here all is cleanliness and order ... there are no visible bellows, each forge being blown when required by admitting air from a great bellows in another part of the house, and wrought by the steam engine. This ... must effect a considerable saving of time ... and is another instance of that remarkable economisation of means which distinguishes all branches of our manufactures.[35]

The scale enabled, but also dictated, a highly tuned system to ensure that 500 workmen functioned efficiently. Tasks were closely defined to maximize economies of scale and precision. Fairbairn made clear the intention: 'In my works a subdivision of labour takes place; I require a good many very superior men, but I can do, by subdividing the work, with some inferior men.'[36] The continuing significance of manual skills in Peter Fairbairn's works is striking. Less-skilled labour was employed, not because machine tools had displaced

29 As late as the 1970s, 70 per cent of metalworking production in the United States was small batch: Sabel and Zeitlin, 'Historical Alternatives to Mass Production', 137.
30 Saul (ed.), *Technological Change*, 145–7.
31 PP Artisans and Machinery, 304.
32 PP Artisans and Machinery, 306, 343.
33 PP Artisans and Machinery, 568.
34 PP Artisans and Machinery, 209; app. 2.
35 *Chambers's Edinburgh Journal*, 513, 27 Nov. 1841.
36 PP Exportation of Machinery, 211.

the skilled, but because shop-floor systems enabled work to be broken down into tasks do-able by men less highly-trained.

This situation, advantageous to large factories, had its obverse: in small workshops, relatively easy tasks must, at least sometimes, have been allocated to skilled workers.[37] But this was offset by the shops' flexibility, subcontracting and mopping up repair and renewal work, a pattern continuing into the industry's recent history. By such means – adaptability, diversification, and disintegration, the features from which the early industry built – a rump of the textile-engineering industry endured.[38]

Most unexpected, though, as in textiles a generation or more earlier, was the variety of arrangements within these factories.[39] It is particularly telling that working by hand (at both high and low skill levels) continued to feature heavily in factories. This indicates that new machine tools – which, as argued above, were successfully used in small establishments, so did not absolutely demand a factory setting – were not the main incentive to introduce factories to engineering. Rather, the major gains in efficiency, of quantity and quality, discipline and control, were achieved through better procedures. Organization compensated where there was still technological deficiency. In first establishing the engineering factory, mechanical handling capabilities, and not machine tools, might just have been the decisive factor.

Responding to the market

Early textile engineers achieved much in small production units. Here, they could be technically flexible while reflecting their artisan roots and limiting risk. Richard Hattersley's small company experimented and kept abreast of developments, but appeared hesitant in extending the product range. Several power looms were built to order in May 1827, but not regularly after that.[40] From 1800, Hattersley's customer Berry Smith established a large business from scratch within seven or eight years.[41] He was at the cutting edge: repairing cotton machinery in 1800, building throstles the following year, producing his own spindles and flyers by 1805, and from 1809 manufacturing a 'modern worsted spinning frame' which he shipped far beyond the local region. But Smith, like Hattersley, held on to routine repair work to ensure an income if

37 More, *Skill and the English Working Class*, 155.
38 Cookson, 'West Yorkshire textile engineering industry', 38–9.
39 See above, pp. 20–1.
40 WYAS Bradford, 32D83/15/2. As the 1830s order books are incomplete this is not definitive.
41 Hodgson, *Textile Manufacture*, 252–6; Hattersley's sales records confirm Smith's component purchases rising rapidly, from a low base in 1800.

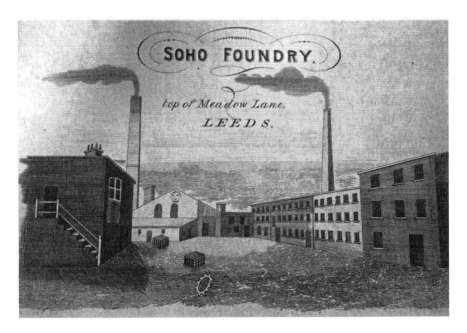

Plate 10. Premises of Zebulon Stirk, Soho Foundry, Hunslet, c. 1840
Source: WYAS Leeds, WYL2537.

the newer work dwindled.[42] Murray and Wood continued to advertise general foundry products in 1796, amidst all their specialisms, presumably as some buffer against a downturn.[43]

So how, in this mood of gradual progression, did change turn more radical? Expansion was financed largely through reinvesting profits and mortgaging new plant. Murray funded the Round Foundry and other developments through a mix of ploughed-back profit, mortgage, and a moneyed sleeping partner. A supportive John Marshall offered part of the site on favourable terms.[44] As Murray built for himself 'a superb house' during those early days, he was clearly not financially overstretched.[45] But not all engineers were as successful as Murray, nor as cautious as Hattersley. There were failures, sometimes through sheer bad luck. Apart from personal problems within family businesses, the market for machinery could be brutally inconsistent, rising and falling rapidly, and varying between localities according to advances in different branches of textiles. Sales in capital goods did not

---

42 Hodgson, *Textile Manufacture*, 254–5.
43 *Leeds Mercury*, 9 July 1796.
44 See above, pp. 111–12.
45 Scott (ed.), *Matthew Murray*, 36.

synchronize with overall trade cycles.[46] In consequence, machine-makers would delay deliveries, recruit more labour and increase overtime until they were sure demand was sustainable.

But a new machine, or other technological breakthrough, might change everything. Certain innovations had the potential to reinvigorate textile engineering, or a sector of it, whatever the overall state of trade. The cotton-mill building boom of 1789–1802, expansion of mechanized worsted spinning in Bradford between 1818 and 1825, and a wave of new textile factories in 1832–36, each provoked a clamour for machines.[47] Around 1810, when many Yorkshire cotton mills converted to worsteds, new or adapted machinery was in high demand.[48] While cotton industry downturns in 1825–26, 1836–42 and 1847–48 immediately squeezed engineers in the sector,[49] worsted machine-makers enjoyed a golden period through the introduction of power looms.[50] The worsted engineers did not appear at the 1841 parliamentary enquiry – perhaps having no grievances to air – and were still working at full capacity in 1843, when the Factory Inspector reported:

> The most extraordinary extension of any trade within a limited period is, perhaps, that which has occurred in the Bradford market … The machine-makers have been for some time, and continue to be, fully occupied in the manufacture of both spinning frames and power looms.[51]

A similarly localized 'extraordinary epoch' in worsted spinning and prepa-ration in Bradford from 1818 prompted Richard Hattersley to open a satellite works in the town.[52] The mechanists of Hyde, near Manchester, were at this same time 'very fully employed, for [cotton] power looms were being introduced, and that kept them in full employment during that time'.[53] The 1838 downturn, which had dire consequences for much of the textile trade, did not affect the rapid growth of Peter Fairbairn's company: 'The improve-ments that have taken place in flax machinery have been very great, and I think the extent to which the trade has gone [since 1828] has arisen chiefly from these improvements.'[54] Textile engineers were sufficiently inundated

---

46   Kirk, 'British textile machinery industry', 134, notes textile engineering in late-nineteenth-century Lancashire lagging about a year behind general economic cycles.

47   Baumber, *Revival to Regency*, 39; Jenkins and Ponting, *British Wool Textile Industry*, 60–70; James, *History of the Worsted Manufacture*, ch. X; Heaton, 'Early Victorian Business Forecaster'.

48   Jenkins and Ponting, *British Wool Textile Industry*, 61; Baumber, *Revival to Regency*, 39.

49   Musson, 'Manchester School', 22.

50   App. 3.

51   PP (HC) 1844, XXVIII, 7.

52   James, *History of the Worsted Manufacture*, 383.

53   PP Artisans and Machinery, 306.

54   PP Exportation of Machinery, 209.

with work in 1824 that they did not express a collective view to parliamentarians about the merits of lifting the machine export embargo.[55] The tone was complacent.

> Your opinion is, that in England we shall always keep the superiority, from our ingenuity and arrangements? – I hope we shall.[56]

The machine-makers' 'ingenuity' had created their market, and perhaps they were entitled to feel smug. For as long as engineers were innovative, producing machines which saved labour or improved quality, textile manufacturers must keep up in order to maintain their own standing.

It seems that machinery was discarded once obsolete, even if it were far from worn out.[57] In difficult trading conditions, the service life of machinery could be prolonged, but still textile manufacturers could not afford to fall far behind. Apparently there was 'very rapid replacement of much machinery installed before 1830'.[58] In New England, machines installed during the 1830s, it is calculated, averaged about 35 years' life, with spinning frames and opening machinery replaced rather more quickly than looms and carding engines.[59] This turnover is slower than in Britain. Babbage estimated in 1832 that textile manufacturers would reckon to recover their outlay in five years, and scrap a machine in 10.[60] In 1841 the Leeds flax-spinner James G. Marshall first claimed that 'a considerable portion' of old machinery remained in use in England, for flax-machinery, though it required 'frequent renewals', was of great durability. But under questioning, he modified this.

> What would you say was the date of the oldest machines which to any extent are now in use; 20 years? – I should think there are not any to that extent.
>
> Then probably most of the improvements that have been introduced in the last 20 years are in general use? – Most of them, and that has led to the displacement of a considerable proportion of old machinery with great rapidity of late years.[61]

Flax-spinning technology was progressing rapidly – 'a considerable improvement each year', as Marshall put it. In the worsted trade, machinery was replaced frequently, although the pace of change did not match that in flax. Robert

---

55   PP Artisans and Machinery, 346.
56   PP Artisans and Machinery, 258, Peter Ewart.
57   Farnie, *English Cotton Industry and the World Market*, 55–6.
58   McGouldrick, *New England Textiles*, 232.
59   McGouldrick, *New England Textiles*, 231, 224–7.
60   Checkland, *Rise of Industrial Society*, 78.
61   PP Exportation of Machinery, 194.

Clough of Keighley constantly re-equipped, replacing some spinning frames after perhaps fifteen years. By 1842 Clough had almost 100 power looms, bought from a number of Keighley suppliers over the previous six years, and subsequently acquired large numbers of looms in 1843, 1847, 1852, 1853 (84 looms) and 1856. But in 1865 the firm owned only 98 looms in total, suggesting high turnover.[62]

Old machinery was not easily modernized, so replacement was often most cost-effective.[63]

> There are very few cases in which you can apply anything very new to an old machine … With regard to the self-acting mule, if the machine be good, we generally put the self-acting part on to it; but if the machine be an old one, the extra expense in attaching the new part to it is often considered as a waste of money, and parties prefer having new machines altogether.[64]

Robert Clough's accounts show old models part-exchanged against new looms and spinning frames, and other obsolete machinery sold on in the textile trade.[65] Whether machine-makers resold, exported, refurbished or scrapped part-exchange machines is not known. Part-exchange may have removed second-hand machinery from circulation, obliging more machine-users to buy new. While many, like Cloughs, frequently updated their plant, others resisted spending more than necessary on machines. Marriners, another Keighley firm of worsted spinners, bought extensively from William Smith and Taylor and Wordsworth but also snapped up second-hand bargains and evidently adapted machinery in their own workshops.[66] By judicious selection, it would be possible to buy the latest technology and use this alongside serviceable second-hand items, perhaps for processes where technology was advancing more slowly. There are suggestions that Leeds flax-machine makers at times sold cheaply outside the immediate locality. Enabling other spinners to compete pressured Leeds flax-spinners to maintain a modern plant.[67]

Once the great waves of innovation subsided, machine-makers must reconsider their strategy. The Select Committee on artisans and machinery in 1824 heard of 70 new cotton-factories around Manchester, and eight or nine in Scotland, which stood empty awaiting machinery.[68] In contrast, the later enquiry of 1841 reported a 'long, dreary depression' which hit engineers hard, following a rise in bank rate in 1836 and lasting until 1842–43.[69] The

62   Smith, 'Robert Clough Ltd', 41–2.
63   PP Exportation of Machinery, 210, 216.
64   PP Exportation of Machinery, 101, William Jenkinson.
65   Smith, 'Robert Clough Ltd.', 42, 51.
66   Ingle, 'History of R. V. Marriner Ltd', 114, 55.
67   Rimmer, Marshalls of Leeds, 233–4.
68   PP Artisans and Machinery, 379, 547.
69   Heaton, 'Early Victorian Business Forecaster', 564.

Lancashire industry worked far below capacity: 'We could produce double the quantity that we have produced in the last twelve months, if it was required'.[70] The cotton-spinner Thomas Ashton of Hyde made a comparison: 'There were [in 1824] many mills standing empty for want of machinery ... there is now more machinery than we can employ ... a very great increase [in machine-making capacity] took place in consequence of the demand.'[71] When prospects of radical new technologies ran out, which happened first in the cotton industry, at last textile engineers lobbied to open overseas markets. The wealth of new foreign business promised to protect margins, circumventing the threat of head-on competition in the home trade.

There is no hard evidence of profit levels in the early industry. Impressionistically, it appears that high returns were possible for competent textile engineers, particularly when offering sought-after technologies. This remained so whatever the state of the general economy. In 1841, when the Lancashire trade was slow, evidence to the Select Committee, while vague about profit levels, suggested still healthy margins. Thomas Marsden of Salford, completing a three-year, £30,000 contract building flax-machinery in France, paid out £6,000 for tools and materials, and over £16,000 in wages.[72] So £8,000 covered fixed costs and profit. William Jenkinson lost a Mexican order, for cotton-spinning machinery and millwork, to Belgium because of the export ban. This was worth £70,000 to £80,000, 80 per cent of which covered profits and paid 1,000 hands for six months.[73] On Marsden's figures for the French contract, where workers including local unskilled labour and apprentices averaged less than £50 a year, the Mexican order would have cost Jenkinson £25,000 in wages, and delivered a similar sum in profit. The Manchester machine- and card-maker Matthew Curtis broke down a £27,000 order for spinning machines: £3,000 for bought-in spindles and rollers, £11,000 on wages, fixed costs of £1,400, £800 covering consumables such as tools and files, leaving £10,800 for materials, profits and depreciation.[74]

With integrated factories the norm, entry to mainstream machine-making was possible only with capital and connections. So the number of significant textile-engineering firms barely increased. Companies were known for certain types of product (as in the pre-factory era), specialization which helped avert head-on competition. This was a sound policy for as long as the market was robust.[75] The older, more collaborative, approach to business perhaps faded first in Lancashire, where cotton mechanization proceeded ahead of woollens.

70 PP Exportation of Machinery, 96, William Jenkinson.
71 PP Exportation of Machinery, 22; and see William Jenkinson, 94.
72 PP Exportation of Machinery, 85.
73 PP Exportation of Machinery, 101–3.
74 PP Exportation of Machinery, 123.
75 Farnie, *English Cotton Industry and the World Market*, 55.

With the working technologies defined for key textile processes, and the home market largely satisfied, new commercial strategies were needed. Lancashire engineers tried refining their machinery, and offering financial incentives to buyers, but the durability of their own products worked against them.[76] The obvious solution was to sell more abroad.

Selling machinery

Where, and how large, was the market? In this 'pre-statistical period' little or no data was collected on machinery output or sales.[77] Working at full capacity, the annual production of cotton machinery was valued in 1824 at £400,000, and in Scotland not more than £40,000, a vague and unsatisfactory estimate.[78] For decades, information was scarce, and any available figures unreliable and difficult to interpret.[79] The Factory Inspectorate itself described official counts of spindles operating in the 1830s as 'not in the least trustworthy'.[80] There is more data for cotton machinery at work – revealing the vast extent of cotton production – than is the case for other types of textiles.[81]

As far as the numbers in Appendix 3 (of power looms working in the 1830s and 1850s) are comprehensive, they must represent almost the entire production to that date. As demand for power looms continued so high, it can be safely assumed that few were scrapped before 1850. All worsted, woollen and flax power looms then operating in England, counted as 50,565, had been made in Yorkshire. Estimating, very roughly, an average selling price of £14, then the total value of domestic power-loom sales in Yorkshire before 1850 was more than £700,000, spread over 15 years. The regional power-loom market in the 1840s, as sales quickened, was therefore worth over £50,000 annually.

Sales of spinning and preparing machinery are even more difficult to quantify. Samuel Crompton, surveying spindles at work in the cotton industry in 1811, reckoned 'this but a partial account of the cotton spinning – the extent of the mule in the woollen trade is not mentioned, tho' extensive'.[82] Nor do spindle figures define numbers of machines: mules might have 50 to

---

76   Farnie, *English Cotton Industry and the World Market*, 55–6.
77   Jenkins, *West Riding Wool Textile Industry*, xiv.
78   PP Artisans and Machinery, 253, 380. Whether the first figure includes Scotland is not stated.
79   Floud, *British Machine Tool Industry*, 4–9.
80   Baines, 'Account of the Woollen Trade', 646; Jenkins, 'Validity of the Factory Returns'; 'Factory Returns'. See app. 3; for more on interpreting official data, Cookson, 'West Yorkshire textile engineering industry', 242–3.
81   See app. 3.
82   Bolton Archives and Local Studies, ZCR/16a/3.

500 spindles, water frames 48 to 160, jennies 48 to 208.[83] Keighley, briefly an Arkwright boom town, soon switched from cotton to worsteds, and never took much to mules.[84] Crompton counted 17 factories there, with a total of 3,312 mule spindles and 14,560 water-frame or throstle spindles.[85] In 1850, across England, 864,874 worsted spindles were in operation (and 1.3 million in 1856).[86] In this period, Keighley held almost a monopoly on manufacturing worsted-spinning frames.[87] So, selling at around 15s. a spindle, the value of frames at work in 1850 was about £650,000. Even with machines kept in service for 25 years – and we know that many were replaced far more frequently[88] – then the market in worsted-spinning frames, mostly produced in Keighley, had an annual value in the 1840s of at least £26,000. The increase in worsted spindleage between 1850 and 1856 was 433,452, amounting to perhaps £325,000, or £54,000 a year. And that is ignoring the value of replacement sales. These rough figures illustrate a huge and accelerating growth in sales of northern machinery.

Local sales always underpinned the trade. Early demand in Yorkshire for textile machines and components was answered first from Lancashire,[89] and between locations with well-established trade routes in textiles. Late-eighteenth-century Keighley and Haworth stuff-makers, for instance, 'principally exposed their goods for sale' in the worsted market of Halifax, from which tools and rudimentary machines came to the Worth valley and Leeds.[90] But textile engineering soon concentrated in the places where its main customers also clustered.

Transport difficulties and costs are an obvious explanation. When Ard Walker brought spinning frames and other machinery from Halifax to his Leeds cotton-factory in 1802, the cost of £168 was inflated by freight charges of £22 15s., plus 15s. to bring the goods from the boat.[91] Benjamin Gott paid £12 15s. 8d to bring 95 cwt (4.75 tons) of machinery from Manchester to Leeds in 1793.[92] Although Keighley, Bingley, Bradford and Leeds, and hence the North Sea and all navigable points beyond, had been connected by canal in 1777,[93] many would-be customers were far from the waterway. The textile outposts in the dales and northern counties, while still numerous, formed

83   Daniels, 'Samuel Crompton's Census', 110.
84   Aspin, *Water-Spinners*, 235.
85   Bolton Archives and Local Studies, ZCR/16a.
86   App. 3.
87   Keighley, *Keighley, Past and Present*, 255.
88   See above, p. 241.
89   See above, p. 52.
90   James, *History of the Worsted Manufacture*, 292.
91   WYAS Leeds, DB23.
92   Crump (ed.), *Leeds Woollen Industry*, 21.
93   See above, p. 50.

a declining proportion of the market after 1800, though not all of them contracted.

Rather, growth concentrated in towns, and it suited machine-makers, for technical reasons and convenience, to have customers close at hand. There are many examples of engineers moving into town, or to a particular neighbourhood, to meet their market: Murray, Lawson and Fairbairn in Leeds; Hattersley family members establishing new companies where clients grouped; Samuel in Bradford, and Jonathan, after trying Burnley and Bradford, in Leeds.[94] Benjamin Berry, from Leeds, found the newly booming town of Bradford more conducive to success.[95]

> [W]herever you can get the most profitable and extensive market there a man would naturally settle … [Machine-makers] establish themselves in those localities where they are most required, provided they have the same facilities for carrying on their business.[96]

But this went beyond costs and convenience. Peter Fairbairn explained the other advantages of a local hub.

> [T]he contiguity of machine-makers to large spinning establishments is of the greatest importance to the extension of that particular branch of manufactures, by the reciprocal feelings which thereby exist between the parties, by being able to come into connexion with each other, and so canvass different improvements, the one trying and suggesting, and the other executing the different mechanical operations.[97]

Hence important innovations came into textile production in Leeds months before the flax-spinners of Ireland, who depended upon Leeds for their machinery, had even heard of the improvement.[98] Established machine-making centres had taken an insuperable position, said Fairbairn, with such technological advantage and no effective competition, for 'a person wanting machinery prefers taking all his machinery of one machine-maker, if he can get it, because the machines are nearly alike, and may be changed from one to another'.[99] The early lead meant that Belfast could not establish itself as an engineering centre, flax-machine making 'having first taken root in Yorkshire'.[100]

94   App. 1 and 2.
95   Koditschek, *Class Formation*, 173–4.
96   PP Exportation of Machinery, 118, Matthew Curtis.
97   PP Exportation of Machinery, 219–20.
98   PP Exportation of Machinery, 220.
99   PP Exportation of Machinery, 223.
100 PP Exportation of Machinery, 220.

At this point, the 1840s, despatching machines from northern textile centres presented little problem. The difficulties complained of by Thomas Cheek Hewes in 1824 no longer applied.

> When we send out a machine, it is taken to pieces like a bedstead, and there is no great care in packing it up; and it is sent to a mill, and set up the very afternoon it is taken out; but if it goes abroad, or even to Aberdeen, we are obliged to make it in a different sort of way, so that it will detach itself in a way that we can pack it, and we find it a very cumbersome thing, and the freight comes to a great deal, in comparison with yarn, and when it gets into the country, it is not portable; and if we do not know the kind of conveyance they have in the country, we may err in that respect.[101]

Hewes had refused a repeat order from Aberdeen, even for components.[102] He did not need the business. Manchester was then three or four years ahead of Scotland in cotton-spinning technology. The Glasgow-based cotton-spinner and machine-maker Henry Houldsworth, more than ordinarily skilled and well-connected, bridged the gap by sourcing the finer parts through his Lancashire associates. He could then fabricate machines by combining them with locally produced heavier components.[103] But Houldsworth was atypical. Generally the dynamic propelled, or at least encouraged, textile manufacturers and machine-makers into close proximity.

But not every textile centre developed its own machine-making cluster. Keighley and Leeds were exceptional in Yorkshire. Richard Hattersley's new machine shop in Bradford in 1818, in response to the town's worsted boom, was soundly judged, as it turned out.[104] Before long, Bradford had several power-loom factories, but the scale of machine-making there never matched the size of its worsted trade.[105] With worsted operations mechanizing, and this branch of textiles concentrating heavily in Yorkshire, the local machinery market was immense. Almost 95 per cent of worsted power looms at work in the United Kingdom in 1850 (30,856 of 32,617) were in the West Riding. In 1856 it remained over 90 per cent, 35,298 of 38,956 looms, and 445 of the country's 525 worsted factories were situated in the county.[106] The small town of Keighley was said in 1879 to 'nearly monopolis[e] the trade of making worsted spinning machinery' as well as the large quantities of looms produced there. What is more, in or near Keighley were a tenth of the

---

101 PP Artisans and Machinery, 349.
102 PP Artisans and Machinery, 342.
103 PP Artisans and Machinery, 378–9.
104 WYAS Wakefield, Deeds GY 658 703.
105 Banks, 'Progress of Engineering in Bradford', 16.
106 PP (HC) 1857 (1) III, 632–3; see app. 3.

factories, an eighth of the spindles and a twelfth of the looms of the United Kingdom worsted trade.[107]

So, much of the local market for machines was very local indeed. Yet out in the Pennines and other marginal areas, while those outlying places lost relative significance, many textile factories remained and long endured. These companies still counted on machine-suppliers in Keighley, Leeds and other engineering centres. Kellett, Brown and Co. made some local purchases when equipping a woollen factory in Calverley during the 1830s and 1840s, but necessarily much of what was needed came from specialist woollen-machinery manufacturers in the Spen Valley, including card-clothing from the concentration of makers around Cleckheaton.[108] Most cotton machinery commissioned in Yorkshire at this time – 126 of the 1,000 mechanically-driven cotton-factories in England in 1835 were in the West Riding[109] – must have come from Lancashire or its fringes.

The trans-Pennine trade in engineering, especially where cotton and woollen districts meshed, was well-established by 1800. Important connections built upon family and apprenticeship links: between Lancashire and Glasgow; west and south Yorkshire; the West Riding and northern counties and Borders; Leeds flax-machine makers and Belfast and Barnsley. From Keighley in c. 1810, Edward Carr sold throstles to Chester and Whitehaven, while Berry Smith equipped a factory in Stockton with spinning frames.[110] A limited set of worsted machinery running in 1824 in Norwich, where there was no indigenous engineering industry, hailed from Yorkshire. The 'spirit of improvement in Norwich', predicted to 'produce, in a short time, a great deal more machinery than we have now in use', failed to deliver.[111] Local specialization brought an inevitable pattern to the inter-regional engineering trade. Fairbairn knew that Leeds, as 'the seat of the chief flax-machine establishments ... for the whole world' had an assured market in Scotland and Belfast, and that his waste-silk machinery would sell in Macclesfield and other silk-spinning centres.[112] This particular market was exclusive, a charmed clique. London, the eighteenth century's leading engineering centre, did not attempt to compete in textiles.[113] Certain older woollen industries maintained suppliers within their region: Borders manufacturers mainly from Glasgow, little from Yorkshire;[114] and the West of England, fairly self-sufficient in

107   Keighley, *Keighley*, 255.
108   Brotherton SC, BUS/Kellett, 1.1, purchase accounts, 1833–c. 1848.
109   Ure, *Philosophy of Manufactures*, 353.
110   Hodgson, *Textile Manufacture*, 251, 255.
111   PP Artisans and Machinery, 154–5, 160.
112   PP Exportation of Machinery, 208–10.
113   PP Artisans and Machinery, 300, 305, 348; PP Exportation of Machinery, 99.
114   Gulvin, *Tweedmakers*, and additional information from Cliff Gulvin.

machinery until after 1850, when a trade with Yorkshire developed.[115] Overall, inter-regional trade in textile machinery (other than flax) can be summarized as modest. This was not because other regions satisfied their own needs for machinery, but rather reflects the textile industry's intense concentration in northern England, and the proximity of manufacturers and engineers to each other.

From the perspective of a migrant building up a machine-making business in Lancashire or west Yorkshire, the home region was not really a market-place.[116] Its significance lay in family affairs, industrial connections, training. Adopting a new district, they held on to earlier contacts and actively used them to advance in trade. Matthew Murray did this, as did Peter Fairbairn. There was a clannish feel about the Chowbent group around William Cannan, and the Wortley Forge hub – both of these places long-established in iron-working.[117] Richard Hattersley, his customers overwhelmingly local to west Yorkshire, nonetheless maintained strong bonds with south Yorkshire suppliers, including steel from Walker and Booth of Rotherham, and files from his native village.[118] It made sense, with Sheffield and district a natural source of tools and special steels. Forty years after Hattersley had left south Yorkshire, following his death in 1829 and his business's failing in 1832, it was an old Sheffield acquaintance who rescued his sons. A steel merchant and tool manufacturer called Samuel Brittain, acting as agent to the assignees, protected the Hattersley interest. This allowed George to resume activity in the Keighley premises, and Samuel to revive the same factory in Bradford as his own business, while cutting adrift the wayward Levi. All the while, Brittain despatched letters of advice and information to George, in the tones of close family friend.[119]

Despite the problems of 1829–32, the Hattersley concern was funda-mentally sound and recovered quickly. It was their good fortune to have technical ability, connections and reputation. George started out afresh with a borrowed £500.[120] The customers for rollers and spindles, at the forefront of whom were Taylor and Wordsworth, stayed loyal. The Leeds partnership had bought from Hattersley almost from the time they started out. The earliest surviving record of this is in 1817, when they ordered spindles modelled on a type Hattersley supplied to Darlington, to the Pease and Backhouse factories.

115   Rogers, 'John Dyer'; information from Ken Rogers.
116   This point relates to textile machinery. Matthew Murray was an exception, but it was steam-engines that he sold to Tyneside collieries.
117   See Angerstein, *Illustrated Travel Diary*, 217–20, 295.
118   WYAS Bradford, 32D83/32/1.
119   WYAS Bradford, 32D83/15/3; /33/1; *Leeds Mercury*, 11, 25 Feb. 1832; 5 May 1832; 21 July 1832; 1, 8, 29 Sept. 1832.
120   See above, p. 109.

After this, Hattersley agreed specifications for a range of parts for Taylor and
Wordsworth – 'done to a gage'. By the early 1820s the partners were among
Richard Hattersley's most significant customers, perhaps the largest of all,
buying spindles, flyers, screws, nuts and rollers in great quantity.[121] They
and other machine makers bought rollers and spindles in 'setts' or 'frames',
continuing the transactions with George's revived business after Richard
died.[122]

Economic doldrums hit some textile-engineering sectors from the 1820s.
As a result, there was a greater effort to promote sales, and a willingness to be
flexible on price.

> [T]he printed list of prices of any machine-maker is not to be depended
> upon; it is well known to those who purchase machinery, that there is a
> great deal of difference between the printed list and the selling price ...
> They sell much cheaper than they print.[123]

The downturn did not apply to worsteds, where significant new technology
was coming on-stream; nor to components, for which markets were generally
buoyant. Then and later, sales to other regions never amounted to much for
Hattersley. Occasionally, there were recorded efforts to sell outside Yorkshire:
Samuel's northern trip in 1821; and brother Levi's apparently unproductive
visits to Scotland, other parts of England, and possibly even the United
States.[124] But if their products did go further afield, more likely it was within
Taylor and Wordsworth machines, or accompanying other customers' consign-
ments, for instance from Horsfall Bros of Bradford to Dublin in 1834.[125]

Hattersley's route into power-loom making was not straightforward. In May
1827, Richard Hattersley noted a clutch of orders for worsted power looms, 10
in all, from five customers.[126] But that was all, and it seems that production
continued thereafter in Bradford. Richard Hattersley and Sons' Silsbridge
Lane branch was described in 1830 as 'spindle, flyer, roller and power-loom
manufacturers'.[127] The Keighley works remained above all a source of
components, and continued so under George after Richard's death. Hattersley
expertise rested in precision parts for spinning, but carving a niche in this new
branch – worsted power looms – came to make sense: the potential was huge,
and avoiding competition with William Smith, already well-established in
Keighley as a spinning-frame maker, was sensible. For George, it was hardly

121 WYAS Bradford, 32D83/15/1.
122 WYAS Bradford, 32D83/15/3.
123 PP Exportation of Machinery, 45.
124 WYAS Bradford, 32D83/15/1; /6/2; /5/5.
125 WYAS Bradford, 32D83/15/3.
126 WYAS Bradford, 32D83/15/2.
127 Parson and White, Dir. (1830), 231, 331–2.

Plate 11. Taylor and Wordsworth's Midland Junction Foundry, Holbeck, c. 1858
Source: Library of Birmingham, LF06, 61999, *Men and Things of Modern England* (M. Billing, c. 1858).

a step into the unknown, for Samuel had already started up in Bradford. The question may rather be why the Keighley business took so long to move into power looms? The hiatus surrounding insolvency and restructuring, in 1832–33, probably delayed it. The brothers perhaps agreed to continue the old division of products until they re-established themselves. It was reported, though it is not certain, that George Hattersley made several looms in 1835. Not until the mid-1840s was he predominantly a loom-manufacturer.[128]

George's rethinking must have been influenced by Ryder's spindle-forging breakthrough in 1840, which made obsolete some of his firm's renowned skills.[129] It seems too that there was a rift with Taylor and Wordsworth. While this may have been merely a commercial relationship reaching its natural end, some unpleasantness is hinted at. The break was at about the time of Joshua Wordsworth's sudden death in 1847, so at some point after George

128 Hodgson, *Textile Manufacture*, 271.
129 See above, pp. 65–6.

Hattersley became a loom-maker.[130] The other change was the involvement of the dynamic and talented Richard L. Hattersley, George's eldest son, who came of age in 1841. He grew increasingly influential within the firm, and from 1846 set a routine of summer trips to the Low Countries, Germany, and later further afield, to sell power looms.[131] By 1860, of 100 looms sold in two months by Hattersleys, a third went to foreign customers. In 1861 829 looms were sold, 298 to export.[132] When George took Richard L. and another son, Edwin, into partnership in 1860, the business's net worth was conservatively estimated as £16,840. Under Richard L. Hattersley in 1888, it was incorporated at a valuation of £100,000.[133]

The end of the export ban

A parliamentary question on the principle of free trade prompted government to revisit the export ban on machinery. In the spring of 1824, a Select Committee took evidence, concluding its investigation in the year following.[134]

This inquiry and its aftermath exposed a stark difference between customers for machinery and those who made it. It came down to economic self-interest. The Manchester Chamber of Commerce had very quickly decided that it was 'highly inexpedient, and injurious to the interests of this country, to allow the exportation of machinery and tools'. Notwithstanding the prevalent free trade orthodoxy, this remained their position.[135] Textile manufacturers stood to gain most from keeping the status quo. Of the Manchester witnesses to the Select Committee, Peter Ewart, John Kennedy and Thomas Ashton – though they had, or had had, interests in textile engineering – were all then heavily involved in cotton-spinning. William Fairbairn and Thomas Cheek Hewes appeared as makers of millwrighting machinery. The flax-spinner John Marshall was the only representative of Yorkshire textiles. Evidently no Yorkshire textile engineer, small-scale or otherwise, was called or offered to be witness.[136]

Shortly after attending the inquiry, John Kennedy produced a pamphlet, *On the Exportation of Machinery*, which was promoted by the Manchester chamber.[137] Here he tried, not very convincingly, to square the incompatible options of free trade versus protectionism in the matter of capital goods.

130   WYAS Bradford, 32D83/32/1, especially letter from Joshua Waddington, 12 Apr. 1847.
131   WYAS Bradford, 32D83/42; /33/6; /33/7.
132   WYAS Bradford, 32D83/42.
133   WYAS Bradford, 32D83/42; /41; also app. 1.
134   PP Artisans and Machinery; for legislative background, see above, pp. 213–14.
135   Musson, 'Manchester School', 23–9; Berg (ed.), *Technology and Toil*, no. 2.
136   PP Artisans and Machinery, 4th, 5th and 6th reports, *passim*.
137   Musson, 'Manchester School', 17–29.

Machinery exports presented free traders with a conundrum. Kennedy argued that a free market in machinery was undesirable, perhaps impossible, for as long as there was great imbalance between what Britain and other nations could offer each other. By selling machines abroad, the superiority built through Britain's own effort would be squandered. Any short-term gains for machine-makers would be far outweighed by damage to the substantially more important British industry, textiles. Kennedy's general line was to stall on the question of machinery exports, but he actually advocated tackling the system's failings through tighter restriction.[138]

Unsurprisingly, the *Manchester Guardian*, vocal supporter of the free trade lobby, pounced on Kennedy's inconsistencies. British advantage, it countered, rested in more than the substance of a machine, and engineers had the same rights as others, to sell their wares in any market. London engineers were also firmly behind unrestricted exports.[139] But northern machine-makers' views are more opaque. They made no collective submission to the Select Committee, and the opinions of those supplying the textile trade were absent. That is itself suggestive – that textile engineers, or at least those in Yorkshire, saw no purpose in pursuing change, nor to have an association act for them, for as long as home demand was strong.

This group evidently still saw mutual purpose with textile manufacturers. Alerted again that the export embargo might be lifted, in 1827 industrialists petitioned the mayor of Leeds to oppose any such move. Signatories included a dozen leading textile companies, and notably two significant machine-makers, Taylor and Wordsworth (good Liberals both), Zebulon Stirk, and the founder John Cawood.[140] In Yorkshire, where new waves of textile technology were still being absorbed, engineers' order books were bursting. The suggestion to end the ban generated concern, while in the cotton districts across the Pennines, slumps in 1825–26, and in the 1830s and 1840s, gave reason to reconsider.[141]

The Select Committee's recommendations sat firmly in the free-trade camp, but the government equivocated much as Kennedy had. A fudged solution almost instantly fuelled a rift between textile manufacturers and engineers in Manchester.[142] So from 1825 to 1843, machine tools, steam-engines and mill gearing could be freely exported, as could most machinery for preparatory textile processes. Export of spinning and weaving machinery was prohibited, unless by Treasury licence recommended by a Board of Trade committee.[143]

138   Musson, 'Manchester School', 26.
139   Musson, 'Manchester School', 26–8.
140   *Leeds Intelligencer*, 25 Jan. 1827.
141   Musson, 'Manchester School', 22.
142   Musson, 'Manchester School', 30–2.
143   *Leeds Intelligencer*, 17 Apr. 1841; and see PP Exportation of Machinery, 3–13, James Deacon Hume, formerly customs and Board of Trade official.

This body had discretion over all machine exports 'as may appear to them not likely to be prejudicial to the trade and manufactures of the United Kingdom'.[144] Witnesses to the later inquiry, in 1841, confirmed the inconsistencies that are obvious from Board of Trade records. The committee, it was said, 'do not understand what they are granting a licence for'.[145] Classes of machinery banned from export to continental Europe were sent in quantity to the colonies. In 1825 Alexander Galloway, agent for an unnamed machine-maker, was allowed to sell 500 (presumably cotton) power looms and other machinery to Egypt. Prohibited exports might be allowed in compliment to a foreign head of state. A Turkish minister took away 'ten models of machinery for the manufacture of cloth' in 1836.[146] Stable doors were closed too late, as with an instruction in 1835 that licences to export waste tow preparing and spinning machinery should in future be refused.[147] As the rules drifted, exporters re-applied in hopes of better luck with a repeat bid. London agents acting for northern engineers obscured exactly what was being exported and by whom. Customs officials were ill-equipped to identify specifics among the range of machinery passing by. Meanwhile old techniques of evasion and illegality were employed by agents: parts inter-mixed to conceal their purpose, whole machines sent through ports where they were unlikely to be recognized, plans and models smuggled in hand luggage.[148]

Frustrated Lancashire cotton-machine makers circumvented the chaos by opening temporary or permanent branches on the continent. This ploy was much easier once artisans were permitted to move freely, from 1825. In 1841, Lancashire machine-makers suggested unsubtly that if the ban remained they might establish a joint stock company on the continent 'and secure to ourselves the advantages which the law now gives to foreigners'.[149] The ultimate proof of regulation's failure was, as Peter Fairbairn put it, that 'they get all our inventions whether we will or not'.[150] Another unwelcome side-effect of protectionism was that denying British machinery sparked creativity abroad. Radically new technology entered Britain, for Americans in particular had 'at once set their minds and ingenuity to work ... a new train of thought has been originated, and ... they have not followed the beaten track which the machine-makers in this country would follow from constantly coming into contact with the machinery which exists'.[151]

But enforcement of the rules had largely collapsed during the 1830s, and

144   TNA, BT6/151. Thanks to David Jeremy for reference and information.
145   PP Exportation of Machinery, 59.
146   PP Exportation of Machinery, 4; TNA, BT6/151.
147   TNA, BT6/151.
148   PP Exportation of Machinery, 3–7.
149   PP Exportation of Machinery, 104, 86.
150   PP Exportation of Machinery, 218.
151   PP Exportation of Machinery, 110–12.

northern engineers came together, particularly in Manchester, in organized opposition.[152] Repeal, by then an acceptance of the inevitable, did not come until 1843. After the 1841 inquiry, Leeds flax-machinery makers jointly lobbied the Board of Trade about the downturn in their branch, calling for free export of their products to the continent. Peter Fairbairn, Joshua Wordsworth, J. O. March and others met Gladstone late in 1842, and a similar deputation, including Maclea, and Samuel Exley, partner in Fenton, Murray and Co., saw the Earl of Ripon in February 1843.[153] Yorkshire machine-makers did not then have foreign branches, and any exporting must have been via London agents.[154] Leeds textile engineers applied directly to the Board of Trade only from the late 1830s, with Lawson, Maclea and March, and Taylor and Wordsworth granted licences to sell flax-spinning and heckling frames in Europe.[155]

Other than Matthew Murray, whose strengthening links with northern Europe started with sales of steam-engines, the Yorkshire engineers showed little inclination to export. Murray sold flax-machinery and steam-engines to Russia and Sweden from c. 1800.[156] Numerous artisans worked abroad, in France, Russia, Sweden and Switzerland,[157] but sending machinery overseas was more tricky. Even when not illegal, it involved expense and effort. So long as orders held up, the domestic market was favoured. London engineers – who in 1824 expressed enthusiasm for free markets in machinery, had a major port on their doorstep, and could charge much more for export goods – nevertheless for pragmatic reasons preferred trading at home.[158] Textile engineers evidently shared the adage of machine-tool manufacturers, that 'a good tool sells itself'.[159] Was this complacency? It made some sense, at least until the home market flattened. British textile machines must then sell themselves abroad, where they were technically in a league of their own, and cheaper than inferior French and Belgian rivals. Export sales, though, demanded a more coherent approach, which was evident in Yorkshire from the 1840s. Exporters to Norway, and presumably to other destinations, including Taylor and Wordsworth of Leeds, developed 'packages' on the older Boulton and Watt model, delivering parts and erecting *in situ*.[160]

152   Musson, 'Manchester School', 41.
153   *Leeds Intelligencer*, 22 Oct. 1842; 25 Feb. 1843; *Leeds Mercury*, 25 Feb. 1843.
154   Holden and Lister's overseas branch was unusual, but came late, after 1848, and with atypical background and product: Honeyman and Goodman, *Technology and Enterprise*, ch. 4.
155   TNA, BT6/151.
156   Turner, 'Fenton, Murray and Wood', 8.5.
157   Turner, 'Fenton, Murray and Wood', 3.23, 8.25; Heaton, 'Yorkshire Mechanic Abroad'; Hodgson, *Textile Manufacture*, 251.
158   Babbage, *On the Economy of Machinery and Manufactures*, 371.
159   Floud, *British Machine Tool Industry*, 83.
160   Bruland, *British Technology and European Industrialization*, app. B, and 20, citing Kirk, 'British textile machinery industry'.

The size of overseas trade before 1843 is impossible to quantify, partly for the obvious reason that illegal exports went unrecorded. Even after 1843, figures for textile machinery were subsumed within steam-engines and millwork, or later, 'other machinery'. While annual totals for engineering exports fluctuated, the overall trend was unsurprisingly on the rise: £600,000 in 1840, £776,000 in 1844, topping £1 million for the first time in 1846, around £2 million in 1853–55.[161] Scrapping the export ban allowed growth without boundaries, and on this foundation textile engineering expanded to immense national importance, commercially as well as technically, and defined itself as a global transmitter of technology.[162]

Textile engineering from the 1840s

To a degree, mechanical engineering can be measured through aggregated census data, starting in 1841. Generally, though, the figures do not distinguish textile engineers from the rest. In 1851 mechanical engineering still represented only about 3.2 per cent of total manufacturing employment, but since 1841 it had grown at an annual rate far higher than other sectors – more than 9 per cent. A typical firm was small: of 677 recorded in 1851, 457 employed fewer than 10 men. Only three companies had between 300 and 349 employees, and 14 in excess of 350. Everywhere, engineering clustered around its customers: in and around London, in Scotland, the west Midlands, Lancashire and the West Riding.[163] In those centres, the industry's significance was far greater than national averages can reveal. In Leeds in 1851, 9 per cent of the occupied population, 7,400 people, almost all male, worked in engineering.[164] It was reported by James Kitson that the Leeds 'iron trades' employed 11,000 hands in 1857; and in 1871 a parliamentary return showed 15,000 engaged in metalworking there, of whom 8,000 to 9,000 were in 'iron mills, foundries and machine-shops'.[165]

For the 1841 Select Committee, Peter Fairbairn's estimates, of firms, workers and capital employed in machine-making in Yorkshire's main engineering towns, supplement that year's census data. He counted 18 Leeds machine-making firms, employing 255 hp, 2,950 hands and £305,000 capital. Additionally, Bradford, Bingley and Keighley together had almost 1,000

161   John Pender and Co., *Statistics of the Trade of the United Kingdom with Foreign Countries from 1840* (1869), 65–7.
162   Bruland, *British Technology and European Industrialization*, 5.
163   MacLeod and Nuvolari, 'Glorious Times', 221–2, drawing in particular on Lee, *British Regional Employment Statistics*.
164   Rimmer, 'Industrial Profile of Leeds'.
165   Walker, *Fortunes Made in Business*, 269.

engineering workers and over £60,000 invested.[166] In total the four Yorkshire towns are said (by another calculation) to have employed 442 hp and 5,000 hands.[167] The 1841 census showed 3,741 working in Leeds engineering, this encompassing growing numbers in machine tools and locomotive engines.[168]

In 11 Lancashire towns there were altogether 115 'mechanical establishments', totalling 1,811 hp and potentially employing 17,382 men, 151 per firm. As in the West Riding, this disguised sharp diversity. Smaller towns averaged 40 or 50 workers to a firm, while in Manchester it was 209, in Salford 280, and in Bolton 321.[169] There were also wide differences between companies, Hibbert and Platt employing 900 and Nasmyth 500.[170] Capital investment reportedly averaged £87 per employee, varying from about £70 in Blackburn and Manchester, to £146 in Burnley.[171] On Fairbairn's figures, the average Leeds firm had £103.39 invested per caput, and 164 workers, close to the overall Lancashire average. Within this, Fairbairn himself employed 550, with Lawson, Maclea and March, and Taylor and Wordsworth each over 100.[172]

Counting heads in this way excludes subcontractors and others not directly or fully employed, and introduces non-engineers to the equation. Many machine-makers also ran a textile business. George Hattersley, for instance, appears in the 1851 census employing 39 women and 29 girls, who can only have been textile workers.[173] Yet without doubt engineering had increased immensely in size during the 1840s. The principal Leeds flax-machine factories were vast. Peter Fairbairn took a dozen or so years to rise from employing two men in Lady Lane, to an establishment of 550 at the Wellington Foundry in 1841; then 850 workers in 1851, over 1,000 in 1858, and doubling again by 1867.[174] Of 7,415 engineering workers in Leeds in 1851, Lawson employed 400, Fairbairn 850, Maclea and March 211, and Taylor and Wordsworth several hundred.[175] But a multitude continued to work in small shops on the traditional pattern. Among these Zebulon Stirk, renowned builder of steam-engines and textile machines but then downwardly mobile in old age, headed a workshop employing just half a dozen. And there was a middling sector of

---

166 PP Exportation of Machinery, 96, 209, 393.
167 PP Exportation of Machinery, 95.
168 Rimmer, 'Industrial Profile of Leeds'.
169 PP Exportation of Machinery, 95–6, 230.
170 Perkin, *Origins of Modern English Society*, 110, suggests the average size of Lancashire establishments falling to 85 by 1871.
171 PP Exportation of Machinery, 95–6, 230.
172 PP Exportation of Machinery, 393; and see app. 2.
173 Keighley census 1851, p. 378.
174 PP Exportation of Machinery, 208; Leeds census 1851 2321/200; Ward, 'Industrial development', 362–4.
175 Rimmer, 'Industrial Profile of Leeds'.

businesses slightly peripheral to the mainstream: the millwrights Stephen and John Whitham making fulling and washing machinery with a complement of 270 at their Kirkstall Road foundry in 1854; and Jonathan Hattersley with 134 men in his roller- and spindle-making factory.[176] In fact George Hattersley, at the apex of textile engineering in Keighley, employed fewer engineering workers than did the medium-sized firm of his lesser known younger brother Jonathan in Leeds.

Peter Fairbairn reckoned in 1841 that his own turnover matched capital invested. He had laid out £50,000 to £60,000 and claimed annual sales of £60,000 – a gross income exceeding £100 per employee.[177] Fairbairn's was a relatively recent start-up, noted for new technologies and streamlined organization.[178] His company's expansion, although exceptional, matched a general trend of substantial investment in engineering plant during the 1830s. If Fairbairn were in any way typical of his peers, then the annual turnover of Leeds engineering, which employed 2,950, would have been in the order of £295,000; and 1,000 workers in the Keighley, Bradford and Bingley industry perhaps produced machinery with a finished value of £100,000. But this is very speculative.

Plainly, the shifting environment encouraged – or obliged – companies to reconsider their approach. The machinery shaping and handling machines in production – that is, machine tools and cranes – had undergone its own revolution. Then, with most textile processes mechanized, innovation plateaued sufficiently that businesses settled their product range. With this, the benefits of factory-based production, economies of scale and consistency of quality, were even better realized. The manufacturing improvements appearing in the 1820s presaged yet finer definition and breakdown of shop-floor tasks. And so with minimal training, as Peter Fairbairn described, men and boys classed as unskilled could be engaged. For employers, this reduced per caput wages, increased flexibility and reduced the power of skilled labour. To the industry, it gave the means to quickly assemble a workforce of thousands. Galloping expansion was then possible, evading the logistical problem of training sufficient numbers through conventional apprenticeship. In fact, as Hattersley demonstrated through the ages, such contingency was nothing new, for flexible specialization had always been the case. 'Conventional' was nothing of long standing.

These shifts in engineering's culture and context presented established firms, and new starters like Fairbairn, with a land of opportunity. It was to be ignored at their peril. The Hattersley experience, in two generations of family between 1790 and 1850, encapsulates the transformation in concrete

176   Ward, 'Industrial development', 353–4.
177   PP Exportation of Machinery, 208.
178   Chambers's Edinburgh Journal, 513, 27 Nov. 1841, 354.

terms. How far, though, had the prevailing ethos moved along? Lifting export restrictions in 1843, and a new patent system after 1850, changed in important ways the framework within which machine-making operated. But while these developments were symbols of a changed culture, they were not in themselves responsible for any fundamental shift in the industry's behaviour and self-image. Textile engineers, in lobbying hard for these new laws, showed a growing strength and autonomy, confidence buoyed by prospects of a lucrative, legitimate, export market. More significant was a loss of harmony. Day-to-day, textile manufacturers and their engineers may have continued as cordial as ever, but in terms of what was advantageous to business, their interests had diverged. Devoid of radical possibilities, their functions gathered into single businesses, the networks once sustaining this industry had run their course.[179]

179   Cookson, 'Quaker Networks', 173.

Appendix 1: Keighley Textile Engineers

Working before 1815

John Brigg

Cut brass for a roving frame when Robert Heaton was building Ponden Mill, 1791–92. Brigg was then contracted for 12 months by Heaton's son as engineer at Royd House Mill, Oxenhope. Hattersley noted 'John Brig clockmaker Keighley'. Nothing found after 1794; no known connection to textile manufacturers of that name.

WYAS Bradford, DB2/6/3, pp. 107, 123, 127; 32D83/5/1; Aspin, *Water-Spinners*, 108–9.

Lodge Calvert (1776–1859)

Trained as a joiner, probably arrived in Keighley from upper Wharfedale in the late 1790s. Bought Hattersley spindles, axles, plates, shafts, etc., from 1799, but Calvert was soon primarily a textile manufacturer. Partner of Thomas Smith (q.v.), 1801–04, converted Ing Row corn-mill for worsted- and cotton-spinning. Reportedly started in worsteds in 1801 with a hand-powered throstle built from Hattersley parts; bought a second machine from William Smith in 1805. Calvert used Hattersley components until c. 1808, then switched to mule spinning. Cotton-spinning enriched Calvert, who claimed to be worth £4,000 in 1818. He gave up cotton c. 1814, joining Samuel Blakey Clapham as worsted manufacturers at Aireworth mill. After 30 years, retired to Bradford. Remained close to Richard Hattersley and was an executor of his will.

WYAS Bradford, 32D83/5/1–2; Hodgson, *Textile Manufacture*, 19–21, 245–6; Ingle, *Yorkshire Cotton*, 165–6; Baumber, *Revival to Regency*, 52–3, 57–8; Keighley St Andrew registers and monumental inscriptions; Leeds St Peter registers; Borthwick, Kettlewell bishops' transcripts, bap. 6 Oct. 1776; J. M. Potter, Kettlewell St Mary index to parish registers, c. 1698–1760, by Wharfedale F.H.S., bap. 1731; *London Gazette*, 20385, Sept. 1844, 3237.

William Carr (c. 1750–1834)

Born into a Catholic family in Scorton, north Lancashire (returning there after retirement c. 1820) Carr was apprenticed as a whitesmith. His sons Edward,

John and Thomas trained as whitesmiths and machine-makers. Edward, who married Susannah Pearson, daughter of Adam (q.v.), carried on Carr's Low Street business, making throstles. His own sons continued in Keighley on a small scale as smiths and iron-moulders. John Carr made and repaired flyers and guides, and was a noted gunsmith. The third brother, Thomas, successfully established himself as engineer and machine-maker in Bingley from c. 1830, the business later converting to manufacturing steam-engines under Thomas's son, John.

William Carr's career, see above, pp. 89–91; Hodgson, *Textile Manufacture*, 249–52; *Craven Muster Roll*; J. P. Smith, *Lancashire Registers III* (Catholic Record Soc., XX, 1916), 214, 233; UGLE, Samaritan Lodge, Keighley; notes of Ian J. Thompson with Ian E. Carr of Surrey, now with Clive Thompson of Clitheroe; Baines, *Dir.* (1822); White, *Dir.* (1837–38), I, 679, 688; (1853), 539, 716.

Thomas Corlass
Cotton twist-spinner, by trade a joiner and cabinet-maker. Built Hope Mill late-eighteenth century, and sourced quantities of Hattersley machine parts, 1800–01, paying fully only in 1804. Gave up this business and dissolved a partnership with William Corlass in 1805. Afterwards, he or his son joined other family members in worsted spinning, and later, cotton. These ventures were unsuccessful, and followed by several more reversals of fortune. A Swedenborgian, in 1805 Corlass gave land for a new church. His son Thomas (b. c. 1785) was a cabinet-maker, freemason from 1806, and sometimes styled gentleman.

WYAS Bradford, 32D83/2/1; /33/7, creditors' meeting, 1847; WYAS Wakefield, Deeds GY, 25 Aug. 1818 and *passim*; Hodgson, *Textile Manufacture*, 225–8; Barfoot and Wilkes, *Dir.*, III, 483; *London Gazette*, 15771, 12 Jan. 1805, 71; Bottomley, 'Keighley New Church', 11; UGLE, Royal Yorkshire Lodge; Ingle, *Yorkshire Cotton*, 166.

James Greenwood
Probably the same man who (aged 21) converted his father's dyehouse at Bridgehouse, Haworth, into a cotton-factory in 1784, Greenwood supervised construction of West Greengate Mill, Keighley, and its machinery, 1784–85. Partnership proposed by the projectors Smith, Watson and Blakey did not materialize. A James Greenwood supplied brass work, 'two pairs of cards Iron Wheels' and oak planks for Robert Heaton's new cotton mill at Ponden, c. 1790. He seems to have returned to Bridgehouse, recorded there as 'cotton-twist spinner and stocking-worsted manufacturer'. If so, Greenwood was among the first to spin worsteds by machine.

Ingle, *Marriner's Yarns*, 13–17, 41; Hodgson, *Textile Manufacture*, xvii–xviii; WYAS Bradford, DB2/6/3, pp. 104–5, 107, 118; WYAS Wakefield, Deeds DH; Barfoot and Wilkes, *Dir.*, III, 483.

Richard Hattersley (1761–1829)
Eldest child of Jonathan Hattersley, nail-maker, of Ecclesfield, and Mary
Parkin (bap. Tankersley, 1741–42). Through his mother and her three siblings,
Hattersley was related to the Drabble family, so cousin to the wives of the
Leeds engineers Taylor, Wordsworth, and Samuel Pollard, and thus a relative
by marriage (rather distantly, and not absolutely certainly) of John Jubb and
the other Drabbles.

Soon after arriving in Keighley, Hattersley joined the Swedenborgian
church, perhaps influenced by his association with Joseph Wright, the
minister. Hattersley became a freemason at the Royal Yorkshire Lodge in
1801.

Hattersley had ten children, including Samuel (1785–1852), George (1789–
1869) and Levi (1795–1858), partners at the time of his death; and Jonathan
(1800–63), a successful textile engineer in Leeds.

For Hattersley, see above, pp. 91–4; other family linkages, see app. 2 for Drabble (especially
regarding Hannah Drabble, Mary Parkin's sister, d. Holbeck aged 68 in 1811), Jonathan
Hattersley and Pollard; C. Smith, Hattersley family bible; registers of Ecclesfield St Mary;
Tankersley St Peter; Sheffield St Peter; Keighley St Andrew; UGLE; P. Whitcombe, unpub.
Hattersley family tree.

Joseph Hindle
A joiner who reportedly made throstles, 1799 to c. 1804. Substantial purchases
from Hattersley in 1800, little afterwards.

WYAS Bradford, 32D83/2/1.

John Inman
Customer of Richard Hattersley, advertised as 'joiner, cabinet-maker and
cotton spinners' machine-maker'. Died or retired in 1800, succeeded by a son,
John, who had £250-worth of parts from Hattersley during 1801, and subsequently c. £130-worth annually until 1805, when he reverted to joinery. Debt
owing to Hattersley was partly settled in kind with items of furniture in 1806.
Sum still outstanding in 1808. Inman occasionally bought Hattersley spindles
and machine parts, 1813–15.

Barfoot and Wilkes, *Dir.*, III, 483; *Craven Muster Roll*; WYAS Bradford, 32D83/5/1; /2/1–2.

William Lawson (?d. 1802) and William Platerous Lawson (b. 1783)
This was a tin-plate worker (not the clock-maker Lawson who made minor
purchases from Hattersley in 1793). Hattersley sold rollers and flyers from
1797 to this tinsmith, presumably for throstle-making. Transactions peaked
in 1800–01, perhaps when Lawson died. His son William Platerous carried
on business as brazier and tinsmith, buying tools from Hattersley in 1806,
supplying unspecified parts to Marriner, 1819 and 1825–26, and John

Brigg, 1825. He was close to the Hattersleys, perhaps visiting America with Levi Hattersley c. 1819. He left permanently for Louisville, Ohio, and then Cincinnati, probably before 1837, again perhaps with Levi, who emigrated to Philadelphia.

Loomes, *Yorkshire Clockmakers*, 21; WYAS Bradford, 32D83/5/1; /2/1; /5/4; /5/5; /15/4; Barfoot and Wilkes, *Dir.*, III, 483; Baines, *Dir.* (1822), 219–21; Brotherton SC, BUS/Marriner, box 118; Keighley Lib., Brigg Box 83.

John (1747–1818) and Titus (1775–1831) Longbottom

John Longbottom, Halifax-born joiner and machinist, worked on Bingley-Skipton canal construction, then settled in Steeton. Regularly bought card rollers, shafts, spindles, flyers, etc. from Hattersley from 1793, for carding and spinning machines. Titus, his apprentice, worked for Berry Smith from 1807, making worsted-spinning frames; then took over the family business with his brother, John, in friendly competition with Smith. These were two of three worsted-spinning frame-makers then in Keighley. Longbottom bought substantially from Hattersley from 1809, and rented room and power from him at North Brook. Took his own premises in 1815, but in 1820 was forced to mortgage them to Hattersley and the ironfounder Thomas Mills, for £620. Bankrupted in 1821, imprisoned, resumed work and repaid some debt, but suffered in the 1825–26 bank crash and never recovered from bankruptcy in 1828. Business closed on Titus's death.

WYAS Bradford, 32D83/5/1; /2/1; /6/1; WYAS Wakefield, Deeds, HF, 24 Aug. 1821; Hodgson, *Textile Manufacture*, 239–60, 59, 26; *London Gazette*, 5 June 1821, 17712, 1223; 14 Aug. 1821, 17737, 1686; R. Longbottom, 'The Longbottoms: Keighley and District Machine-Makers and Mechanics', *Old West Riding*, 6(1) (1986), 1–5.

Michael Merrall (1775–1819)

Apprenticed as blacksmith to William Parker of Keighley, worked for Richard Hattersley in 1796. Left by 1808 to set up in business at Clubhouses. Merrall and Hattersley supplied each other, 1809–19, exchanging iron and iron turnings. Merrall produced rollers, spindles, flyers and guides, his customers including Berry Smith, and from 1817, the worsted spinner Marriner. Made one of the first steam boilers in Keighley, for Corlass, and repaired and maintained pumping engines at Morton Banks colliery. He employed about 20 by 1819, when killed in a steam-engine accident. His assets were valued under £300 and the firm was wound up.

Keighley St Andrew registers 1813, 1816, 1819; WYAS Bradford, 32D83/6/1; /2/1; WYAS Wakefield, Deeds GH (1815); GX (1818); Hodgson, *Textile Manufacture*, 262, 160; Baumber, *Revival to Regency*, 55; Brotherton SC, BUS/Marriner, Box 118; Borthwick, Craven, Aug. 1820; *London Gazette*, 17921, 10 May 1823, 766; 17931, 14 June 1823, 973.

John Nicholson
Printer, bookseller and stationer, said to have co-invented the hand throstle with John Weatherhead (q.v.). But Nicholson was not an engineer, and the technical input was probably Weatherhead's. Afterwards he was partner in a worsted-twist spinners and manufacturers, presumably operating improved worsted throstles. John Nickelsen & Co., and Turner and Nicholson, bought flyers and spindles from Hattersley in the 1790s, to 1802. Nicholson remained a bookseller and was afterwards a printer, perhaps in Bradford.

WYAS Bradford, 32D83/2/1; /5/1; Keighley, *Keighley*, 110; Barfoot and Wilkes, *Dir.*, III, 483–4; A. L. Cooper, 'George Nicholson (1760–1825), printer', *DNB*.

Adam Pearson (b. c. 1756)
Origins not known, noted as 'a skilful mechanic', Pearson was foreman/mill engineer at Low Mill, the county's first Arkwright-style factory, 1780s to perhaps 1796. Supervised smiths, joiners and wood-turners, and trained the young William Smith as machine-maker. Perhaps involved in Low Mill's building and fitting out in 1780, certainly in Keighley by 1781. Very likely trained in specifics at Cromford, or by Arkwright associates elsewhere. A small purchase from Hattersley c. 1800 indicates that Pearson may have become a twist-spinner.

Hodgson *Textile Manufacture*, 212–14, 244; Keighley St Andrew registers; Aspin, *Water-Spinners*, 76–82; WYAS Bradford, 32D83/2/1, p. 65; Notes of I. J. Thompson (see William Carr, above).

George Richardson (b. 1771)
Brass-founder, briefly partner of William Carr (q.v.) c. 1793, as founders and machine-makers. Afterwards mainly a brass- and iron-founder and jobbing metalworker. Perhaps built further machines: bought spindles and flyers from Hattersley, c. 1800–02. Partner of Thomas Mills (q.v.) c. 1814, in a foundry converted from a barn. Died or declined business before 1820. Samaritan Lodge member from 1794.

Barfoot and Wilkes, *Dir.*, III, 483; *Craven Muster Roll*; WYAS Bradford, 32D83/2/1–2; WYAS Wakefield, Deeds EO, FC, GH; UGLE.

Berry Smith (1772–1836)
Reportedly Carr's first apprentice in Keighley, c. 1790, the only man listed specifically as machine-maker on the muster roll. Journeyman mechanic at West Greengate cotton mill, 1797–1800. In business in 1800, buying Hattersley spindles, flyers and rollers worth £35, then £140 in 1801, over £300 in 1802, and rising. By 1810 produced worsted-spinning frames and repaired cotton machinery; perhaps made some spindles and flyers for himself from

c. 1804. Built a new machine shop that year, later extending Acres Mill for room and power tenants.

By his mid-30s Smith, born illegitimate in Bingley parish, was wealthy enough to qualify as a West Riding elector, and in 1824 proved assets of over £1,000 to become a member of the Keighley Improvement Commission. He shipped worsted machinery across the country, yet never advanced beyond 'wood ends and tin carrying rollers'. C. 1810, converted Acres Mill to commission worsted spinning. At some point he gave up machine-making. Employed 60 people in his spinning business in 1834.

Hodgson, *Textile Manufacture*, 252–5, 59–60, 243; *Craven Muster Roll*; Baumber, *Revival to Regency*, 54; Ingle, *Marriner's Yarns*, 35; Baines, *Dir.* (1822), 220; WYAS Bradford, 32D83/2/1; WYAS Wakefield, Deeds, EX, KG; Keighley Lib., rate books, 1829–35, 1837–38, 1842; Brotherton SC, YAS0966, Yorkshire Poll Book, 1807, 367; Dewhirst, *History of Keighley*, 23–4, 27–8; PP (HC) 1834 XX (167) C1, 220–1; Bingley All Saints register; Bottomley, 'Keighley New Church', 11, 15.

Thomas Smith

Made substantial purchases of spindles and machine parts from Hattersley, from 1793, and noted as partner of Lodge Calvert (q.v.), 1801–04. Subsequent history unknown, and evidently unconnected with the later machine-maker Thomas Smith, a Berry Smith apprentice.

WYAS Bradford, 32D83/5/1; /2/1.

William Smith (1774–1850)

Smith's father James (1726–1800) was a corn-miller at Stockbridge, across the Aire from Keighley, and evidently poor. William worked at Low Mill from age nine, later apprenticed there under Adam Pearson (q.v.) as mechanic. Set up in business when about 21, making components and then throstles, supplying Berry Smith and others. William Smith later developed an improved spinning frame.

Smith's seven sons were brought up within the business, and by 1847 four were partners. Smith then retired with a £3,000 settlement. Probate value of his personal estate was £4,000. The main family company broke up in 1865, its most successful and enduring offshoot, of many Smith engineering and textile enterprises, a vast business at Burlington Shed belonging to the fourth son, Prince.

For Smith's career, see above, p. 95 and (for relationship with clock-making) pp. 83–4. Smith family tree researched by Stephen Hattersley Smith and Christopher S. Smith; Feather, 'Nineteenth-century entrepreneurs'; Borthwick, bishop's transcripts, Bingley; Borthwick, Craven, Oct. 1851. Prog.; *Keighley News*, 29 Mar. 1890; 21 Oct. 1922; Hodgson, *Textile Manufacture*, 246–9; Jeremy (ed.), *Dictionary of Business Biography*, V (1984–87), 213.

Joseph Tempest (1753–1836)
Joseph Tempest, carpenter by trade and from Sutton-in-Craven, was employed
by Craven, Brigg and Shackleton as millwright at Walk Mill in 1783. At Royd
House, Oxenhope, in 1790, Tempest planned and supervised construction
of a cotton-spinning factory with 30-ft wheel. Regular purchases of rollers
and other components from Hattersley in the 1790s suggest he was building
spinning frames. By 1822 back in Sutton, where his brother William (1748–
1834) was a watch- and clock-maker, Tempest was listed as a millwright.
Member of the Royal Yorkshire Lodge from 1788.

Hodgson, *Textile Manufacture*, 36; WYAS Bradford, 32D83/5/1; DB2/6/3; UGLE; Kildwick
St Andrew register, 1753; Baines, *Dir.* (1822), 613; Aspin, *Water-Spinners*, 109–10.

John Weatherhead (?1754–?1798)
Weatherhead, always called a joiner, brought rollers from Ashton-under-Lyne
in 1789/90 while helping fit out Ponden Mill. Single most important customer
during Hattersley's first year in business, 1793, Weatherhead took spindles,
shafts and bayonets, brought flyers for alteration and worsted rollers to
be turned, supplied iron, and had Hattersley repair a vice. He became less
important to Hattersley with the growth of other custom.

Evidence about Weatherhead and Nicholson's collaboration to improve
the worsted throstle is sparse. Perhaps Weatherhead, with relevant skills
and knowledge, had ideas and was supported financially by Nicholson.
Weatherhead's last recorded transactions with Hattersley were in 1798, when
Hattersley bought old iron and rollers, first from Weatherhead and then from
his wife Mary. It appears that Weatherhead had died, and his son John, later
cabinet-maker and freemason, was not old enough to take over the business.

WYAS Bradford, DB/6/3; 32D83/2/1; /6/1; Keighley, *Keighley*, 110; Aspin, *Water-Spinners*,
106–10; Keighley St Andrew registers.

In business 1851–53

Businesses listed in the 1851 Keighley census and/or in White, *Dir.* (1853),
539–45.

Richard Sharp Bailey
Small-scale and apparently short-lived supplier of wool-combing machinery.

George Bland (1796–1864)
George Bland, Addingham-born blacksmith, supplied Marriners with
components, 1821. Partnership with Charles Fox established c. 1835 at Acres
Mill, noted for high quality products. Clough of Grove Mill bought their

first power looms from Fox and Bland, £100 each, in 1836, and more in 1841. Uninsured, Fox and Bland were hit by a serious fire c. 1840, losing all tools and designs. Business rebuilt in a machine shop and foundry in Low Street, expanded significantly under Bland and his sons John and William in the 1850s. Employed 12 men in 1851.

Hodgson, *Textile Manufacture*, 269–71; Addingham St Peter register and information from Kate Mason; Brotherton SC, BUS/Marriner, Box 118; Smith, 'Robert Clough Ltd.', 41–2; Keighley Lib., rate books, 1867, 1870; *Keighley News*, 23 Jan. 1864.

Briggs and Banks

'Spindle, fly and roller makers' in South Street in 1848. Partners in 1851 were William Brigg, aged 35, and Samuel Brigg and Abraham Banks, both 29, employing nine men and 19 boys. Sold power looms to Clough in 1852, taking old models in part exchange. By 1863, company had split into new enterprises under Samuel Brigg at Dalton Works, and Banks in Bradford.

Keighley Lib., Brigg box 83; rate books, 1853–54; Smith, 'Robert Clough Ltd.', 42–3; Jones, *Mercantile Dir. of Bradford* (1863), 245.

Brown, Darling and Sellers

Darling and Sellers, later famed for machine tools, started as machine- and tool-makers at Low Bridge, 1850–51. William Darling (b. c. 1828), mechanic and Charles Brown (b. c. 1817), machine-maker, both Leeds-born, recently come to Keighley, employed half a dozen in 1851. Robert Sellers, from Wyke, newly out of apprenticeship, joined as partner, and Brown left in 1854.

London Gazette, 13 Oct. 1854, 21609, 3107.

George Hattersley

George Hattersley's business was thoroughly revived by 1851, producing power looms, rollers, spindles, etc. Hattersley also manufactured worsteds. Of 60 men, 40 boys, 39 women and 29 girls employed, the females undoubtedly worked in the textile factory. Despite the hiatus in 1830–32, this business descended directly from Richard Hattersley's, where George was apprenticed as roller- and spindle-maker, worked from 1798, and was a partner from c. 1818.

Above, app. 1.

John Midgley

Titus Longbottom's former apprentice, of Newsholme, produced power looms from c. 1837. Continued in business after 1850, though Midgley may by then have forsaken machine-making for textiles.

Hodgson, *Textile Manufacture*, 275–6, 28.

Thomas Mills (c. 1786–?1861)

Iron- and brass-founder, arrived from Huddersfield c. 1809. That Mills was an executor of Hattersley's partner Thomas Binns in 1810 suggests a prior relationship. Briefly associated with George Richardson (q.v.), c. 1814, Mills' business by 1851 employed 15 men and seven boys. Supplied significant quantities of iron to Hattersley, and was, less so, a customer; sold cast-iron parts to William Smith until 1830; engaged significantly with Marriners as they equipped with worsted machinery, 1819–26. At times Mills ventured into machine-making and worsted spinning. Planning retirement, he let his premises to a machine-making and ironfounding partnership, Smith, Pickles and Mills, c. 1852, in which he was at first a partner, alongside his sons Thomas and William, and Joseph Smith and Thomas Pickles. A year after his withdrawal in 1853, the business folded. Liabilities of £885 were almost matched by the value of stock, but 'his two sons are the losers'. Thomas Mills, presumably the son, re-established the foundry in the same Low Street premises.

White, *Dir.* (1837), I, 687–8; WYAS Bradford, 32D83/6/1; /32/1; /2/2; /2/5; /6/1; Brotherton SC, BUS/Marriner, box 118; Keighley census, 1841, 1851, Low Street; Keighley Lib., poor rate books, 1831, 1854; rate books, 1851, 1853, 1858; *London Gazette*, 21446, 7 June 1853, 1601.

Jesse Ross

Henry Ross patented a wool-combing machine in 1837, significant enough to have influenced Holden and Donisthorpe. The rights passed to Jesse, perhaps a son, who took further patents, in 1841, 1851 and 1853. Though the 1853 directory called him a maker of wool-combs, more likely he was licenser of patent rights.

Burnley, *History of Wool and Wool-Combing*, 294, 407, 426–7, 429, 431; *Bradford Observer*, 28 Oct. 1852.

Charles and Allan Smith

Charles (b. 1818) and Allan (b. c. 1821) were sons of Thomas Smith, Berry Smith's first indentured apprentice. They made spinning frames, preparing machinery, rollers, spindles and flyers, employing three men and three boys in 1851. Company had grown from Thomas's partnership with his brother-in-law, the clock-maker William Keighley, c. 1815–20, making wooden-framed machinery using hand-powered tools. Thomas continued alone, settling in Acres Mill in 1834 in adjacent workshop to Fox and Bland (q.v.). He suffered uninsured damage, losing benches, tools and models, in their fire c. 1840, and continued with some difficulty. He died in 1850, and his sons gave up the business c. 1853.

Hodgson, *Textile Manufacture*, 263–4; Keighley St Andrew, registers.

John and Samuel Smith

Hattersley-trained brothers, set up c. 1818 at Low Bridge, making rollers, spindles and flyers for worsted, cotton and flax. After a destructive fire in 1821, resumed production at Long Croft. Both had died by c. 1850. Keeping their name, the firm expanded under a brother and nephew, William and Samuel, employing 80 workers in 1851, 400 to 500 in 1866. Product range grew to encompass machine tools and spinning frames. Suffered a major fire in 1869.

Hodgson, *Textile Manufacture*, 256–9; Dewhirst, *History of Keighley*, 24; WYAS Wakefield, Deeds GP, 13 Feb. 1817; KE, 7 Aug. 1827; LZ, 10 Nov. 1834; Baines, *Dir.* (1822), 220; White, *Dir.* (1837), 687; Keighley Lib., rate books, 1837–38, *passim*; *Keighley News*, 1 Dec. 1866; 20 Mar. 1869.

William Smith and Sons

Founded c. 1795. In 1850 made worsted-spinning frames, rollers, spindles and flyers; also worsted spinners and manufacturers. No employee figures for 1851.

Hodgson, *Textile Manufacture*, 244–9; Jeremy (ed.), *Dictionary of Business Biography*, V (1984–87), 213; above, William Smith.

Appendix 2: Leeds Engineering Businesses Established Before 1830

Major figures and leading businesses

William and Joseph Drabble

Occupied the Silver Street works in Holbeck after Jubb left in 1796, and before Taylor and Wordsworth. The brothers were not especially important technically, but very significant as their extensive clan connected leading textile engineers, then and later. Through a series of marriages, Drabbles were linked to Jubb, Taylor, Wordsworth and John Pollard in Leeds, and Hattersley in Keighley.

Connections are not fully established but the weight of evidence is compelling, centring upon descendants of Joseph Drabble of Wortley by Penistone, his sons William (b. 1743) and John (dates unconfirmed); and daughter Sarah (b. 1752). William was father of William (b. 1769) and Joseph (b. 1773) Drabble of Silver Street. Sarah was the first wife of John Jubb the elder. John Drabble apparently married Hannah Parkin (b. 1743), seemingly aunt of Richard Hattersley (q.v.). Daughters of John and Hannah married Samuel Pollard, Joshua Wordsworth and Joseph Taylor. The elder John Jubb seems to have been uncle by marriage not only to the Drabbles of Silver Street, but also to Mary Pollard, Martha Wordsworth and Hannah Taylor, and great uncle of the second Martha Wordsworth.

William and Joseph Drabble established their Silver Street business probably in 1796, certainly by 1798, while still in their 20s. Conceivably they had been Jubb's apprentices, so versed in woollen, cotton and worsted machinery. Their main business became flax and hemp machine-making. They employed both Wordsworth (after he married their cousin Martha) and Taylor (who later married Martha's sister).

In 1800 the brothers bought neighbouring land to expand Jubb's workshops. Wordsworth in 1834 noted that the oldest Silver Street buildings were erected 'nearly 40 years since'. But Joseph pulled out of the partnership in 1806, advertising the following year a modern 'extensive manufactory' at the Steander, producing flax, tow and hemp machinery. From 1809, he struck a deal with William Farmery (q.v.) to make new and adapt old machinery on Farmery's patented system. Soon afterwards he became insolvent, and the Steander works and its stock of flax-spinning, roving and carding machinery were sold.

William continued with a range of hemp, flax, tow and worsted machinery. A new line, patent axle-trees for coaches and wagons, perhaps precipitated his bankruptcy in 1812. His assignees, presumably main creditors, were local ironfounders, John Cawood and Richard Gothard. The bankruptcy sale included complete and unfinished carding engines, roving and spinning frames, joiners' tools, benches and wood, lathes, fluting engines, smiths' tools and hearths, and Drabble's household goods. The extensive freehold factory was sold in 1813. Taylor and Wordsworth moved their new business into the works in 1814. They and Richard Cluderay both seem to have successfully produced patent axles, so William Drabble's problem could have been cash flow, after buying out his brother. The Drabbles disappear from Leeds records after Martin Cawood paid final dividends in 1819.

Wortley Chapelry, Tankersley, bap. 1743, 1743, 1752, 1769; 1773; 1776; 1779; 1785; mar. 1763; 1803; Leeds St Peter, mar. 1798; Wordsworth, 'Joshua Wordsworth'; *Leeds Dir.* (1798); PP (HC) 1834 XX (167) C1, 47; WYAS Wakefield, Deeds, EH 140 182; *London Gazette*, 4 Nov. 1806, 15972, 1452; 20 Oct. 1812, 16660, 2130; 16 Mar. 1819, 17490, 494; Baines, *Dir.* (1822); *Leeds Mercury*, 10 Oct. 1807; 7 Nov. 1812; 19 Dec 1812; 11 June 1814; 3 Sept. 1814; *Leeds Intelligencer*, 10 Nov. 1806; 19 Oct. 1807; 10 July 1809; 13 Aug. 1810; 18 May 1811; 18 July 1812; 16 Nov. 1812; 10 May 1813; 22 Mar. 1819. Key evidence tying Leeds Drabbles to John (who was not certainly William and Martha's brother, though probably so) is that his widow lived with a daughter in Holbeck. Hannah Drabble died aged 68 in 1811: *Leeds Intelligencer*, 11 Nov. 1811; Leeds St John, bur., 2 Nov. 1811.

Peter Fairbairn (1799–1861)

Kelso-born son of a farm steward, youngest brother of the renowned William, Peter Fairbairn was a renowned innovator who revolutionized flax and hemp preparation, enabling superior yarns to be produced at low cost. His became the largest engineering business in Leeds, said to be 'most notable in its particular line of operation in the world'. The family moved around, settling on Tyneside c. 1804. Peter reportedly started work in a colliery at eleven, and aged fourteen was apprenticed to John Casson, Newcastle millwright and engineer. Broadened his experience in Glasgow, Manchester, London and France, consulting his brother before moving to Leeds mid-1828, capitalizing on the Round Foundry's decline.

With £500 lent by William, Fairbairn bought out of his Glasgow partnership with Houldsworth. Perhaps William supported his brief period of experimentation in Lady Lane, Leeds, where a former Houldsworth employee was 'modeller', and 'a stalwart Irishman' lathe-turner and 'man about'. Fairbairn's models impressed John Marshall, who helped establish the works near Wellington bridge, ordered the novel designs to re-equip his own factory, and underwrote wage costs until the firm was self-sustaining. This happened quickly, thanks to a general clamour for the machines. Fairbairn took an existing iron and brass foundry with workshops and 4-hp engine, buying the site with a mortgage in 1829. He built a new machine shop, installed a 6-hp engine, then reconstructed the main factory in 1841, fireproofed and raised it from two to three storeys. Noted for a fine division of labour, Fairbairn employed 550 by 1841; 850 in 1851, 1,400 in 1861, 2,000 to 2,500 in 1900. Early on, he substituted iron for wood in woollen machinery; made special machine tools for armament producers during the Crimean War; and extended into general engineering tools.

With £50,000 to £60,000 capital employed in 1841, 550 workers produced c. £70,000-worth of machinery annually. Fairbairn's commanding position was built on innovation, in organization as much as products. He employed, but did not bind, many apprentices aged around 14, and was criticized for training unskilled men to his specific needs, cause of the one industrial dispute at Wellington Foundry in his lifetime, in 1833.

Fairbairn took partners only in 1848, apparently thinking of expansion into machine tools. He met Thomas Greenwood (1807–73), a former woollen-machine maker admired for elegant machine-tool designs, when buying tools from Stephen and Joseph Whitham, who were primarily millwrights. Greenwood joined Fairbairn in 1843 as chief draughtsman, soon rising to works manager. The other new partner, John Batley, came to Wellington Foundry as chief cashier. The company focused more upon machine tools after 1850, while still turning out 20 flax-spinning machines a week. The partners quarrelled in 1856, Fairbairn taking out a loan from Beckett's Bank to buy out Greenwood and Batley, who became famed machine tool-makers in Armley. Wellington Foundry was then valued at £78,946.

After this, and following Fairbairn's death in 1861, there was a succession of new partners: his brother-in-law Thomas Kennedy, son Andrew, nephew T. S. Kennedy, and apprentices who had worked their way into management, John William Naylor and Alexander Sinclair McPherson. Adopted limited liability in 1882, as Fairbairn, Naylor, McPherson & Co. Ltd. Amalgamating in 1900 with Samuel Lawson and Combe Barbour of Belfast to form a giant flax-making machinery conglomerate, Fairbairn's was valued at £85,251.

Peter Fairbairn was impressively energetic in public life, a Whig associate of Charles G. Maclea and John Marshall. An overseer, member of the reformed corporation from 1836, and mayor of Leeds, 1858–60, as a widely respected moderate Liberal. He was knighted when as mayor he entertained the Queen at his mansion, Woodsley House, for the opening of Leeds Town Hall. His funeral at Adel was attended by 700 workpeople, and he left personal assets worth £45,000.

G. Cookson, 'Sir Peter Fairbairn, 1799–1861', DNB; Walker, *Fortunes Made in Business*, 252–90; Taylor (ed.), *Biographia Leodiensis*, 31, 491–6; WYAS Leeds, Acc. 2371, bundle 23, notes on Fairbairn history (1897); box 76, valuation and notes (1969); box 13; *Chambers's*

Edinburgh Journal, 513, 27 Nov. 1841, 354; Ward, 'Industrial development and location', 362–6; Beresford, *East End, West End*, 131, 286, 288, 295, 338–40; PP (HC) 1834 XX (167) C1, 31; PP Exportation of Machinery, 208–10; WYAS Wakefield, Deeds (1829), KO 743 651; 745 652; 746 653; (1830), KU 681 670; Baines and Newsome, *Dir.*; White, *Dir.* (1837), I, 564; *Repertory of Patent Inventions*, XVIII (July–Dec. 1851), 169; *The Engineer*, XI, 11 Jan. 1861, 26; *London Gazette*, 1 Feb. 1831, 18772, 200; 13 May 1856, 21883, 1768; J. Lindsay, 'Falls Foundry, 1900–14', *Textile History*, 1/3 (1968–70), 352; *Leeds Intelligencer*, 9 Nov. 1833; 31 Jan. 1835; 21 Aug. 1841; *Leeds Times*, 11 Apr. 1833; 2 Jan. 1836; 19 Oct. 1839; 3 Oct. 1840; 7 Nov. 1840; 18 Feb. 1843.

(William Fairbairn): J. Sutherland, 'Sir William Fairbairn, FRS (1789–1874)', *Biographical Dictionary of Civil Engineers*, 272; Hayward, 'Fairbairn's of Manchester' 1.2–1.20; Byrom, 'William Fairbairn', ch. 4.

(Greenwood and Batley): Floud, *British Machine-Tool Industry*, especially 120–1; 'Thomas Greenwood', in Jeremy (ed.), *Dictionary of Business Biography*, 645–6; 1851 census, Leeds 2321/200; Gildersome Baptist registers, 1814; *The Engineer*, XXXV, 21 Feb. 1873, 113; Anon., *Industries of Yorkshire*, I, 166; M. Blackburn, transcript of report, evidently from a Leeds newspaper, 9 Feb. 1873.

John Jubb sen. (1748–1808) and jun. (1775–1816)

The older Jubb, a millwright by profession, originated in south Yorkshire. His was a common name, but his details most closely match the baptism near Barnsley of a son of William Jubb of Monk Bretton. In 1774 married Sarah Drabble (1752–90) in Doncaster; sons, John and Joseph, were baptized in 1775 and 1777 in Sarah's birthplace, Wortley. Most likely, therefore, Jubb worked at Wortley forge. He then moved to Churwell, Morley, the first of several children baptized at Topcliffe Congregational (Independent) chapel in 1778. Jubb was partner, with Samuel, John and Joseph Wetherill, clothiers and staunch Topcliffe chapel-goers, in Churwell mill, a water-driven Arkwright-style cotton-factory insured for £1,000 in 1784. He seems to have lived on the premises, while pursuing a separate business as millwright and 'engine-maker' producing 'engines for cotton and wool, and … improved machines for carding, scribbling &c.' In 1784 Jubb advertised 'more improvements than ever in constructing machines for scribbling, carding &c of fleece wool …'. He was in great demand, his standing as master millwright qualifying him for insurance and legal commissions, working across the Yorkshire textile districts as a fire loss assessor, installer of steam-engines, and broker in factory insolvencies.

Jubb moved to central Leeds in late 1787 or 1788. He bought machine parts including spindles and screws from Kirkstall Forge; sold scribbling and carding machines, willeys, and fulling stocks, and updated older models; advertised for mechanics, joiners and whitesmiths who knew about cotton and worsted machinery, and millwrights with textile experience; trained premium and trade apprentices; and in 1794 developed a sideline in threshing and winnowing machinery. Jubb's first Leeds workshop, in the newly laid Silver Street, Holbeck, later evolved into Taylor and Wordsworth's Midland

Junction Foundry. With a growing reputation for woollen machinery, he left in 1796 for 'more commodious premises' in Meadow Lane, Hunslet, later called Soho works.

In managing insolvencies and estates, and sometimes himself a creditor owed for machines or millwrighting or as mortgagee, business opportunities came Jubb's way, in Leeds and elsewhere. The commissions reflect his professional rank as millwright, higher than most engaged in engineering. Other indicators of status are that he was married a second time by licence and described as 'yeoman'; and his daughters' marriages, to a Sheffield gentleman and a dissenting minister.

Dying aged 60 in 1808, he left an estate of £3,000 and the Meadow Lane property to trustees, Jubb's friends William Varley of Hunslet (q.v.), and Robert Cookson of Holbeck, clothier. He intended the business continue under his surviving sons, John and Joseph, millwrights and machine-makers, assisted by loans from the estate. John bought the real estate for something over £1,900. Announcing a readiness to carry on, and confirming the importance still of timber to their activities, the sons advertised a large stock of dry and well-seasoned materials. But a series of disasters beset them, and the partnership lasted only four years. John jun. lost his wife and then his 12-year-old son. The last mention of J. & J. Jubb, in 1812, was a donation to the Leeds General Infirmary, where Joseph was probably being treated. Only days later 'after a long and painful affliction', he died aged 35. John jun. must have shouldered much responsibility himself, and had not been held back. When Salt and Gothard's longstanding ironfounding partnership was dissolved, he took their nearby works, in 1810 advertising his brass and iron foundry there. His work was a continuation of his father's, including supervising machinery auctions and insolvencies.

The firm was derailed by Jubb's premature death in 1816, at 41. His sons were children, not even apprentices. His second wife was to direct the business, advised by executors and trustees, John Raper, carpenter, and David Nell, common brewer, both of Holbeck, instructed to bind the sons as machine-makers and iron- and brass-founders. Jubb's estate was valued at £5,000, and with valuable industrial property. Martha Jubb announced she would continue, the foreman of over 20 years acting as manager, and retaining all the same workmen. But this was optimistic without Jubb's active direction. He had foreseen the difficulty, giving the trustees discretion to wind up. Perhaps indeed it proved unmanageable, for withdrawal was soon decided upon. Martha had another offer, marrying a Wakefield gentleman a year after Jubb's death. Her stepsons' fate is unknown. The Soho Foundry premises were advertised for sale in 1817, and taken in 1818 by James Procter & Sons, machine-makers.

Royston St John, bap. 1748; Doncaster St George, 1774; Wortley Chapelry, Tankersley; Leeds St Peter; Ferry Fryston St Andrew (mar. 1813); W. Smith (ed.), *The Registers of Topcliffe and*

Morley (1888), 71–7, 124, 132, 138, 141, 147, 150, 165; W. Smith, *Morley Ancient and Modern* (Longmans, Green, 1886), 233–4; Aspin, *Water-Spinners*, 238, 460; Jenkins, *West Riding Wool Textile Industry*, 109, 199–200, 283; Crump, *Leeds Woollen Industry*, 213, 220, 321, 323; Crump and Ghorbal, *Huddersfield Woollen Industry*, 76; Connell, 'Industrial development', II, no. 64; WYAS Leeds, 6257/1–2; *Leeds Dir.* (1798), 31; *London Gazette*, 11 Mar. 1809, 16236, 333; G. D. Lumb (ed.), *Extracts from the Leeds Intelligencer, 1791–6*, Thoresby Soc., XLIV (1955), 16; *Leeds Intelligencer*, 6 Jan. 1789; 14 Apr. 1789; 8 Nov. 1791; 2 June 1794; 22 Feb. 1796; 17 Oct. 1796; 2 Oct. 1797; 6 May 1799; 27 May 1799; 17 June 1799; 1 July 1799; 19 Aug, 1799; 2 Dec. 1799; 1 Sept. 1800; 22 Feb. 1802; 18 Feb. 1805; 14 Apr. 1806; 25 July 1808; 8 Aug. 1808; 11 Dec. 1809; 11 Jan. 1813; 13 Mar. 1815; 2 Feb. 1818; 4 May 1818; *Leeds Mercury*, 23 Nov. 1784; 23 July 1808; 6 Aug. 1808; 16 Dec. 1809; 9 June 1810; 29 Sept. 1810; 7 Mar. 1812; 13 Apr. 1812; 2 May 1812; 13 Aug. 1814; 22 Apr. 1815; 8 Apr. 1816; 20 Apr. 1816; 19 Apr. 1817; 6 Sept. 1817; 2 Feb. 1818; 28 Mar. 1818; Plan of Leeds made 1767–70, pub. 1775 by R. Sayer and J. Bennett; N. & F. Giles, Plan of the Town of Leeds and its Environs, 1815; Borthwick, Ainsty, Sept. 1809; Exch. Oct. 1816.

Samuel Lawson (1782–1866)

If, as a descendant believed, Samuel Lawson was apprenticed to Murray and Wood, then he must have been among their first, and in Leeds long before his father Thomas arrived in 1803. More likely the Keighley-born Lawson trained at Greenholme mill, Burley-in-Wharfedale, where Thomas was mill engineer and agent, moving to Leeds with his father. So if indeed he worked for Murray and Wood, it was probably post-apprenticeship as improver, and this would be his first encounter with flax-machinery. The first reference to Samuel in Leeds, and the only one as 'clock-maker', covers four weeks' work, 1803–04, building machinery for Ard Walker's new cotton-factory. Thomas then worked for J. & J. Holroyd at a new cotton-factory in Mabgate; his subsequent movements are unknown.

Lawson, styling himself blacksmith and flax-spinning machine-maker, set up in business in Mabgate in 1812. He was in a partnership of four until 1816, then reduced to two, with Mark Walker (1787–1874) until 1831. Walker left to establish a flax and tow mill off North Street. Next to his engineering works, Lawson's flax-dressing and spinning factory was run by managers, employing 66, mainly children and young women, in 1834. Two sons, John and Edward, joined the company that year, to form Samuel Lawson & Sons. For reasons unclear, perhaps when Lawson was short of funds after buying out Walker, Joshua Wordsworth was named as his trustee in 1835. If this were a stumble, it was brief, the firm continuing to grow. The textile side converted to fine spinning in 1840, then (like much of the Leeds flax industry) ceased altogether c. 1850. In engineering, 400 employees in 1851 grew to 1,400 in 1888, on a 12-acre site, the largest factory in north Leeds.

Samuel Lawson's precision skills show in his instrument-making, a leisure pursuit that confirms his professional reputation for intricacy. Lawson's planetarium was shown in the 1839 Leeds exhibition. His flax-machinery patents, though few in number, recorded some significant advances.

In common with other Leeds engineers, Lawson was active as a borough councillor, though unusually a conservative opposed to reform in 1832. He died aged 85, three years after retirement. His son, John (1805–83), took over the company, later introducing his own sons and those of Edward (d. 1857). John Lawson was deaf, perhaps explaining why he did not engage in public affairs. He was reckoned 'one of the most resourceful mechanics of his day', had several patents to his name, and under his direction the firm grew to an immense size. His own sons, Arthur Tredgold (1844–1915) (created baronet in 1900) and Frederick William (1845–1915) were both directors of Fairbairn Lawson Combe Barbour Ltd, Sir Arthur the founding chairman and his son Sir Digby a later chairman of the conglomerate.

WYAS Leeds, Acc 2371, box 76; box 80/2, notes by Capt. E. A. C. Lawson, 1946; DB23; Aspin, *Water-Spinners*, 436; Beresford, *East End, West End*, 241–4; PP (HC) 1834 XX (167) C1, 249; WYAS Wakefield, Deeds, LY 425 363; Ward, 'Industrial development and location', 422–3; Anon., *Industries of Yorkshire*, I, 162; *London Gazette*, 8 Nov. 1831, 18869, 2304; 8 Sept. 1863, 22769, 4395; White, *Dir.* (1837), 613; *Dir.* (1853), 240; Leeds census 1851, 2319/670, John Lawson of York Road; Leeds St Peter, bap. 1806, 1812; *Leeds Intelligencer*, 28 Apr. 1831; 30 July 1836; 10 Mar. 1838; *Leeds Mercury*, 10 Aug. 1839; 3 Oct. 1840; 15 Dec. 1866; *Leeds Times*, 19 Sept. 1840; *Yorkshire Post*, 8 July 1926; 25 Feb. 1915; 2 June 1915; *Proc. Inst. Mech. Eng.*, Oct.–Dec. 1915, 481.

Maclea and March

Charles Gascoigne Maclea (1792–1864) and Joseph Ogdin March (1799–1888) trained with Matthew Murray and became his sons-in-law. They established a separate business as brass- and iron-founders and flax-machinery makers in 1825.

In background, Maclea was unlike any other Leeds machine-maker. Edinburgh-born and 'descended from a good family' of Church of Scotland ministers, details of his early life are opaque, probably because of his illegitimacy. The forenames must derive from Charles Gascoigne (?1738–1806), ironmaster and member of the Yorkshire gentry, who managed and part-owned Carron ironworks, Scotland's first, in Falkirk. After bankruptcy in 1786, Gascoigne lived in Russia, establishing foundries, rolling mills and other facilities for the government. Maclea's father, Col. Duncan Maclea (c. 1772–1828), joined the Russian Imperial Army soon after Charles' birth. He must already have known Gascoigne, who possibly arranged the army commission. Apprenticeship for Charles Maclea at the Round Foundry may also have been promoted by Gascoigne. Maclea turned 14 in 1806, just as Gascoigne negotiated on the Tsar's behalf a large order for steam-engines and machine tools from Murray. The earliest concrete record of Maclea in Holbeck comes only in 1815, when he witnessed Richard Jackson's wedding to Murray's eldest daughter, Margaret. The following year, noted as 'engineer', Maclea married Ann Murray. Later, as a leading industrialist and mayor of Leeds, illegitimacy might have been embarrassing. For Murray, though, Maclea's engineering talent, connections, education and respectable background made him a perfectly acceptable son-in-law.

March, born in Holbeck to a woollen-worker too lowly to figure in local directories, joined Matthew Murray as apprentice in 1814. He quickly established a position above the status of 'ordinary workmen'. But while Richard Jackson was promoted Round Foundry factory manager by 1818, none of the sons-in-law became a partner. That may have prompted Maclea and March's departure. In the year that March married Murray's youngest daughter, they launched in 'very nice and convenient' premises in Dewsbury Road. Union Foundry, with a 6-hp Murray engine, was afterwards greatly enlarged; in 1834 it employed 82, in two-storey workshops around a courtyard. The partners registered no patents, but Maclea's flax-spinning machines found 'a European fame'. The company was also noted for machine tools, their drawings published as exemplars in 1841. Maclea joined a deputation of Leeds machine-makers lobbying the Board of Trade in 1843 to end export controls, and served as a Great Exhibition juror. Both partners were publicly very active, Liberal members of the reformed corporation, church trustees, and railway and insurance company directors. Both served as mayor of Leeds – Maclea in 1846 and March in 1862–63. Maclea retired early from business, withdrawing from the partnership late in 1842, and curtailing his mayoral term as his health worsened. Childless, he left most of his property to March's family. March continued alone, employing 211 workmen in 1851, and up to 300 in the 1860s. Only the elder of his surviving sons, George, joined the business. March retired through ill health in c. 1880 and died in 1888. Over the following year, George closed Union Foundry and sold the premises.

Woodhouse St Mark, monumental inscription to Maclea; Leeds St Peter, mar. 1797; Queen Street Independent, bap. 1799, 1828, 1833; Taylor, *Biographia Leodiensis*, 516–18; Smiles, *Industrial Biography*, 133–7, 179–80, 260; Thompson, *Matthew Murray*, 154–6, 225–7; Scott, *Matthew Murray*, 44–5, 49, 89, 113; Connell, 'Industrial development', II, no. 62; Harris, *Industrial Espionage*, 487–90; E. H. Robinson, 'Charles Gascoigne, 1738?–1806, ironmaster', *DNB*; 'The transference of British technology to Russia, 1760–1820', in B. M. Ratcliffe (ed.), *Great Britain and her World, 1750–1914* (1975), 8–10; R. H. Campbell, *Carron Company* (1961), 7–12, 144, 146, 152–3; *London Gazette*, 14 Dec. 1849, 21049, 3836; *Leeds Intelligencer*, 8 Jan. 1816; 21 July 1825; 26 Apr. 1832; 2 Nov. 1839; 25 Feb. 1843; 28 May 1864; *Leeds Mercury*, 7 Mar. 1818; 25 Feb. 1843; 27 May 1864; 28 Feb., 3 Mar. 1888; WYAS Wakefield, Deeds, KL 720 615, 1829; LE 380 373, 1832; PP (HC) 1834 XX (167) C1, 251; J. Weale, *Catalogue of Books on Architecture and Engineering, Civil, Mechanical, Military and Naval, New and Old* (1854), 27, ref. to supplement to Tredgold's edn of R. Buchanan, *Practical Treatise on Millwork and other Machinery* (1841); 1851 Leeds census, 2321/573, Beech Grove House.

Murray and Wood

Matthew Murray (1765–1826) was born in Newcastle upon Tyne, into a dynasty of Northumberland smiths. While still apprenticed, he married Mary Thompson of Wickham in 1785. Near Wickham was Crowley's long-established and technically influential ironworks; possibly, though this is speculation, Murray worked there. Employed as a mechanic in Stockton-on-Tees, 1787 to late 1788/89, Murray encountered John Marshall, who visited Darlington when negotiating a licence for Kendrew and Porthouse's flax-spinning machine. Murray then joined Marshall in Adel, Leeds, where they experimented to improve the mechanism. From 1790, Murray fitted out Marshall's new factory in Holbeck with flax-machinery, taking charge of and enhancing a new Boulton and Watt steam-engine in 1793. Several flax-processing patents were procured at this time. Murray and Marshall remained close, and while Murray continued to supply all Marshall's machinery, he inclined increasingly towards steam and other fields of engineering.

The Murray–Wood partnership started at Mill Green, Holbeck, in 1794 or 1795, continuing from 1796 in Water Lane, near Marshall. David Wood (1761–1820) was a blacksmith, apprenticed to his father in Ulleskelf, outside Tadcaster. He moved to Leeds c. 1790. Married three times, of his numerous children only two sons outlived him: Joseph (d. 1821, aged 18) and David (c. 1798–1830). Wood perhaps met Murray through Marshall, later Wood's great friend. According to James Watt jun., Wood was 'the steady man of business who directs the works'; as a mechanic, he was called 'a man of genius', and in character, 'upright, humble, humane and charitable'. Boulton and Watt thought of enticing Wood to Soho, as a way of ruining Murray, but concluded he was incorruptible. Like Samuel Lawson, he made instruments. After the younger David Wood's death, there followed a sale of 'very desirable' mechanical, mathematical and optical instruments made for personal use: lathes with their tools, a portable gas appliance, a drawing table with instruments; and 'choice optical and mathematical instruments principally applicable to the higher and more refined parts of mechanics'. Wood had also designed a domestic washing machine for his home.

Yet Wood was overshadowed by Murray, not being named on Murray's patents, nor in technical literature. In taking care of business, he allowed Murray to focus upon innovating, particularly with steam-engines. A third active partner, James Fenton (1754–1834), was recruited in 1799, selling his share of Marshall's business, bringing fresh capital (amount unknown) to Murray and Wood, and relieving Murray of the book-keeping. Fenton, a Unitarian, was related to prominent local colliery-owners, though Watt jun. claimed he was 'not very respectable', with a brother, an attorney, 'well skilled in all the nefarious practices of his profession'. Fenton supervised four clerks, and was 'generally busied in the counting house and probably keeps the ledger and writes the letters'. William Lister of Bramley was a fourth partner, 1804–11, purely an investor though styling himself ironfounder. The new investments, with mortgages and sale of surplus land, funded large-scale expansion of the works, by then called the Round Foundry.

The renowned engineer Samuel Owen, formerly of Boulton and Watt and one of Murray's engine erectors c. 1800–05, classed the Leeds firm as 'the best manufacturers of steam engines in England'. They were regarded by Rees in 1816 as unmatched 'in beauty and perfection of workmanship', made in a large, well-organised and labour-efficient factory. According to March, Murray 'touched nothing that did not come out of his hands a new thing', with 'real genius ... For clever tools and implements, and especially for the forgings of beat-iron work, such as parallel motions and the like, he was far in advance of others'. Smiles thought Murray's revolutionary system of sponge weights and wet spinning of flax his greatest achievement. Murray's heckling machine won the Society of Arts' gold medal in 1809; he continued to design and construct beam engines, his work from 1811 with Trevithick producing a high-pressure engine which, fitted to a boat, proved a pioneering application of steam to passenger traffic. Murray is best known in Leeds, for steam locomotives built for the Middleton railway from 1812, the first commercially successful technology of the type, and the earliest sustained demonstration of steam locomotion's possibilities. The 4-hp engines ran on Blenkinsop's patent rack-rail, and remained in service until the 1830s. Another Murray engine powered a Mississippi steam tug, from 1815–16. After this, he worked on machine tools, dyehouse plant, marsh drainage, and gas- and waterworks, and was consulting engineer to factories, mines, and other industrial installations.

David Wood died in 1820, and his son Joseph in 1821. The survivor, David jun., described as a gentleman, wound up affairs but never joined the company, dying in Germany in 1830. Neither did Murray's only son, Matthew, participate in the business. He left for Russia in c. 1821, working as an engineer in Moscow until his death in 1835. When Murray himself died, in 1826, his son-in-law Jackson was executor. Murray's most prized bequests, including mechanical drawings, the gold medal, and a diamond ring from the Empress of Russia, went to Jackson's own family. Richard Jackson, called a bookkeeper, late of the Bradley Ironworks in Staffordshire, had some familiarity with steam-engines. He appeared as manager of Murray's engine manufactory when witness at an 1818 inquest, having inspected a Murray boiler which exploded at Brandling's colliery.

Until 1832, James Fenton directed the business alone, as Fenton and Murray. Marshall's support was no longer a given. Peter Fairbairn's flax-spinning innovations attracted John Marshall's custom from 1828. On quality, Fairbairn beat the Round Foundry, which had upset its oldest customer by chasing sales among Marshall's Irish competitors. By c. 1833, Marshall fully switched to Fairbairn. Finally, in 1832, the ageing Fenton did what Murray had not, confronting the succession problem. Samuel Exley (c. 1796–c. 1881) was promoted manager and partner of the machine-making side, Fenton, Murray and Co., salaried and with a profit share. Fenton then similarly admitted Jackson to partnership, creating a jointly run foundry, millwright and engine branch called Fenton, Murray and Jackson.

Fenton's interest was inherited in 1834 by his brother William, a lawyer in Surrey. While all appeared as before, there were problems: a court case about marine engine patents, orders delivered late or cancelled, disputes with workers. In 1837–38 a locomotive shop was built in Marshall Street, to equip for the railway boom. Beckett's bank held the Holbeck deeds as surety. Then William Fenton died, his interest left in trust for a grandson, Richard Yale, a minor. In 1843, Exley discovered the extent of a crisis previously concealed from him. Assets of the venture in which he was partner were being used to discharge Jackson's company's debts. Within three months, pressed by Exley to protect his own interest, Fenton, Murray and Co. was wound up. Murray's works closed and the contents were sold. Jackson and Yale were personally and jointly bankrupted. Over-ambitious expansion and poor management had been the final blow. Several former employees, apparently with the assignees' blessing, continued the business at Water Lane. As the number of partners reduced, the company became Smith, Beacock and Tannett, machine tool makers. The fitting shop, the Round Foundry, was badly damaged by fire in 1875, and demolished in 1895.

Newcastle All Saints, bap. 1765; Gateshead St Mary, mar. 1785; Kirkby Wharfe St John the Baptist, bap. 1761; mar. 1760, 1783 (Wood's sister Ruth Smurfitt of Leeds confirming the Kirkby Wharfe link); Leeds Ref. Lib., YAHS monumental inscriptions, Balm Lane Methodists, 18, 24; Local Notes and Queries, 1918–20, p. 32; Borthwick, Ainsty, May 1813, Prog.; Dec. 1820; June 1826; Brotherton SC, MS165/39; MS165/23; Thoresby Soc., MS Box VIII, Killingbeck/ Hunslet; Thompson, *Matthew Murray*, especially 1–5, 251, 254, 286. 289–92, 306–7, 349, 371–80, 479; Turner, 'History of Fenton, Murray and Wood', especially 2.9, 8.1–2, 8.12, 8.25, 9.5, 9.7, 9.9, 10.4; Scott (ed.), *Matthew Murray*, especially 18–19, 36, 40, 41, 42, 47, 49, 88–90; Taylor, *Biographia Leodiensis*, 298–302, especially 300 fn (correcting misconceptions in Smiles, *Industrial Biography*, 260–4); Cossons, *Rees*, V, 139–40; Cookson, 'Matthew Murray', *DNB*; M. Chrimes, 'Matthew Murray', in Skempton (ed.), *Biographical Dictionary*, 461–2. White, *Dir.* (1822), I, 558; Anon., *Industries of Yorkshire*, I, 84; S. Bye, 'The Rise and Demise of Mr Murray's Round Building', *YAS Industrial History Section newsletter*, 38 (1993); Cookson (ed.), *VCH Durham IV*, 154–5; for Crowley, Angerstein, *Illustrated Travel Diary*, 258–66; Rimmer, *Marshalls of Leeds*; *Leeds Intelligencer*, 3 Nov. 1800; 29 Feb. 1808 *et seq.*; 5 June 1809; 8 Mar. 1813; 28 Feb. 1814; 9 Oct. 1820; 21 Jan. 1822; 23 Feb., 9 Mar. 1826; 2 Dec., 3 June 1830; *Leeds Mercury*, 4 June 1808; 1 July 1815; 7 Mar. 1818; 4 Nov. 1820; 20 Dec. 1834; 8 Nov. 1844; additional information from Ron Fitzgerald and Paul Murray Thompson.

Zebulon Stirk (1782–1853)

Stirk, born in Otley, was a machine-maker and an accomplished steam-engine manufacturer. Marrying in Leeds in 1803, around the time his apprenticeship as a whitesmith ended, he witnessed with his mark. Whether apprenticed in Otley or Leeds is unknown, but most likely Stirk advanced under a Leeds flax-machinery and engine-maker, Murray or Jubb, for these would be the products of his own business. This launched in or before 1813, so Stirk could have been another victim of Drabble's failure. With a mortgage, he bought a factory and warehouse on the east of town, off York Street, near

Timble (Sheepscar) beck. By 1821 Stirk's premises comprised a 'steam-engine manufactory, machine-maker's shop and engine house', insured for £800. A partnership with Mary Vickers ended in 1816. In 1821 Stirk took as partner William Horsfield, for 17 years Matthew Murray's foreman, and then boiler-maker with Joseph Shaw. Stirk planned to add boiler manufacture to his iron and brass foundry. Horsfield withdrew in 1825.

Stirk never patented, though ambitious and technically proficient. He ran a flax-processing operation in 1819. By 1822 he made steam-engines, flax-spinning and mill machinery, water presses and gaslight apparatus, and later, patent boilers. By 1824, to Leeds factories alone Stirk had supplied nine steam-engines, an aggregate 114 hp. His own 10-hp engine heated by steam a works then including a counting house, foundry, joiners' and smiths' shops, value without contents £2,200. The steam-engine was insured in 1824 for £400, the stock for £1,000. In 1826, Stirk's new foundry produced the largest iron casting ever made in Leeds, weighing almost nine tons and destined for Brown's ironworks, under construction near Nether Mills. By the 1830s he also had a 3,000-spindle flax-spinning factory on the site.

Various misfortunes hit, including a fatal industrial accident, an accidental killing of one worker by another with a shovel, a lightning strike, a hurricane which destroyed a foundry chimney, and a serious fire starting in the flax-mill dryhouse which spread and destroyed foundry models, though the £500 loss was insured. But none of these explains Stirk's perennial financial difficulties. The Bowling Iron Co. rescued him from insolvency c. 1834, channelling cash through their Leeds agent to keep a valued customer afloat. In 1837 came further trouble. Stirk offered for sale his flax business, in a six-storey building with 36-hp engine. Soon, trustees stepped in to sell the York Street engineering- and flax-mills, other properties, foundry equipment, machine tools and flax-spinning frames.

Stirk had at least eight children, and trained his older sons as machine-makers. For some reason they never joined the firm. One claimed that ill-treatment forced him away; another, John, had a business making clay and mortar mills off Meadow Lane; Joseph, living near his father in St Peter's Square, was perhaps employed at York Street; James was apparently responsible for the 1840 memorandum book. But in 1837, Stirk had recently taken partners: Zebulon (b. 1816), only just of age; and a stepson, John Wade Thornton, evidently the grandson of John Wade, a machine-maker in Meadow Lane c. 1807–09. The insolvency of Stirk and his young partners was perhaps triggered by the Leeds Commercial Banking Co. Creditors received final dividends of 10s. in the pound in 1840. Stirk moved to the Soho Foundry, Meadow Lane, probably in 1838, certainly by 1842, into premises previously occupied by Lambert, Jackson and Vickers, iron- and brass-founders (and presumably related to Mary Vickers).

The products remained the same, according to his business card, but in a scaled-down operation. In 1843 Stirk exported to Hamburg six spinning frames adapted for worsteds, and then 24 carding engines, 18 hackling machines and 150 cylinders into Europe. New creditors emerged, and bankruptcy proceedings resumed in 1844. His trustees – including John Hick, of Bowling, bookkeeper, presumably of the iron company – took over Stirk's property. Still business continued, with Stirk retained as manager. It seemed to suit the Bowling company that he continue, for they even took successful action on his behalf, backed by evidence from the younger Zebulon, to recover £70 withheld by their own former agent.

Early in 1845, Stirk's stock and tools were sold by the trustees: 'a very complete set of engine models' for plant of 4 to 80 hp; new tow and line spinning frames; machine tools; moulding boxes and foundry equipment. 'Commodious premises of engine and machine shops, with foundry' were quickly relet. Stirk moved again, setting up as engineer, machinist and ironfounder at School Close, near Mill Hill, again much reduced and in rented premises, with six employees. After Stirk's death, his executors offered an impressive range of machinery, including a 25-hp condensing portable beam engine, 'quite new, only just finished on the premises'; a Whitworth 2-hp oscillating horizontal steam-engine; and a substantial catalogue of high quality machine tools, some made in-house, others by well-known Leeds firms including Maclea and March. The younger Zebulon evidently predeceased him, and other sons were not involved. John Stirk of Halifax (1838–1917), the well-known machine-tool maker, had served an apprenticeship with J. O. March and afterwards worked for Peter Fairbairn, Francis Berry of Sowerby Bridge, Darling and Sellers of Keighley, and several others, before setting up for himself in 1866. He could have been a grandson of Zebulon Stirk's first family, but the relationship, if any, is unconfirmed.

Otley All Saints, bap. 1782; Leeds St Peter, mar. 1803; bap. 1807, 1809; 1816, 1821; WYAS Leeds, WYL2537, Stirk memorandum book, late 1830s; WYAS Wakefield, Deeds, FW 633 659, 634 660 (1813); GC 513 606 (1815); Brotherton SC, MS18; Guildhall Lib., Sun CR 11937/130, 969376 (1821); /133, 982279 (1822); /145, 1018179 (1824); TNA, BT 6/152; Calderdale Ref. Lib, P621; 1851 census, Leeds 2321/329, Bishopgate St.; Ward, 'Industrial development and location', 412; Connell, 'Industrial development', II, no. 64; Long, 'Bowling Ironworks'; Wilson, *Dir.* (1807); *Leeds Dir.* (1809); Baines, *Dir.* (1822), 81; Parson, *Dir.* (1826), 168; Baines and Newsome, *Dir.*; White, *Dir.* (1837), I, 605; *Dir.* (1853), 149; *London Gazette*, 27 Feb. 1816, 17144, 385; May 1825, 18138, 860; 16 Feb. 1844, 20317, 547; *Leeds Mercury*, 27 Mar., 3 Apr. 1819; 1 Dec. 1821; 11 July 1835; 8 Feb. 1845; 10 Apr. 1852; *Leeds Intelligencer*, 12 May 1825; 7 Dec. 1826; 25 June, 13 Aug. 1829; 4 Jan. 1834; 13 May 1837; 15 Dec. 1838; 5 Jan. 1839; 22 Feb. 1840; 17 Feb., 24 Feb. 1844; 25 Jan., 1 Mar. 1845; *Leeds Times*, 17 Jan., 14 Feb. 1835; 4 & 11 Mar. 1837; 27 June, 25 July 1840; 3 Apr. 1841; 23 Apr. 1842; 27 July 1844; 16 Apr. 1853; 7 June 1856; 28 July 1866; *Law Journal*, Feb. 1840, 12; *Yorkshire Gazette*, 25 Apr. 1840.

Taylor and Wordsworth

Joshua Wordsworth (1780–1846), trained as a carpenter, was from an agricultural worker's large family in Thurgoland, Silkstone. He later supported older brothers, wire-drawers, who had continued there in poverty, and brought several nephews to train and work in Leeds. Wordsworth married Martha Drabble in Tankersley in 1803, and then, it seems, moved to work for his wife's cousins in Holbeck. His engineering talent was exceptional. Less is known of the early life of Joseph Taylor (1777–1848), a mechanic perhaps trained up by Jubb or Drabble. Certainly Taylor worked for Drabble at Silver Street, becoming Wordsworth's brother-in-law on marrying Martha's sister Hannah in 1805. Wordsworth's second wife was another Martha Drabble, presumed niece of the first. Three daughters and a son, Joshua Taylor Wordsworth (1826–95), lived to adulthood.

After William Drabble failed in 1812, Taylor and Wordsworth joined another former Drabble workman, Nathaniel Marshall, as flax, tow and worsted machine-makers and axle-makers, in 'a commodious place in Holbeck'. Two years later, in Drabble's former premises, they advertised for iron turners and vice-men. Marshall withdrew in 1816. Their 'mechanics workshop' and engine house were insured in 1817 for £800. Drabble's 6-hp engine was later replaced by an 8-hp Murray model. A major expansion in their machine-making in 1830 brought in large numbers of vice-men, iron-and wood-turners, and smiths. The company gathered sites around Silver Street, and by 1834 had added sizeable extensions, including a 10-hp engine, brass and iron foundries, turning and filing shops, pattern- and model-making departments. A three-storey workshop and other original structures were lost to a fire in 1844.

The firm's success built on Wordsworth's flair for innovation. By 1818 they produced woollen, flax and worsted machinery, though never cotton. Their nearby woollen and worsted factory tried and showcased these products. A Merino Society award in 1821 recognized the firm's new machines as 'spinning the best 6 gross of worsted yarn of British Merino wool'. Their textile business enjoyed long-term success: Wordsworth later had interests in a Barnsley flax and linen company too.

John Whitehead and John Pollard became partners in or before 1840. Pollard was a nephew of Hannah Taylor and of the first Martha Wordsworth, and probably a cousin of the second. The new partners actively managed a vast undertaking, with almost 300 employees in 1839.

Taylor and Wordsworth shared political and social interests: they were Liberal representatives of Holbeck ward in the reformed Leeds corporation; Congregationalists and principal sponsors of Salem Independent chapel, Holbeck; and generous supporters of charity. Joshua Wordsworth died suddenly in 1846, his personal estate worth £25,000. Joseph Taylor died childless 18 months later, leaving valuable bequests to John Pollard, including personal and family items, and other estate to Pollard's mother and other family members.

Whitehead and Pollard continued as Taylor, Wordsworth and Co., along with Wordsworth's solicitor and executor, James W. H. Richardson, who withdrew when Joshua Taylor Wordsworth joined the company on coming of age in 1852. But the young man left in 1856. Retaining the name, the partners were joined by Pollard's son Benjamin Mallinson Pollard, and two sons of Whitehead. Joshua Wordsworth's linen factory in Barnsley was sold and closed in 1848, though the Leeds worsted operation continued a while longer. Taylor and Wordsworth were known in the twentieth century for woollen and synthetic fibres machines. They had been pioneers in flax-dressing and screw gill machinery; and in wool-combing, first to manufacture the Noble comb.

Silkstone All Saints, bap. 1780; Leeds St Peter, mar. 1805; 1811; Wordsworth, 'Joshua Wordsworth'; Hey, 'Militia men'; WYAS Wakefield, Deeds, KG 170 178 (1821); HM 347 307 (1823); LI 136 139 (1832); GZ 589 633; HM 472 440; HU 583 571; KH 711 599 (1829); KR 408 353 (1830); LI 133 136, 135 138, 136 139 (1832); Guildhall Lib., Sun CR 116/920393; Brotherton, MS18; PP (HC) 1834 XX (167) C1, 47; Taylor, *Biographia Leodiensis*, 430–1; Borthwick, Ainsty, Prog. Sept. 1846; Mar. 1848; Baines, *Dir.* (1822), 118; Anon., *Industries of Yorkshire*, I, 90; D. Hey, *A History of Penistone and District* (Wharncliffe Books, 2002), 27–8, 81–3; *Fiery Blades*, 220, 269; Carpmael (ed.), *Law Reports*, II, 151; *Leeds Intelligencer*, 23 June 1825; 11 Mar. 1830; 6 Sept. 1834; 2, 9 Mar. 1839; 26 Dec. 1840; 27 Mar. 1841; 17 Feb. 1844; 14 Feb. 1846; 5 Feb., 28 Oct. 1848; 11 Sept. 1852; *Leeds Mercury*, 7 Nov. 1812; 11 June 1814; 30 May 1818; 7 Apr., 19 May 1821; 21 Aug. 1824; 27 June 1835; 12 Mar. 1836; 21 Jan. 1837; 29 Aug. 1840; 23 Apr. 1842; 8, 15 Aug. 1846; 15 Dec. 1849; *Leeds Times*, 19 Nov. 1836; 17 Feb. 1844; 8 Aug. 1846; 5 Feb. 1848; *Leeds Journal*, 22 (4), Apr. 1951, 126; *London Gazette*, 23 Mar. 1816, 17121, 562; 13 July 1824, 18044, 1158; 25 Feb. 1842, 20075, 546; 3 Sept. 1852, 21355, 2400; 20 June 1856, 21894, 2178.

Foundries, forges, engine-makers, lesser workshops

Martin Cawood

Reportedly arrivals from Birmingham in 1791, Martin and John Cawood had a small brass foundry in Duke Street. Partnership ended in 1799. Martin then opened an iron foundry, with 7-hp Matthew Murray engine, at Quarry Hill. He had a cupola furnace (technology patented 1793). Bought the works, valued at £1,600, c. 1804–05, while retaining Duke Street foundry. His son John became partner then.

Very innovative, briefly making 'improved scribbling and carding machines … wholly of cast iron'. Core business was brass and iron castings for 'collieries, engines, machinery, mills, merchants, dyehouses &c'; also domestic ovens and household goods, some patented. Later supplied and fitted gas works, installing six in Leeds factories, 1818–19. Focus by 1820s was general castings and structural work for fireproof buildings. John Cawood headed the firm by 1828, retired in 1834, handing over to four sons, who continued (along with a flax- and tow-spinning factory) until 1849.

Ward, 'Industrial development and location', 409–10; Binns and Brown, *Dir.*; Wilson, *Dir.*; Baines, *Dir.* (1822), 45; Pigot, *Dir.* (1828), 1013; White, *Dir.* (1837), I, 530, 549; Brotherton SC, MS18; *Leeds Intelligencer*, 17 July 1797; 11 Nov. 1799; 6 Oct. 1800; 2 Apr. 1804; 11 Feb. 1805; 20 Jan., 6 Oct. 1806; 7 Mar., 22 Aug. 1808; 26 Apr. 1813, 1 Mar., 7 June 1819; *Leeds Mercury*, 15 Aug. 1818; 24 Oct. 1840; *Leeds Times*, 3 Oct. 1835.

Richard Cluderay (1778/9–1844)

Probably first a whitesmith, later called iron- and brass-founder, textile-machine maker, even millwright. Soon after Drabble's failure, Cluderay established Star Foundry near his Holbeck Lane End home, c. 1815, like Drabble making patent axle-trees, so possibly a redundant employee. His son William was a machine-maker at the Round Foundry; another, John, was a mechanic. After Cluderay's death, a modest-sized business continued as C. & W. Cluderay, employing 13, all ironworkers, in 1867.

Leeds St Peter, mar. 1797; bap. 1806; YAHS, monumental inscriptions, Holbeck St Matthew, 78; Connell, 'Industrial development', II, no. 7; Baines, *Dir.*, 526; Pigot, *Dir.* (1828), 1013; White, *Dir.* (1837), I, 646, 649; *Leeds Intelligencer*, 1 Apr. 1805; *Leeds Times*, 4 & 11 July 1833; 27 Aug. 1842; 20 Jan. 1844; *Leeds Mercury*, 29 Feb. 1840.

Charles Crosland

Jenny, billy and flax-machine maker in Holbeck, recorded 1816–22.

Pigot, *Dir.* (1816–17), 144–5; Baines, *Dir.*, 526.

William Farmery

By trade a coach-maker, called himself machine-maker c. 1800 when leasing room in Marsh Lane Mill. Supplied rollers and spindles and executed work for Ard Walker, 1803–04. Farmery was agent for his landlord, the magnate Richard Paley, on two factory properties, 1803–c. 1805, but cut adrift by Paley's assignees. Was himself bankrupted in 1806. His stock-in-trade included smith's tools, spindles, rollers, lathes, fluting engines, a vice and files. In 1809 his new spinning method was marketed under licence, including to Joseph Drabble (q.v.).

Leeds St Peter, mar. 1794; Ward, 'Industrial development and location', 410; WYAS Leeds, DB23; *Leeds Intelligencer*, 8 Aug. 1803; 11 Feb. 1805; 9 June 1806; 6 Apr. 1807; 25 Sept. 1809; *London Gazette*, 21 June 1806, 15930, 788.

Jonathan Hattersley (1800–63)

Fourth of Richard Hattersley's five surviving sons, left Keighley soon after his father's death. Not a partner in the business, signed away any interest to his brothers' assignees in 1832, and presumably left jobless. Found work

c. 1831–33 at Moscow Mills, Accrington, then Burnley, then moved to Leeds. Retained cordial but somewhat distant commercial links with his brothers.

Jonathan advertised in 1834 as spindle- and flyer-maker, later also roller manufacturer and ironfounder, off North Street. In 1848 developed a plant at New Wortley, close to canal and railways, employing 134 in 1851. He took up residence in Armley Old Hall, and left personal estate valued at £10,000. John Pollard, machinist, was an executor. Son and partner Thomas Hattersley continued the company.

Keighley St Andrew, bap. 1831, 1835, 1837; bur. 1833; WYAS Wakefield, Deeds, LI 529 525; QE 571 601; QZ 358 367; XP 412 465; WYAS Bradford, 32D83/33/2; /4; /6; Baines and Newsome, Dir., 94; White, Dir. (1837), I, 661; (1853), 128; (1861), 132; Leeds census, 1851, 2321/39; 2321/36; will proved at Wakefield, 3 Feb. 1863.

Thomas Marriott

Noted variously as washing-machine maker, joiner, cabinet- and machine-maker in Lady Lane, 1798–1809.

Leeds Dir. (1798), (1809); Wilson, Dir.; Holden, Dir., 251–8.

Joseph Matthews

Made patent axles and machines, in Water Lane, Holbeck, noticed in directories from 1816. Conceivably another start-up by a former Drabble workman. Matthews continued in Neville Street, running a brass and iron foundry, extant in 1853.

Pigot, Dir. (1816–17), 144–5; Baines, Dir. (1822), 68; Parson, Dir., 168; White, Dir. (1837), I, 583; (1853), 114.

John and Samuel Pollard

Most interesting for links, via Drabble, to Joshua Wordsworth and John Jubb. John Pollard jun. recorded 1787–89 buying from Kirkstall Forge. Presumed relative/partner of Samuel Pollard, Rotherham carpenter who married Mary Drabble in Leeds in 1798. Samuel's son John (b. 1802) closely connected professionally with Wordsworth, probably his apprentice, then a close associate, eventually partner, and ultimately successor.

See Taylor and Wordsworth, above; Leeds St Peter, bap. 1802; mar. 1798; WYAS Leeds, 6257/2, p. 139.

James Procter

A John Proctor, whitesmith, was in Leeds, 1798–1800; and a Prockter and [Thomas] Bedford, machine-makers, in Meadow Lane, 1807–09. James Procter, partner of William and Samuel Marsden as flax- and tow-spinners and machine-makers in Hunslet Lane, was bankrupted in 1813, though continuing afterwards as machine-maker. James Procter &

Sons, machine-makers, took over Jubb's works in 1818 and advertised as his successor, offering modern 'woollen, flax, tow, hemp and worsted machinery' as well as millwright's work, and spindles, flyers and rollers. The Meadow Lane premises were insured in 1821 for £2,100, John Procter occupying brass and iron foundries, and James the machine-makers' shop, the pair living there in adjoining houses. In 1826 their presumable successors, James and Samuel Procter, machine-makers in Wellington Street, became insolvent.

Guildhall Lib., Sun CR 11937/131, no. 973498; WYAS Leeds, LO/HU5; Wilson, *Dir.*; *Leeds Dir.* (1809); Pigot, *Dir.* (1816–17), 144–5, 198; Baines, *Dir.*, 117–18; Parson, *Dir.*, 168; *Leeds Mercury*, 28 Mar. 1818; *Leeds Intelligencer*, 10 May 1813; 24 Jan. 1814; 2 Feb., 20 Apr., 4 May 1818; 1 Nov. 1819; 4 Jan. 1827; 17 Jan. 1828.

Richard Pullan & Sons
Richard Pullan, iron- and brass-founder of Hunslet, made steam-engines recognized for power and reliability. In local sales, Pullan led the pack chasing Murray (who had made 77 of 129 engines working in Leeds in 1824), with 22, generally quite small engines.

Benjamin Pullan (c. 1734–1800), a smith active in Hunslet in 1770, was probably Richard's father. Richard set up as an ironfounder in 1785, bought from Kirkstall Forge, 1787–90, and was for a time partner in Popplewell, Pullan and Shaw. By 1815 Richard Pullan and Sons had wide interests in Hunslet companies: Bower's chemical works, a glassworks, and Lowgate scribbling mill and dyehouse. Pullan withdrew from these ventures, 1813–17, probably to fund expansion of a foundry at Soho Ironworks. Many workers were recruited: engine-builders, smiths, turners, cylinder borers. After Richard's death in 1823, his sons ended their association. William became a plumber, brass-founder and gas fitter at Mill Hill. Benjamin retained the company name and Hunslet premises, continuing much as before. He died in 1838, after which his widow carried on the business, closing c. 1845.

Connell, 'Industrial development', II, no. 203; WYAS Leeds, 6257/2, p. 155; LO/HU5; WYAS Wakefield, Deeds, EM 474 631; EQ 49 66; Brotherton SC, MS18; *Leeds Intelligencer*, 14 June 1785; 22 Aug. 1812; 6 Feb., 23 Sept. 1815; 2 Oct. 1823; 15 Apr. 1830; 23 June 1838; *Leeds Mercury*, 24 Oct. 1818, 16 Jan. 1819; 19 Apr. 1823; *Leeds Times*, 8 Mar. 1845; *London Gazette*, 13 July 1813, 16752, 1389; 14 Jan. 1817, 17209, 90; White, *Dir.* (1837), I, 646; (1853), 130.

Salt and Gothard
An early instance of Leeds and south Yorkshire engineering connection. Titus Salt, whitesmith with family links in Sheffield, bought property at Hunslet Moor in 1755. Presumably the same man married a widow in Sheffield in 1763, thus acquiring further real estate. Here too he must have gained specialist skills, for a 1772 partnership agreement called him cast steel-maker. Timothy Gothard (1723–1805), the name Huguenot, was a millwright born at Silkstone, later working in Rotherham. Salt and Gothard were partners

at Hunslet Moor by 1770, recorded buying coal on credit. By 1793 a major customer for Middleton coal, they took 300 tons annually and had their own rail-side staith.

Their foundry was probably Leeds' oldest, opened c. 1750 by R. Howitt. Under Salt and Gothard a booming, very local, trade developed in colliery and waggon-way castings, including wheels and plates for Brandling's line, and parts for Rothwell colliery's Newcomen-type pumping engine installed c. 1750. The value of sales to Middleton colliery exceeded purchases. They bought from Kirkstall Forge, 1787–91. The partners retired in 1802, giving way to Titus Salt jun. and John Gothard. This younger partnership dissolved in 1809. Other sons of Gothard then stepped forward, with Salt's son Daniel, who later sold out to John Gothard. Jubb (q.v.) took over their main brass and iron foundry premises in 1810, while the Gothards split into two branches, Timothy at Balm Road Foundry, with John and Richard Gothard evidently occupying part of the older site. Salt assignees had involvement into the 1820s, though the premises were partly empty and semi-derelict, perhaps vacated after Jubb's death. John Gothard died in 1824, succeeded at Hunslet Foundry by a son-in-law, John Gledhill, until it passed in 1855 to Richard Kilburn & Sons.

Silkstone All Saints, bap. 1723, 1762; mar. 1786; Tankersley St Peter, mar. 1745; WYAS Leeds, LO/HU5; 6257/2, p. 24; Thoresby Soc., MS Box VIII, Killingbeck Mss; Guildhall Lib., Sun 11936/385/597243, 1792; obit., *Methodist Magazine*, XXIX (1806), 325; R. Balgarnie, *Sir Titus Salt, Baronet* (1877 [1970]), 6–8; E. K. Scott, 'Hunslet Foundry, Leeds', *Edgar Allen News*, Oct. 1935 (in Leeds Ref. Lib.); Ball, 'Millwrights', 39; May, 'Real estate', 239, 241, 258, 277, 280–3, 295; Scott (ed.), *Matthew Murray*, 67–8, 105; Connell, 'Industrial development', II, no. 211; Barfoot and Wilkes, *Dir.*; Baines, *Dir.*, 534; Pigot, *Dir.* (1828), 1013; *Leeds Intelligencer*, 13 Mar. 1809; *Leeds Mercury*, 29 Sept. 1810; *London Gazette*, 11 Mar. 1809, 16236, 333; *Monthly Magazine*, 1 June 1805, 516.

George and Joseph Shaw

George Shaw, merchant, of Cross, Briggate, supplied iron to the Middleton colliery from 1778. Joseph (b. 1765), presumably his son, moved the business into manufacturing c. 1794, taking a stake in Hunslet Ironworks (or Forge) at Low Mills, sharing an island in the Aire with a fulling mill. Unlike William Hodgson's iron forge, next to a scribbling (etc.) mill on Balm beck, which adopted steam power from 1797, Shaw's stayed water-powered into the 1820s. At first partnered with Fenton and Walker, Shaw became sole owner and made Hunslet Ironworks a slitting mill in 1799, at a time when he and the Low Moor Co. dominated iron supply to Middleton colliery. An affluent merchant living in Park Square, Shaw belonged to the Iron Masters' Association, a price-regulating cartel.

Butler, *History of Kirkstall Forge*, 58; May, 'Real estate', 246, 287–9, 295, 141–2, 275; OS 6″ Yorks. 218, surv. 1846–47 pub. 1852; Leeds St John, bap. 1765; Beresford, *East End, West End*,

479; Guildhall Lib., Sun 44/726392, 1801; 649650 f. 457, 1796; Brotherton SC, MS18; Baines, *Dir.* (1822), 78, 534; Baines and Newsome, *Dir.*; *Leeds Mercury*, 1 Dec. 1821.

William Varley

William Varley – father and son – established as wire-workers in Hunslet since 1740, supplied woollen cards, spindles, flyers and other components. In the 1770s, Varley twice compensated and apologized to a patentee for counterfeiting a wire cylinder for flour-dressing. The son had taken over the business some years before his father's death in 1794.

Sometimes called gentleman, Varley jun. (1750–1834), like his friend Jubb the elder, involved himself in the affairs of insolvents and others. He was Jubb's trustee, and helped the younger Jubb's executors wind up the business. He lived in a substantial house near his workshops, and owned considerable other property. The legitimate Varley line died out, but the business continued through Sedgwicks, and later Procters (seemingly unconnected to James, q.v.), into more general engineering.

Andrea Hetherington, *History of Procter Brothers Ltd* (2016); WYAS Leeds, LO/HU5; Connell, 'Industrial development', II, 206; May, 'Real estate', 285; Crump (ed.), *Leeds Woollen Industry*, 321; White, *Dir.* (1837), I, 611, 661, 669; (1853), 159; *Leeds Intelligencer*, 11 Mar. 1777; 7 Sept. 1779; 3 Feb., 3 Mar. 1794; 12 June 1797; 18 Feb. 1799; 24 Nov. 1806; 6 Sept. 1817.

Warwick & Co.

Noted as machine-makers in Lindley's steam-engine survey, 1824 (with a 5-hp Pullan engine). Otherwise recorded as iron- and brass-founders, from c. 1799 when Joseph Warwick had Leeds Bridge foundry.

Brotherton SC, MS18, p. 6; Ward 'Industrial development and location', 391; Binns and Brown, *Dir.* (1800, 1809); Baines, *Dir.*, 86, 115; Baines and Newsome, *Dir.*

Appendix 3: Estimates of Textile Machinery at Work in the United Kingdom, 1835–56

Spindles and looms at work in the UK textile industry, 1850 and 1856

	1850	1856
Spindles	25,638,716	33,503,580
Looms	301,445	369,205

Source: PP (HC) 1857 (Sess. 1), III, 572.
Note: Figures for Lancashire's woollen mills have evidently been excluded from the 1850 totals. These should presumably therefore show a further 223,778 spindles and 4,839 power looms (Jenkins, 'Factory Returns', 60).

Worsted power looms at work in the West Riding, 1836–56

1836	1841	1843	1845	1850	1856
2,768*	11,458	16,870	19,121	30,856	35,298

Sources: PP (HC) 1845 (639) XXV, 477; 1857 (1) III, 633.
* Cf. figure of 2,856 given in PP (HC) 1836 (24) XLV, 150–1.

Power looms and spindles at work in England and the West Riding, 1835–56

Power looms

		1835	1836	1850	1856
England	Wool	2,045	2,150	9,439[a]	14,453
	Worsted	3,082	2,969	32,617	38,956
	Silk	1,714	1,714	6,092	9,260
	Flax	309	209	3,670/1,141[b]	7,689
	Cotton	108,632	108,751	249,627	298,847
West Riding[c]	Wool	175[d]	272		
	Worsted	2,953	2,856	30,856	35,298
	Silk		Nil		
	Flax		Nil		
	Cotton		3,114		

Spindles

		c. 1833	1850	1856
England	Wool			
	Worsted		864,874	1,298,326
	Cotton	9,333,000		
West Riding				
	Worsted		746,281	1,212,587

Sources: PP (HC) 1836 (24) XLV, 145; 1851 (1304), XXIII, 217; 1857 (Sess. 1), III, 559; Baines, *History of the Cotton Manufacture*, 431; Ure, *Cotton Manufacture*, lxii; James, *Worsted Manufacture*, 536; Baines, 'Account of the Woollen Trade', 636.

Notes:
[a] The woollen power loom figure for 1850 should include a further 4,839 (Jenkins, 'Factory Returns', 60).
[b] Figures given for the flax industry differ between PP (HC) 1851 (1304), XXIII, 232, and 1857 (Sess. 1), III, 574, though those for other textile branches are identical.
[c] Information for 1836 relates to only part of the West Riding, though apparently including the major woollen and worsted areas (PP (HC) 1836 (24) XLV, pp. 150–1).
[d] Incomplete. A further 226 looms were said to have been used for both woollen and worsted fibres (Jenkins, *West Riding Wool Textile Industry*, 126–7).

Bibliography

Manuscript and archival sources

Bolton Archives and Local Studies
ZCR, papers of Samuel Crompton

Borthwick Institute for Archives, University of York
Records of probate

Brotherton Library Special Collections, University of Leeds
BUS/Marriner, R. V. Marriner Ltd, business archive
MS18 William Lindley's survey of steam-engines in Leeds, 1824
MS165, E. Kilburn Scott collection, including notes of Samuel Owen
MS193, Gott papers, business records
MS194, Gott papers, family records
MS200, Marshall and Co., business archive

Calderdale Reference Library
P621, John Stirk (1838–1917)

Durham Record Office
D/HP/1, records of Henry Pease and Co., woollen manufacturers

Fall River Historical Society, Mass.
William C. Davol diary, journal of a trip to England, 1838–39

Guildhall Library/London Metropolitan Archives
Sun and Royal Exchange fire insurance records

John Rylands Library Special Collections, University of Manchester
GB 133 MCK, McConnel and Kennedy, master cotton-spinners

Keighley Library
Apprenticeship indentures

Brigg Box 83
Rate books and poor rate books

Leeds Reference Library
Local Notes and Queries
YAHS monumental inscriptions

North of England Institute of Mining and Mechanical Engineers, Newcastle
NEIMME 3410, papers of colliery viewers: /Bud (John Buddle); /For (Forster collection); /John (George and John Johnson); /Wat (Watson)

Rhode Island Historical Society, Rhode Island
MS254/VI, Zachariah Allen papers, Journal of European Trip 1825

The National Archives
BT6/151, Board of Trade, machinery exports 1825–42
T1/568/281–6, correspondence of Leeds woollen manufacturers re industrial espionage, 1781

Thoresby Society, Leeds
MS Box VIII, Killingbeck/Hunslet
Plans of Leeds including Giles (1815) and Fowler (1831)

United Grand Lodge of England, Library and Museum
Membership lists of Keighley, Leeds, Halifax and other lodges

West Yorkshire Archive Service
(Bradford)
32D83, George Hattersley and Sons Ltd of Keighley, records
DB2, Journal of Robert Heaton
SpSt, Spencer Stanhope of Horsforth, family and estate records

(Calderdale)
Handlist to the archive of Pollitt and Wigzell, Bank Foundry, Sowerby Bridge

(Leeds)
Acc. 2371, Fairbairn, Lawson, engineers, Leeds
DB23, Ard Walker, engine and machinery accounts, 1800–04
LO/HU/4–5, Hunslet fieldbook, 1791, and valuation, 1823–24
WYL76, KF4/4, 6755 and 6257, records of Kirkstall Forge

(Wakefield)
BEA, Beaumount of Bretton Hall
Registry of Deeds

Yorkshire Archaeological and Historical Society, Brotherton Library Special Collections
YAS/DD61, Addingham deeds etc.
YAS/MD292, Taylor family of Gomersal, deeds and documents

Printed primary sources

Craven Muster Roll, 1803 (NYCRO no. 9, 1976), transcript of NYCRO, ZYU
PP (HC) 1824 (51) V, Select Committee on Artisans and Machinery
PP (HC) 1834 (167) Cl, Factories Inquiry Commission
PP (HC) 1841 (201) VII, Select Committee on the Operation of Laws affecting the Exportation of Machinery
PP (HC) 1843 XIV [431], RC on Children's Employment in Mines and Manufactories. Second Report
PP (1912–13) CIX c. 6320, Final Report on the First Census of Production of the United Kingdom, 1907
J. Wolffe (ed.), *Yorkshire Returns of Religious Worship*, vol. 2: *West Riding* (North), Borthwick Texts and Studies 31 (2005); (South), 32 (2002)

Directories

Bailey, W., *Northern Directory* (1781)
Baines, E., *History, Directory and Gazetteer of the County of York* (1822)
Baines and Newsome, *General and Commercial Directory of the Borough of Leeds* (1834)
Barfoot, P., and J. Wilkes, *Universal British Directory* (5 vols, 1790–99)
Binns and Brown, *Directory for the Town of Leeds* (1800)
Holden, *Triennial Directory* (1809–11)
Parson, W., *General and Commercial Directory of the Borough of Leeds* (1826)
Parson, W, and White, W., *Directory of the Borough of Leeds, the City of York, and the Clothing District of Yorkshire* (1830)
Pigot & Co., *Commercial Directory* (1816–17)
Pigot & Co., *Yorkshire Directory* (1828–29)
The Leeds Directory for the Year 1798 (1798)
The Leeds Directory for 1809 (1809)
White, W., *History, Gazetteer and Directory of the West Riding of Yorkshire* (2 vols, 1837–38)
White, W., *Directory and Gazetteer of Leeds, Bradford and the Clothing Districts of the West Riding of Yorkshire* (1853)
Wilson, G., *A New and Complete Directory for the Town of Leeds* (1807)

Secondary works

Aikin, J., *A Description of the Country From Thirty to Forty Miles Round Manchester* (John Stockdale, 1795)

Allen, R. C., *The British Industrial Revolution in Global Perspective* (Cambridge University Press, 2009)

Allen, Z., *The Practical Tourist* (A. S. Beckwith, 1832)

Andrews, C. R., *The Story of Wortley Ironworks* (Milward, Nottingham, 1956)

Angerstein, R. R., *Illustrated Travel Diary, 1753–1755: Industry in England and Wales from a Swedish Perspective*, trans. Torsten and Peter Berg (Science Museum, 2001)

Ankarloo, D., 'New Institutional Economics and Economic History', *Capital and Class*, 78 (2002), 9–36

Anon., *Industries of Yorkshire*, 2 vols (Historical Publishing Co., 1888–90)

Ashton, T. S., *An Eighteenth-Century Industrialist: Peter Stubs of Warrington* (A. M. Kelley, 1939)

——, *Iron and Steel in the Industrial Revolution* (Manchester University Press, 1963)

Aspin, C., *The Decoy: How the Portuguese Learned to Spin Like Arkwright* (Helmshore Local History Society, 2011)

——, *The Water-Spinners* (Helmshore Local History Society, 2003)

Babbage, C., *On the Economy of Machinery and Manufactures*, 3rd edn (John Murray, 1833)

Baines, E., *Account of the Woollen Manufacture* [1858], ed. K. G. Ponting (David and Charles, 1970)

——, 'An Account of the Woollen Trade of Yorkshire', in T. Baines (ed.), *Yorkshire, Past and Present*, II (William Mackenzie, 1873), 629–95

——, *History of the Cotton Manufacture in Great Britain* (n.p., 1835)

Banks, J., *On the Power of Machines* (Pennington, 1803)

——, *A Treatise on Mills* (Pennington, 1795)

Banks, J. W., 'The Progress of Engineering in Bradford', *Bradford Engineering Society Journal* (1925–26), 1–17

Baumber, M., *From Revival to Regency: a History of Keighley and Haworth, 1740–1820* (M. L. Baumber, 1983)

Bayliss, D. G., 'Sowerby Bridge, 1750–1800: The Rise of Industry', *Transactions of the Halifax Antiquarian Society* (1985)

Bennett, H. F., 'The Journal of George Brownell on a Voyage to England in 1839', *Contributions of the Lowell Historical Society*, 2/3 (1921), 325–71

Benson, A. P., *Textile Machines* (Shire, 1983)

Beresford, M. W., *East End, West End: the Face of Leeds during Urbanization, 1684–1842* (Thoresby Society, LX–LXI, 1988)

——, *The Leeds Chambers of Commerce* (Leeds Chamber of Commerce, 1951)

Berg, M. (ed.), *The Age of Manufactures 1700–1820: Industry, Innovation and Work in Britain* (Routledge, 1994)

———, 'On the Origins of Capitalist Hierarchy', in Bo Gustafsson (ed.), *Power and Economic Institutions: Reinterpretations in Economic History* (Edward Elgar, 1991)

———, 'Small Producer Capitalism in Eighteenth-Century England', *Business History*, 35/1 (1993), 17–39

———, *Technology and Toil in Nineteenth-Century Britain* (CSE, 1979)

Biernacki, R., 'Culture and Know-How in the 'Satanic Mills': An Anglo-German Comparison', *Textile History*, 33/2 (2002), 219–37

Bindman, D. and G. Riemann (eds), *'The English Journey': Journal of a Visit to France and Britain in 1826 by Karl Friedrich Schinkel* (Yale, 1993)

Brown, J. K., 'Design Plans, Working Drawings, National Styles: Engineering Practice in Great Britain and the United States, 1775–1945', *Technology and Culture*, 41/2 (2000), 195–238

Brown, J. and M. B. Rose (eds), *Entrepreneurship, Networks and Modern Business* (Manchester University Press, 1993)

Bruland, K., *British Technology and European Industrialization: The Norwegian Textile Industry in the Mid-Nineteenth Century* (Cambridge University Press, 1989)

Brunton, R., *A Compendium of Mechanics*, 4th edn (John Niven, 1828)

Buchanan, R., *Practical Essays on Millwork* (J. Taylor, 1814)

Buchanan, R. A., *Industrial Archaeology in Britain* (Pelican, 1974)

Burnett, J. (ed.), *Useful Toil: Autobiographies of Working People from the 1820s to the 1920s* (Allen Lane, 1974)

Burnley, J., *The History of Wool and Wool-Combing* (Sampson Low, 1889)

Butler, A. E., B. F. and H. M. (eds), *The Diary of Thomas Butler of Kirkstall Forge, Yorkshire, 1796–9* (privately printed, 1906)

Butler, R., *The History of Kirkstall Forge through Seven Centuries, 1200–1954* (H. Jenkinson, 1945)

Butterworth, R., 'The Ecclesfield Nailers' Agreement', *Transactions of the Hunter Archaeological Society*, II (1920–24), 114–18

Campbell, R., *The London Tradesman* (T. Gardner, 1757)

Cantrell, J. A., *James Nasmyth and the Bridgewater Foundry: a Study of Entrepreneurship in the Early Engineering Industry* (Chetham Society, XXXI, 3rd series, 1984)

Cantrell, J. A. and G. Cookson (eds), *Henry Maudslay and the Pioneers of the Machine Age* (Tempus Publishing, 2003)

Cardwell, D. S. L., *The Organisation of Science in England* (Heinemann, 1972)

Carpmael, W. (ed.), *Law Reports of Patent Cases*, I (1843); II (1851)

Casson, M. and C., *The Entrepreneur in History: From Medieval Merchant to Modern Business Leader* (Palgrave Macmillan, 2013)

Catling, H., *The Spinning Mule* (Lancashire County Council, 1986)

Chaloner, W. H., 'New Light on Richard Roberts, Textile Engineer (1789–1864)', *Transactions of the Newcomen Society*, XLI (1968–69), 27–44

Chapman, S. D., 'The Textile Factory before Arkwright: A Typology of Factory Development', *Business History Review*, 48/4 (1974), 451–78

Checkland, S. G., *The Rise of Industrial Society in England, 1815–1885* (Longmans, 1964)

Clay, J. W. (ed.), *Familiae Minorum Gentium* (Harleian Society, XXXVII, 1894)

Colls, R., *The Pitmen of the Northern Coalfield: Work, Culture and Protest, 1790–1850* (Manchester University Press, 1987)

Cookson, G., 'A City in Search of Yarn: the Journal of Edward Taylor of Norwich, 1817', *Textile History*, 37/1 (2006), 38–51

———, 'Early Textile Engineers in Leeds, 1780–1850', *Publications of the Thoresby Society*, 2nd ser., 4 (1994), 40–61

———, 'Family Firms and Business Networks: Textile Engineering in Yorkshire, 1780–1830', *Business History*, 39/1 (1997), 1–20

———, 'The Mechanization of Yorkshire Card-Making', *Textile History*, 29/1 (1998), 41–61

———, 'Millwrights, Clockmakers and the Origins of Textile Machine-Making in Yorkshire', *Textile History*, 27/1 (1996), 43–57

———, 'Quaker Families and Business Networks in Nineteenth-Century Darlington', *Quaker Studies*, 8/2 (2004), 119–40

———, 'Quaker Networks and the Industrial Development of Darlington, 1780–1870', in Wilson and Popp (eds), *Industrial Clusters and Regional Business Networks*, 155–73

——— (ed.), *Victoria County History of Co. Durham. IV. Darlington* (University of London, 2005)

Cookson, G. and N. A., *Gomersal: a Window on the Past* (Kirklees Borough Council, 1992)

Cookson, G. and C. A. Hempstead, *A Victorian Scientist and Engineer: Fleeming Jenkin and the Birth of Electrical Engineering* (Ashgate, 2000)

Cooper, C. C., 'Making Inventions Patent', *Technology and Culture*, 32/4 (1991), 837–45

Cossons, N., *The BP Book of Industrial Archaeology* (David and Charles, 1993)

Court, W. H. B., *The Rise of the Midland Industries, 1600–1838* (Oxford University Press, 1953)

Cressy, E., *A Hundred Years of Mechanical Engineering* (Duckworth, 1937)

Crosby, A. G. (ed.), *Family Records of Benjamin Shaw, Mechanic of Dent, Dolphinholme and Preston, 1772–1841* (Record Society of Lancashire and Cheshire, CXXX, 1991)

Cross-Rudkin, P. and M. M. Chrimes (eds), *Biographical Dictionary of Civil*

Engineers in Great Britain and Ireland 2: 1830–1890 (Institution of Civil Engineers, 2008)

Cruickshank, J. L., *Headingley-cum-Burley, c. 1540–1784* (Thoresby Society, 2nd ser., 22, 2012)

Crump, W. B. (ed.), *The Leeds Woollen Industry, 1780–1820* (Thoresby Society, XXXII, 1931)

Crump, W. B. and G. Ghorbal, *History of the Huddersfield Woollen Industry* (Tolson Museum, 1935)

Dakin, G., 'A Review of the Development of Cotton-Spinning Machinery', *Journal of the Textile Institute Proceedings*, 42/8 (1951), 457–78

Dane, E. Surrey, *Peter Stubs and the Lancashire Hand-Tool Industry* (Sherratt, 1973)

Daniels, G. W., 'Samuel Crompton's Census of the Cotton Industry, 1811', *Economic History*, II (1930), 107–10

Davies, K., 'Peter Atherton, Cotton Machinery Manufacturer, 1741–99', *Transactions of the Lancashire and Cheshire Antiquarian Society*, 106 (2011), 73–101

Davies, R., A. Petford and J. Senior (eds), *The Diaries of Cornelius Ashworth, 1782–1816* (Hebden Bridge Local History Society, 2011)

Derry, T. K. and T. I. Williams, *A Short History of Technology* (Clarendon, 1960)

Dewhirst, I., *A History of Keighley* (Keighley Borough Council, 1974)

Dobson, C. R., *Masters and Journeymen: a Prehistory of Industrial Relations, 1717–1800* (Croom Helm, 1980)

Dodsworth, C., 'The Low Moor Ironworks, Bradford', *Industrial Archaeology*, 8 (1971), 122–59

Dupin, C., *The Commercial Power of Great Britain* (Knight, 1825)

Dutton, H. I., *The Patent System and Inventive Activity During the Industrial Revolution, 1750–1852* (Manchester University Press, 1984)

Eden, F. M., *The State of the Poor* (Routledge, 1928 [1797])

Emmerson, G. S., *Engineering Education: a Social History* (David and Charles, 1973)

English, W., *The Textile Industry: an Account of the Early Inventions of Spinning, Weaving and Knitting Machines* (Longmans, 1969)

Enros, P. C., 'Cambridge University and the Adoption of Analytics in Early Nineteenth-Century England', in Herbert Mehrtens (ed.), *Social History of Nineteenth-Century Mathematics* (Birkhäuser, 1981), 135–48

Fairbairn, W., 'An Account of the Rise and Progress of Manufactures and Commerce and Civil and Mechanical Engineering in these Districts', in T. Baines (ed.) *Lancashire and Cheshire, Past and Present*, II (William Mackenzie, 1867), i–clxxx

———, 'An Experimental Inquiry into the Strength of Wrought-Iron Plates and Their Riveted Joints as Applied to Ship-Building and Vessels Exposed to Severe Strains', *Philosophical Transactions of the Royal Society*, 140 (1850), 677–725

———, 'On Metallic Constructions', *Civil Engineer and Architect's Journal*, XV (1852)

———, *Treatise on Mills and Millwork*, II (Longman, Green, 1865)

———, *Useful Information for Engineers* (Longman, Green, 1860)

Farnie, D. A., *The English Cotton Industry and the World Market, 1815–1896* (Clarendon, 1979)

———, 'The Textile Machine-making Industry and the World Market, 1870–1960', *Business History*, 32/4 (1990), 150–70

Felkin, W., *A History of the Machine-Wrought Hosiery and Lace Manufactures* (Longmans, Green, 1867)

Fisher, D. R. (ed.), *The History of Parliament: The House of Commons 1820–1832* (Cambridge University Press, 2009)

Floud, R. C., *The British Machine Tool Industry, 1850–1914* (Cambridge University Press, 1976)

Fraser, D. (ed.), *A History of Modern Leeds* (Manchester University Press, 1980)

French, G. J., *Life and Times of Samuel Crompton* (Thomas Dinham & Co., 1860)

Gilbert, K. R., *Machine Tools: Catalogue of the Science Museum Collection* (HMSO, 1966)

Giles, C. P. and I. H. Goodall, *Yorkshire Textile Mills: the Buildings of the Yorkshire Textile Industry, 1770–1930* (HMSO, 1992)

Gilfillan, S. C., *The Sociology of Invention* (MIT Press, 1970 [1935])

Goodchild, J., 'A Case of Industrial Espionage?', *Old West Riding* 3/1 (1983), 16–17

———, 'Pildacre Mill: an Early West Riding Factory', *Textile History*, 1/3 (1968–70), 337–49

Gordon, R. B., 'Who Turned the Mechanical Ideal into Mechanical Reality?', *Technology and Culture*, 29/4 (1988), 744–78

Grady, K., *The Georgian Public Buildings of Leeds and the West Riding* (Thoresby Society, LXII, 1987)

Griffiths, T., P. A. Hunt and P. K. O'Brien, 'Inventive Activity in the British Textile Industry, 1700–1800', *Journal of Economic History*, 52/4 (1992), 881–906

Gross, L. F., 'Wool-Carding: a Study of Skills and Technology', *Technology and Culture*, 28/4 (1987), 804–27

Guest, R., *A Compendious History of the Cotton Manufacture* (Joseph Pratt, 1823)

Gulvin, C., *The Tweedmakers: a History of the Scottish Fancy Woollen Industry, 1600–1914* (David and Charles, 1973)

Harris, J. R., 'Attempts to Transfer English Steel Techniques to France in the Eighteenth Century', in S. Marriner (ed.), *Business and Businessmen* (Liverpool University Press, 1978), 199–233

———, *Industrial Espionage and Technology Transfer: Britain and France in the Eighteenth Century* (Ashgate, 1998)

———, 'Industrial Espionage in the Eighteenth Century', *Industrial Archaeology Review*, 7/2 (1985), 127–138

Harrison, J. K., *Eight Centuries of Milling in North-East Yorkshire* (North York Moors National Park Authority, 2001)

Harte, N. B., 'On Rees's *Cyclopaedia* as a Source for the History of the Textile Industries in the Early Nineteenth Century', *Textile History*, 5 (1974), 119–27

Hawkes, A. J., *The Clockmakers and Watchmakers of Wigan, 1650–1850* (privately printed, 1950)

Hayman, R. A., *Ironmaking: the History and Archaeology of the Iron Industry* (History Press, 2011)

Heaton, H., 'Benjamin Gott and the Industrial Revolution in Yorkshire', *Economic History Review*, 3/1 (1931), 45–61

———, 'An Early Victorian Business Forecaster in the Woollen Industry', *Economic History*, II (1933), 553–74

———, 'A Yorkshire Mechanic Abroad', in L. S. Pressnell (ed.), *Studies in the Industrial Revolution: Essays Presented to T. S. Ashton* (Athlone Press, 1960), 281–312

———, *The Yorkshire Woollen and Worsted Industries from the earliest time up to the Industrial Revolution* (Oxford University Press, 1965)

Henderson, W. O., *Britain and Industrial Europe, 1750–1870* (Leicester University Press, 1965)

Henderson, W. O., *J. C. Fischer and his Diary of Industrial England, 1814–51* (Frank Cass, 1966)

Hey, D. G., *The Fiery Blades of Hallamshire: Sheffield and its Neighbourhood, 1660–1740* (Leicester University Press, 1991)

———, 'The Nail-making Background of the Walkers and the Booths', *Transactions of the Hunter Archaeological Society*, X (1971–79), 31–6

———, *The Village of Ecclesfield* (Huddersfield Advertiser, 1968)

Hills, R. L., *Power in the Industrial Revolution* (Manchester University Press, 1970)

Hirst, W., *History of the Woollen Trade for the last Sixty Years* (n.p., Leeds, 1844)

Hodgson, J., *Textile Manufacture and Other Industries in Keighley* [1879], ed. G. Cookson and G. Ingle (Shaun Tyas, 1999)

Honeyman, K., *Child Workers in England, 1780–1820: Parish Apprentices and the Making of the Early Industrial Labour Force* (Ashgate, 2007)

———, *Origins of Enterprise: Business Leadership in the Industrial Revolution* (Manchester University Press, 1982)

Honeyman, K. and J. Goodman, *Technology and Enterprise: Isaac Holden and the Mechanisation of Woolcombing in France, 1848–1914* (Scolar, 1986)

Hoppit, J., *Risk and Failure in English Business, 1700–1800* (Cambridge University Press, 1987)

Hudson, P., *The Industrial Revolution* (Edward Arnold, 1992)

Humphries, J. and B. Schneider, 'Spinning the Industrial Revolution', *University of Oxford Discussion Papers in Economic and Social History*, 145, June 2016

Hunter, James, *The Making of the Crofting Community* (Birlinn, 2010)

Ingle, G., *Marriner's Yarns: the Story of the Keighley Knitting Wool Spinners* (Carnegie, 2004)

———, *Trouble At T'Mill: the 1826 Yorkshire Weavers' Riots* (Royd Press, 2013)

———, *Yorkshire Cotton: the Yorkshire Cotton Industry, 1780–1835* (Carnegie, 1997)

———, *Yorkshire Dales Textile Mills* (Royd Press, 2009)

Inkster, I., 'Mental Capital: Transfers of Knowledge and Technique in Eighteenth-Century Europe', *Journal of European Economic History*, 19 (1990), 403–41

Jacob, M. C., *The First Knowledge Economy: Human Capital and the European Economy, 1750–1850* (Cambridge University Press, 2014)

James, J., *The History of Bradford and its Parish* (Longmans, Green, 1866)

———, *History of the Worsted Manufacture in England* (Longman, Brown, Green, 1857)

James, K. J., 'The Hand-Loom in Ulster's Post-Famine Linen Industry: The Limits of Mechanization in Textiles' "Factory Age"', *Textile History*, 35/2 (2004), 178–91

Jefferys, J. B., *The Story of the Engineers, 1800–1945* (Lawrence and Wishart, 1970)

Jenkins, D. T. (ed.), *Cambridge History of Western Textiles* (Pasold, 2003)

———, 'The Factory Returns: 1850–1905', *Textile History*, 9 (1978), 58–74

———, 'The Validity of the Factory Returns 1833–50', *Textile History*, 4 (1973), 26–46

———, *The West Riding Wool Textile Industry, 1770–1835: a Study in Fixed Capital Formation* (Pasold, 1975)

Jenkins, D. T. and K. G. Ponting, *The British Wool Textile Industry, 1770–1914* (Pasold, 1982)

Jenkins, J. G. (ed.), *The Wool Textile Industry in Great Britain* (Routledge and Kegan Paul, 1972)

Jenkins, M. and G. Johnson, 'Entrepreneurial Intentions and Outcomes: a Comparative Causal Mapping Study', *Journal of Management Studies*, 34/6 (1997), 895–920

Jennings, B. (ed.), *A History of Nidderdale* (Sessions, 1983)

Jeremy, D. J., 'British Textile Technology Transmission to the United States: The Philadelphia Region Experience, 1770–1820', *Business History Review*, 47/1 (1973), 24–52

––––––, 'Damming the Flood: British Government Efforts to Check the Outflow of Technicians and Machinery, 1780–1843', *Business History Review*, 51/1 (1977), 1–34

–––––– (ed.), *Dictionary of Business Biography: a Biographical Dictionary of Business Leaders, 1860–1980*, 5 vols (Butterworths, 1984–86)

––––––, 'Immigrant Textile Machine Makers along the Brandywine, 1810–1820' *Textile History*, 13/2 (1982), 225–48

–––––– (ed.), *International Technology Transfer: Europe, Japan and the USA, 1700–1914* (Elgar, 1991)

–––––– (ed.), *Technology and Power in the Early American Cotton Industry* (Memoirs of the American Philosophical Soc., 189, 1990)

––––––, *Transatlantic Industrial Revolution: the Diffusion of Textile Technologies between Britain and America, 1790–1830s* (Blackwell, 1981)

Jeremy, D. J. and P. C. Darnell, *Visual Mechanic Knowledge: The Workshop Drawings of Isaac Ebenezer Markham (1795–1825), New England Textile Mechanic* (American Philosophical Society, Philadelphia, 2010)

Johnson, M. P. and P. Worrall, *Top Forge, Wortley* (Sheffield Trades Historical Society, 1983)

Jordan, E., 'The Exclusion of Women from Industry in Nineteenth-Century Britain' *Comparative Studies in Society and History*, 31/2 (1989), 273–96

Keighley, W., *Keighley, Past and Present* (A. Hey, 1879)

Kerridge, E., *Textile Manufactures in Early Modern England* (Manchester University Press, 1985)

Koditschek, T., *Class Formation and Industrial Society: Bradford, 1750–1850* (Cambridge University Press, 1990)

Koorey, S., *Fall River Revisited* (Arcadia, 2012)

Kuhn, T. S., *The Structure of Scientific Revolutions*, 2nd edn (University of Chicago Press, 1970)

Landes, D. S., *A Revolution in Time: Clocks and the Making of the Modern World* (Harvard University Press, 1983)

––––––, *The Unbound Prometheus: Technological Change and Industrial Development in Western Europe from 1750 to the Present* (Cambridge University Press, 1969)

Lawson, J., *Letters to the Young on Progress in Pudsey* (Caliban, 1978 [1887])

Lawton, R., 'The Economic Geography of Craven in the Early-Nineteenth Century', *Transactions of the Institute of British Geographers*, 20 (1954), 93–111

Lee, C. H., *British Regional Employment Statistics, 1841–1971* (Cambridge University Press, 1979)

————, *A Cotton Enterprise, 1795–1840: a History of M'Connel and Kennedy, Fine Cotton Spinners* (Manchester University Press, 1972)

Lemon, H., 'Some Aspects of the Early History of Spinning, with Special Reference to Wool', *Journal of the Textile Institute Proceedings*, 42/8 (1951), 479–501

Lipscomb, A. A. and A. E. Bergh (eds), *The Writings of Thomas Jefferson* (Washington, 1905)

Lister, S. C., *Lord Masham's Inventions: Written by Himself* (Lund, Humphries, 1905)

Long, H., 'The Bowling Ironworks', *Industrial Archaeology*, 5 (1968), 171–7

Longstaffe, W. H. D., *The History and Antiquities of the Parish of Darlington* (Darlington and Stockton Times, 1854)

Loomes, B., *Yorkshire Clockmakers* (Dalesman, 1972)

Lowe, N., *The Lancashire Textile Industry in the Sixteenth Century* (Chetham Society, XX, 3rd series, 1972)

MacLeod, C., *Heroes of Invention: Technology, Liberalism and British Identity, 1750–1914* (Cambridge University Press, 2007)

————, *Inventing the Industrial Revolution: the English Patent System 1660–1800* (Cambridge University Press, 1988)

————, 'Negotiating the Rewards of Invention: The Shop-Floor Inventor in Victorian Britain', *Business History*, 41/2 (1999), 17–36

————, 'The Paradoxes of Patenting: Invention and its Diffusion in Eighteenth- and Nineteenth-century Britain, France and North America', *Technology and Culture*, 32/4 (1991), 885–910

————, 'Strategies for Innovation: the Diffusion of New Technology in Nineteenth-Century British Industry', *Economic History Review*, 45/2 (1992), 285–307

MacLeod, C. and A. Nuvolari, '"Glorious Times": the Emergence of Mechanical Engineering in Early Industrial Britain, c. 1700–1850', *Brussels Economic Review*, 52 (2009), 215–37

McGouldrick, P. F., *New England Textiles in the Nineteenth Century: Profits and Investment* (Harvard University Press, 1968)

McNeil, I., *Joseph Bramah: A Century of Invention, 1749–1851* (David and Charles, 1968)

Mantoux, P., *The Industrial Revolution in the Eighteenth Century* (Cape, 1948)

Marglin, S. A., 'What Do Bosses Do?: The Origins and Functions of Hierarchy in Capitalist Production', *Review of Radical Political Economics*, 6/2 (1974), 60–112

Marsden, B., *Watt's Perfect Engine: Steam and the Age of Invention* (Columbia University Press, 2002)

Mason, K. M., *Woolcombers, Worsteds and Watermills: Addingham's Industrial Revolution* (Addingham Civic Society, 1989)

Mason, P. F., *The Pit Sinkers of Northumberland and Durham* (History Press, 2012)

Mason, R., *Pennine Village* (Craven Herald, 1971)

Mathias, P., *The Transformation of England* (Methuen, 1979)

Meisenzahl, R. R. and J. Mokyr, 'The Rate and Direction of Invention in the British Industrial Revolution: Incentives and Institutions', in J. Lerner and S. Stern (eds), *The Rate and Direction of Inventive Activity Revisited* (University of Chicago Press, 2012), 443–79

Milligan, E. H., *Biographical Dictionary of British Quakers in Commerce and Industry, 1775–1920* (Sessions, 2007)

Mokyr, J., *The Lever of Riches: Technological Creativity and Economic Progress* (Oxford University Press, 1990)

More, C., *Skill and the English Working Class, 1870–1914* (Croom Helm, 1980)

Morehouse, H. J., *The History and Topography of the Parish of Kirkburton and of the Graveship of Holme, including Holmfirth* (n.p., 1861)

Morrell, J. B., 'Bourgeois Scientific Societies and Industrial Innovation in Britain, 1780–1850', *Journal of European Economic History*, 24/2 (1995), 311–32

Morris, R. J., *Class, Sect and Party: the Making of the British Middle Class: Leeds 1820–50* (Manchester University Press, 1990)

Morrison-Low, A. D., *Making Scientific Instruments in the Industrial Revolution* (Ashgate, 2007)

Muirhead, J. P., *The Life of James Watt, with Selections from his Correspondence* (D. Appleton, 1859)

Musson, A. E., 'The Engineering Industry', in R. Church (ed.), *The Dynamics of Victorian Business* (Allen and Unwin, 1980), ch. 4

———, 'The 'Manchester School' and Exportation of Machinery', *Business History*, 14/1 (1972), 17–50

Musson, A. E. and E. Robinson, *Science and Technology in the Industrial Revolution* (Manchester University Press, 1969)

Newton, G. D., 'Early Coal Mining in Leeds, 1560–1700', *Publications of the Thoresby Society*, 2nd ser., 24 (2014), 1–23

Nicholson, J., *The Millwright's Guide* (n.p., 1830)

———, *The Operative Mechanic and British Machinist* (Knight and Lacey, 1825)

Nowotny, H., *The Cunning of Uncertainty* (Polity Press, 2016)

Ogden, J., *A Description of Manchester by a Native of the Town* (Heywood reprint, 1860 [1783])

Ogilvie, S., 'The Economics of Guilds', *Journal of Economic Perspectives*, 28/4 (2014), 169–92

Ó Gráda, C., 'Did Science Cause the Industrial Revolution?', *Journal of Economic Literature*, 54/1 (2016), 224–39

O'Brien, P., 'The Micro Foundations of Macro Invention: The Case of the Reverend Edmund Cartwright', *Textile History*, 28/2 (1997), 201–33

Pacey, A., *The Maze of Ingenuity: Ideas and Idealism in the Development of Technology* (Allen Lane, 1974)

——, *Technology in World Civilization: A Thousand-Year History* (MIT Press, 1990)

Parker, J., *Illustrated History of Wibsey, Low Moor, Oakenshaw, Wike, Norwood Green, Judy Brig, Royds Hall, Coley and Shelf* (J. Feather, 1902)

Peel, F., *Spen Valley Past and Present* (Senior, 1893)

Perkin, H., *The Origins of Modern English Society, 1780–1880* (Routledge and Kegan Paul, 1969)

Pole, W. (ed.), *The Life of Sir William Fairbairn, Bart. Partly Written by Himself* (David and Charles, 1970 [1877])

Pollard, S., *The Genesis of Modern Management* (Edward Arnold, 1968)

Ponting, K. G., *Leonardo da Vinci: Drawings of Textile Machines* (Moonraker/Pasold, 1979)

Potts, M. S., 'William Potts of Leeds, Clockmaker', *Publications of the Thoresby Society*, 2nd ser., 13 (2003), 25–45

Prickett, S. (ed.), *The Romantics: the Context of English Literature* (Holmes and Meier, 1981)

Priestley, J., *Historical Account of the Navigable Rivers, Canals and Railways of Great Britain* (n.p., 1831)

Rae, J. B., 'Engineers are People', *Technology and Culture*, 16/3 (1975), 404–18

Raistrick, A., *Quakers in Science and Industry* (David and Charles, 1968)

Raistrick, A. and E. Allen, 'The South Yorkshire Ironmasters (1690–1750)', *Economic History Review*, 9/2 (1939), 168–85

Randall, A., *Before the Luddites: Custom, Community and Machinery in the English Woollen Industry, 1776–1809* (Cambridge University Press, 1991)

——, 'The Philosophy of Luddism: The Case of the West of England Woollen Workers, c. 1790–1809', *Technology and Culture*, 27/1 (1986), 1–17

Rees, A., *Cyclopaedia* [1802–09], ed. N. Cossons, 5 vols (David and Charles, 1972)

Rimmer, W. G., 'The Industrial Profile of Leeds, 1740–1840', *Publications of the Thoresby Society*, L (1967), 130–57

——, *Marshalls of Leeds, Flax-Spinners, 1788–1886* (Cambridge University Press, 1960)

Robertson, P. L. and L. J. Alston, 'Technological Choice and the Organization of Work in Capitalist Firms', *Economic History Review*, 45/2 (1992), 330–49

Robinson, E. and A. E. Musson, *James Watt and the Steam Revolution* (Adams and Dart, 1969)

Rogers, K. H., 'John Dyer, Engineer and Inventor', *Trowbridge History* I (1991), 15–18

Roll, E., *An Early Experiment in Industrial Organisation: Being a History of the Firm of Boulton & Watt, 1775–1805* (Frank Cass, 1968 [1930])

Rolt, L. T. C., *The Mechanicals: Progress of a Profession* (Heinemann, 1967)

———, *Tools for the Job: a History of Machine Tools to 1950* (Science Museum, 1986)

Rosenberg, N., *Inside the Black Box: Technology and Economics* (Cambridge University Press, 1982)

———, *Perspectives on Technology* (Cambridge University Press, 1976)

Rowlands, M. B., *Masters and Men in the West Midland Metalware Trades before the Industrial Revolution* (Manchester University Press, 1975)

Rule, J., *The Labouring Classes in Early Industrial England, 1750–1850* (Longman, 1986)

Rydén, G., *Production and Work in the British Iron Trade in the Eighteenth Century: a Swedish Perspective* (Uppsala Papers in Economic History, Research Report 45, 1998)

Sabel, C. and J. Zeitlin, 'Historical Alternatives to Mass Production: Politics, Markets and Technology in Nineteenth-Century Industrialization', *Past and Present*, 108 (1985), 133–76

Saul, S. B. (ed.), *Technological Change: the United States and Britain in the Nineteenth Century* (Methuen, 1970)

Saxonhouse, G. R. and G. Wright, 'New Evidence on the Stubborn English Mule and the Cotton Industry', *Economic History Review*, 37/4 (1984), 507–19

Schmitt, J-M., 'Relations between England and the Mulhouse Textile Industry in the Nineteenth-Century', *Textile History*, 17/1 (1986), 27–38

Scott, E. Kilburn, 'Early Cloth Fulling and its Machinery', *Transactions of the Newcomen Society*, XII (1931–32), 31–52

——— (ed.), *Matthew Murray, Pioneer Engineer: Records from 1765–1826* (privately printed, 1928)

———, 'Memorials to Pioneer Leeds Engineers', *Transactions of the Newcomen Society*, XI (1930–31), 164–7

Sellars, M., 'Iron and Hardware', in W. Page (ed.), *Victoria County History of the County of York*, II (1912), 398–400

Sennett, R., *Together: The Rituals, Pleasures and Politics of Co-operation* (Allen Lane, 2012)

Sigsworth, E. M., *Black Dyke Mills: a History. With Introductory Chapters on the Development of the Worsted Industry in the Nineteenth Century* (Liverpool University Press, 1958)

Skempton, A. W. (ed.), *Biographical Dictionary of Civil Engineers in Great Britain and Ireland*, I, 1500–1830 (Institution of Civil Engineers, 2002)

Smail, J., 'Manufacturer or Artisan? The Relationship between Economic and Cultural Change in the Early Stages of the Eighteenth-Century Industrialization', *Journal of Social History*, 25/4 (1991–92), 791–814

————, *Merchants, Markets and Manufacture: the English Wool Textile Industry in the Eighteenth Century* (Macmillan, 1999)

———— (ed.), *Woollen Manufacturing in Yorkshire: the memorandum books of John Brearley, Cloth Frizzer at Wakefield, 1758–1762* (Yorkshire Archaeological Society Record Series, CLV, 2001)

Smiles, S., *Industrial Biography: Iron Workers and Tool Makers* (John Murray, 1863)

———— (ed.), *James Nasmyth, Engineer: an Autobiography* (John Murray, 1897)

Smith, A. (ed.), *A Catalogue of Tools for Watch- and Clock-makers by John Wyke of Liverpool* (Henry Francis du Pont Winterthur Museum, 1977)

Sokoloff, K. L., 'Inventive Activity in Early Industrial America: Evidence from Patent Records, 1790–1846', *Journal of Economic History*, 48/4 (1988), 813–50

Sokoloff, K. L. and B. Z. Khan, 'The Democratization of Invention During Early Industrialization: Evidence from the United States, 1790–1846', *Journal of Economic History*, 50/2 (1990), 363–78

Steeds, W., *A History of Machine Tools, 1700–1910* (Clarendon, 1969)

Strickland, M. F., *A Memoir of the Life, Writings and Mechanical Inventions of Dr Edmund Cartwright* (Saunders and Otley, 1843)

Sturt, G., *The Wheelwright's Shop* (Cambridge University Press, 1963 [1923])

Styles, J., 'Spinners and the Law: Regulating Yarn Standards in the English Worsted Industries, 1550–1800', *Textile History*, 44/2 (2013), 145–70

Sullivan, R. J., 'The Revolution of Ideas: Widespread Patenting and Invention During the English Industrial Revolution', *Journal of Economic History*, 50/2 (1990), 349–62

Sutcliffe, J., *A Treatise on Canals and Reservoirs* (n.p., 1816)

Sykes, R., *The Spinning Jenny: a Revolution in Yarn Production* (Colne Valley Museum, 1992)

Tann, J., *The Development of the Factory* (Cornmarket Press, 1970)

————, 'Marketing Methods in the International Steam Engine Market: The Case of Boulton and Watt', *Journal of Economic History*, 38/2 (1978), 363–89

————, 'The Textile Millwright in the Early Industrial Revolution', *Textile History*, 5 (1974), 80–9

Tann, J. and A. Burton, *Matthew Boulton: Industry's Great Innovator* (History Press, 2013)

Tann, J. and M. J. Breckin, 'The International Diffusion of the Watt Engine, 1775–1825', *Economic History Review*, 31/4 (1978), 541–64

Taylor, R. V. (ed.), *The Biographia Leodiensis: or Biographical Sketches of the Worthies of Leeds and Neighbourhood from the Norman Conquest to the Present Time* (Simpkin, Marshall, 1865)

Thaler, R. R., *Misbehaving: The Making of Behavioural Economics* (Allen Lane, 2015)

Thompson, P. M., *Matthew Murray 1765–1826 and the Firm of Fenton Murray and Co. 1795–1844* (privately published, 2015)

Thorne, R. (ed.), *The History of Parliament: The House of Commons 1790–1820* (History of Parliament Trust, 1986)

Tomory, L., 'Fostering a New Industry in the Industrial Revolution: Boulton & Watt and Gaslight 1800–1812', *British Journal for the History of Science*, 46/2 (2013), 199–229

———, 'Science and the Arts in William Henry's Research into Inflammable Air during the Early-Nineteenth Century', *Annals of Science*, 71/1 (2014), 61–81

———, 'Technology in the British Industrial Revolution', *History Compass*, 14/4 (2016), 152–67

Tupling, G. H., 'The Early Metal Trades and the Beginnings of Engineering in Lancashire', *Transactions of the Lancashire and Cheshire Antiquarian Society*, LXI (1949), 1–34

Tweedale, G., *Steel City: Entrepreneurship, Strategy and Technology in Sheffield, 1743–1993* (Clarendon, 1995)

Uglow, J., *Elizabeth Gaskell* (Faber and Faber, 1993)

Ure, A., *The Cotton Manufacture of Great Britain*, I (n.p., 1836)

———, *The Philosophy of Manufactures* (Charles Knight, 1835)

Usher, A. P., *A History of Mechanical Inventions* (Dover Books, 1982)

Wadsworth, A. P. and J. de Lacy Mann, *The Cotton Trade and Industrial Lancashire, 1600–1780* (Manchester University Press, 1965)

Walker, J., *Fortunes Made in Business* (Sampson Low, 1884)

Waller, T., *A General Description of All Trades* (privately printed, 1747)

Walsh, D., 'The Lancashire "Rising" of 1826', *Albion* 26 (1994), 601–21

Whitaker, T. D., *History and Antiquities of the Deanery of Craven*, 3rd edn (Dodgson, 1878)

White, G. S., *Memoir of Samuel Slater, the Father of American Manufactures* (A. M. Kelley, 1967 [1836])

Wilson, J. F. and A. Popp, *Industrial Clusters and Regional Business Networks in England, 1750–1970* (Ashgate, 2003)

Wilson, R. G., *Gentlemen Merchants: the Merchant Community of Leeds, 1700–1880* (Manchester University Press, 1971)

Winder, T. (ed.), *An Old Ecclesfield Diary, 1775–1845* (Northend, 1921)

Woodbury, R. S., *Studies in the History of Machine Tools* (MIT Technology Press, 1972)

Woodcroft, B., *Brief Biographies of Inventors of Machines for the Manufacture of Textile Fabrics* (Longman, Green, 1863)

Woolrich, A. P., *Mechanical Arts and Merchandise: Industrial Espionage and Travellers' Accounts as a Source for Technical Historians* (De Archaeologische Pers, Netherlands, 1986)

Wright, T., *Some Habits and Customs of the Working Classes, by a Journeyman Engineer* (Tinsley Brothers, 1867)

Unpublished papers and theses

Ball, C. A., 'Millwrights in Sheffield and South Yorkshire, 1550–1950' (University of Sheffield, M.A., 1992)

Bayliss, D., 'Report on Damstead Works, Dronfield' (South Yorkshire Industrial History Society, 1998)

Bottomley, M. V., 'Keighley New Church: the first two hundred years' (1989, copy in Keighley Ref. Lib.)

Byrom, R., 'William Fairbairn – experimental engineer and mill builder' (Huddersfield University, Ph.D., 2015)

Connell, E. J., 'Industrial development in South Leeds, 1790–1914' (University of Leeds, Ph.D., 1975)

Cookson, G., 'The West Yorkshire textile engineering industry, 1780–1850' (University of York, D.Phil., 1994)

Feather, K. M., 'Nineteenth-century entrepreneurs in Keighley' (University of Liverpool, B.A. diss. 1983)

Hayward, R. A., 'Fairbairns of Manchester: the history of an engineering works in the nineteenth century' (UMIST, M.Sc., 1971)

Hey, D. (ed.), 'The militia men of the Barnsley district, 1806: an analysis of the Staincross militia returns' (University of Sheffield extramural class, 1998; copies at WYAS Wakefield, Goodchild collection; and Barnsley Lib.)

Ingle, G., 'History of R. V. Marriner Ltd., worsted spinners, Keighley' (University of Leeds, M.Phil., 1974)

Kirk, R. M., 'The economic development of the British textile machinery industry c. 1850–1939' (University of Salford, Ph.D., 1983)

Lumby, V. E., 'A study of some of the aspects of the Keighley Mechanics' Institute from its inception in 1825 to 1875' (University of Leeds, M.A., 1982)

May, B. C., 'Real estate and the development of an industrial village: Hunslet, Leeds, 1750–1800' (University of Leeds, M.Phil., 1980)

Moher, J. G., 'The London millwrights and engineers, 1775–1825' (Royal Holloway London, Ph.D., 1988)

Smith, M. G., 'Robert Clough Ltd., Grove Mill, Keighley: a study in technological redundancy, 1835–65' (University of Leeds, M.A., 1982)

Smith, S. B., 'Thomas Cheek Hewes, 1768–1832: an ingenious engineer and mechanic of Manchester' (University of Manchester, M.Sc.Tech, 1969)

Turner, T., 'History of Fenton, Murray and Wood' (University of Manchester, M.Sc.Tech., 1966)

Ward, M. F., 'Industrial development and location in Leeds north of the River Aire, 1775–1914' (University of Leeds, Ph.D., 1972)

Wordsworth, S., 'Joshua Wordsworth, machine-maker of Leeds, 1780–1846' (2016, copies in Leeds Central Lib.; Society of Genealogists, London)

Index

Page numbers in parentheses refer to images.

PEOPLE, MARKETS, GOODS:
ECONOMIES AND SOCIETIES IN HISTORY

ISSN: 2051-7467